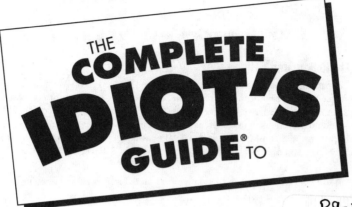

THE
COMPLETE
IDIOT'S
GUIDE® TO

P9-DTQ-884

D0123496

Nazi Germany

by Robert Smith Thompson

ALPHA

A Pearson Education Company

Again, as always and forever, to Judy.

International Standard Book Number: 0-02-864475-1
Library of Congress Catalog Card Number: 2002116798

05   04   03   8   7   6   5   4   3   2   1

Interpretation of the printing code: The rightmost number of the first series of numbers is the year of the book's printing; the rightmost number of the second series of numbers is the number of the book's printing. For example, a printing code of 03-1 shows that the first printing occurred in 2003.

Printed in the United States of America

Note: This publication contains the opinions and ideas of its author. It is intended to provide helpful and informative material on the subject matter covered. It is sold with the understanding that the author and publisher are not engaged in rendering professional services in the book. If the reader requires personal assistance or advice, a competent professional should be consulted.

The author and publisher specifically disclaim any responsibility for any liability, loss, or risk, personal or otherwise, which is incurred as a consequence, directly or indirectly, of the use and application of any of the contents of this book.

For marketing and publicity, please call: 317-581-3722.

The publisher offers discounts on this book when ordered in quantity for bulk purchases and special sales.

For sales within the United States, please contact: Corporate and Government Sales, 1-800-382-3419 or corpsales@pearsontechgroup.com.

Outside the United States, please contact: International Sales, 317-581-3793 or international@pearsontechgroup.com.

Publisher: *Marie Butler-Knight*
Product Manager: *Phil Kitchel*
Managing Editor: *Jennifer Chisholm*
Senior Acquisitions Editor: *Randy Ladenheim-Gil*
Development Editor: *Ginny Bess Munroe*
Copy Editor: *Catherine Schwenk*
Illustrator: *Jody Schaeffer*
Cover/Book Designer: *Trina Wurst*
Indexer: *Brad Herriman*
Layout/Proofreading: *John Etchison, Becky Harmon*

Contents at a Glance

Contents

Foreword

According to Adolf Hitler, the Third Reich would last 1,000 years. It ended up lasting 12. Hitler's favorite architect, Albert Speer, designed buildings for the Nazi regime employing a "theory of ruin value" that was supposed to have the structures looking as noble as ancient Greek and Roman temples when they lay in ruins after a thousand years. Alas, Allied bombings in World War II put Speer's theory to the test rather sooner than he expected, and the results were not noble at all.

The ignominious end and short duration of the Third Reich have not in the least dampened our interest in the Hitler regime, which remains lively over a half-century since the failed Führer committed suicide in his bunker under Berlin. One of the reasons for our abiding interest, of course, is the old "fascination of the abomination," but the Third Reich also piques our intellectual curiosity: We want to know how it was that a highly advanced and sophisticated nation like Germany could relapse into the political and moral barbarism of Nazism. We want to know this partly because we sense that if the Germans could do it, so, just possibly, could we.

All serious students of modern German history know there are no easy explanations for the Third Reich. So does Robert Thompson, the author of this excellent guide to Nazi Germany. Although in his closing observations he cites *hubris* as a "fatal flaw" running through most of German history—a perfectly defensible position—in general he avoids overarching explanations and focuses on specific political, socio-economic, and cultural developments to help us understand the German conundrum. Throughout his analysis, which encompasses the rise of German nationalism when there was not yet a Germany, national unification via Otto von Bismarck's policies of "Blood and Iron," Kaiser William II's ill-fated campaign to give Germany an imperial "Place in the Sun," the traumatizing effects of military defeat in World War I, and the economic and political turmoil of the Weimar Republic, Thompson illuminates the German scene by making insightful comparisons with events in other nations, including our own. For example, he points out that in times of economic malaise, America, too, has been highly susceptible to racist and xenophobic nostrums. In the end, while Thompson's tour through German history won't give the reader many sound-bite answers to the question "Why Hitler?" it will certainly give him or her a better understanding of how the nation of "Dichter und Denker" (poets and thinkers) could have so run amok in the modern era.

As for Hitler himself, Thompson is equally resistant to one-stop-serves-all explanations, including such psychological answers that focus on the Führer's unhappy childhood, alleged homosexuality, or monorchidism (single testicle). Hitler was certainly a megalomaniac, but his madness generally had a method to it, and he was capable of learning from his mistakes. As Thompson reminds us, he came to power legally—assuming the chancellorship in January 1933 by dint of his control of the largest party in the German parliament. By that time, the democratic process had already been severely compromised, but the facility with which Hitler was able to deliver the coup de grâce should remind us that the electoral process by itself is no guarantee against tyranny. And the fact that the majority of the German people continued to support this tyranny throughout its short but brutal career should also remind us that the "will of the masses" can be an evil will indeed.

One persistent—albeit highly inaccurate—image of Nazi Germany has it functioning like a well-oiled Mercedes. In fact—as even *Complete Idiot's Guide* readers should know—the Third Reich was a hodgepodge of competing fiefdoms run by a motley crew of ambitious infighters who (for good reason) despised and distrusted each other. Hitler himself encouraged the back-stabbing among his satraps because this prevented any one of them from effectively challenging his own power. But in the end this was no way to run a Reich, and the Nazi regime would probably not have lasted 50 years, much less 1,000, even if Hitler had not hastened its demise by taking on most of the world between 1939 and 1945. Yet the final tragedy, of course, is that the Third Reich did not have to last more than a few years to leave a legacy of destruction and political criminality that seems millennial in its dimensions.

David Clay Large

David Clay Large is a professor of history at Montana State University in Bozeman. His specialty is modern German history, and his most recent books include *Where Ghosts Walked: Munich's Road to the Third Reich; Berlin;* and *And the World Closed Its Doors: One Family's Struggle to Escape the Holocaust.*

Introduction

What happens when an educated and cultured people, famed not only for their industrial prowess and military might but also their traditions in philosophy, science, and the arts, put aside their critical faculties to follow what George Orwell, the English writer, called the tom-tom beat of modern tribalism? What happens when such a people abandon the ordinary politics of barter and compromise for the extraordinary politics of faith, hope, and hatred? What happens when, instead of facing problems squarely and working out reasonable solutions, such a people become seduced by visions of a utopia with no problems at all and solutions based on the extermination of their enemies, real or perceived? And what happens when, poisoned by the prejudices of the past and the propaganda of the present, such a people turn to warfare and mass murder? Then you get Nazi Germany.

This isn't to say that all Germans were Nazis. From the very moment of Hitler's illegal seizure of power in 1933, many Germans raised their voices in protest. Most of those who did so, however, ended up jailed, killed, or both. Or, like the physicist Albert Einstein, the novelist Thomas Mann, and the conductor Erich Leinsdorf, they managed to escape. Less notable figures also made their way to Florida, Indiana, and other safe havens. Even among those who had no choice but to stay behind, such as an elderly working-class couple who would risk their lives by distributing anti-Hitler postcards, there were Germans who withheld their hearts and minds from the Nazi regime.

But most Germans did support the Nazis. As Daniel Goldhagen showed in his book, *Hitler's Willing Executioners*, published just a few years ago, the vast majority of the German people applauded the killing of Jews.

So we come to the question of the present book: Why did the Germans, on the surface at least as civilized as any people on earth, become swallowed up in a movement of mayhem, murder, and military aggression?

There's no single answer to this question. But as *The Complete Idiot's Guide to Nazi Germany* points out, any explanation of Nazism has to start with the historical background. For in important ways Germany was not like other European countries. Except for Russia it had a bigger population than any other European country and no other country on the continent could match its wealth and power. Yet, compared to England, France, and Spain, Germany as a country was a Johnny-come-lately. Until the middle of the nineteenth century, Germany as such didn't even exist and then it started demanding its place in the sun. The tragedy that befell all who lived in Germany was that the majority of the German people eventually succumbed to the illusion that they could attain that place by following Adolf Hitler.

How to Use This Book

For your ease of use, this book is organized into five different parts, plus three appendixes:

Part 1, "The German Colossus," traces out the rise of Germany under Bismarck and its defeat in the First World War under Kaiser Wilhelm II.

Part 2, "The Ascendancy of Evil," takes us through Hitler's rise to power in 1933.

Part 3, "The Nazi State," shows how Hitler consolidated his power at home and started on his course of aggression abroad.

Part 4, "The Rising Tide," goes from Hitler's first conquests to the turning point at Stalingrad.

Part 5, "The Decline and Fall of Nazi Germany," portrays Germany's defeat and Hitler's death.

Additional Features

You'll notice notes that I've inserted in the margins and throughout the pages of this book. These extras take the following forms:

> ### Memorable Places
>
> Germany was full of beautiful cities and famous locales. As you encounter them, you'll see that they formed the stage-setting of the drama that was the story of the Third Reich.

> ### Terms and Translations
>
> These bits of text define terms or provide translations to explain German words you might not be familiar with.

> ### Supporting Actors
>
> If Hitler was the greatest villain in that drama, he certainly had a good supporting cast. You'll meet them—Himmler, Goebbels, and others.

> ### Modern Day Parallels
>
> Was Nazi Germany completely different from the world today? Unfortunately, the answer is no. You will find mention of a number of similarities in present-day countries.

Bet You Didn't Know

You're probably familiar, at least generally, with the story of Nazi Germany. The story, nonetheless, has lots of unfamiliar details, mostly having to do with the economic and political background of the German tragedy.

Acknowledgments

The staff at the reference desk of the Thomas Cooper Library at the University of South Carolina has been kind, patient, and most helpful. So have two colleagues, Richard Mandell and Robert Herzstein, both experts on Nazi Germany; their assistance has been far greater than they realize. My thanks above all, for her kind and ever-patient help with the author's computer problems, as well as her support, to Polly Thompson.

Trademarks

All terms mentioned in this book that are known to be or are suspected of being trademarks or service marks have been appropriately capitalized. Alpha Books and Pearson Education, Inc., cannot attest to the accuracy of this information. Use of a term in this book should not be regarded as affecting the validity of any trademark or service mark.

Part 1

The German Colossus

After the First World War, a lot of people (and not just Germans) believed that Germany had legitimate grievances. But what grievances? Didn't Germany start the war? Yes, the German armies got the war started. And Germany certainly had developed into a colossus astride the continent of Europe. However, Kaiser Wilhelm II had ordered his forces into what he thought was a preemptive war: Hit them before they hit you. So was Germany's going to war in 1914 an act of offense or defense? You be the judge. And you decide whether the peace settlement of 1919 was a just settlement.

Before There Was a Germany: 1815–1866

In This Chapter

- ◆ Germany poor and divided
- ◆ The rise of nationalism after Napoleon
- ◆ The post-Napoleonic balance of power
- ◆ The first steps toward unity

On April 30, 1945, Adolph Hitler, the *Führer* (leader) of Nazi Germany, climbed the stairs to the top of his bunker, which had been dug and fortified with concrete in the center of Berlin. With him was Eva Braun, who had been his mistress and only days before became his wife. As they stepped into the sunlight, they could hear the rumble of Russian artillery all around the edge of the city; overhead, they could make out the shapes of Russian bombers. Around them as far as they could see, the once-magnificent buildings of the German capital were no more than smoldering ruins. No German forces were available to meet the attackers and the fall of Berlin was inevitable, only hours away. Knowing that they were personally doomed, Hitler and Eva Braun committed double suicide.

The Nazi radio network was still functioning, barely, and it reported that the *Führer* had died heroically on the field of battle. With that news, Germany's resistance to the Allies—primarily Russia, Great Britain, and the United States—collapsed altogether. After 12 years of existence, Nazi Germany (the Third Reich that Hitler had boasted would last a thousand years) came to an end. The greatest horror of modern times had passed into history.

But why had that horror arisen? What were its roots? Its origins?

After World War I, Nazism and political movements like it had great appeal in Spain, France, Italy, and several of the countries of Eastern Europe. But it reached its most virulent form in Germany. Why?

Nazi Germany was more than the creation of that warped political genius, Hitler. To understand how it came to be, we have to go back in German history—way back. For what we call Germany—for centuries, really, Germanies—was never a typical European nation. Its similarities to Western Europe were only superficial. That uniqueness helps explain the eventual rise of the Third Reich.

The Land

Germany lies in the center of Europe. When the country was in its military prime, from the middle of the nineteenth century to the end of World War II, this obvious fact about its location was a source of strength. Germany could strike eastward and westward at almost the same time, believing that it could defeat its enemies on both fronts. But before that, the location was a source of weakness. Germany had no well-defined natural boundaries. The British became identified with a large island, the Italians with a peninsula, and the French with sharp seacoast boundaries. Yet the Germans lived within frontiers that were artificial and not lasting. From the Middle Ages onward, German borders expanded and contracted like an accordion, depending on wars, treaties, and royal marriages. So before the nineteenth century, people who spoke German (or its many dialects) could not say with any assurance: "This is our country!" Unlike the British and the French, the Germans had little or no sense of *national identity*.

More than any other major European area, what became Germany was also split up by mountain ranges, valleys, plateaus, ridges, lakes, and rivers. Intersecting the northern German plain were four substantial rivers—the Rhine, the Elbe, the Oder, and the Vistula. Complicating these geographical barriers, what we call Germany even in the late eighteenth century was split up among hundreds of kingdoms, duchies, principalities, bishoprics, archbishoprics, and free cities. "Germany" barely existed.

Terms and Translations

Whatever our ethnic origins, we Americans share a **national identity**. Most of us speak the same language and share a common history, and we know that if born or naturalized within the 50 states we are legally Americans. But suppose our regional dialects—the way people speak in Maine versus South Carolina versus Oregon, etc.— were so different that we could not understand each other. What if people in Michigan and Texas knew nothing of the American Revolution? And imagine, as once was the case, that Florida was still Spanish, Louisiana and most of the land up the Mississippi and the Missouri Rivers was French, and California was Mexican. Could we then say that we were all Americans—as opposed to New Yorkers, Virginians, or Hawaiians? Old Germany was something like this.

Compared to Great Britain, Germany was economically inferior. By the end of the eighteenth century, Britain was fully into its industrial revolution, the manufacturing center of the world, but the German-speaking peoples were still largely nobles in their castles and peasants in their fields. In no sense could "Germany" be considered a great power. At least not back then.

The Culture

Still, the German-speaking peoples were unsurpassed in poetry, drama, music, and philosophy. In fact, the late eighteenth century and the early nineteenth century in Germany was the age of the *Aufklärung*, the Enlightenment.

The most renowned dramatist of the age was Gotthold Lessing, who wrote *Nathan the Wise* (1779). The play was a plea for religious and racial tolerance; Hitler would ban it from the stages of Nazi Germany. The poets Friedrich von Schiller and Johann Wolfgang von Goethe likewise stressed the liberation of the human spirit. So did the genius composer Ludwig von Beethoven (who eventually resided in Vienna) and the philosopher Immanuel Kant.

Another writer carried the idea of liberation to an extreme. He was a Lutheran pastor and

Terms and Translations

Believe it or not, German is not a difficult language. It has long words, but so does English. So let's take a look at the word **Aufklärung**. The first part is *Auf*, like the English *up*. The second part, *klärung*, is the same as *clearing*. Take a look. *Klär* is pronounced like the name Clare and means "clear." The *ung* in German is *ing* in English. So Aufklärung means "clearing up"— or "enlightenment."

theologian named J. G. Herder. Interested in the songs and popular writings of the German past, Herder came up with the idea of *Volksgeist*, or spirit of the people.

Herder believed that the various peoples of Europe should develop their own spirit in their own ways; for him, such diversity would reflect the richness of humanity and God. Now, a crucial point: Herder did *not* espouse the idea of the superiority of the Germans to other peoples. The Nazis later would distort his teachings, claiming exactly the supremacy that Herder had rejected. But Herder *did* give voice to the notion of *nationalism* and in particular German nationalism: the right to be free of oppression.

Were the Germans an oppressed people? Some came to think they were. The years 1789 to 1815 saw the French under Napoleon Bonaparte coming to reign supreme over the German people.

> **Terms and Translations**
>
> Let's break down the word **Volksgeist**. In German, the letter *v* is pronounced *f*. So **Volks** means "folk." Ghost and *geist* are cognate words. You've heard of a poltergeist? It's a kind of ghost. And a ghost is a spirit. So Volksgeist means "spirit of the people."

> **Terms and Translations**
>
> **Nationalism** means more than national identity. Nationalism suggests that a nation—a people with a common past, a common heritage, and a common sense of being oppressed—has a common right to be freed from that oppression. The American Revolutionary War was an example of nationalism in action.

The Birth of German Nationalism Under Napoleon's Oppression

We all know of Napoleon—Napoleon I, Emperor of the French, King of Italy, and Protector of the Confederation of the Rhine—the little emperor who conquered nearly all of Europe; the Napoleon who in 1812 invaded Russia only to be driven back by snow, hunger, and Russian guerrillas; the Napoleon exiled first to the island of Elba in the Mediterranean; the Napoleon who returned to the European continent in 1814 only to be defeated by the British at Waterloo and exiled again, for the rest of his life, to the island of St. Helena in the South Atlantic.

But there was more to Napoleon than just the story of the rise and fall of a conqueror. Though based on military success, Napoleon's impact on conquered peoples reshaped institutions. This was true of the Poles, the Dutch, the Italians, and especially the Germans. In the German-speaking regions to the east of France, Napoleon introduced a common legal code and the beginnings of political unity.

An example was the Duchy of Württemberg in southern Germany. Take a look at the following two maps. In 1800, the duchy possessed islands of territory well separated from its main mass. Only 50 miles wide, Württemberg was surrounded by a mosaic of tiny, independent political units ruled, nominally, by something called the Holy Roman Empire (which someone said was not holy nor Roman nor an empire). But in 1810, after Napoleon had overrun central Europe, what was now the Kingdom of Württemberg was consolidated and enlarged, sticking down across the Danube, touching the border of Switzerland, and in the west extending almost to the Rhine.

Similar consolidations under Napoleon all over Germany reduced the number of states to about 40 and added to the efficiency of law and government. And in Württemberg, the duke, having been made king, was grateful to Napoleon. A line from Mel Brooks's musical *The Producers* describes how rulers must have felt: "It's good to be the king!"

Bet You Didn't Know

Napoleon defeated Prussia in the field of battle, a loss Prussia resented, and yet well-to-do Germans adored French culture.

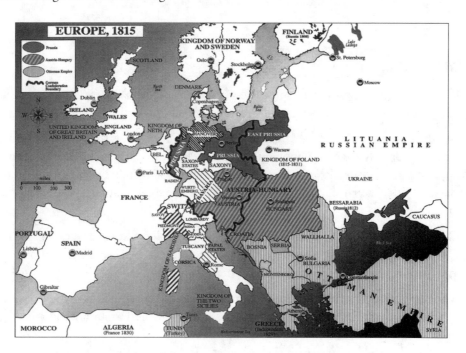

Map of Europe in 1815.

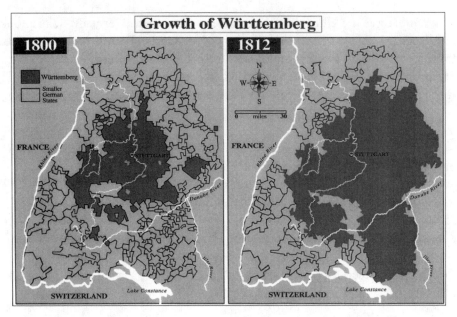

The Congress of Vienna.

Rise of Nationalism

If Napoleon got thanks from some, he got resistance from others. All across Europe, nationalism (the longing for freedom from French oppression) became the big idea.

Nowhere was the idea bigger than in Germany. There, after 1800, nationalism was directed not only against Napoleon and the French, but also against the Frenchified upper classes. Nationalism in Germany was felt most acutely by the middle and lower classes; Hitler later would pitch his appeals to the descendants of these same elements.

German nationalism, as it arose in the time of Napoleon, set the stage for Hitler. Ordinary Germans became fascinated with the idea of political unity and national greatness, largely because they had neither.

A pastor named Friedrich Ludwig Jahn (1778–1852) put together a youth movement in which young men carried out physical exercise for the Fatherland. He led them on long hikes in the countryside and staged rallies in which they screamed denunciations of German-speaking, pro-French aristocrats. In fact, he taught them to be suspicious of foreigners, Jews, and others who would supposedly corrupt the purity of the German *Volk* (folk).

The organization was a forerunner of the *Hitlerjugend,* or Hitler Youth. But the Hitler Youth organization was a long-term effect of the German revolt against the French.

In the short run, the major effect was the political transformation of Prussia and its rulers, the Hohenzollerns. An ancient German-speaking family, the Zollerns boasted an ancestral home in a castle on the Danube. During the Middle Ages they migrated northward, and they added "Hohen"—high—to their name, establishing themselves as rulers of Prussia.

Bet You Didn't Know

Did you know that the last of the Zollerns was still ruling during the first four decades of the twentieth century and then died in exile in Holland in 1941? The ruler was Kaiser Wilhelm II.

Kingdom of Prussia

By the time of Napoleon, Prussia was the biggest kingdom in northeastern Germany. It spread out along the Baltic roughly from Berlin, its capital, in the west, to Lithuania in the east.

Because Prussia lay along the Baltic, its geographical position ensured that the kingdom of Poland was land-locked. That geographical detainment would explode into World War II.

Prussia was an agricultural land, ruled by the Hohenzollerns and their aristocratic allies, wealthy landowners called the Junkers. The king and his nobles were a rigid caste, authoritarian in view, despising the merchant classes of western Germany, keeping their peasants in a state of serfdom, and worshipping all things military.

There was only one catch. Prussia had lost to Napoleon during the Napoleon Wars. So how was the kingdom to strengthen itself enough to get revenge against the French? One high-ranking officer in the Prussian army, a Baron von Stein, who had moved from western Germany where he had a castle on the Rhine, came up with an answer. Give the people, or at least some of the people, Stein contended, a stake in preserving Prussia. Stein was not advocating democracy. No way. Prussia was an *absolutist* state.

Terms and Translations

Absolutism is the idea that the monarch (or his equivalent, such as Stalin or Hitler) rules with an iron fist, tolerating no opposition and regarding himself as above the law. So the ruler's authority is absolute. But a warning: If you aspire to be such a dictator, you had better be good at it. Any display of weakness invites your enemies to try to overthrow you. This almost happened to Hitler.

Baron Stein also proposed that the old Prussian caste structure be made less rigid. Under Stein, in 1807, the peasants were liberated from serfdom. Many of them were allowed to move away from their villages. But those who stayed became hired farm hands, impoverished people without political or legal power. So far, thus, Stein's reforms were more apparent than real: Prussia's lower classes remained at the bottom of society.

But Stein's reforms also permitted the small merchant class in Prussia to buy land and to serve as officers in the army. The mercantile elements thereby could develop a sense of citizenship. This part of Stein's reform package was clever. Many of the merchants were bankers. Bankers always had money and kings always needed money. Prussia's financiers began funding Prussia's rulers, a pattern to be repeated when Hitler rose to power.

Militarily, however, Prussia was still weak, unable to provide a match for Napoleon. For Prussia, victory over France came about only when Napoleon retreated from Russia and Prussia joined a coalition of other European nations. In fact, when Napoleon suffered his final defeat at Waterloo in 1815, it was largely at the hands of the British general, the Duke of Wellington. Actually, the peace settlement produced at Vienna in 1814 and 1815 left Germany—the Germanies—almost as divided as before.

The Congress of Vienna

In October 1814, Prince Klement von Metternich, the foreign minister of Austria, Tsar Alexander I of Russia, Lord Castlereagh, the foreign secretary of Great Britain, Charles Talleyrand, the French foreign minister, and Prince Karl August von Hardenberg, the chancellor of Prussia, gathered in Vienna to redraw the map of Europe. Despite the differences among their countries, they shared an all-important conviction: Nothing like the Napoleonic wars should ever be allowed to occur again. The method they used to make sure of it was called the *balance of power*.

The conference took place in the Austrian capital. At the heart of the city stood an immense mass of buildings known as the Hofburg. This was the Austrian imperial residence, a town within the city.

Here were the territorial arrangements: Great Britain, with the mightiest fleet in the world, needed no land on the continent, although Lord Castlereagh reserved the right to intervene again if another power upset the

Terms and Translations

The idea of **balance of power** is this: If all the European great powers—Britain, France, Austria, Russia, and Prussia—were equal in military strength, then no one could get away with Napoleon-style aggression. What made up military strength? Largely, the number of soldiers. So a great power's population base and its territorial extent were important.

balance. France had to withdraw from Holland, the Rhineland, and Belgium to within its pre-revolutionary borders; Russia expanded into Poland; Austria got control of Lombardy and Venetia, the two provinces of northern Italy; and Prussia got the right to rule a patch of western Germany that bordered on Luxembourg, Belgium, and Holland.

Memorable Places

Having been built and added to over many centuries, the palace was full of contrasts. A dark fifteenth-century courtyard opened through an archway into a wide expanse of wall. Inside the huge windows, the chambers were done in gilt and white paneling and hung with glittering chandeliers. At green baize–covered tables under those chandeliers, the statesmen of Europe decided their continent's future.

But no one at the Congress of Vienna wanted Prussia, with its militaristic tradition, to gain too much territory, thus too many new inhabitants and a much larger army. So between Prussia proper and its new western acquisition, the statesmen at Vienna set up what was called the *German Confederation.*

The German Confederation

The membership of the German Confederation sounded like a street full of German beer gardens: the Kingdoms of Bavaria, Saxony, Württemberg, and Hanover; the Grand Duchies of Baden, Hesse-Darmstadt;, Mecklenburg-Schwerin, and Strelitz, Saxe-Weimar, and Oldenburg; the Electorate of Hesse-Cassel; the Duchies of Brunswick, Nassau, Saxe-Coburg-Gotha, Meiningun and Hildburghausen, Anhalt-Dessau, Bernburg, and Cöthen; the four free cities of Lübeck, Bremen, Hamburg, and Frankfurt-am-Main; and several smaller principalities. No member of the confederation could declare war on any other member—and no member could form an alliance with a foreign country that would hurt any other member. There was a central government called the Bundestag or Diet, but it was no more than a gathering of ambassadors from the various members; it did not even have the power to create its own army.

The creation of the confederation left German nationalists disappointed. Prussia and Austria (nominally part of the confederation) were separate monarchies. Although the free cities of the confederation respected individual liberties, kingdoms such as Bavaria did not. In many of the entities of the confederation, patriots who spoke out often landed in jail. The dream of a united German nation seemed impossible to attain.

The Germanies after 1815 furthermore appeared as economically inferior as ever. Three quarters of the people lived in villages or small towns: In Prussia, only Berlin, Breslau, and Königsberg had more than 50,000 inhabitants. Travel and communications were primitive: Many of the roads were only paths through the forests. Most Germans were farmers; artisans worked much as they had done in the Middle Ages. Silesia in the south was famous for its weaving and the Black Forest for its toy-making. The Germanies had no modern factories, no steam engines, no signs at all of economic modernity.

Economic and Social Change, 1815–1848

Germany, of course, is renowned for its industrial prowess. Its automobiles, watches, coffeemakers, and the like are the best in the world. And in the first half of the twentieth century, its military machine was fearsome. Yet in the two decades or so after the end of the Napoleonic wars, Germany was the least advanced of all the big European countries (except Russia). What brought about the growth?

The times, they were a changin'. Here and there, ambitious German investors began to copy Great Britain's manufacturing cornucopia. In 1835, the first German railroad was laid between Nürnberg and Fürth; by 1840, there were 282 miles of track; by 1850, 5,134 miles; and by 1860, more than 6,600 miles. Locomotive factories were constructed in Essen, steel plants in Solingen, and textile sheds in Silesia. In 1850, the Germanies produced only 208,000 tons of iron; by 1860, the output had risen to 1,391,555 tons. Using mechanized equipment, German farmers increased their food output. The German postal system became the most efficient in the world.

How do we explain Germany's rapid economic growth? It is a cliché, naturally, to talk of German organization and efficiency. But something else was involved. Isaac Watt, an eighteenth-century Scottish inventor, figured out how to put a tea kettle on something with wheels and use the power of the steam to make the wheels turn. After much work, Watt invented the steam engine. But the Germans didn't have to waste time inventing. They sent agents to Great Britain and copied Watt's designs. Germans did the same in America: They copied the McCormick reaper. They didn't bother reinventing the wheel, they copied it.

These remarkable economic developments were accompanied by shifts in the German social order. In line with medieval practice, the various monarchies and dukedoms of the German Confederation had excluded the middle classes from any role in public life. The newly rich business families, however, saw no reason why they should not share in political decisions. They would soon make their voices heard.

Another innovation was also underway: The very divisions among the Germanies of the confederation presented barriers to further economic growth. Trade in the region was impeded by a bewildering variety of water, inland, and provincial tolls. Some 2,775 articles were subject to duties, which were collected by some 8,000 customs officials. The following may seem imaginary, but it was true: A merchant who traded between Hamburg and Austria, or between Berlin and Switzerland, had to cross 10 borders, be familiar with 10 sets of tariffs, and pay 10 sets of duties. Prussia itself encompassed 67 different tolls and 119 different currencies.

The Zollverein (Customs Unions)

Gradually, between 1818 and 1834, merchants and manufacturers in the various Germanies consulted, demanded, and finally got a customs union called the *Zollverein*.

Terms and Translations

Zollverein is easy to translate as well. The German *Zoll* (pronounced *tsoll*) is the English toll, something you have to pay when you drive across many of our bridges. The German prefix *ver* often conveys the sense of bringing something about, or moving toward something. *Ein* means "one" or "un," as in "unity." So the Zollverein was a customs union, meaning an agreement among the various entities of the German Confederation to move toward the elimination of duties, tariffs, and quotas on goods that crossed their mutual borders. The European Community today is, among other things, a customs union or a Zollverein.

The idea of a Zollverein came originally from Friedrich List (1789–1846), an early economist who lived in Württemberg. It is hard to imagine that any professor of economics, the "dismal science," would be held up to public ridicule and persecution. Yet such was the case with List. Secret police agents spied on him, statesmen denounced him as a tool of German manufacturers, and newspapers branded him a traitor. What was his alleged crime? Aside from knowing that he was right and that just about everybody else was wrong, List preached a revolutionary (and, by the way, a non-Marxist) economic doctrine.

Up to a point, List, like German capitalists, aped the British. Many British economists, such as Adam Smith and David Ricardo, advocated free trade. So did List. Yet he wrote as a German. Maybe free trade, he admitted, was fine for the British. But if Germany were to achieve greatness, List was convinced, it had to enjoy free trade internally. However, externally Germany should erect tariff walls against foreign competition. Thus, Germany would protect its recent economic gains and, at the same time, free itself from the inefficiency of internal tariffs. Only with a free market inside, List held, could the Germanies become as efficient and productive as possible.

His ideas made sense to the businessmen. But the various kings, dukes, princes, and so forth of the German Confederation made tidy profits from the tolls they collected. So List was hitting them where it hurt—in their pocketbooks. That is why they treated him like dirt.

> **Bet You Didn't Know**
>
> List would be hailed as a patron saint throughout Germany. But while he was alive, his actual influence amounted to nothing—except that the government of Prussia saw the virtue of his ideas. Indeed, the leadership of the Zollverein movement came from the Prussians. Starting with their two separated geographical units, where they reduced tariffs and quotas, Prussian administrators slowly but surely, one by one, pressured the other German states into joining the Prussian customs union.

Announced on January 1, 1834, the Zollverein included 18 German states and a population of more than 23 million people, all under Prussian leadership. Economically speaking, the Germanies at last were on the way to becoming a united Germany.

But what kind of Germany? The Revolution of 1848 provided a tragic answer to that question.

The Revolution of 1848

For the aristocratic classes all over Europe, the year 1848 was nothing less than a nightmare. As in some kind of spontaneous combustion, screaming mobs milled through city streets, kings and ministers fled their palaces, and revolutionaries proclaimed republics. The movement spread from Copenhagen to Palermo and from Paris to Budapest, lasting from the early spring to late in the summertime.

Yet the revolutions of 1848 lacked enduring strength. Revolutionaries in various countries had little contact with each other and, poorly armed, had little means of defense against the police forces and armies of the great powers. The movement soon collapsed.

Such was the story of the Revolution of 1848 in the Germanies. Although the mercantile classes had little or no sympathy for the rabble in the streets, in May 1848, a group of professors, judges, lawyers, bureaucrats, clergy (both Protestant and Catholic), and businessmen met in Frankfurt. They were called the Frankfurt

Assembly and they talked a lot about tolerance, democracy, and even an all-German constitution.

But the talk came to nothing. As the tide of revolution receded, liberalism was submerged in the stronger sentiment of nationalism. Throughout the Germanies people were left with a legacy of Prussian discipline, efficiency, and authoritarianism. The revolutionaries of 1848 had hoped that German unity could lead to freedom. They had it backward. After 1848, the prevailing view was that unity could come about only through force and that force, in turn, would produce not freedom but cohesion. As the political liberalism of 1848 faded away, the idea of German unification through *Eisen und Blut* (iron and blood) became the prevailing doctrine.

So by the early 1860s, the Germanies were ready for the advent of the political and diplomatic genius who would forge just such a unification. He was Otto von Bismarck.

The Least You Need to Know

- ◆ What we call Germany as late as the mid-nineteenth century was not even a country at all.

- ◆ Compared to France and Great Britain, the region called Germany was economically poor.

- ◆ Many Germans envisioned a united nation.

- ◆ Although revolutionaries had hoped the unification of Germany would result in freedom, German nationalism continued to be marked by stressed authority and military power.

- ◆ By the beginning of the nineteenth century, Germans were attaining economic unity, which would provide the foundation of the political unification soon to be brought about by Otto von Bismarck.

The German Empire: 1866–1871

In This Chapter

- ◆ Germany just before Bismarck
- ◆ Bismarck's rise to power
- ◆ Bismarck's little war with Denmark
- ◆ Bismarck wages war with Austria
- ◆ A part of France falls into Bismarck's hands
- ◆ Bismarck's dream is realized; Germany unites

As we have seen, even after the Revolution of 1848, the Germans were a politically divided people. As far as France and Russia were concerned, this state of affairs was just fine. Ever since the Protestant Reformation, which made northern Germany largely Lutheran, largely Catholic France sought deliberately to keep the Germans in rivalry with each other: Paris had no desire for a strong power just to the east; keeping Germany divided was official French policy. And later, when Russia had begun to take part in European affairs, St. Petersburg, too, saw benefit in the pulverization of the Germanic world—the benefit being a chance for expansion along the Baltic and into Poland.

Terms and Translations

Divisa et impera is a term of Latin origin, meaning "divide and conquer," a classic strategy used by great powers for ruling others. The premise of divide and conquer is that if you can get the locals to fight among themselves, their ensuing weakness allows you room to rule. Such had been the fate of Germany before the middle of the nineteenth century.

Gradually, though, again as we have seen, a lot of Germans came to resent being divided up. They became nationalistic. But unlike nationalism in France and Great Britain, where patriots lauded their liberties, German nationalism took on a special hue. Regarding the individualism of the Western powers as fundamentally selfish, and sneering at the principle of liberty so cherished west of the Rhine, German nationalists tended to glorify group values, collectivism, and, above all, the state. German nationalism became hooked up with the idea of authoritarianism.

It was also linked with the sentiments of ethnic superiority. Although the Nazis eventually trumpeted the supposed supremacy of so-called Aryans over Jews, German racism in the early to mid-nineteenth century had to do mainly with the assumption of the inferiority of the Slavic peoples, Poles, Czechs, Slovaks, and other such Eastern Europeans.

Before we go on, we should recognize that, whatever the borders of Germany from time to time, throughout much of Eastern Europe, Germans, Poles, Czechs, Slovaks, Hungarians, Romanians, and Ukrainians lived closely together, sometimes in nearby towns and villages and sometimes even side by side. Eastern Europe was a marbled cake in which peoples of different ethnicities were swirled together. Often they intermarried and followed the same occupations.

Yet German nationalists extracted from this intermixture of similar people the myth of their own genius. And, until Hitler, no one capitalized better on the myth than did Otto von Bismarck, the Iron Chancellor of Prussia.

Bismarck Expands the Military During His Reign

Of all the European great powers, Prussia had always been the smallest and weakest. Although the Congress of Vienna had allowed Prussia to expand westward, leaders in Berlin after the Revolution of 1848 were frightened. The state had survived the uprisings, but who knew what lay ahead? Then, in the middle of the 1850s, the British and French on the one side and the Russians on the other had gone to war (the Crimean

War) over Russia's desire to expand into the Mediterranean. Britain and France had won, without bothering to seek Prussian help. And by 1861, Italy had unified, driving the Austrians from most of the area north of the peninsula and without any Prussian saying of "yes" or "no." High-ranking Prussians saw their country as becoming irrelevant in European affairs.

Such was the general background to the ascendancy of Bismarck. More specifically, the Prussian king, Wilhelm I, believed that he had to double the size of his army and wanted a new *Diet*, or parliament, to fork out the money. This legislative body should not be confused with the British House of Commons or the French Chamber of Deputies, where the middle classes had at least some representation. The Prussian Diet was dominated by men of great wealth. Unfortunately for the king, the wealthiest men in his domains were the new capitalists from along the Rhineland. They all professed patriotism, naturally. But they also despised standing armies and all the militarist traditions of the Prussian *Junkers* (the land-owning class), from whom the officer corps was almost entirely recruited and whom they despised as antiquated agriculturalists. So the Diet refused to put up the money to increase military numbers.

Desperate to strengthen the military, the king cast about for help. The person he turned to was Otto von Bismarck. Born in 1815, Bismarck was a tall, bulky man of aristocratic Junker background but with a reputation for utter rebelliousness. As a youth he had been a playboy, an indifferent student, a classic devotee of wine, women, and song, and of duels (supposedly 25 in all), and a wastrel who had indifferently occupied minor governmental posts. He had abandoned one position to run off to Switzerland in the hopes of marrying a young woman who rejected him. He had then returned bankrupt to his ancestral manor house in East Prussia; there he had made a pretense of being a stolid, unimaginative, dull Junker landlord. As a manager of his estates, he had been an utter failure.

Yet he was an aristocrat and so he came to the attention of the king. Bismarck was no German nationalist and he did not look upon Germany as the Fatherland. He was a Prussian, although far more intelligent and worldly than most of those who stayed on their East Prussian estates. Still, as a Prussian he regarded the members of the Diet as unwelcome free-thinkers and liberals. When the king chose him as chancellor in 1862, he had but one goal—buttressing the might of Prussia. And if Prussia became strengthened at the expense of the liberals, too bad.

By Blood and Iron

So Bismarck did have a principle: Prussian supremacy. But no other principle bound him for long; he accepted no formal ideology or any conventional morality. Once in high office, he became the classic practitioner of *Realpolitik*.

Terms and Translations

When the Spanish conquered the New World, they used the word *real* to mean the wishes of the king. In time, the French picked up the word, and then the Germans under Bismarck. Because the king was supposed to be above the law, *Realpolitik*, the German version of the term, meant a foreign policy uninhibited by considerations of morality, religion, or ethics, but rather one based on what the king—or his first minister—considered to be the Prussian national interest.

For Bismarck, the only thing that mattered was Prussia's national interest, at least as he saw it. Nothing else made any difference. The king would fear him, the Junkers would consider him a traitor to his class, and the liberals of the West would think him their friend, only to later consider him their enemy. To Bismarck, enemies and friends were about the same: The friend of today might be the opponent of tomorrow. He loathed making long-range plans. Instead, he was practical and opportunistic. When he saw his opportunities, he took them.

When Bismarck became chancellor in 1862, his job, or duty, was to get the capitalists in the Diet to fork out money to enhance the army. The struggle went on for four years. The members of the body simply refused to raise taxes. But under Bismarck, government officials collected the revenues anyway. Bismarck did not care what the Diet thought. The people of Prussia were docile and respectful of uniforms. And they were intimidated. Military needs won out over any doctrine of government by consent.

There was another reason people paid up. Nationalism was strong enough to lead people to believe that an army reorganized, retrained, and re-equipped was the key to the reunification of Germany.

Members of the Diet argued that Bismarck's tax policy was unconstitutional. The constitution, he replied, was hardly intended to weaken the state. Bismarck was undermining freedom, and the liberals fought back. What Germans admired in Prussia, Bismarck retorted coldly, was its power.

Bismarck went even further. The borders of Prussia, as established by the Congress of Vienna in 1815, he declared, had to be changed; Prussia must be ready and willing to seize any and all chances for expansion. To this, he added his most memorable utterance: "Not by speeches and majority votes are the great questions of the day decided—that was the great error of 1848—but by blood and iron!"

Something Is Rotten in the State of Denmark

One of Bismarck's opportunities arose in 1867, only a year after his victory over the parliamentarians. The northernmost provinces of the German Federation were Holstein and, just south of Denmark, Schleswig. The population of Schleswig was about half German and half Danish. Like Bismarck, the king of Denmark wanted to expand, so he set his sights on the acquisition of Schleswig. Yet Germans of all stripes could agree on one thing: Denmark was not going to have Schleswig. So the legislative body of the German Confederation called for an all-German war against Denmark.

Did Bismarck, the man of "iron and blood," go along with this? Absolutely not! He didn't want the confederation strengthened at all and he certainly did not want German unity unless Prussia could be the unifier. But at the same time, he didn't want to frighten the Germans outside of Prussia into forming an alliance against him. So he formed his own alliance with Austria.

> **Terms and Translations**
>
> An **alliance** is a formal pact between nations in a common cause. Are alliances enduring? The answer to this depends on what the partners want.

In 1864, Prussia and Austria together went to war against Denmark and easily won. So Schleswig was safe from Danish control. But Bismarck wanted more than that. He wanted to join both Schleswig and Holstein to Prussia. Again, he chose to act by stealth. So he got the Austrians to agree to a Prussian occupation of Schleswig while they, the Austrians, marched into Holstein. The Austrians thought it was a fair deal. We come back, though, to the old business of tariffs and other rights of transit. Despite the *Zollverein*, Bismarck made it difficult for farmers in Holstein to sell their goods across the border in Schleswig. This seems like a trivial matter. Yet while Bismarck pretended to regulate border disputes, he actually allowed them to get nasty. Soon they would provide him with a pretext for another war, this one against Austria.

In the meantime, Bismarck worked to isolate Austria diplomatically. This was not hard to do. The British were deliberately staying out of continental conflicts. In 1863, Bismarck had taken care to join Russia in suppressing a Polish rebellion, so St. Petersburg was well disposed toward Prussia and Bismarck. Italy had just become unified, driving the Austrians out of Lombardy; to win over the new Italian king, Bismarck held out the lure of Venetia, the province around Venice.

What about France? France had a new emperor, Napoleon III. But unlike his famous ancestor, he faced a lot of discontent at home. Having committed himself to trying (unsuccessfully) to create an empire in Mexico, he was not paying much attention to what was going on in the Rhineland. Besides, Bismarck met with Napoleon III at Biarritz, a popular resort on the southwestern coast of France. Usually gruff and forbidding, Bismarck was charm itself. In his meeting with the French monarch, Bismarck hinted vaguely that he would allow France to expand somewhere. He did not specify just where. But the tactic worked. Napoleon III agreed to condone a Prussian war against Austria.

But Bismarck was still not finished. He wanted widespread German support against Austria, so he presented himself as a democrat. He said that he was all for reform in the German Confederation: It could have a real legislature elected by universal male suffrage. (As in the United States at the time, women did not have the right to vote.) He figured that most Germans were not supporters of either the capitalists or the various governmental entities of the confederation. Like Hitler later, Bismarck would use mass support to undermine all established interests that stood in his way. Bismarck was now ready for his war with Austria.

Bismarck Coaxes Austria into War

Bismarck had made sure that Prussia and Austria would keep on squabbling over transit rights between Schleswig and Holstsein. Things got so bad that Austria went before the German Confederation to ask for help. Convinced of the justice of the Austrian cause, the ambassadors to the confederation demanded that Bismarck end the border disputes. Rather than give way, Bismarck sneered at the confederation as having no authority, accused Austria of aggression, and ordered Prussian troops to march into Holstein, which had earlier been occupied by Austria. Austria in turn declared war on Prussia and persuaded the confederation to send an all-German force against Prussia. So now, in 1866, Bismarck was at war not only with Austria but also with most of the other German states along the Rhine.

His enemies didn't have a chance. The Prussian army was the best-trained in Europe. Its troops were also equipped with the new needle-gun, with which infantrymen could fire off five rounds in a minute. Commanded by the brilliant General Helmuth von Moltke, the Prussian troops rode off to battle most of the way aboard trains that by the mid-1860s steamed along the most sophisticated railroad network in Europe. The opposition was no match for Prussia's troops. The confederation troops had no unified command and Austria's troops were mainly Czechs, Slovaks, Hungarians, and others who had little or no motivation to fight for the German-speaking emperor in Vienna.

The decisive battle took place at a town called Königsgrätz near Prague. The Austrian defeat was humiliating, and Moltke soon defeated the other German states, picking them off one by one.

The Austro–Prussian War lasted only seven weeks. Bismarck brought it to a close before the other European great powers even realized what had happened.

Bismarck Forms the North German Confederation

Bismarck annexed both Schleswig and Holstein, along with Hanover (a big state just south of Holstein), the Duchies of Nassau and Hesse-Cassel, and the free city of Frankfurt. These acquisitions joined Prussia proper with the western territories gained at the Congress of Vienna. In those captured territories, old governments simply disappeared. So did the German Confederation.

In its place, Bismarck created a North German Confederation in 1867. It included the newly expanded Prussia and 21 other German states.

South of the Main River, in the middle of Germany, Bavaria, Baden, Württemberg, Hesse-Darmstadt, and Austria were outside Bismarck's new group, with no kind of union among themselves. Italy had taken advantage of Austria's defeat to take over Venetia, just as Bismarck had promised it could do.

Bismarck next busied himself with organizing the North German Confederation. He made it much stronger than the older German Confederation. The Prussian king became the hereditary monarch. Ministers of all the states were responsible to him. Bismarck set up a parliament with two chambers. In the upper house, as in the United States, the states as such were represented. Members of the lower house, again as in the United States, were elected by universal male suffrage. Bismarck *seemed* to be modeling his new confederation on the Constitution of the United States of America.

Recall that Bismarck had made the Prussian king monarch of the new confederation. However, at that time, the king, Wilhelm I, was weak. So while the constitution made the ministers of the various states responsible to the king, in practice they had to report to Bismarck. Bismarck, in effect, was a dictator, backed by secret police and the potent Prussian army.

Why did Bismarck implement the parliament (an American style of government)? Because Bismarck wanted allies against the wealthy industrialists whose factories lined the banks of the Rhine and its tributaries. What allies? The socialists and the labor unions that in the 1850s and 1860s had arisen in protest against the excesses of the capitalists.

However, when we say socialists here we are not talking about Marxists. During the Revolution of 1848, Karl Marx had fled Germany and eventually settled in London, where in 1867 he published his huge work, *Das Kapital.*

The socialist leader in Germany at the time was Ferdinand Lassalle. Unlike Marx, Lassalle believed it possible to improve the conditions of the working class through the existing political system rather than by overthrowing it.

" " Supporting Actors

We usually associate "socialism" with Karl Marx. Ironically, however, the heart of his doctrine—that a revolution by the workers in the industrialized countries was inevitable—has never come true. The major socialist or communist revolutions have taken place in Russia and China, two countries that until well into the twentieth century were agricultural lands. Marx underestimated the power, wealth, and simple survivability of the capitalist classes in Western and Central Europe. But the socialism of Lassalle was not revolutionary: It called for the use of *political* power.

So Bismarck, the archconservative from East Prussia, formed an alliance with Lassalle, the nonrevolutionary socialist. In so doing, Bismarck linked nationalism and socialism to support his empire. This concept of nationalism and socialism developed by Bismarck became ingrained in German thinking.

The French Are Next to Fall

The situation on both sides of the Rhine, however, was unstable. The remaining states in southern Germany were floating in empty space; sooner or later, they were probably going to drift into a larger orbit—Austrian, Prussian, or French. France itself was having troubles. Napoleon III's intervention in Mexico was a fiasco; a united Italy had arisen on France's southeastern frontier. And in violation of the cardinal principle of French foreign policy for centuries—the disunion of Germany—most of the German people were now citizens of a single and powerful state.

In Paris, Napoleon III, or at least some of his advisors, began to talk of war toward the east. If only France could seize the moment and defeat Germany! The defeat in Mexico would be forgotten! Italy would no longer be a factor! And the old divisions of Germany could be restored.

In Berlin, Bismarck heard these rumors of war. He must have been pleased. At a minimum, he could use them to frighten the southern German states into an alignment with Prussia and the North German Confederation.

Luck played right into Bismarck's hands. A revolution had taken place in Spain and the queen had fled into exile. Then a provisional government in Madrid invited Prince

Leopold of Hohenzollern, a cousin of Prussia's Wilhelm I, to be Spain's constitutional monarch: He would reign, but the Spanish parliament would rule. Upon learning of the offer, Paris was aghast. Just imagine: Hohenzollerns to the east of them and Hohenzollerns to the south of them!

As it turned out, Prince Leopold had no interest in going to Spain and three times refused the offer. Enter Bismarck: He persuaded the Spanish to try again, and on July 2, 1870, news of Leopold's acceptance reached Paris. Outraged, Paris instructed Vincente Benedetti, its ambassador to Prussia, to protest. Benedetti met Wilhelm I at the spa of Ems, officially demanding that the acceptance be withdrawn. The king complied, and on July 12, Leopold stated definitively that he would not be the Spanish king. This disappointed Bismarck.

But then the French government cabled Benedetti to see the Prussian king again at Ems and to demand that never again should a Hohenzollern be named king of Spain. Refusing to make a commitment, Wilhelm I wired a report of the conversation to Bismarck in Berlin. Bismarck saw another opportunity. He doctored the Ems telegram so that when it was published, Prussian readers would think their king had been insulted and the French would think their ambassador had been treated rudely. Bismarck's editing produced the results he wanted. In both France and Prussia, people demanded war.

The issue of the Spanish throne had already been settled. However, on July 19, 1870, the government of Napoleon III made the fatal mistake of declaring war on Prussia.

Bet You Didn't Know

You might have the idea that countries disregard treaties at will. Usually they don't, or if they do, there are good reasons for doing so. In tearing up the 1856 treaty, Russia took advantage of France's weakness. However, as you'll soon learn, Russia later entered into a treaty *with* France. There's an old expression: The enemy of my enemy is my friend. After Bismarck's invasion of France, who do you think Paris and St. Petersburg saw as their enemy? Germany, of course.

Bismarck had done the work to isolate France. The British frowned upon Napoleon's adventure in Mexico. Italy had not yet taken Rome, because French troops were there; but with the outbreak of war between France and Prussia, Paris withdrew those troops and the Italians waltzed right into the Eternal City. The Russians also had no love for France: According to the peace treaty of 1856, which ended the Crimean War, Russia had been forbidden to keep naval ships on the Black Sea. With Prussia and France on the brink of war, Russia gleefully broke the treaty.

France didn't have a chance without allies and because they weren't as advanced militarily and economically compared to Prussia. The Franco–Prussian War (later called the Franco–German) began on July 19, 1870. Prussia now had the support of the southern German states (with the exception of Austria). Crossing Luxembourg, Bismarck's army simply crashed into France. As the troops marched in their pointed helmets, gray uniforms, and jackboots across the pleasant countryside of northeastern France, huge columns of dust rose against the blue late summer sky. Moving as fast as they could, thousands of French peasants and refugees clogged the roadways; their numbers were more effective than the French army in slowing the German advance.

Then came the Battle of Sedan in a frontier fortress town. When the principal French general was seriously wounded and had to be evacuated, Napoleon III himself showed up on the scene. The Germans captured Napoleon III and made him a prisoner. Later they released him and, along with the Empress Eugénie, he high-tailed it to England.

But Bismarck wasn't finished. He ordered General von Moltke to proceed into Paris. For four months in the winter of 1870 to 1871, the Germans besieged the French capital. Paris did not surrender, but people in the city were reduced to eating rats and sparrows.

At the palace of Versailles, outside Paris, on January 18, 1871, Bismarck proclaimed the creation of the German Empire, the Second *Reich*. He also staged a ceremony whereby his king, Wilhelm I, received the hereditary title of Emperor of Germany. The rulers of the lesser German states (except, of course, Austria) accepted Wilhelm's imperial authority.

Ten days later, the people of Paris, shivering and starving, at last opened the gates to the Teutonic troops. Entering the city, Bismarck imposed harsh terms of peace.

Terms and Translations

The German word **reich** is a cognate of the English *rich*. An empire is supposed to be rich, so the Germans called their empire a Reich. The First Reich was buried in the mystical mists of medieval history. Bismarck's was the Second Reich. Hitler's was the Third Reich.

France had to pay Germany an indemnity of five billion gold francs, an enormous sum and without precedent in European history. They also had to forfeit most of two provinces along the eastern border, Alsace and Lorraine.

The Alsatians spoke German, but they considered themselves to be French, and they protested vigorously over being moved around like cattle. They protested in vain. In Frankfurt on May 10, 1871, Bismarck dictated the peace treaty. Alsace and Lorraine were now part of the German Empire—an amputation that the French were not about to forget.

Germany Finally Unites

The consolidation of Germany (except for Austria) under Bismarck changed the face of Europe. Reversing the arrangements of the Congress of Vienna, it created a geographical, political, and economic German colossus astride the center of Europe. Germany was by far the strongest state on the continent and, industrializing rapidly after 1871, it became even stronger.

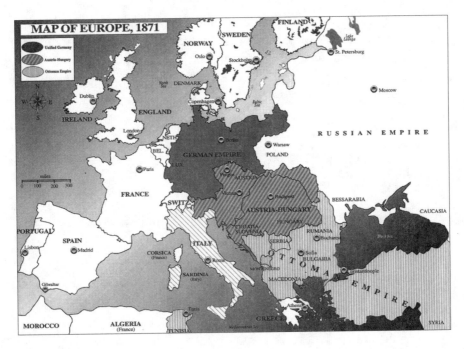

Map of Europe, 1871.

And the consolidation of the German Empire was by Bismarck's creation. In bringing the German Empire into existence, he had outfoxed many, including Germans themselves. He allowed each of the German states to keep their own laws, government, and constitution. On paper, the German Empire looked like a federation; however, make no mistake, Bismarck's new Germany was based on the coupling of authoritarianism with nationalism and socialism.

Otto von Bismarck never heard of Adolph Hitler or Nazi Germany. But he created exactly the institutions, the culture, and the sentiments that Hitler would exploit to the fullest.

The Least You Need to Know

◆ After Napoleon, Bismarck was the political genius of the nineteenth century.

◆ Bismarck used an old tactic to weaken geographic areas that he wished to takeover: Divide and conquer.

◆ Blood, iron, and superb diplomatic skills where the tools Bismarck used to bring about the unification of the German Empire.

◆ The methods by which Bismarck expanded Prussia into that German Empire laid the groundwork for Hitler's Third Reich: an authoritarian state supported by the ideas of nationalism and socialism.

Wilhelm's Germany: 1871–1914

In This Chapter

- ◆ Bismarck's hidden agenda, the Kulturkampf
- ◆ Kaiser Wilhelm II's attempts at imperialization
- ◆ Germany's expansion attempts and political actions put neighboring countries on the defense
- ◆ Germany fights fire with fire, attempting to create a great naval fleet to rival Great Britain
- ◆ Serbian nationalists' desire for freedom sparks the First World War

Bismarck has been called a "white revolutionary"—as opposed to a "red revolutionary" conservative as opposed to a Communist—who overturned the existing order in Europe. But with Bismarck gone, could any German leader maintain international order? Could Kaiser Wilhelm II? Sadly for the future of Germany, he could not.

Bismarck's Final Years of Power

After Bismarck's unification of Germany, the sense of safety that had marked international relations since the Congress of Vienna began to turn into fear. The statesmen at Vienna had pinned their hopes for peace on the disunity of Germany; an effective union of Germany, they believed, would revolutionize European affairs. Events proved them right. Once united (or almost united, because it still lacked Austria), Germany embarked on a period of unprecedented industrial expansion. Manufacturing, finance, and shipping grew phenomenally. In 1865, for example, Germany had produced less steel than France; by 1900 it was outproducing France and Great Britain together. Not surprisingly, German nationalists craved a Europe-wide recognition of Germany's superpower status.

Bismarck saw the dangers of such a position. Germany, he realized, was powerful but fragile. Its divisions were deep: peasants versus landowners; workers versus capitalists; northerners versus southerners; Protestants versus Catholics; and just about everybody, overtly or covertly, against Slavs, Jews, and other "foreigners." Any one of these divisions, Bismarck feared, could tear his creation apart.

Modern Day Parallels

A diplomatic term: honest broker. A modern parallel: In 1978, President Jimmy Carter led the Egyptian president and the Israeli prime minister to enter into full diplomatic relations. Under Carter, the United States sought no territory, only peace. What did Carter have to gain from his work? A reputation as a peacemaker. So it was with Bismarck. He didn't want any land in the Balkans. But he did want to show the leaders of the other European great powers that he could be trusted to keep the peace. That was his way of ensuring Germany's safety abroad.

So, having overturned the balance of power, he tried to restore it. He forged alliances with both Russia and Austria-Hungary (as Austria was renamed after its loss of most of northern Italy), even though those two empires were competitors in the Balkans. And in 1878, he staged a new European convocation, the Congress of Berlin. The issue had to do with who would control the Balkans. The Ottoman Empire (or Turkey), the ruler of the region for centuries, was the "sick man of Europe," receding fast. Russia, in an expansionist mood again, had ambitions in the region; so did the French and the Austrians. Although wanting no colonies in the area, Great Britain wanted to keep the Russians out of the Mediterranean and hence out of the Balkans. At the Congress of Berlin, Bismarck brought about a solution to the problem. Russia could make advances down the Black Sea into Romania, but no farther; France could trade with the locals; and Austria-Hungary got control of Croatia (basically along the northern Adriatic) and Slovenia in the north, and influence in the provinces of Bosnia and Herzegovina, right in the middle of what one day became (and then ceased to be) Yugoslavia. Bismarck came out of the affair with the reputation of being an honest broker.

The Kulturkampf

Bismarck-the-honest-broker, however, had not suddenly become a liberal at home. In the last two decades of his time in power (from 1871 to 1890), he restricted the power of the parliament, crushed press freedoms, and drove many of the socialists underground. Ironically, he became a sort of socialist himself, using the resources of the German state to insure workers against sickness, accident, and incapacity in old age; thus he lifted the lid from the pressure cooker of social discontent. Imperial Germany under Bismarck was years ahead of the more democratic France, Great Britain, and the United States. Bismarck was the pioneer of the welfare state, even if his motive was to keep the masses content with bread (welfare policies) and circuses (public displays of German military might).

Above all, Bismarck wanted to keep the masses under his control. So starting in 1871, he launched a political campaign called the *Kulturkampf.*

The Kulturkampf, in which the Protestant liberals of western Germany joined eagerly, was an anti-Catholic campaign. Under Bismarck's rule, laws imposed restrictions on Catholic worship and education, the Jesuits were expelled from Germany, and many Catholic bishops throughout Germany were arrested or sent into exile.

Terms and Translations

Kulturkampf. *Kultur,* obviously, means "culture." What about **kampf?** Look at the first four letters of the English word *campaign. Kampf* and *camp* are almost the same. So *kampf* means a "campaign" or "struggle." Hitler's later infamous autobiography, *Mein Kampf,* meant, simply, *My Struggle.*

Bismarck Is Fired

In time, Bismarck came to believe that his anti-Catholic efforts were fruitless; Catholicism was deeply engrained in southern Germany. Besides, he wanted the political support of Catholics for his social reform programs.

Many of the Catholics living within the borders of the German Empire were Poles. And the Kulturkampf took on an aspect of anti-foreignism. Like other Slavs, the

Poles were supposed to be racially inferior to those of *pure* Germanic stock. Later, it would be an easy step for those pure Germans to target another foreign group, the Jews.

And Bismarck himself, in his later years, came to think that the socialists, Poles, and Jews, together or as individual groups, would try to destroy his empire from within. He even contemplated military action through which he could overthrow civilian rule altogether.

He never quite got to that point. In 1890, when he was 75 years old, the new emperor, Wilhelm II, forced him to retire.

When he learned of his dismissal, Bismarck was furious. He had been the political genius who had brought Germany to its pinnacle of power. And here he was dumped. The pilot was gone from the ship. Yet Bismarck was also a Prussian royalist and in the end he accepted his monarch's decision.

The Kaiser and His Character

Kaiser Wilhelm I died in 1888. And his son, Kaiser Friedrich III, ill with cancer, passed away after only three months on the throne. Thus began the reign (1888–1918) of Wilhelm's grandson and Friedrich's son, Kaiser Wilhelm II. From the outset, he was determined to be what his grandfather had not been, Bismarck's true superior.

Born in 1859 of then-Prince Friedrich and Princess Victoria (a daughter of England's Queen Victoria), Wilhelm had been a rambunctious, energetic, bright child with a withered left arm and hand. As he grew up, he could not use a knife and fork, and at state dinners he had to rely on a partner or footman to cut his meat. The left sleeves of his coats and uniforms had to be cut short. As he matured, his formal photographs almost always showed his miniature left hand holding a pair of gloves, an optical illusion intended to elongate the arm.

Did the handicap affect his character? Perhaps so, but he certainly was no recluse. Although no more than 5'9" in height, Wilhelm carried himself as if he were taller, strutting into a room with the stiff stride of a Prussian officer. "If he laughed," a British observer commented, "which he is sure to do a good many times, he will laugh with absolute abandonment, throwing back his head, opening his mouth to the fullest extent possible, and often stamping with one foot to show his excessive enjoyment of any joke ..." He was wholehearted about everything. He spoke English fluently and idiomatically, with no trace of a German accent. He worshipped his grandmother, Queen Victoria, and all things English.

The world outside Germany saw the kaiser as a caricature, with the upturned moustaches, the metallic snarling voice, the pointed Prussian helmet, the uniforms, and the parade-ground manner that itself looked like a declaration of war. Behind the image, though, was the human being: His barber visited him every morning to wax the facial hair into position; the flat and lifeless tone of his voice was the result of a throat operation; and offstage his public bellicosity turned into private timidity. Like his father and grandfather before him, he was afraid of Bismarck. He was also jealous of the great man and, convinced that he himself could lead Germany on a new course, he fired the old chancellor abruptly.

Around Europe, people referred to Wilhelm's action as "dropping the pilot." And despite the four chancellors who succeeded Bismarck, it was Wilhelm II who dominated policy. But whether he was as good a pilot as Bismarck remained an open question.

Domestically, the kaiser's new course was only partly new. True, there was no Kulturkampf; the anti-socialist laws were abandoned; the social welfare programs were expanded; elections were permitted; and a few political parties were allowed to exist. But Wilhelm II inaugurated no serious moves toward democracy. He was obsessed with what he believed to be the divinely ordained rights and privileges of the House of Hohenzollern. And the German Empire still rested on the power of the various local princes, the arms, the industrialists, and the ancient landowning class, the Junkers.

Nevertheless, a democratic spirit was growing. A new party, the Social Democrats, called for political reforms, especially by allowing majority rule in the Reichstag, or federal parliament. From Wilhelm's point of view, the Social Democrats really got out of hand. In the election of 1912, they got four and a quarter million votes, about one third of all cast, and they were the largest single party in the assembly.

All the same, they were excluded from the highest posts in the government. Even without the coming of the First World War, the German Empire, created by Bismarck, was moving toward a political crisis: The issue was whether Germany should at last be a democracy.

But Germany under the kaiser was also moving toward something else: a reaching for world, or at least European, domination.

Germany's Place in the Sun

In the late nineteenth century, all the major European powers were engaged in imperialism. Great Britain led the way with colonies or dominions (such as Canada) stretching all around the world; India was considered the jewel in the British imperial crown. The French acquired colonies in North and sub-Saharan Africa and in Vietnam. Belgium got the Congo. Russia had expanded all across Manchuria to Vladivostok, the port city on the North Pacific. Japan, too, got into the act, defeating China in a war fought in 1894 to 1895 and taking Taiwan and Korea as colonies.

Germany got what was left over: Tanganyika (now Tanzania) on the East African coast, a scattering of Pacific islands spread out above New Guinea, and Shandong, a Chinese peninsula that jutted up toward Korea. This was, however, not much of an overseas empire, and to German imperialists its small size was an embarrassment.

Building a Strong Navy

In much the same way that Bismarck had built German nationalism, by official governmental policy, Wilhelm II and his ministers sought deliberately to infuse the German population with the doctrine of imperialism. Why did they have to preach? Because building an empire overseas meant the construction of a powerful new German navy. But navies are expensive and many throughout Germany wanted the government to spend more money on social welfare. So the kaiser's imperialism, however sincere, served the political purpose of defeating his opponents. In speech after speech, the kaiser announced that "our future lies on the seas" and "the trident must pass into our hands." "Our navy," he went as far as to say, "will grow and flourish, during peaceful times to promote the peaceable interests of the Fatherland, and in war times to destroy the enemy, if God helps us."

Wilhelm did not name the enemy. But he did raise the possibility of a general war.

> **Terms and Translations**
>
> Obviously, **imperialism** is related to empire. But an empire, such as Germany's under Bismarck, does not necessarily try to expand. Imperialism thus is a doctrine that says the empire has a *right* to expand. So imperialism is nationalism taken a step further: Nationalism talks about a people's common destiny and imperialism says that such a destiny lies in taking over other people's lands.

> **Bet You Didn't Know**
>
> If you go to a Chinese restaurant or supermarket, you might encounter Tsingtao Beer. The name is Chinese and it is imported from China. But from its strong taste, you think it must be a German beer. That's because it is. Tsingtao (now spelled Qingdao) is the capital of Shandong Province and the Chinese have preserved a brewery that was commissioned by Kaiser Wilhelm II.

The kaiser's diplomacy was certainly personal. Once Bismarck had consolidated the German Empire, he presented a peaceful face to the rest of Europe—but not so with Wilhelm. Careful to maintain his personal rule, he followed Bismarck with a string of weak chancellors: General von Caprivi (1890–1894), an old soldier; Prince Hohenlohe

(1894–1900), aged uncle of the emperor; Prince Bernhard von Bülow (1900–1909), a courtier whose principal quality was his ability to flatter; and Theodor Bethmann Hollweg (1909–1917), an inexperienced administrator. So Wilhelm kept control of German diplomacy in his own hands.

Wilhelm's Political Faux Pas

Unlike Bismarck, however, the kaiser was deplorably inept. In January 1896, when a British raid against the Boers in South Africa failed, Wilhelm II sent a telegram of congratulations to Paul Kruger, president of the Transvaal Republic. "I express to you my sincere congratulations that, supported by your people and without appealing from help to friendly powers, you have succeeded by your energetic action against armed bands that invaded your country as disturbers of the peace, and have therefore been able to restore peace and safeguard the independence of the country against outside attacks." When the message was published in England, it aroused a storm of protest. Three years later, Lord Salisbury, the prime minister, said: "The raid was folly, but the telegram was even more foolish."

It was foolish because it made Wilhelm look as if he were trying to stir up trouble with London. Maybe he was. What is clear is that the telegram was wildly popular throughout Germany and even most of the European continent. The continentals loathed the British Empire and its aggression in South Africa. Nonetheless, the British portrayed Wilhelm as the aggressor.

More diplomatic clashes followed. In March 1905, Kaiser Wilhelm II disembarked from a German warship at the port of Tangier in Morocco. Morocco had become a French colony. Riding ashore on a white horse, Wilhelm gave a strongly worded speech in favor of Moroccan independence. After the speech, Germany demanded and got an international conference at Algeciras in Spain to resolve the French–Moroccan issue. Representatives of all the European great powers, as well as the United States, were in attendance. The gathering took place in 1906. To Germany's consternation, however, the conference supported France's claims in Morocco. Only Austria-Hungary voted with Germany. Living as we do in an age in which we deem colonialism a bad thing, we might have had some sympathy with Wilhelm. After all, he was trying to undermine the French colonial empire. But why was he doing so? Out of altruism? At the time, the fellow heads of state thought he was trying to push the French out of the way so that he could grab more colonies for Germany. That certainly was the impression he gave.

Wilhelm was his own enemy. In October 1908, the *Daily Telegraph*, a British newspaper, published an account of an interview between the kaiser and an unnamed British subject. In the course of the interview, Wilhelm presented himself as a lover of peace. These were his words:

> What more can I do than I have done? I declared with all the emphasis at my command, in my speech at Guildhall [in London] that my heart is set upon peace, and that it is one of my clearest wishes to live on the best of terms with England … I have said time after time that I am a friend of England, and you press—or, at least, a considerable section of it—bids the people of England refuse my proferred hand and insinuates that the other holds a dagger …

A Chip off the Old Block

The next move Wilhelm made showed him to be more of a disciple of the man he had dismissed, Bismarck, advocating sheer force in international relations.

A second Moroccan crisis came in 1911. A German gunboat, the Panzer, steamed into the port of Agadir to "protect German interests." Berlin promised no further such incidents in Morocco if Germany could take over the French Congo. In the end, Germany obtained only trifling concessions in sub-Saharan Africa. But the damage was done. All three of Germany's major enemies were convinced that the kaiser was on the march toward world domination.

A Ring of Enemies

Once he had created the German behemoth, Bismarck tried through diplomacy to present his empire as peace-loving. But keeping all Germany's potential enemies at bay required all the Iron Chancellor's diplomatic skill. Had he remained in office after 1890, no one knows what might have happened. But none of Bismarck's successors, neither the kaiser nor the subsequent chancellors, came close to possessing Bismarck's acumen. Or maybe the gathering of enemies was inevitable: By the end of the nineteenth century and the beginning of the twentieth century, the leaders of France, Russia, and Great Britain were intent on restoring a balance of power—aimed at Germany.

The first to become allies, in 1896, were France and Russia. Now remember this: France, once the great revolutionary power, was still a hotbed of democracy, and Russia, headed by the tsar, the Orthodox church, and the secret police, was an *autarchy*. So what did

Terms and Translations

An **autarchy** refers to a country under absolute rule, complete control from the top. Old Prussia and then Germany had come close to being autarchies, but they didn't come close to the Russian model. Russia allowed hardly even a whiff of liberalism.

France and Russia have in common? The countries had nothing in common except the principle that the enemy of my enemy is my friend. Russia feared the new Germany and France wanted revenge for the loss to Bismarck. As a result, Paris and St. Petersburg signed the Dual Alliance in 1896.

The third great power, Great Britain, was not far behind Russia and France. Ever since the Napoleonic Wars, London had maintained a policy of "splendid isolation," concentrating on affairs of the empire and remaining neutral in the Franco–German War. Faced with the rise of German commercial and naval competition, however, the sea lords of Britannia began to reassess their isolation policy when it came to Germany. In 1904, British and French generals and admirals got together in Paris and agreed to coordinate their military planning. This was not exactly an alliance, but it was close to one. The agreement was called an *entente cordiale*, French for a "cordial understanding." It was aimed against Germany, and Berlin knew it.

Then, as if drawing the ring around Germany even tighter, Great Britain and Russia signed a treaty. In the nineteenth century, during the Crimean War, the British had seen the Russians as their main enemy. This was no longer the case. In 1907, Great Britain agreed that Russia could have a *sphere of influence* in northern Persia (now Iran).

> **Terms and Translations**
>
> A **sphere of influence** is not quite a colony, but a region that certain countries, such as country A, B, and C, agree that another country (for this example, country D) can pretty much run as it sees fit.

Why Persia? Britain and Russia had been contesting the country for a century, the British to protect India and Russia to gain access to warm water ports. London wanted an alignment with Russia against Germany: hence the Persian concession.

Finally, in 1912—as German intelligence strongly suspected—Great Britain and France entered into a secret alliance. If Germany invaded France, the agreement was that the British navy would defend the French ports along the English Channel.

The governments of France, Russia, and Great Britain, now called the Triple Entente, saw this network of ties as defensive. The German government saw it as offensive, and was determined, accordingly, to hang on to its one ally, Austria-Hungary.

An Inferior Ally (but the Only One They've Got)

Having lost to Bismarck and being thrown out of northern Italy, the Austrian Empire had nearly fallen apart. Stretched out over a multitude of linguistic and ethnic groups in Eastern Europe, it was like an old cracked jar held together by wire. The wire was the so-called Compromise of 1867: In theory, the Austrian emperor, Franz Josef, ruled; but in practice, Hungary had acquired an equal share of the government: hence Austria-Hungary.

However, the Austrian troubles had not ended with the creation of the so-called Dual Monarchy. All sorts of groups—Czechs, Poles, Slovaks, Jews, Romanians, Croats, and, most significant for what was to come, down in the Balkans, the Serbs—were demanding various degrees of independence.

To stifle the demands, especially in the Balkans, Austria-Hungary in 1908 formalized its occupation of Bosnia and Herzegovina, placed under its administrative control by Bismarck at the Congress of Berlin. (Soon after that meeting, a grateful Vienna accepted an alliance with Germany.) What these abstract terms meant was that in 1906 Austria-Hungary transformed a half-hearted occupation into a full-fledged one.

This next point is crucial: Germany consistently approved the occupation of Bosnia and Herzegovina. In Chapter 4, you'll see why Germany's approval had world-shattering consequences.

Austria-Hungary, an ally, although not very good in the field of battle, was content with its exertion of power, and Germany could turn its attention to its naval rivalry with Great Britain.

Tirpitz's Navy

Alfred Thayer Mahan, an American admiral who taught at the Naval War College in Rhode Island, had written extensively of the importance of sea power in international relations. Taking his examples largely from British history, he had contended that sea power was the foundation of imperial greatness; he concluded that in the long run, as had been the case in the Napoleonic wars when British ships had blockaded the European continent, a powerful navy could always choke off and through attrition destroy a land power. Nowhere were Mahan's books read with more interest than in Germany. Led by Admiral Alfred von Tirpitz, chief of staff of the German fleet, in 1898 Germany strenuously began a naval building program.

Now let's have a dose of political reality. Germany then in some ways was like America now: Interservice rivalry was rife. Tirpitz's naval program cost money, and the German army, proud of its traditions and successes, was hostile to the upstart navy. And the socialists wanted a share of the imperial budget for their various welfare causes. And while Kaiser Wilhelm II was indeed the monarch, he still had to mediate among these competing claims. So the Tirpitz naval construction measures never produced a fleet that could match, much less beat, the British fleet.

In international relations, perception is often as important as reality. Facts aside, the British government persuaded itself that Germany's naval growth was a threat.

Or did the British misperceive Germany's intent? Berlin insisted that a high-seas fleet was essential to secure its colonies, protect its trade, and safeguard its home waters. London held with equal resolution that, because Great Britain was almost wholly dependent on imports for food, it must at all costs maintain control of the sea lanes. And, besides, why *was* Germany seemingly so hell-bent on a naval competition?

Berlin and London saw each other from the point of view of a zero-sum game: Your gain is my loss.

The Road to War

The crisis that produced the First World War, however, was far removed, at least at first, from British–German relations. We come back again to nationalism. By the beginning of the twentieth century, Serbian nationalists down in the Balkans had begun to work for the breakup of the Austro–Hungarian Empire. Right next to Bosnia and Herzegovina, Serbia was the center of anti-Austrian agitation; Serbia looked forward to the expulsion of the Austrians from Bosnia and Herzegovina, as well as the northern Balkan provinces of Croatia and Slovenia, and the unification of those territories under the monarchy in Belgrade. So after Austria-Hungary's outright annexation of Bosnia-Herzegovina in 1908, Serb nationalists, who had targeted the two provinces as their own, swore revenge against Vienna.

In the three years after 1908, Balkan tensions subsided. But then, in 1911, the Balkans erupted in warfare. Serbia, Bulgaria, and Greece ganged up against Turkey, expelling the "sick man of Europe" from the Balkans altogether. But Bulgaria and Serbia squabbled over Macedonia, and in two wars fought in 1912 and 1913 Serbia, Greece, and Romania defeated Bulgaria. Serbia and Greece then nearly went to war over control of Albania. But to keep the peace, the great powers created Albania as an independent kingdom.

So despite verbal support from Russia, Serbia had failed to gain access to the sea. Frustrated and inflamed, factions among the Serbian nationalists vowed to try again.

The result of their resolution was the great international explosion of the First World War. The fuse that lit the explosion started in Sarajevo, the provincial capital of Bosnia. And all this had the most profound effect on Germany: Nazi Germany was the direct product of the First World War.

The Least You Need to Know

♦ Bismarck, the genius of nineteenth-century international relations, followed his forcible unification of Germany with sustained efforts to preserve the general peace. However, he was fired by Kaiser Wilhelm II.

♦ Wilhelm was not necessarily a warmonger, but he certainly gave a good impression of one. Under his leadership, Germany sought, or seemed to seek, its place in the international sun, and thus became a rival to Great Britain and its preeminent world position.

♦ In response to German expansionism, France, Russia, and Great Britain formed an interlocking series of understandings and alliances, which Germany took to be a hostile, encircling ring.

♦ Germany had only one ally, the decrepit Austro–Hungarian Empire. But Kaiser Wilhelm II believed in the need to preserve that alliance; as we'll see, that belief led to disaster for Germany; the catalyst of that disaster lay down in the obscurity of the Balkans.

Chapter 4

The Coming of the First World War: June 28, 1914–August 4, 1914

In This Chapter

- ◆ Two murders in Sarajevo spark a declaration of war
- ◆ The kaiser underestimates the likelihood of a full-fledged war involving all the great powers in Europe
- ◆ Russia, France, and Great Britain align with the Serbs—and therefore, against Germany
- ◆ Wilhelm declares war on the Serbs in support of Germany's ally, the Austro–Hungarian Empire
- ◆ As the clock tolls 11 P.M., Great Britain enters the war, spelling doom for Germany

Sarajevo, the provincial capital of Bosnia, was shaped like a bowl. The mountains that surrounded it sloped down past farmlands and orchards, then whitewashed houses, scatterings of churches, mosques, and synagogues, and at last the shops and bazaars of the town. At the bottom of the bowl ran the major thoroughfare, the Appel Quay, which lay alongside the Miljaćka River, a stream that divided Sarajevo in two.

Landlocked in the middle of all those mountains, Bosnia had become an Austrian territory. For some years before 1914, however, elements in Serbia next door (Serbia lay between Bosnia and the Danube River; Austria-Hungary stretched north from the Danube) had been fomenting revolution. These people were Serb nationalists who dreamed of unifying all the Slavs of the Balkans (Yugoslavia means "southern Slav") as Italy and Germany before them had been unified. But unification meant expelling the Austrians from the region, just as earlier the Austrians had been expelled from Italy. So the Serbian nationalists had been using the classic techniques of a weak people: propaganda; boycotts; and, on occasion, murder. Whenever they could they targeted Austro–Hungarian officials for assassination.

> **Modern Day Parallels**
>
> Were the Serb assassins patriots or terrorists? It may have depended on your point of view. For the Austrians, they were clearly terrorists. To many Serbs, they were patriots. Are there any parallels to this in the world today?

Not wanting to lose Bosnia as it had lost Lombardy and Venetia earlier, Vienna, the capital of the Austro–Hungarian Empire, had increased its military presence in the province and, late in June 1914, had sent Archduke Franz Ferdinand, heir to the throne of the Austro–Hungarian Empire, to inspect the troop maneuvers. His observations completed, Franz Ferdinand and his wife, Sophie, planned to pay an official visit to Sarajevo.

So on the morning of June 28, 1914, in a display of Austro–Hungarian rule, a royal motorcade drove down the Appel Quay. In the third car, which was open, rode the archduke and his wife. After he gave a speech at the town hall, just beyond the end of the embankment, the procession returned toward the river, heading up into the hills for a visit to the Bosnian museum.

Just as the archduke's automobile slowed to make the turn up a side street, however, a young Bosnian Serb named Gavrilo Princip stepped forward from the crowd that was lining the curb. Trained and financed by a secret society called the Black Hand in Belgrade, the capital of Serbia, Princip was armed with a revolver. When he neared the imperial car, he fired twice. Within the hour the archduke and archduchess were dead. Six weeks later, Europe was at war.

Why? And what on earth did a pair of murders, however ghastly, down in the Balkans have to do with Germany? Not much—except that Sarajevo paved the way to the rise of Nazi Germany.

Austria-Hungary Devises a Final Solution

Up in Vienna, Franz Josef, the Austro–Hungarian emperor, and his top ministers did not think they had much of a choice. Almost the moment they learned of the Sarajevo murders and that Serbia was implicated—police officers in Sarajevo quickly arrested Princip and half a dozen co-conspirators, and through interrogations learned of the connection with the Black Hand in Belgrade—they made the determination to bring South Slav separatism to an end. More precisely, they wanted to reach what they called a final solution, exterminating their Serbian opponents.

Terms and Translations

The Austro–Hungarian use of the phrase **final solution** had nothing to do with Jews. Vienna's target was Serbian nationalism. And the Austro–Hungarian authorities were not trying to eradicate an entire population. Their attitude, nonetheless, was that the time had come to deal decisively with a people they regarded as subhuman and therefore worthy of any kind of abuse. The Austrian-born Adolf Hitler would transfer that attitude to the Jews.

Without any significant opposition within the ranks of government, Austria-Hungary decided to go to war. Before it did so, however, Vienna dispatched an emissary to Germany, its ally, to assure itself of Berlin's support. Kaiser Wilhelm in response issued a "blank check," recognizing Austria-Hungary's need to stop the agitation in the Balkans and urging Vienna to stand firm.

Despite what many said about him later, the kaiser was not looking for a war, at least not at this moment. He was, however, giving his full support to Austria-Hungary's imperialist and racist policy in the Balkans. If he thought that Vienna could carry out such a policy without triggering a war, he was only deluding himself.

Encouraged, Vienna concealed its intent from the other great powers. But in the last week of July 1914, it presented Belgrade with an ultimatum.

The ultimatum demanded other things, such as Serbia ending its anti-Austrian propaganda and removing boycotts to Austrian trade. It also insisted that Austrian officials be allowed to go to Serbia and work with Serbian police in investigating just who was behind the Sarajevo murders. Belgrade accepted every point of the ultimatum except one: the bit about having Austrian police on their soil. That, they believed, would be a breach of their country's independence.

Vienna seized on that one objection as a reason to issue a declaration of war. On July 28, 1914, Austro–Hungarian artillery began to shell Belgrade, just across the Danube River.

The Kaiser's Misjudgment Leads to a Fatal Delusion

As he had done for years, Kaiser Wilhelm II devoted the month of July to a North Sea excursion aboard the royal steam yacht, the *Hohenzollern*. (He took his family name very seriously.) The cruise along the Norwegian fjords was peaceful. The meals aboard were excellent and during the white nights the kaiser and his chosen ministers gathered in the smoking room for cards. All was uneventful.

On July 25, though, the ship's radio picked up the text of the Austro–Hungarian ultimatum to Serbia. Admiral George Müller, chief of the naval cabinet, took a copy of the ultimatum to Wilhelm after breakfast. He found the kaiser walking the deck.

> Reading the document, Wilhelm commented, "*Was, das ist doch einmal eine forsche Note.*" ("Well, for once that's a strong note.")

> Müller replied: "*Ja, forsche ist die Note, aber sie bedeutet Krieg!*" ("Yes, the note is strong, but it signifies war!")

The kaiser countered that Serbia would surely capitulate and that no war would ensue. Soon, though, another message reached the yacht: This one stated that Austria-Hungary was on the verge of war *and* that Russia was willing to engage in military preparations and thus deciding to fight on behalf of Serbia. At that point, at 6 P.M. on the afternoon of July 25, Wilhelm ordered the ship back to Germany.

"It was a beautiful summer evening," Admiral Müller wrote. The kaiser stood for a long time on the bridge enjoying the peaceful picture of forests, mountains, and farmhouses as we sailed out of Sognefjord. I said to him: "In times of political tension such as these, one could almost look with envy upon this land which lies outside the great conflicts of world history ...." His Majesty agreed and maintained that at the last moment the leaders of the states involved would shrink from the appalling responsibility of starting a war.

Wilhelm II utterly lacked Bismarck's ability to read reality. True, Russia, a Slavic nation, was allied to Serbia, committed to that tiny country's defense. But, Wilhelm believed, he could use what he considered his extraordinary powers of persuasion, showing his first cousin, Tsar Nicholas II, the folly of going to war.

Here was Wilhelm's fatal delusion. He had a choice. He could disown Austria-Hungary, refusing to sanction Vienna's final solution. But he did not avail himself of this option. Instead, he accepted the coming of war and thought that he could keep it "localized"—his term—in the Balkans.

That conviction underlay a series of telegrams he exchanged with the Russian tsar. They have been nicknamed the Willy-Nicky telegrams. One, from kaiser to tsar, on July 29 at 1:45 A.M., read:

> It is with the gravest concern that I hear of the impression which the action of Austria against Serbia is creating in your country. The unscrupulous agitation that has been going on in Serbia for years has resulted in the outrageous crime, to which Archduke Franz Ferdinand fell a victim .... You will doubtless agree with me that we both, you and me, have a common interest as well as all sovereigns to insist that the persons morally responsible for the dastardly murder should received their deserved punishment. In this case politics plays no part at all.
>
> On the other hand, I fully understand how difficult it is for you and your government to face the drift of your [pro-Slavic] public opinion. Therefore, with regard to the hearty and tender friendship, which binds us both from long ago with firm ties, I am exerting my utmost influence to induce the Austrians to deal straightly to arrive to a satisfactory understanding with you. I confidently hope that you will help me in my efforts to smooth over difficulties that may still arrive.
>
> Your very sincere and devoted friend and cousin,
> Willy

Wilhelm sounded sincere. But there was not a word about his getting Vienna to step back from war. And that was exactly what Nicholas II wanted him to do. On July 29, at 8:20 P.M., the tsar sent this message to the kaiser:

> Am glad you are back. In this serious moment, I appeal to you to help me. An ignoble war has been declared to a weak country. The indignation in Russia shared fully by me is enormous. I foresee that very soon I shall be overwhelmed by the pressure forced upon me and be forced to take extreme measures which will lead to war. To try and avoid such a calamity as a European war I beg you in the name of our old friendship to do what you can to stop your allies from going too far.

Wilhelm wanted peace. He just didn't want to stop Austria-Hungary from going too far. His response to the tsar on July 29, follows:

> ... I think a direct understanding between your government and Vienna possible and desirable, and as I already telegraphed to you, my government is continuing its exercises to promote it. Of course military measures on the part of Russia

would be looked upon by Austria as a calamity we both wish to avoid and jeopardize my position as mediator which I readily accepted on your appeal to my friendship and help.

At the Congress of Berlin in 1878, Bismarck also had been the mediator. Wilhelm, however, forgot—or refused to recognize—that you cannot be a mediator if you favor one side. The tsar to the kaiser, July 30:

Thank you heartily for your quick answer .... The military measures, which have now come into force were decided five days ago for reasons of defense on account of Austria's preparations. I hope from all my heart that these measures won't in any way interfere with your part as mediator, which I greatly value. We need your strong pressure on Austria to come to an understanding with us.

That pressure the tsar desired was not forthcoming from the kaiser.

The Allies Close In

So here were the issues:

◆ Austria-Hungary was determined to crush Serbian nationalism once and for all.

◆ Refusing to recognize that Serbia had any justice on its side, Kaiser Wilhelm II sympathized wholly with Vienna; his claim to being a mediator was a gross exaggeration.

◆ Russia was allied to Serbia and was determined to go to that small state's defense.

So far there was nothing that would have led Germany into a war. But the technical word for Russia's military preparations was "mobilization." That meant that Russia was calling up the reserves and putting them aboard troop trains that were headed for Austria. And the train tracks ran along the German border.

Even so, the kaiser and his government might have overlooked a Russia troop movement; after all, Russia's trains were poor and the troops were not well trained. But Berlin also had to concern itself with France.

Russian–French Alliance

Now remember that from 1896 onward, Russia and France had been allies. That alliance had been aimed against Germany. And in the middle of July 1914, after the

Sarajevo murders, the French president and premier paid an official state visit to Nicholas II and the imperial court at St. Petersburg. The purpose of the visit was to reinforce the treaty of alliance and it ended with the French president solemnly assuring Nicholas that in case of war, France would march against Germany.

Back in France, late in July, most of the French public and the Chamber of Deputies were in favor of war with Germany. The mood was that of avenging the loss of Alsace and Lorraine to Bismarck. A few on the political scene, to be sure, wanted peace, and the most prominent of them was Jean Jaurès, the head of the French Socialist Party. Jaurès believed that for the working classes of Europe a war would be a calamity, and in speeches and editorials published in his party's newspaper, he said so. On the night of July 31, as he was eating dinner in a Parisian café, however, an assassin gunned him down. Was the assassin a government agent? Possibly. But with this new murder, just about all calls in France for peace were silenced. And so, as Austria-Hungary went to war against Serbia, France began to mobilize against Germany.

Archduke Franz Ferdinand.

(Culver Pictures)

The German government had long foreseen a two-front war with Russia and France. So the German army had developed the Schlieffen Plan, named for General Alfred von Schlieffen, Berlin's turn-of-the-century chief of staff. The idea was that if Germany had to fight a two-front war, it would attack France first. The most mechanized in Europe, the German army would move quickly through Belgium (ignoring Belgium's neutrality) in a gigantic scythelike sweep—so that the right sleeve of the soldier the farthest on the right would brush against the English Channel—and pin the French back against the Argonne Forest (just above Switzerland) and the Swiss Alps. Victorious, the Germans would take Paris, much as they had done under Bismarck. Then the German army would turn back toward the east and overwhelm the slow-moving Russian army.

The German high command was confident that the Schlieffen Plan would bring about the defeat of Germany's enemies (which it did in the case of the Russians). All the same, in the last days of July 1914, Kaiser Wilhelm II was reluctant to unleash it. Perhaps he was more nervous than his generals; perhaps he did not want to be blamed for starting a continental war; perhaps he had inherited Bismarck's fear that a continental war would tear Germany apart (which it did). Whatever the explanation or explanations, even as Russia and France were mobilizing, Wilhelm held back, withholding his final approval for war.

The British Arrive

What may have led Wilhelm to change his mind was the action undertaken by Great Britain. The British, remember, for a century had stayed aloof from continental quarrels. But now all that was about to change.

In July 1914, much of the British navy had been staging annual maneuvers off the Isle of Wight in the English Channel. The fleet customarily had returned to its battle stations at Gibraltar, Malta, Cyprus, Suez, and beyond. At the end of July 1914, however, after obtaining the approval of H. H. Asquith, the prime minister, the first lord of the admiralty ordered most of the ships to proceed to Scapa Flow, a huge naval base in the Orkney Islands, high above Scotland.

Bet You Didn't Know

Guess the name of the first lord of the admiralty who ordered the ships to proceed to Scapa Flow. It was Winston S. Churchill.

From Scapa Flow the British fleet had a straight shot down the North Sea at the northwestern coast of Germany and at the Kiel Canal, Germany's lifeline between the North Sea and the Baltic.

In Berlin, the kaiser and his top officials had long feared such a strike: They called it *die englische Gefahr* (the English danger). So by the morning of July 31, 1914, the kaiser knew that the time for a decision had come.

Wilhelm Decides on War

That morning, a huge crowd gathered in the center of Berlin, hoping for news. Good news or bad news, it almost didn't matter. People wanted to hear anything that would remove their sense of uncertainty.

The people were gathered in the *Lustgarten*, a park in front of the kaiser's *schloss* (castle). Over the turrets floated the yellow imperial standard, the sign of the presence of His Majesty.

People came and went constantly, some standing for an hour or two, then going off to attend to necessary affairs, and returning as quickly as they could. But whether they stayed or went, the question was always the same: Would there be war?

As the morning progressed, the air became warm, even sultry. The huge crowd grew restless. A month had gone by since the Sarajevo assassinations, a month of diplomatic to-ings and fro-ings with endless negotiations, threats, and assurances of peace.

Peddlers with sausages and newspapers worked their way through the throng. They did not sell much because in the heat people were not hungry and because the news would be out of date as soon as it was printed. The people of Berlin wanted to learn of the kaiser's decision.

Terms and Translations

In English, *lust* suggests sexual desire. It does in German, too. To Germans, it also means pleasure or delight, and so the *Lustgarten* was an amusement park where ordinary Berliners could go for enjoyment.

At about 10:30 A.M., the crowd suddenly went silent. People stared up at the windows of the castle. They thought they had seen a motion on a balcony. There was nothing. They tried to peer up through the panes, but the glass only reflected the sunshine. In the park below, people could glean nothing of what was taking place behind the heavy yellow draperies of the palace windows.

Noon came, and there still was no news. More and more people, husbands and wives and their children, joined the multitude. In the tower over the castle the clock struck five.

Then, ever so slowly, a door opened. The people could see a policeman emerge. He walked out onto the balcony and, moving to one side, slowly took off his helmet. He held it in front of his chest. The policeman opened his mouth and the crowd leaned forward. Then they could hear his words: "His Majesty Kaiser Wilhelm II."

In that moment, Wilhelm himself, in full uniform, with spiked helmet, tunic covered with medals and medallions, high, polished boots, and a sword at his side, strode into view. There, on the balcony of the Berlin Castle, he made his declaration of war:

> A momentous hour has struck for Germany. Envious rivals everywhere force us to legitimate defense. The sword has been forced into our hands. I hope that in the event that my efforts to the very last moment do not succeed in bringing our opponents to reason and in preserving peace, we may use the sword, with the help of God, so that we may sheath it again with honor. War will demand enormous sacrifices by the German people, but we shall show the enemy what it means to attack Germany. Go forth into the churches, kneel down before God, and implore his help for our brave army.

He then told his people that Germany had declared war on Russia and France. Then the kaiser disappeared again into the castle.

As Wilhelm exited, a few voices below, then hundreds and thousands, joined together in singing the German chorale of thanksgiving, written in the seventeenth century and eventually harmonized by the composer Felix Mendelssohn, "*Nun danket alle Gott*" ("Now Thank We All Our God"):

> Now thank we all our God,
> With heart, and hands, and voices,
> Who wondrous things hath done,
> In whom the world rejoices;
> Who from our mother's arms
> Hath blessed us on our way
> With countless gifts of love,
> And still is ours today.

On August 1, another crowd gathered, this one in Munich. A photograph of that demonstration shows at least 100,000 people jammed together. The faces are blurred and are almost indistinguishable. But a magnifying glass brings one of those faces to life. The hair is dark, plastered down over the left side of the forehead; a brush moustache adorns the upper lip. The man is small and young, but unmistakable. He is Adolf Hitler.

Big Ben Sounds Doom, Doom, Doom

The morning of August 4, 1914, brought gloomy weather to London. Dark clouds scudded up from the Channel, spitting down flurries of rain and brushing in patches of fog. The English capital was shrouded in gray, the atmosphere being, in the word of *The Westminster Gazette*, "unsettled." The term described the sky above as well as the mood below.

German troops, British intelligence had reported the day before, had crossed the border into neutral Belgium. In response, the House of Commons had authorized Prime Minister Asquith and his foreign secretary, Sir Edward Grey, to send an ultimatum to Berlin. If Germany did not withdraw from Belgium by 11 P.M. that night (midnight Berlin time), Great Britain would declare war.

Shortly before 3 P.M., Asquith went to the House to announce that the ultimatum had been sent. The announcement was greeted with cheers.

Shortly after the House adjourned, Walter Hines Page, the American ambassador, called on Grey. Tall, worn, and pallid, Grey was standing against the mantelpiece in his ornate room in the Foreign Office, right across the street from Ten Downing Street. "England would be forever contemptible," Grey said, "if it should sit by and see this treaty [for Belgian neutrality, signed in the 1830s] violated. Its position would be gone if Germany were thus permitted to dominate Europe. ... We have told Germany that, if this assault on Belgium's neutrality is not reversed, England will declare war."

"Do you expect Germany to accept it?" Page asked.

Grey shook his head. "No," he said. "Of course everybody knows that there will be war."

That evening, as the rain stopped, a huge crowd filled the center of London. After dark, a multitude surged around the Victoria Memorial and toward Buckingham Palace. On one of the balconies appeared King George V: He also was a first cousin of Kaiser Wilhelm II. As one, a million voices sang, "God Save the King!"

After dinner at Ten Downing Street that night, Asquith, Grey, and a few others from the ministry gathered in the Cabinet Room. David Lloyd George, serving then as chancellor of the exchequer, joined them.

By 9 o'clock they had heard nothing from Berlin. Ten o'clock came. Only an hour remained until the ultimatum to Berlin would expire; still nothing from Berlin. The clock on the mantelpiece showed 10:55 P.M. Every one seated around the green baize–covered table in the Cabinet Room was watching that clock, encased in the most private of thoughts. The room, dimly lit, was still.

Then, from down the Whitehall and across Parliament Square and high in the tower beside the Houses of Parliament resounded the bells of the most famous clock in the world, the deep sonorities of Big Ben. The time was 11 P.M.

In the Cabinet Room, Lloyd George later wrote, "Every face was suddenly contracted in a painful intensity. 'Doom!' 'Doom!' 'Doom!' down to the last stroke." Great Britain and Imperial Germany were at war.

In that same moment, out of the harbor at Portsmouth, on the Channel coast, a ship called the *Telconia* slipped out into the sea. *Telconia* was an unarmed vessel equipped with a huge crane, for its task had been that of laying underwater cables. On this night, however, its mission was different. Under the cover of a fog, it chugged over to the German coastline, between Holland and Denmark. There the crane dipped down and lowered huge shears to the seabed below. There lay five cables, intended to transmit messages from Germany to South America, Mexico, and the United States. In a swift motion, the *Telconia* cut those cables and hauled the severed parts aboard. Mission completed, the ship returned to Portsmouth.

No single mission, on land or sea, could have done more harm to the German cause. Whatever the rights or wrongs of their cause, in going to war the leaders of Wilhelm's Germany had forgotten an overwhelmingly crucial fact: If they could not get their side of the story to the United States, and with their trans-Atlantic cables cut they could not, then British propagandists could have a field day in the pastures of American public opinion.

For if the United States were to enter the war on the side of the British and the French, then Germany was indeed doomed.

The Least You Need to Know

- Two murders in Sarajevo, an obscure town in the faraway Balkans, triggered the First World War.

- Austria-Hungary's response to the murders in Sarajevo, with its imperialist and racist overtones, foreshadowed Hitler's "final solution" for the Jews.

- Contrary to legend, Kaiser Wilhelm II may not have been seeking an aggressive war. Nevertheless, he succumbed to the fatal delusion that he could have his strudel and eat it too: He could support Austria-Hungary and not face a general war.

- Britain's entry into the war, and in support of Britain, the probability of America's entry, practically guaranteed that Germany would face disaster.

Chapter **5**

The Great War: 1914–1918

In This Chapter

- ◆ An early victory over the Russians has Austria-Hungary thinking everything will go according to plan

- ◆ Austria-Hungary's failure to execute the Schlieffen Plan causes them to face two armies (France and Britain), making them greatly outnumbered

- ◆ After countless casualties on both sides and a stalemate on land, the battlefront moves to sea

- ◆ A German telegram intercepted by British Intelligence sends the United States to war

- ◆ The war ends, but it's not over for the German people; Kaiser Wilhelm is exiled, and a revolution sets in

- ◆ Without a government, Germany is in chaos and the Austro–Hungarian Empire collapses, resulting in several independent states

The First World War began in a burst of optimism. The cheering crowds in the capitals of all the great powers believed that the war would be over soon, by the time the leaves fell in the autumn. It was not to be. The stalemate of war was to drag Germany ever deeper into ruin.

War Breaks Out

Let's start with something often overlooked but crucial. Hitler, by birth, was an Austrian. In a sense, by attacking Serbia, Austria-Hungary had started the war. Germany and Austria-Hungary were allies (although their high commands never really coordinated their efforts with each other). And in time, Hitler would unite Germany and Austria. So as we look at the First World War, it seems reasonable to treat Germany and Austria-Hungary together: certainly the First World War brought them tumbling down together.

When war came, the Viennese were as excited as the citizens of Berlin and Munich. Throngs of people in the *Ringstrasse* (the Ring Street, Vienna's central avenue) waved flags and sang anthems. The city's Friedrich Cardinal Piffl called upon the imperial forces to strike down "the enemies of God," meaning the Serbs. And as in Germany, the socialists, as nationalist as they were socialist, whole-heartedly endorsed the war.

Indeed, for Austria-Hungary as well as Germany, the war got off to a glorious start. Crossing the Danube in gunboats, ferries, and barges, the forces of Austria-Hungary marched into Belgrade with ease. Transporting an army of almost 4,000,000 men, Germany's trains thundered across the Rhine bridges and poured across Belgium into northeastern France. Born in England and no lover of Prussia, a princess named Evelyn Blücher wrote in her diary that the Germans "take to war as a duck takes to water."

On August 18, Kaiser Wilhelm spoke to troops from a balcony in his castle at Potsdam, just outside Berlin. The "entire German nation to the last man has grasped the sword," he declared. "And so I draw the sword which with the help of God I have kept in its scabbard for decades." At this point he drew his sword and held it high above his head. "The sword is drawn, and I cannot sheathe it again without victory and honor. All of you shall and will see to it that only in honor is it returned to the scabbard. You are my guarantee that I can dictate peace to my enemies. Up and at the enemy … Three cheers for our army!"

Memorable Places

Like his English cousin, George V, Wilhelm had a lot of castles. His favorite was at Potsdam, then a medieval town about 10 miles from Berlin. Because it had been his principal residence, at the end of World War II the victorious Big Three, Marshal Josef Stalin, Prime Minister Winston S. Churchill, and President Harry S Truman, chose the Potsdam palace as the site for their summer, 1945, so-called peacemaking conference.

Soon afterward, the kaiser took the royal train to still another castle, this one at Coblenz high on a bluff where the Mosel and Rhine Rivers flowed together. During Bismarck's war with France, Wilhelm's grandfather, Wilhelm I, had ensconced himself in the same *schloss* (castle). Wilhelm II was determined to stay there until Germany once again defeated France.

He had every reason to believe that his wait would not be long. Out in East Prussia, a region of hills, lakes, and scrub pines, near a town called Tannenberg, the Germans destroyed an advancing Russian force. And along the western front, the German armies in August 1914 were swinging like a hammer in a wide arc toward Paris, according to the Schlieffen Plan. Everything was proceeding like clockwork.

The Schlieffen Plan was a design of brilliance—on paper. But what the German high command forgot, as have many other military planners, was the human element. A war plan is no better than the people who have to carry it out.

Gloomy Gus

The German commander on the western front was General von Moltke, nephew of the victor of Bismarck's wars. Tall and heavy, with a perpetual air of distress, he had received from the kaiser the nickname of *der traurige Julius*, or in American slang, Gloomy Gus. Actually, like his uncle, his given name was *Helmuth*, meaning bright courage. He turned out to be neither bright nor courageous. Shortly before the German victory at Tannenberg, von Moltke learned that the Russians had pushed two armies into Germany, penetrating East Prussia. He panicked, withdrawing troops from the German right wing, the one that was supposed to sweep along the English Channel, and sent them to the eastern front. There they brought about the victory over the Russians.

But at such a cost! General von Moltke had ruined the workings of the Schlieffen Plan in the west. Realizing through intelligence sources that the German attacking force was diminished, the French commander in chief, General Joseph Joffre, regrouped. With support from the British contingent, which was still small, he ordered a counterattack at the Marne River.

Normally, the Marne had been a peaceful stream, flowing gently through the fields of Flanders as it meandered its way to the sea. Now, between September 5 and 12, 1914, it flowed with blood. The German advance stopped at the Marne. Berlin's hope of felling France in a single blow was ended.

The Stalemate

By the end of 1914 and on into 1915, Germany's initial victories over the Russians in the east were of little help. The Germans pushed on into the tsarist empire, inflicting huge losses—in 1915 alone, the Russians lost more than 2 million men—but the spaces to be covered were enormous and the Russians kept fighting.

The Austro–Hungarians had taken Belgrade with ease. But Serbia is a mountainous country, ideal for guerrilla warfare. Heading for the hills and then staging ambushes, Serb peasants stopped the Austrian advance and inflicted huge casualties.

Most important, on the western front what had promised to be a war of movement had become one of position. In August 1914, the German cavalry had pranced off to war in high spirits. By the end of the year the horses were gone. Instead there were the trenches, hundreds of miles of interconnected ditches filled with mud, lice, and rats, sometimes as big as cats. Between the two lines of trenches, which stretched all the way from the English Channel to Luxembourg, was a no-man's-land. Troops from either side ran into deadly machine-gun fire.

In terms of efficiency and training, the German army was still the best in Europe. But because the Germans had not completed the Schlieffen Plan—because they had not come close to reaching Paris—French–British communications across the Channel remained uninterrupted. So by the end of 1914, the Germans were facing two armies, the French and the British, and they were outnumbered. The result was a stalemate all along the western front.

The Diplomatic Stalemate

Now we have to go back to look at the diplomatic front. For a couple of decades, Italy had been allied with Germany and Austria-Hungary (the three together were called the Central Powers). But once the war broke out, Rome broke off the tie, holding out for the highest bidder. Central and Allied officials alike rushed to the Italian capital, offering what they didn't have to offer, money and land. At last the Allies won out, promising that once the war was over, Italy could have an empire in North and East Africa. So Italy went to war on the Allied side, attacked Austria-Hungary, and the fighting in the mountains between Italy and Austria also fell into stalemate.

On the other hand, Bulgaria and Turkey had allied themselves with the Central Powers: The Bulgarians hated the Russians, and Turkey had been receiving military aid from Berlin. Bulgaria and Turkey clearly could not do much for Germany on the western front. But they *could* block access by the British and the French to Russia, their own other ally. London and Paris could send no aid to St. Petersburg.

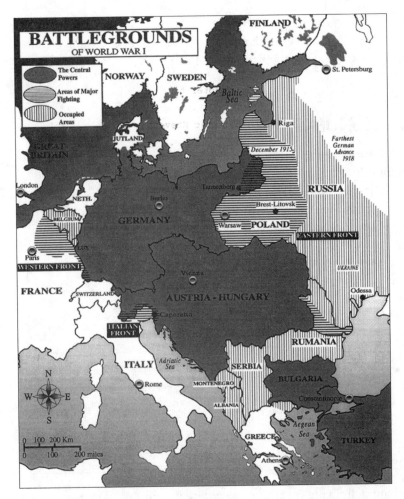

Map of battlegrounds in World War I.

(Eric Stevens)

Now we come to one of the great disasters of the war. Hoping to open up communications with Russia (the German navy had closed the Baltic), Great Britain in the spring of 1915 launched an attack on Turkey. They hoped to take Constantinople (now Istanbul), which lay at the entrance to the Black Sea. But to get to Constantinople, the British had to get up through a strait called the Dardanelles, a narrow body of water formed by the Asiatic part of Turkey along the southeast and, along the northwest, a peninsula called Gallipoli.

On its western flank Gallipoli had a long beach, backed by cliffs. Atop the cliffs was a row of fortresses. The idea was that British ships could steam up the strait, blast away at the forts, then land troops on the beach. But the Germans had strewn the strait with mines. That stopped the ships. The Turks stopped the troops. Well armed and trained by the Germans, Turkish forces in the forts let loose murderous gunfire upon the British (mostly Australians and New Zealanders) who landed on the sand. Within a few days after the start of the assault, the British had lost nearly 150,000 men. They soon gave up the mission.

The Paralysis of the Fronts

In 1916, both sides tried to break the deadlock in northern France. In February, the Germans hurled a million men at Verdun, a French fortress town near the southern end of the front. The French commander, Joffre, put General Philippe Pétain in charge of holding the fortress and its environs. Pétain and his troops had to take on nearly the full weight of the German army. Lasting six months, the Battle of Verdun drew the horrified attention of the world: Despite more than 300,000 casualties on both sides, the Germans could not break through.

The British and the French in the meantime had been planning their own offensive at the Somme River.

Bet You Didn't Know

The Somme, Marne, and Meuse rivers in northeastern France took on the reputations as being sites of some of the most horrific battles in history. But the important thing to remember is that, as they meandered through the fields of Flanders, they were very close together. Once the Germans were stopped at the Marne in 1914, the front lines did not move more than about 10 miles in either direction. Such was the nature of the paralysis of the war.

Factories in Great Britain had finally cranked out artillery in unheard of amounts and, through military conscription, the government in London had raised a huge new army. So the idea in the British high command was to break through at the Somme simply by applying stupendous pressure. It didn't work. In the first day of the attack, the British lost 60,000 men. After a week they had advanced no more than a mile and after a month, only two and a half miles. The Battle of the Somme, lasting from July to October 1916, cost the British 400,000 men and the Germans 500,000. And no one had gained anything of any value.

With the armies locked together on the land, both sides looked to the sea for help. Here the Germans were at a disadvantage from the very beginning of the war. The *englische Gefahr* (English danger) that the British fleet would attack the Kiel Canal never materialized. But an even greater danger to Germany was that of a British naval blockade.

As an industrialized country, Germany was heavily dependent on imports for food; Germany also had no oil reserves to speak of, except in the Austro–Hungarian Empire, and its war production could not function without shipments of iron ore from northern Sweden. So the British used their much larger fleet, based in Scapa Flow, to control the English Channel and the North Sea, and thus to grip Germany in a stranglehold.

Early on in the war, Germany's admirals tried to break the encircling ring. At the Battle of Jutland, off the Danish coast, the German High Seas Fleet took on the Royal Navy. After several hours of combat, during which Germany sank more British ships than they themselves lost, the kaiser's vessels were able to withdraw into the mined waters around Kiel. The Germans had not exactly lost the battle, but their big surface warships never came out again to challenge the British dominance at sea. So day by day, week by week, and month by month, the British blockade, which stopped mainly the Americans, the Dutch, and the Scandinavians from exporting anything at all to German ports, impaired Germany's ability to fight the war.

Desperate, Berlin turned to another kind of naval vessel, the submarine. Germany would try to put a counterblockade into place: In February 1915, Berlin declared all the waters around the British Isles to be a war zone. Within that area, any Allied vessel could be torpedoed and even neutral vessels would be in danger.

At first, British ships seemed helpless against the submarine threat. Then the Germans made a fateful mistake. Early in May 1915, the British-owned *Lusitania*, the largest and fastest passenger ship in the world, set sail from New York, heading for Liverpool. Before the ship left the United States, the German embassy placed notices in the New York papers, warning people not to take passage; indeed, the *Lusitania* was carrying munitions manufactured in America and purchased for Allied use. The *Lusitania* was sunk off the Irish coast. About 1,200 persons were drowned; 128 of them were American citizens.

The American public was shocked and President Woodrow Wilson, in a strong note to Berlin, informed Germany that Washington would consider another such sinking as "deliberately unfriendly." Fearful of a U.S. entry into the war on the side of the Allied Forces, Germany refrained from making full use of its submarine fleet for two years.

So Germany could not use the one weapon that might have brought Great Britain to its knees. And the pythonlike envelopment of the British blockade continued to tighten around the German economy.

The Domestic Scene in Germany

From the very beginning of the war, Germany had engaged in a total mobilization of the home front. All able-bodied men were forced into the military, and huge numbers of women were drafted to work in the factories. Women were liberated from their traditional roles of cooking and cleaning. But their new income contributed to an unforeseen consequence: *inflation.*

Christmas, 1915, illustrated the mounting shortages on the home front. Most people could no longer afford Christmas trees. In Stuttgart, bakers produced only two modest forms of Christmas cake. In Berlin, pancakes and fritters fell victims to the shortage of fat. Even traditionally festive Christmas markets looked sad: The usual chocolates, wooden toys, and tree ornaments were missing.

Other kinds of shortages were felt. Throughout Germany and Austria-Hungary in 1916, consumer-related industries were closed down altogether. Workers went through old slag heaps in hope of recovering anything metal. Chemical industries had to turn over their supplies for war production. Barns were scraped to recover nitrates, used in explosives. Church bells came down to be melted and recast as guns. The governments of Germany and Austria-Hungary alike appealed to their citizens to turn in doorknobs and brass ornaments. Princess Evelyn Blücher wrote of this war effort: "It is an interesting sight … to see cartloads of old pots and kettles and candlesticks, door-handles, chandeliers, etc., being driven along the street, and a poor woman or schoolboy carrying a copper kettle or brass lamp to the collecting offices to be weighed and paid for." And all along, the governments claimed that there was no metal shortage; the propagandists tried to maintain morale at all costs.

Terms and Translations

Inflation is a complicated topic but here a simple point will do. Germans had more money to spend than ever before. Yet because industry was producing almost wholly for the war, there were fewer consumer goods than ever before. More money chasing fewer goods is a classic formula for inflation.

But the governments could hardly explain away the hunger that was setting in. In both Germany and Austria-Hungary, staples such as flour and potatoes were in short supply. "I noticed strings of poorly dressed women and children held in line by police, waiting for milk, vessel in hand," wrote an official at the American embassy in Vienna late in 1916. "Latecomers went home empty-handed, while lucky ones obtained only half as much as they expected. Similar lines … can be observed standing in the morning hours in front of the bakers' shops and stores where coffee, tea, and sugar are being sold."

Economic Conditions: From Bad to Worse

Economic conditions were turning from bad to worse. Shortages of corn and oats for horses and cattle led to their widespread slaughter—just as the governments in Berlin and Vienna were demanding more meat for the troops on the fronts. Austria-Hungary itself was starting to break apart. Hungary banned food exports to Austria, which gave rise to cries of treason. And remember the *Zollverein* (Custom Union)? The idea was to break down barriers to trade. Now, in Austria in 1916, provinces, districts, and villages *raised* trade barriers against each other.

On into 1917, Germany and Austria-Hungary were turning to *Ersatz* (substitutes) to meet food shortages. Roasted acorns and beechnuts replaced coffee beans. Tea was made of grasses and wild flowers. Plant fats took the place of animal fats. And then came that favorite German snack, the sausage.

A black market arose, meaning that given the shortages, some persons sold food products above the state-set price. Some were caught doing so. Princess Evelyn Blücher at the Breslau train station said, "A well-dressed, dignified-looking lady appeared at the luggage-room with the object of checking her trunk. Her flurried mien, and the obvious nervousness with which she hurried on the porter to weigh her trunk, aroused the suspicion of the station-master. The trunk was promptly opened, and to the surprise of the amused onlookers a whole pig was discovered in it. It was confiscated and sold in the town at the official price, to the great discomfiture of the stately lady."

Terms and Translations

In German the noun *Satz* has several meanings; the most common are "part" or "ingredient." *Ersatz* means "equivalent" or "substitute."

Bet You Didn't Know

Bismarck once remarked that there are two things you don't want to see being made: laws and sausages. Sausages came to be stuffed with sawdust and, get this, pigeon droppings.

The Russian Revolution and the Berlin Blunders

In the spring of 1917, an event took place that promised to alleviate all the privations. A combination of military reverses, incompetent leadership, and popular disaffection led in March to a revolution in Russia. All indications were that Russia would soon leave the war. That meant the German high command could withdraw forces from the eastern front or launch a last great offensive in France. For the people of Germany and Austria-Hungary, victory seemed in sight.

However, in early 1917, Berlin committed two blunders of world-class proportions. First, it announced the resumption of unrestricted submarine warfare; that steeply threatened another *Lusitania*-type incident. Second, on January 19, 1917, Alfred Zimmermann, the German foreign secretary, sent over the radiowaves a note to the German ambassador in Mexico City proposing to Mexico an alliance in a joint war against the United States. British intelligence decoded the message and passed it along to President Wilson. On April 6, 1917, at Wilson's request, Congress declared war on Germany. Now, with the vast manpower and resources of the United States thrown into the mix, and with the unexpected speed in which the United States entered into the European war, the scales tipped in favor of the Allies.

Bet You Didn't Know

"On the first of February we intend to begin submarine warfare unrestricted. In spite of this, it is our intention to endeavor to keep neutral the United States of America. If this attempt is not successful, we propose an alliance on the following basis with Mexico: That we shall make war together and together make peace. We shall give general financial support, and it is understood that Mexico is to reconquer the lost territory in New Mexico, Texas, and Arizona ..."

Just how Mexico was to retake the territories lost in the 1840s war with the United States, Zimmermann failed to make clear; nor did he explain how Germany was to cross the Atlantic Ocean when its fleet was bottled up in Kiel.

In March 1918, the German general staff indeed organized a final offensive toward the west. Germany again won some victories but could not break through the Allied lines decisively. In the middle of July of the same year, the British and the French, reinforced by American divisions, launched a counterattack. The new push from the west so weakened the German positions that Berlin initiated inquiries about the possibility of an armistice.

Peace Ploys

On July 15, the Germans had reached their farthest advance along the Marne River, much as they had done in 1914. This time, however, nine American divisions were waiting for them; the new French commander in chief, Ferdinand Foch, had used the Yanks as the advance guard of his July 18 counterattack. Badly overstrained, the Germans had faltered. The ensuing American assault through and beyond the zone of the trenches had proven more than the Germans could withstand. With its forces in pell-mell retreat, the German high command informed the government in Berlin that Germany could not win the war.

The foreign office had already made overtures of peace to Wilson through neutral embassies.

Early in 1918, Wilson had gone to the Congress, spelling out his Fourteen Points, which he considered to be the American objectives in the war. In his address, Wilson made it clear that he wanted not only to end the war but also to eliminate the empires of France and Britain. Berlin concluded that Wilson wanted a balanced peace, with Germany kept intact.

Wilson did want a balanced peace. But he also laid down a condition for an armistice: Kaiser Wilhelm II must go. And that was the deal. On November 10, an unwilling and embittered Wilhelm, this time taking orders from his general staff, fled Germany for exile in Holland. Then, at the eleventh hour of the eleventh day, November 11, 1918, the First World War came to an end.

However, the story of Germany continued. Created by Otto von Bismarck and sustained by Kaiser Wilhelm II, the Second Reich imploded in revolution.

Germany's Revolution

When the war broke out, the German government succeeded in gaining the support of the Socialists, the largest opposition party in the country. Remember that Bismarck had forged a coalition of nationalists and socialists. And working class patriotism carried over into the war itself.

But as the British blockade took its toll, as inflation set in and *real incomes* fell, as the wounded came back to the hospitals and the dead were lowered into graves, and the costs of the war became manifest, it became increasingly clear that the support of the Socialists was only provisional. As early as December 1915, a group of 20 Social Democrats in the parliament refused to approve the government's request for war credits.

Later, discontent among the workers showed up in a series of sporadic strikes. The most violent center of unrest, however, was not on the home front but in the German navy itself, where disparities in privileges between officers and enlisted personnel created a genuinely revolutionary situation. When the officers tried to launch a last suicidal attack on the British Royal Navy, still maintaining the blockade in the North Sea, open revolt broke out on October 30, 1918, at the naval base at Kiel.

Terms and Translations

Real income is a fairly straightforward concept. If I pay one dollar for a bushel of potatoes today but because of inflation I have to pay a dollar and a half tomorrow, my actual purchasing power has declined. My real income has gone down.

Suddenly, the German revolution was full blown. The sailors at Kiel called upon sympathetic groups in the army and throughout the country to assume political power. The call was answered, particularly in the large cities.

Before this revolt, the government in Berlin had been keenly aware of Germany's political instability. Along with the defeat on the western front, that awareness led the authorities to make their approach to President Wilson. But they hardly realized the consequences of their dealings with Wilson. When the kaiser abdicated and departed abruptly, Germany no longer had a government.

Collapse

With Wilhelm gone, the revolutionary groups had to struggle among themselves for the power Wilhelm's departure left behind. In time, Hitler would emerge supreme from the midst of that struggle. But in the meantime, the Bismarckian–Wilhelmine German Empire disappeared in the rubble of defeat.

So did the Austro–Hungarian Empire. With Vienna's armies suffering humiliating defeats on the Italian and Serbian fronts, the various subject nationalities (Czech, Slovak, Hungarian, Romanian, Croatian, and so on), and their national councils who represented them in the western capitals, obtained increasing recognition from the Allies. In October 1918, they declared their independence.

Terms and Translations

"... And to the **republic** for which it stands," we say in the Pledge of Allegiance. But what are we saying? The word *republic* emerged from the French Revolution and traced back to ancient Rome. It means simply a country that is not a monarchy.

In the meantime, the aged Emperor Franz Josef had passed on to the great Viennese coffee shop in the sky. His successor, Charles I, a distant relative, abdicated on November 12, 1918, and on the next day Austria was proclaimed a *republic*, and the tie with Hungary was dissolved. Within a week, Hungary, Czechoslovakia, Romania, and Yugoslavia (centered around Serbia) had proclaimed their own existence as countries independent from the now-defunct Austro–Hungarian Empire. And Austria was left a miniature German-speaking state, free to wallow in nostalgia over its lost glories, if that's what they had been.

We are now at a crucial juncture on the road to Nazi Germany. Just about everything that German nationalists (from the days of Napoleon Bonaparte onward) had longed for was gone. Both Germanies, Germany itself and Austria, had suffered unacceptable defeats in the fields of battle. Yet rather than accept responsibility for those defeats— Austria's grievance against Serbia and Germany's blind support of Austria when the German economy would not support a sustained war—the mood in German-Austrian nationalist circles was to blame someone else.

But whom? The answer to that question would emerge from the 1919 peace talks that took place in guess where—the Hall of Mirrors at Versailles, where Otto von Bismarck initially had proclaimed the existence of the German Empire.

The Least You Need to Know

◆ Despite Germany's high hopes, the movement of its troops into France in the autumn of 1914 ended in a stalemate.

◆ Despite Germany's vaunted industrial and military strength, the British Royal Navy played a major part in reducing Germany to surrender: Germany could never counter the naval embargo.

◆ Not surprisingly, given the embargo of food and raw materials, the German and Austrian populations became increasingly restive. Late in 1918, that restiveness turned into outright revolution.

◆ The First World War led to the collapse of the German and Austrian Empires. Nationalists began looking for scapegoats.

Chapter 6

The Peace to End All Peace: January 18, 1919–June 28, 1919

In This Chapter

- ◆ Paris is the site for the signing of the new peace treaty
- ◆ The negotiation process and its major players—although Germany is shut out from these procedures
- ◆ The major changes brought about by the Versailles Treaty
- ◆ A new German government, called the Weimar Republic, is formed after the Versailles Treaty

In November and December 1918, the leaders of France, Great Britain, and the United States agreed to hold peace talks the following spring. The last great peace talks had taken place at the Congress of Vienna in 1814 and 1815. This time, however, the victors had no intention of establishing a balance of power. Quite the contrary.

How the Paris Peace Talks Opened

The peace talks opened in Paris on January 18, 1919. What was the significance of that date? It was 48 years to the day after Bismarck had proclaimed the creation of the German Empire. The spirit of the Iron Chancellor still hung over Europe.

Europe, however, looked different than it had in Bismarck's time. The Russian Empire was gone and its former capital, now called Leningrad, was in the hands of the Bolsheviks; a brutal civil war was raging all across Russia. The German and Austro–Hungarian Empires were also defunct, with revolutionary regimes struggling to establish themselves in Berlin and Vienna. In Estonia, Latvia, and Lithuania down the Baltic coast, as well as in Poland and along the basin of the Danube, new republics had sprung into being, but these were without strong leaders or even borders on which everyone could agree. East of the Rhine and Italy, Europe was anarchic, with criminal gangs and warlords terrorizing the people and looting at will. France and Great Britain, although victorious, had lost a million men each and their treasuries were empty; northeastern France was so pocked from shells that it looked like a moonscape.

Bet You Didn't Know

At the Congress of Vienna, the victors brought the defeated French into their councils, allowing France a say in its own future. And what we might call the Vienna system lasted for a century because it was legitimate: All the great powers (not necessarily the lesser ones and certainly not the various nationalists) had a stake in keeping international relations pretty much as they were. They had their squabbles, as with the Crimean War; however, until the coming of Bismarck, none of the great powers was willing to risk a continental war; and even he, after creating the German Empire, tried to make Germany look as if it respected the rights and privileges of the other great powers. But the victors at Paris excluded the Germans; therefore, Germany would have no reason to see any arrangements made at Paris as legitimate.

What do you think? Should Germany have been included in the peace talks? Would the world possibly have been spared its future horrors?

Germany had been spared an invasion, but otherwise it was a devastated land. Everywhere people were gaunt from hunger; even as the peace talks began, the British maintained their naval blockade. Although not as ruinous as it would become later, inflation was steadily mounting. The women who worked in the factories had long since given up hope of buying new clothing. The soldiers who hobbled back from the front, many of them on crutches, were dressed in rags. And Kaiser Wilhelm II, whom the German people had been taught to revere as a god, was gone, disgraced. His empire, once so seemingly stable, was showing signs of social and moral disintegration.

Worst of all, the victors in Paris were not allowing the Germans to take part in the peace talks. The French, the British, and the Americans had also excluded the Bolsheviks. To the Germans this was fine, because the Communists in the new Soviet Union were just scruffy barbarians. But to keep Germany out of discussions regarding the future? This seemed outrageous. The Germans did not accept the thesis that the Central Powers alone should bear the guilt for the coming of the war. So even as the Paris talks were barely underway, Germany subscribed to a sense of grievance.

The Big Four

Twenty-seven countries were represented at the Paris peace talks. Even China, so far away, had sent a contingent to fight on the side of the Allies and believed it was entitled to something of a share of the spoils. The full sessions, however, were unimportant. What did matter were the talks among the Big Four—Premier Vittorio Orlando of Italy, Prime Minister David Lloyd George of Great Britain, Premier Georges Clemenceau of France, and President Woodrow Wilson of the United States.

Italy had sided with the Allies only after a bribery to do so. And Italy's military contribution to the Allied cause, by comparison to the British and French efforts, had been minimal. A small man with a bushy mustache, Vittorio Orlando, the Italian prime minister, carried the least weight among the Big Four.

David Lloyd George had taken over the British premiership at the end of 1916. A fiery and mercurial politician with a mane of white hair, his primary interests before the war had lain in the realm of domestic reforms. Finely tuned to the nuances of British public opinion, he wanted an acknowledgement of Germany's defeat but he also realized that Britain had beaten back Germany's challenge to its empire. Lloyd George was not obsessed with the desire for revenge.

Clemenceau, on the other hand, desired revenge. The premier of France, Georges Clemenceau, with a drooping mustache and sweeping white hair, was known as the "tiger of France." An aged patriot, he had been born in 1841, and he well remembered the humiliation of the Franco–German War. Clemenceau would have been quite happy to see Germany pulverized again and returned to its pre-Bismarckian disunity. Actually, he would have been delighted to see all Germany turned into a pasture.

Woodrow Wilson wanted a just peace. It's hard now to imagine the hopes that just about everyone in Europe, including the Germans, placed on the narrow shoulders and frail frame of President Woodrow Wilson. Once a college professor who had become the head of Princeton University and then, in the election of 1912, had been elevated to the awesome heights of the American presidency, Wilson was looked upon with awe and expectation. When he reached Europe in January 1919, he was welcomed as if he represented the second coming of Christ. In Paris, as Wilson entered the city in an open carriage, people threw roses, violets, and holly from their windows. As he stood in the carriage, raising his silk top hat, French citizens screamed in holy fervor. He rode under red, white, and blue bunting and draped flags. Military bands beat drums and sounded bugles. The noise was lost in the roaring cheers for the man who would save France from another 1870 and another 1914. A huge banner stretched across the Champs Élysées: "Wilson the Just."

> **Supporting Actors**
>
> Wilson might have been the hero, but he was a very sick man. He didn't have the strength to insist on a lenient treaty for Germany.

The Germans, too, looked to Wilson for justice. The Fourteen Points had seemed so promising: "open covenants openly arrived at"; freedom of the seas "alike in peace and in war"; world-wide free trade; arms limitations; readjustments of colonies; the self-determination of peoples and the redrawing of the map of Europe along national lines; and, above all, a League of Nations, an international organization intended to keep the peace. Wilson's principles were democratic, liberal, and progressive, apparently in tune with the prevailing ideas in the Germany of 1919.

Germany looked to Woodrow Wilson to create a new era. But still there was that sinister—from the German point of view—aspect to the Paris peace talks. Germany was not to be included.

Negotiations Without the Germans

In the first week of the peace conference, the Allies and Wilson agreed to establish the League of Nations. Then they got down to shaping the peace.

Almost immediately, the Allies began to fight among themselves. Just how great a victory should they claim? Clemenceau wanted a whole lot. He wanted France to occupy not only the Saarland, the industrialized region in southwestern Germany that bordered on Luxembourg and eastern France, but also the entire left bank of the Rhine. Wilson and Lloyd George objected: They considered Clemenceau's territorial demands excessive and injurious to peace.

Lloyd George and Clemenceau did agree that Germany should pay all their war costs. Wilson disputed the demand: He thought that peace would rest on a Germany that was prosperous, not saddled with the need to pay huge reparations.

Orlando threatened to walk out of the conference if Italy's claims along the eastern Adriatic coast were rejected. Two cities there, Trieste and Fiume, were Italian-speaking, although they had been part of the Austro–Hungarian Empire. The Italians wanted still another poke at the Austrians.

The principals at Paris disagreed over the form of Poland. But they did agree that Germany should be punished. The most important decisions at Paris certainly did punish Germany. Germany lost all its colonies. Actually, they were gone anyway, over-run by the British and the Japanese. Under the agreement for the League of Nations, the Allies agreed to call the former colonies of Germany and its own allies "mandates." The word was a way of pretending that those colonies did not have new colonial masters. So Turkey's domains to the south, Syria and Lebanon, and Palestine (the present-day Israel, Jordan, Kuwait, and Iraq) became respectively French and British "mandates." The Union of South Africa (part of the British Commonwealth) took over German Southwest Africa (now Namibia). Australia got German New Guinea and the Solomon Islands; New Zealand took over German Samoa. Japan got other once-German islands in the Pacific, most notably the Marshalls and the Carolines, as well as China's Shandong Peninsula.

Then came the German war machine. The British and the French asserted their authority over the German fleet at Kiel; rather than surrender their vessels, German crews scuttled them. The Allies also decided to limit the German military to 100,000 men; because they also forbade conscription, the reduced German army became exclusively professional. It could possess up to six warships but no aircraft or submarines. Germany was to place no troops on the left bank of the Rhine or within 30 miles of the river's right bank. All German rivers, including the Rhine, were to be open to international shipping.

Next were the territorial provisions. Alsace and Lorraine went back to France. Three cities along the border became Belgian. Out in the east, two provinces, Posen and West Prussia, were made part of the newly created Poland. Poland got a corridor of land to the Baltic; the German city of Danzig (now Gdansk) was put under the control of the League of Nations. Memel, a German-speaking port on the Baltic, was handed over to Lithuania. And all along the borders of France, Denmark, Belgium, and Poland, areas that were ethnically mixed, residents could vote on which country to join.

Last but not least was the matter of money. Deeply in debt to the United States, the British and the French were determined to restore their own finances from German pockets. So they insisted that Germany accept total responsibility for starting the war and therefore total payment for all the costs; those payments were called *reparations*.

Terms and Translations

The word **reparation** implies giving compensation to satisfy someone who has suffered injury, loss, or wrong at the hands of another. Thus, it assumes that one party or another is exclusively guilty of wrongdoing. And that was precisely what the vast majority of the German people denied: They insisted that the Russian and French mobilizations and the British move of the fleet to Scapa Flow had been precipitative acts that had forced Germany to launch a preemptive war; that Germany had struck first for reasons of self-defense.

Do you agree with the Germans? Why or why not?

Germany was supposed to pay the Allies for both military and civilian losses. Germany was to start payments immediately and the bill eventually was figured at nearly $32 billion. But that wasn't all. Germany had to hand over most of its merchant and fishing boats, hand over most of its coal, and give up all property owned by German private citizens in other countries. This last bit meant that Germany could no longer invest abroad, as it had done before the war.

Bet You Didn't Know

You've heard the old expression, "You can't get blood out of a turnip." Germany was the turnip and the reparations were the blood. How was Germany supposed to pay up when it had lost so much of its productive capacity? The answer was that it couldn't. At the end of the Second World War, the British and the Americans (not the Soviets) did not repeat this demand for reparations. They believed that it was in their own economic interest to see Germany restored and able to trade with the rest of the world.

Understanding the Treaty of Versailles

The Paris peace negotiations produced separate treaties dealing with German's alliance partners, Austria, Hungary, Bulgaria, and Turkey. The most famous of the treaties was signed at Versailles. Here (as they exactly appeared) were its major provisions:

> **ARTICLE 31:** "Germany, recognizing that the Treaties of 1839, which established the status of Belgium before the war, no longer conform to the requirements of the situation, consents to the abrogation of said treaties. ..."

Translation: In 1839, the great powers of Europe had agreed that Belgium should be independent of Holland and neutral. Now Germany was to consent to Belgium being aided by the Allies.

ARTICLE 42: "Germany is forbidden to maintain or construct any fortifications either on the left bank of the Rhine or on the right bank to the west of a line drawn 50 km [30 miles] to the east of the Rhine. ..."

Translation: The Rhineland was to be a demilitarized zone.

ARTICLE 45: "As compensation for the destruction of the coal mines in the north of France and as part payment toward the total reparation due from Germany for the damage resulting from the war, Germany cedes to France in full and absolute possession, with exclusive rights of exploitation, unencumbered and free from all debts and charges of any kind, the coal mines situated in the Saar Basin. ..."

Translation: Coal had been the fuel of the mighty German economy. Now that fuel was to be turned over to France.

ARTICLE 51: "The territories which were ceded to Germany [in 1871] are restored to French sovereignty. ..."

Translation: Alsace and Lorraine were to be returned to France.

ARTICLE 80: "Germany acknowledges and will respect strictly the independence of Austria. ..."

> ### Memorable Places
>
> Back in the seventeenth century, France's King Louis XIV had built a whole new city at the old village of Versailles about ten miles from Paris. Fitted out with polished mirrors, glittering chandeliers, and tall windows that looked out on formal gardens, the palace was a monument to wealth and power.

Translation: Germany could not force German-speaking Austrians to join their country.

ARTICLE 81: "Germany ... recognizes the complete independence of the Czecho–Slovak state. ..."

Translation: A newly created country, Czechoslovakia contained a sizable German-speaking population. This article meant that Germany was to leave those German-speaking people alone.

ARTICLE 87: "Germany ... recognizes the complete independence of Poland. ..."

Translation: Germany was to accept the transfer of some of its pre-war territories to the new Polish state.

ARTICLE 119: "Germany renounces in favor of the principal Allied and associated powers all her rights and titles over her overseas possessions. ..."

Translation: Germany's colonies were gone.

ARTICLE 160: "By a date which must not be later than March 31, 1920, the German army must not comprise more than seven divisions of infantry and three divisions of cavalry. After that date the total number of effectives in the army of the states constituting Germany must not exceed 100,000 men, including officers and establishments of depots. The army shall be devoted exclusively to the maintenance of order within the territory and to the control of the frontiers. The total effective strength of officers, including the personnel of staffs, whatever their composition, must not exceed 4,000. ... The German general staff and all similar organizations shall be dissolved and may not be reconstituted in any form."

Translation: Except for police and border functions, Germany was disarmed.

ARTICLE 180: "All fortified works, fortresses, and field works situated in German territory to the west of a line drawn 50 km to the east of the Rhine shall be disarmed and dismantled."

Translation: Germany was shorn of all defenses along its frontier with France.

ARTICLE 181: "After the expiration of a period of two months from the coming into force of the present treaty the German naval forces in commission must not exceed: 6 battleships, 6 light cruisers, 12 destroyers, 12 torpedo boats, or an equal number of ships constructed to replace them. ... No submarines are to be included. All other warships, except where there is a provision to the contrary in the present treaty, must be placed in reserve or devoted to commercial purposes. ..."

Translation: The kaiser's high seas fleet was reduced to the status of a coast guard.

ARTICLE 198: "The armed forces of Germany must not include any military or naval air forces."

Translation: Toward the end of the First World War, the airplane had come into play over the battlefields. Because it could bomb the trenches, its use may have given Germany a decided advantage. Under this article, Germany was prevented from taking advantage of her airplanes.

ARTICLE 231: "The Allied and Associated governments affirm and Germany accepts the responsibility of Germany and her allies for causing all the loss and damage to which the Allied and Associated governments and their nationals have been subjected as a consequence of the war imposed on them by the aggression of Germany and her allies. ..."

Translation: First of all, the major "Associated" government was the United States: President Wilson resolutely refused to consider the United States technically an ally of Great Britain and France. This on his part was a sop to American isolationists. More broadly, this was the war guilt clause: The Versailles treaty pinned all the blame for the war on Germany, which justified the requirement for Germany to pay up.

ARTICLE 245: "Within six months after the coming into force of the present treaty, the German government must restore to the French government the trophies, archives, historical souvenirs or works of art carried away from France by the German authorities in the course of the war of 1870 to 1871 and during this last war. ..."

Translation: Germany had to return the spoils of war, past and present.

ARTICLE 428: "As a guarantee for the execution of the present treaty by Germany, the German territory situated to the west of the Rhine, together with the bridgeheads, will be occupied by Allied and Associated troops for a period of 15 years from the coming into force of the present treaty. ..."

Translation: The French especially were likely to occupy the western part of Germany for 15 years to come.

ARTICLE 431: "If before the expiration of the period of 15 years Germany complies with all the undertakings resulting from the present treaty, the occupying forces will be withdrawn immediately."

Translation: Germany might get time off for good behavior.

The Versailles Treaty was unquestionably harsh, and almost everyone in Germany was outraged. Their government had made a deal with President Wilson—the departure of the kaiser in return for the country's being kept intact—and Berlin had lived up to its side of the arrangement. Now, when news of the treaty got around, people in Germany felt betrayed and they saw Wilson as the betrayer. To almost all Germans, the war guilt and reparations clauses were utterly repugnant. No one wanted to sign the treaty damning himself, his party, and his principles in the eyes of fellow Germans.

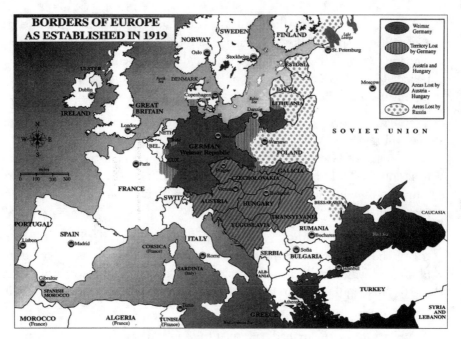

Map of Germany after the Treaty of Versailles.

(Eric Stevens)

But the Germans had no choice. With their country in political turmoil, starved by the British blockade, and faced with the threat of an actual invasion, the Germans had no choice but to sign the treaty. So leaders of the Catholic and Social Democratic Parties agreed to shoulder the hateful burden: They would regretfully provide the signers.

Two virtually unknown and deeply embarrassed German representatives showed up at the Hall of Mirrors at Versailles and, in the presence of a huge number of European and American dignitaries, signed the treaty. The date was June 28, 1919, five years to the day after the assassination of Archduke Franz Ferdinand in that obscure town so far away in the Balkans, Sarajevo.

Ever since that day, diplomats, journalists, historians, and others have debated the wisdom of the Treaty of Versailles. They thought it was too harsh. But this much is clear: From the very beginning, well before Hitler and the Nazis rose to power, Germany had no real intention of abiding by the treaty.

The Weimar Republic

Some elements in Germany, to be sure, wanted to fashion a western-style democracy. Indeed, after several months of discussions in Weimar, a town about 50 miles southwest of Berlin, a group of political moderates in July 1919 drew up a constitution remarkably similar to the United States Constitution. The Weimar Constitution, adopted on August 11, 1919, preserved the word *Reich* but declared that Germany was a republic; no more kaiser. It went on to create a *Reichstag*, which acted much like the American Congress.

The members of the Reichstag were to be elected by the people, as in the American House of Representatives. There was also to be a *Reichsrat*, in which each of the German *Länder* were to be represented: Think of the U.S. Senate.

Terms and Translations

The first part of *Reich-stag* is easy: *Reich* means "rich" or "realm," hence a country. *Tag* seems obscure, but isn't really. It is a cognate of the English *day*. T and d are both pronounced at the tip of the tongue. We also usually consider y to be a consonant, as in "yes." G is also a consonant. Indeed, *Tag* means "day." And who sits in deliberation every day, or nearly every day? Congress, or the Reichstag. The Reichstag became very important in Hitler's rise to power.

Terms and Translations

No, *Reichsrat* does not mean a rich German rodent. When you be*rate* somebody, you are telling that person off, saying that he or should not have done such and such. So you're giving a kind of advice. *Rat* in German means advice. The Reichsrat was supposed to supply counsel, as the American Senate supposedly does. A *Ratskeller* is a town-hall cellar that doubles as a restaurant or beer hall. Now, *Länder*. When we say land, we can mean the soil or an area. The old areas or states of Germany persisted into the Weimar period. The umlaut and the *-er* ending make the word plural. It's pronounced almost like the English word *lender*. So the German Senate was composed of the states. Sound familiar?

The Weimar Constitution was also strong on the rights of free expression, as in the American First Amendment, and it made a lengthy provision for the "general welfare," a phrase found twice in the U.S. Constitution.

So far, so good. The Weimar Republic looked like a democracy, on paper. But its major supporters were the parties in the center of the political spectrum, the Catholics and the Social Democrats, precisely the groups associated with the signing of the hated Treaty of Versailles.

But remember this, too. The U.S. Constitution in the beginning was no guarantee of democracy. Only white, male property owners could vote. And under the Alien and Sedition Acts, passed by Congress in the time of President John Adams, the Bill of Rights was virtually overthrown. Democracy in America has been the product of a long, slow evolution. But the Weimar Republicans were trying to establish a German democracy overnight.

And the Germans had had little or no experience with democracy. Before Bismarck, a few of the free cities did respect individual rights. But most of the kingdoms and duchies had been authoritarian—as had Prussia. True, in the nineteenth century a lot of Germans did seek freedom, but by and large they were the ones who came to the United States. To those who remained behind, democracy was an alien phenomenon.

So right from the start of the Weimar Republic, most Germans still adhered to the traditional authoritarianism. Yes, Germany was again deeply divided.

On the left were the so-called Spartacists, named for a Roman slave who led a slave revolt in southern Italy in 72 B.C.E.; they were led by two out-and-out Communists, Karl Liebknecht and Rosa Luxemburg, who, in January 1919, took over Berlin and tried to make it a Bolshevik city. Their revolution failed and Liebknecht and Luxemburg were arrested, and were shot to death while "trying to escape." Even in failure, however, their revolt signaled the contempt of the German left for democracy.

And then there was the right. In 1920, a cabal of army officers staged a *Putsch*, or armed revolt, in Berlin. (*Putsch* is a cognate of the English word *push*, as when you push someone out of power.) They put the republican government to flight and tried to put in place a new government of their own, headed by a figure named Dr. Wolfgang Kapp. Shutting down the public utilities, workers in Berlin stopped the takeover.

Lacking widespread support, however, the Weimar government was weak, unwilling or unable to take serious measures against private armed gangs led by anti-democratic, authoritarian agitators. As early as 1923, one of those agitators led another failed revolt, this one in Munich. His name was Adolf Hitler.

The Least You Need to Know

- Probably the most significant decision made at the Paris peace talks of 1919 was that of excluding the Germans from the deliberations. For better or worse, this meant that whatever treaty the conversations produced was bound to be illegitimate in the eyes of the German people.

♦ Of all the world leaders who met in Paris, starting in January 1919, the most important was Woodrow Wilson. He put forth a vision of peace based on justice. To the German people, though, he seemed to betray his own principles, leaving Germany to the mercy of the French and others who wanted to take chunks of the German Empire.

♦ The Treaty of Versailles was based on the assumption that Germany was solely responsible for the advent of the war. The treaty therefore left Germany geographically shrunken, militarily weakened, and financially ruined.

♦ The German government that emerged after the signing of the Versailles Treaty was called the Weimar Republic, named for the town where the new German constitution had been drafted. But it was a weak government, unable to withstand the buffetings from the Communists on the left and the forces led by Hitler on the right.

Part 2

The Ascendancy of Evil

Defeated in the First World War, Germany was a dissatisfied country. But why did it fall under the spell of Adolf Hitler, turn to Nazism, and become an aggressive machine of war? The answers, spelled out in the next five chapters, lie in the organizational and speech-making techniques Hitler learned in his youth, the sense of crisis in Germany in the 1920s, the hardships caused by the Great Depression, Hitler's political appeals to a suffering nation, and, finally, his seizure of power in 1933.

Chapter 7

Hitler's Youth: 1889–1923

In This Chapter

- Hitler's dysfunctional childhood
- Down and out in Vienna and Munich
- Hitler's military career
- The formation of the Nazi Party
- How membership in the Nazi Party slowly grows, through passionate speeches in beer halls

We saw Germany emerge from an almost medieval land of political divisions—with various kings and dukes in their independent castles—and a land of farmers and artisans, with smatterings of hugely talented poets, musicians, and philosophers, to an ostensibly unified and certainly economically powerful giant of a country. We also saw *that* Germany entered into a war of unprecedented mass destruction and a war its leaders should have known it could not win. We saw Germany defeated, humiliated, and scorned. And we saw the beginnings of the spirit that was to overwhelm Germany and indeed much of the world—the widespread desire to recapture the glories of the German past.

Throughout Germany immediately after the signing of the Versailles Treaty was the intense, even obsessive, desire for the reconstruction of the country—socially, politically, and internationally. Germany had to be a great power once again, even a greater power than before.

Was this desire for greatness megalomania? Probably so. And that brings us to Hitler.

A Look at Hitler's Character

Before we go into the details of the rise of Hitler, we should briefly look at Hitler's character and some of the questions that are often asked about his character.

Was Hitler crazy? Many have thought so; in the end he certainly was out of touch with reality. But we've got to be careful here. We Americans often brand our enemies as crazy. In the beginning, at least, Hitler was "crazy like a fox." As we'll learn in this chapter, in the early 1920s Hitler was perfectly in touch with what multitudes of Germans believed.

Was Hitler anti-Semitic? Of course. However, he was no more anti-Semitic than most Christian Germans of the time and, for that matter, most non-German Europeans.

Was Hitler a homosexual? Some of his contemporaries thought so. There is a story that when he was a teenager in rural Austria, he fled from the advances of an amorous milkmaid. However, others who knew him attested to his interest in women.

And then there's the old business about Hitler's love for dogs. As an adult he always seemed to have a dog. Did that make him weird? President Harry S Truman once said of Washington, D.C., "If you want a friend in this town, buy a dog."

We've got to remember that Hitler started life as a nobody. He eventually discovered his gift for mesmerizing crowds. His extreme right-wing, anti-Semitic, anti-foreign rantings and ravings appealed to ever-larger audiences. He was an utterly cynical manipulator of public opinion who used his skill on the platform to elevate himself to a position of power. He craved power and prestige at all costs, for they covered up an inner void. Hitler had no real ideas or concept of what was ideal; he desired only the untrammeled quest for power.

Hitler was a lower-class version of Bismarck, a seeker of power for power's sake, but without the Iron Chancellor's brilliance and certainly without his sense of limits. Or so it seems to this author. Interpretations of Hitler are endlessly fascinating. Let's see what you come up with. Here are the known facts.

Hitler's Birth and Boyhood

Hitler's parents grew up in the *Waldviertel* (the Wood Quarter), an Austrian farming region northwest of Vienna and not far from the current border of Czechoslovakia. The region was hilly with lots of forests and occasional fields from which the peasants laboriously had cleared away the stones. Hitler's father, Alois Hitler (born illegitimate as Alois Schicklgruber and legitimized by a priest as Hitler—a name that over the generations had undergone several spelling changes), had risen above the status of peasantry by becoming a minor figure in the Austro–Hungarian Empire. He was a brutal man who drank heavily and regularly beat his wife and two children who lived to adulthood. (Four died in infancy.) Adolf Hitler, born in 1889, came to hate his father.

Born in a remote village, Hitler learned the local dialect. German is a language of many dialects, some of which most Germans cannot understand. Hitler's first language was just such a dialect. For many years Hitler could not speak standard German (*Hochdeutsch*) with correct grammar.

> **Modern Day Parallels**
>
> Many studies of abused children show that when they grow up, they often become abusers themselves. Some people, of course, break the chain of abuse. Without question, though, Hitler grew up in an atmosphere of domestic violence that foreshadowed his role in bringing greater violence.

In describing where some people come from, the Germans have an expression: "*Aus Buxtehude*," which means "from the back of beyond." This is where some might say Hitler came from; in other words, Hitler was a hick.

He also showed all the makings of a drifter. He went off to school at the nearby town of Linz, but he was an indifferent student at best; by the time he was 16 years old, he had become a school dropout. That year his father died, and, inheriting a bit of money, Adolf started to lead a Bohemian existence. Hooking up with another youth, August Kubizek, he rented a small apartment. While Kubizek practiced various musical instruments, Hitler whiled away his time reading, filling sketchbooks with drawings, and going to the opera. Wagner especially enchanted him. He dreamed vaguely of becoming an architect.

In the spring of 1906, his mother let him visit Vienna. For a month he roamed the romantic old city, staying with his godparents, and gawking with awe and admiration at the baroque buildings of the Austrian capital.

He returned to Linz; in his imagination, he was already an architect. Why did Hitler choose architecture? Hitler had not yet discovered politics. But according to what his friend Kubizek said many years later, he would stand in front of the Linz cathedral, praising some features and in his sketchpads showing how he would redesign others. In fact, on paper he redesigned almost all of Linz, planning a new railroad station and a public park. He was showing an urge to create—as well as a politician's drive to be in control.

Late in December 1907, Hitler's mother Klara died of cancer. Unlike his father, she had been kind and undemanding. Her death heightened Hitler's growing sense of emptiness, and the next year he and his friend headed to Vienna, Hitler thought forever.

Once in the metropolis, Kubizek won admission to the Academy of Music. Hitler's application to the Academy of Art, however, was rejected twice. The architectural drawings Hitler had submitted were accurate but without flair. Yet he could not qualify for the Academy of Architecture: The authorities there required a serious educational background. Kubizek's success, and his own failure, led Hitler to break off the friendship. Now he was in Vienna alone, with the funds from his small inheritance running low.

Down and Out in Vienna and Munich

By late summer 1909, with his funds dwindling, Hitler had lived in a series of rooms, each sleazier than the last and each farther out into the slums that surrounded Vienna. Each time he moved, he registered his changes of address with the police; that was a requirement in the Austro–Hungarian Empire. His last registration was dated August 22. Within a month, however, he dropped from sight, entering the underworld of poverty. Unable or unwilling to work, he spent the autumn as a wandering tramp. For a while his home was a bench in the *Prater*, the famed amusement park with the Ferris wheel. Selling a few paintings and most of his clothing, Hitler met the coming of winter without a coat. He resigned himself to lining up for dinners and a bed at a Viennese asylum for the homeless.

For Hitler the asylum turned out to be a significant place: Along with other down-and-outers, for the first time in his life, apparently, he began to discuss politics. Like his fellow bums, Hitler blamed his plight on the upper classes of Vienna, and especially the Jews. Yet his anti-Semitism was not yet the all-consuming passion he was characterized for during his later years. There, in that shelter, he began to harbor his political ambitions. In Hitler's memoirs, *Mein Kampf*, he said:

> You know—without exaggeration—I always believe that the world has lost a great deal in that I could not attend the Academy [of Art] and learn the technical end of the art of painting. Or has fate chosen me for something else?

In time, Hitler was able to sell some of his paintings and move into another cheap room of his own. But after five years of a love-hate relationship with Vienna, he was ready to move on. Upon leaving Vienna, he hung a placard over his bed that read:

> We look free and open
> We look steadfastly,
> We look joyously across
> To the German Fatherland!
> Heil!

On May 25, 1913, Hitler got off the train from Vienna and made his way through the lobby of Munich's Hauptbahnhof, or main railroad station. Full of hope, he found a room and immediately began to paint his pictures. But the art market in Munich was small and Hitler made only a few sales. The winter of 1913 to 1914 found Hitler again on the brink of starvation.

Then a peculiar incident took place. On the afternoon of January 18, Hitler heard a knock on his door. When he opened it, he was confronted by a Munich police officer. The officer handed over a summons. The document was from Vienna. It ordered Hitler to report for military duty back in Linz within two days. If he failed to do so, he would be charged with leaving Austria-Hungary "with the object of evading military service"; if found guilty, he would be subject to imprisonment and a heavy fine.

Terms and Translations

Hauptbahnhof. *Haupt* means "head," or "main." You've heard of the famous German *Autobahns*. *Bahn* means "road," as in "railroad." *Hof* doesn't seem to have any cognates in English, but it suggests a court or palace.

The officer ordered Hitler to go with him to a Munich police station. The next morning he was escorted to the Austro-Hungarian consulate general.

Here we gain a bit of insight into Hitler's character: His ability to win sympathy from others. On seeing his ragged clothes and skinny body, the consul-general took pity on this young man, especially after hearing his tale of woe. Back in 1911, Hitler claimed, he had tried to register for military service in Vienna but had heard nothing since. The summons had taken him by surprise and gave him no time to return to Linz by the deadline, and he had no money for the trip. Relenting, the official let him go to Salzburg at government expense, arriving there on February 5. Here is how Hitler described his sorrowful story:

> I was a young, inexperienced person, without financial help and also too proud to seek assistance from anyone or beg. Without any support, depending only on myself, the kronen and heller received for my work were often only enough to

provide a place to sleep. For two years my only girl friend was Sorrow and Need, and I had no other companion except constant unsatisfied hunger. I never learned to know the beautiful word "youth." Today, after five years, my memories are still in the form of frostbitten fingers, hands, and feet. ... I kept my name clean, and am not guilty in the face of the law and have a clear conscience. ...

Back in Austria, Hitler was found physically unqualified for military service. A report found him "unfit for combat and auxiliary duties. Unable to bear arms." Returning to Munich, Hitler resumed his efforts to sell his paintings and his dreams of a career as an architect. Again, though, everything changed. On the afternoon of June 28, 1914, his landlady told him the news: "The Austrian heir, Archduke Franz Ferdinand, has been assassinated!"

War came a month later. Swept up in the patriotic fervor, Hitler volunteered for service, this time in Munich. This time he was accepted. On August 16, he reported for duty at the barracks of the First Bavarian Infantry Regiment.

Now his immediate problems were solved. He would have food, clothing, and shelter. He would have companionship. And he would have a purpose in life.

Hitler the Soldier

Taking place on the grounds of a public school, Hitler's training was short but intensive. Soon he was transferred to the Sixteenth Bavarian Reserve Infantry Regiment. Still in Munich, the boot camp was even tougher than before. Lots of the men groaned under the strain. Not Hitler. He loved every minute of it. One of his fellow soldiers was later quoted as saying that when Hitler held his rifle, he "looked at it with a delight that a woman looks at her jewelry."

On October 17, Hitler's unit marched out of Munich, heading for more training still at a military camp 40 miles to the west. The drilling was even more strenuous, with extensive rifle practice and long night marches. At last, on October 20, Hitler's unit was ready to move out. He wrote to his Munich landlady: "I'm so happy."

At daybreak, Hitler's train was puffing along above the Rhine. As the river mists cleared, the rising sun burst upon an immense statue called Germania, standing high on the bank of the river. Throughout the train, the soldiers burst into "*Wacht am Rhein*," or "Watch on the Rhine," a patriotic song from the days of Bismarck. Eight days later, Hitler and his comrades were in battle at the front lines.

"Now the first shrapnel hisses over us and explodes at the edge of the forest, splintering trees as if they were straws," Hitler wrote to an acquaintance back in Munich.

"We watch with curiosity. We have no idea as yet of the danger. None of us is afraid. Everyone is waiting impatiently for the command, 'Forward!' ... We crawl on our stomachs to the edge of the forest. Above us are howls and hisses, splintered branches and trees surround us. Then again shells explode at the edge of the forest and hurl clouds of stones, earth and sand into the air, tear the heaviest trees out by their roots, and choke everything in a yellow-green, terribly stinking steam. We cannot lie here forever, and if we have to fall, it's better to be killed outside [the trenches]."

Finally, Hitler and his fellow soldiers heard the order to go over the top. Hitler again: "Four times we advance and have to go back; from my whole batch only one remains beside me; finally, he also falls. A shot tears off my right coat sleeve, but like a miracle I remain safe and alive. At two o'clock we finally go forward for the fifth time, and this time we occupy the edge of the forest and the farms."

Bet You Didn't Know

On both sides of the fighting, the Allies on the west and the Germans on the east, soldiers had little idea of what was happening even as close as a mile away. We have many accounts of the trench warfare, and they all seem to focus, as did Hitler's, on what was close by, the trees, the trenches, and the deaths of people all around. Although Hitler could not see it, the difficulties of his unit's advance were part of the overall German slowdown.

A couple things stand out from Hitler's account. He did have a way with words: Although untutored, he had an innate sense of style that later would underlie the hypnotic quality of his speeches. And he also was getting a sense of invulnerability. In stark contrast to his days as a bum in Vienna and Munich, he was starting to feel that he was being preserved for some kind of mission:

"I was eating my dinner in a trench with several comrades," he said years later to a British journalist. "Suddenly a voice seemed to be saying to me, 'Get up and go over there [through no-man's land].' It was so clear and insistent that I obeyed mechanically, as if it had been a military order. I rose at once to my feet and walked 20 yards along the trench, carrying my dinner in its tin-can with me. Then I sat down to go on eating, my mind being once more at rest. Hardly had I done so when a flash and deafening report came from the part of the trench I had just left. A stray shell had burst over the group in which I had been sitting, and every member of it was killed."

Was Hitler making this up? Who knows? But we do know that a few weeks later he told fellow soldiers, "You will hear much about me. Just wait until my time comes."

Maybe it was in the trenches that Hitler acquired his sense of destiny. And although toward the end of the war he was gassed and had to undergo medical treatment, he did receive the Iron Cross, a medal awarded for valor.

Corporal Hitler, in uniform and wearing the Iron Cross.

(Found in John Toland's Adolph Hitler; *U.S. Army*)

When the end of the war came in November 1918, a representative of the post-Wilhelm German government entered the private railroad car of France's Marshal Ferdinand Foch and signed the armistice. Hitler would not forget that moment.

The Right-Wing Revolutionary

Demobilized in 1919, Hitler, embittered over Germany's defeat, returned to Munich. Once again he was dirt poor, hungry, and living in a squalid room. This time, however, at least he had the consolation of being not much different from everyone else. "1919 in Munich was a sad time," he wrote. "Little light, lots of dirt, poorly dressed people, impoverished soldiers, in short, the picture resulting from four years of war and the scandal of revolution."

In *Mein Kampf*, Hitler undoubtedly lied frequently and exaggerated much. This particular passage, though, rings true. We know from many sources that life in post-war Germany was grim.

The discontent was also real, as Hitler quickly found out. Somehow he became involved with a small circle of men, only half a dozen or so, who called themselves the *Deutsche Arbeiterpartei.* Later Hitler would expand the name to the *National Sozialistische Deutsche Arbeiterpartie* (NSDAP, the National Socialist German Workers' Party, or, simply, the Nazis).

The group at first did not look very menacing. Hitler described them as clothed in "military pants, dyed coats, hats of indefinable shapes but shiny from wear, our feet in remodeled war boots ..." The group was hardly a party and certainly not a political movement. It was just a ragtag collection of veterans who met in the back room of a clubhouse to lament their fate.

Terms and Translations

Nazi is simply the abbreviation made up of the first syllables of "National" and "Socialist." **Deutsche** is German, as in "Pennsylvania Dutch." **Arbeit** means "work."

But Hitler had other ideas for the group. He persuaded one of them, who had access to a mimeograph machine, to run off invitations for membership. Slowly the number of those in attendance rose to about 35.

At the larger meetings Hitler passed the hat. With the collection in hand, he bought advertising space in the *Münchener Beobachter* (the *Munich Observer*), a *völkisch*, anti-Semitic newspaper. Hitler was calling for a mass meeting in Munich's *Hofbräuhaus*, a beer hall, to be held on the evening of October 16, 1919.

Terms and Translations

Here, the use of the German word **Völkisch** seems appropriate. *Völkisch* obviously can be translated as "folkish." But we don't use that word in English. In German, it takes on the meaning of folk tradition, folk-lore, some kind of mythic past. More exactly, it implies the so-called Aryan "race" as distinct from the Jews.

The evening marked the start of Hitler's rise to power. About 70 people showed up. After some preliminaries, Hitler walked to a lectern that someone had placed on the head table. At first he talked quietly, so much so that the audience had to strain to hear his words. Then his voice grew stronger and his message became violent. For half an hour he ranted, spewing out denunciations of the English and the French, Communists, the people who supposedly had stabbed Germany in the back by arranging the defeat (actually it had been the German high command), and, above all, the Jews. He spoke without restraint, grimacing, scowling, waving his arms, calling for revenge against any and all of Germany's enemies. The crowd loved it and he finished to deafening applause.

Hitler built on his success. More meetings followed, larger crowds assembled, and ever more vociferous speeches were delivered. Hitler's appeal was especially great to the army veterans who, like him, had survived the trenches; these former troops, anti-Marxist and anti-Semite alike, formed the nucleus of a private army.

Hitler went further. Around the end of 1919, he sat down in his room with some of these former troops and worked out a series of 25 points to be delivered at a mass meeting. He called these points "theses." His choice of that word was not at all accidental. Back in the early sixteenth century, Martin Luther had nailed his "95 theses" to the door of the Wittenberg Cathedral. And although he had broken with the Catholic Church, Luther had propagated what the Catholic Church then held, that Jews had been responsible for the death of Jesus.

The meeting at which Hitler was going to pronounce his own theses was scheduled for 7:30 P.M., February 24, 1920. All over Munich posters printed in bright red were plastered on walls and doors. Hitler had initiated the use of red in his propaganda: It symbolized blood.

The propaganda certainly had its effect. When the meeting opened in the large room of the *Hofbräuhaus*, more than 2,000 persons were in attendance. The audience was quiet, even when Hitler got to his feet. Wearing a shiny old blue suit, he looked like anything but a demagogue. He began, as usual, in a low voice. Almost like a professor, he traced out the recent history of Germany. So far, no histrionics. Then he came to the revolutions that had swept Germany in 1918 and 1919. Now he showed some emotion, especially as he denounced the leftists.

At that point, trouble broke out. Some of those in the audience were socialists. They shouted back at Hitler. Soon beer mugs were flying through the air, many of them aimed at Hitler's head. Then Hitler's army buddies went into action. Armed with whips and billy clubs, they beat up on the troublemakers, driving most of them outside.

Terms and Translations

In German, the prefix *ent* conveys the sense of "away." *fernung*, related to the English word *far*, means "distance." So *entfernung* meant "removal." But it also has an extended meaning: "elimination."

Hitler was able to continue his speech. He spelled out all his theses. They were the foundation of what would become his official ideology: the restoration of the colonies; the overturning of the Treaty of Versailles; the creation of a new army; social welfare for the workers; the union of all German-speakers in a new *Reich*; a ruthless battle against the socialists; and the *entfernung* of the Jews. Right there, in the Munich Hofbräuhaus on the night of February 24, 1920, Hitler was calling for the Holocaust.

Those who had not been expelled from the audience reacted with rapturous joy. Hitler's theses had something for everyone—he was emerging as a shrewd politician— except the Jews. So great was Hitler's popularity that 11 months later, on January 22, 1921, Munich hosted the first national congress of the Nazi Party. Hitler's magnetism on stage, and his anti-Semitism, had made him a respected force, at least in Bavaria.

He was also coming to be feared. The brawl at the Hofbräuhaus told him that he could attain eventual victory through the use of violence. And by 1922, he had begun to win disciples who also were attracted to the use of force. One of these was Herman Göring, an extroverted, flamboyant pilot who had been a flying ace in the First World War; another was also a pilot, but a grayer personality than Göring, Rudolf Hess. An un-questioning follower of Hitler, Julius Streicher, joined the ranks: Stocky, bald, and crude, he was if anything even more anti-Semitic than Hitler. Streicher soon founded an anti-Semitic newspaper called *Der Stürmer*. It meant *The Stormer*, as in the later Nazi Storm Troops.

The name of the paper was no accident. Hitler was already organizing the Nazi Party as a paramilitary organization.

On the Brink of the Beer Hall *Putsch*

An army costs money. Hitler had another ally, the German-born, Harvard-graduated, handsome and cultured Ernst Hanfstängl. The suave and persuasive Hanfstängl knew how to ingratiate himself with the people who had the money, the industrialists of the Rhineland. Their fortunes, to be sure, had been much diminished. Before and during the war, however, those fortunes had been based largely on sales of munitions to the German military. The industrialists therefore had every reason to give financial support to someone who promised to restore the German state. That someone was Hitler.

Hitler's ability to appeal to workers and businessmen alike speaks volumes. Whatever else he was, he was as good as Bismarck at forging political coalitions.

By 1923, he was even beginning to see himself as the new Bismarck, the man who had conquered all Germany. And why not? Only the year before, Benito Mussolini had marched a private army into Rome and seized the Italian government. If Mussolini, why not Hitler? He was determined to do it.

Hanfstängl's wife, Helene, would recall that "absolutely no one could ever persuade [Hitler] to change his mind. On a number of occasions … I noticed the faraway expression in his eyes; it was as though he had closed his mind to all ideas but his own."

In the summer of 1923, Hitler's idea was that, in emulation of Mussolini, he would lead his Nazis to Berlin. But first they would take over Munich. And the starting point there would be the Hofbräuhaus, the beer hall.

The Least You Need to Know

◆ Adolf Hitler was born into a backwoods family in rural Austria. His schooling was desultory, for he was in constant rebellion against all forms of authority—his father, his teachers, and his Austro–Hungarian overlords. But he did not turn out to be a left-winger. Like Bismarck, he would be a "white revolutionary," white as opposed to red, or Communist.

◆ Hitler spent several years as an adolescent and a young adult living the Bohemian life, if not that of just a bum. He manifested artistic yearnings, but he by no means found himself as an artist.

◆ Vienna was crucial for Hitler's development. It was almost two cities: One put on display the glitter of imperial pomp; the other was a vast slum of poverty and disease. From the former, Hitler learned how to stage political theater; from the latter, he imbibed a radicalism that he later linked with German nationalism.

◆ Hitler's formative experience was as a soldier in the trenches of northeastern France. There he came to worship the German state and to see himself eventually as a politician.

◆ Hitler would aspire to be no ordinary politician. Once decommissioned, he discovered that he had a gift as a rabble-rouser, indeed one with an undoubted talent for political dramaturgy. Thus, as early as 1923, he decided to make a stab at seizing power in Germany.

Chapter 8

The Beer Hall *Putsch:* 1919–1923

In This Chapter

- How Germany tries to function with a weakened government and no true political leader
- The Ruhr crisis and how limiting industrial production creates hyperinflation
- The problems with the German army and its troops' lack of true allegiance to the government
- The attempted putsch and Hitler's imprisonment

Germany in the early 1920s was in chaos: Hitler's was not the only right-wing revolutionary society. Conspirators murdered Matthias Erzberger, a political moderate who had signed the Versailles Treaty, and Walter Rathenau, a financier who had organized the German economy during the war. Rathenau's sins were that he supported international conciliation and that he was Jewish.

Everywhere leftists battled rightists in the streets. Criminal gangs robbed banks almost unimpeded. Jews lived in a state of constant fear. The police barely functioned, at least as protectors of the public safety. And the government, seated at Weimar, was a government in name only.

Weaknesses of the Weimar Republic

The Weimar government was far from legitimate. Remember that word *legitimacy?* In this context, it means "accepted by the people."

Let's contrast the Weimar Republic with Great Britain in the early 1920s. Britain also had suffered in the war and its economy was in shambles. But its government was stable. Presiding over the government was the crown: King George V was a much-loved monarch. But real power lay in the hands of the prime minister, who presided over the majority party (in the early 1920s, the Conservative or Tory Party). For more than two centuries, British politicians had evolved a two-party system. Labour was now replacing the older Liberal Party, but the principle of one party in power and the other playing the part of the "loyal opposition" was deeply engrained. It meant that if Britons were dissatisfied with their government, they had a respected alternative to which they could turn.

Terms and Translations

Political culture simply represents the fundamental political values of a country.

Great Britain had seen plenty of workers' strikes, but no revolution. Revolution wasn't necessary. Britons with a grievance could get redress, or much of a redress, through peaceful means. The British political culture had stressed evolution, not revolution; it had placed a premium on compromise and orderly change. Most Britons had a sense of having a stake in the way things were. This was not the case with the Weimar Republic.

The glue that had held the political system together was the German monarch, and he was gone. But because it had been an absolutist state, Germany had had little or no tradition of political parties. After the First World War, a host of parties sprang up, but none of them could build a clear majority. There was no loyal opposition. Between 1920 and the end of 1923, the Weimar Republic consequently went through seven different cabinets.

The government's weakness was hardly surprising. For example, the government couldn't collect taxes very well. Bismarck and the kaiser both had had no trouble bringing in the revenues: The public had been deferential to authority. German political culture had been authoritarian. And when you have a culture that is authoritarian but no source of authority, then you've got big trouble. Each group grabs what it can, with no interest in compromise. No one has a stake in the system.

Hitler's was not the only paramilitary group. By the time Hitler was organizing the Nazis, a *putsch*, or revolt, led by Gustav von Kahr, had already turned the state of Bavaria into a haven for right-wing extremists. In fact, a map of western and central Germany between 1918 and 1923 showed nearly 30 different cities to be centers of revolutionary and counter-revolutionary activity.

Power early on in the Weimar Republic lay almost wholly in the hands of the several states and cities, as if the old French dream of a pulverized Germany had come true again. Indeed, the Germans had not been able to get the French off their backs. In 1919 came the Ruhr crisis.

The Ruhr Crisis

In the bend where the Rhine River wound its way down through the foothills of the Alps and turned upward on its course toward Holland, there lay the valley of the Ruhr. (The Germans called it the *Ruhrgebiet*, the Ruhr territory.) The area was small, no larger than metropolitan New York, really just a dot on the continent of Europe.

But its significance was immense. Its mines yielded more coal than all the rest of Europe combined. It also produced fine steel. The relation of its coal mining and steel producing was not accidental. The Ruhr was Europe's main source of coke— pure carbon, acquired by cooking coal to draw off its gases—and coke was indispensable for the conversion of iron into steel.

The valley of the Ruhr had been the engine of Germany's economic prowess. "The German Empire," John Maynard Keynes, the British economist, once noted, "has been built more truly on coal and iron than on blood and iron."

So it's little wonder that the French gazed upon the valley of the Ruhr, right across the border, with greedy eyes. In fact, early in 1923, Paris claimed that Germany had defaulted on reparations payments and sent an army into the Ruhr to seize the coal and iron industries.

Wilhelm Cuno, the head of the German government at the time, reacted by canceling all reparations, period. He also asked businessmen, workers, and public officials in the region not to cooperate in any way with the French. For once the Weimar government had done a popular thing: Germans in general cheered this defiance and people in the Ruhr engaged in work stoppages.

But that meant that the engine of the German economy had ceased to function. The production of goods came to a grinding halt. That meant fewer goods being chased by a constant amount of money, a classic device for aggravating inflation.

Before the Ruhr crisis, the value of the German currency, the deutsche mark, had already fallen from 8.9 to over 190 to the U.S. dollar. Internally, Germany had been experiencing pronounced inflation.

Bet You Didn't Know

In America we buy things with the dollar and in Europe now with the euro. So when a European comes here or an American goes to Europe, that person must obtain dollars or euros. This means you buy the other side's currency, pretty much as you buy a loaf of bread at the store. Pretty much. But usually the price of the loaf of bread doesn't change much, at least in the short run. Sometimes, currencies do change in their value dramatically. This happened with the deutsche mark before the Ruhr crisis. Americans could buy a lot more of the German currency than before. Now imagine: Suppose that today a loaf of bread costs $1 and tomorrow, say 20¢; so you can buy a lot of bread. That's what happened in Germany in the early 1920s. Americans could buy a lot of the German currency.

Then came the peace settlement. Two years after the Paris peace talks, the Allies presented Germany with a reparations bill set at 132 billion gold marks; all the major countries had reserves of gold, which was more stable in value than paper money. John Maynard Keynes calculated that the amount was three times more than Germany could afford to pay.

Hyperinflation

Do you remember the war in Vietnam? The American economy in the early 1960s was pretty much at full production, and then the government's spending on the military skyrocketed. But President Lyndon B. Johnson was reluctant to ask Congress for a tax hike to pay for the war. So the government had to borrow the money, which put more money in circulation, which triggered an inflation that lasted until the early Reagan years.

Much the same thing had happened in Germany. During the First World War, the increased arms production came about by curtailing consumer manufacturing. But Kaiser Wilhelm and his ministers lacked the will to impose a progressive taxation system. Instead of extracting funds from the rich, the government in Berlin covered its mountain of debt by issuing war bonds. As the war progressed, the purchase of such bonds by the German public was increasingly less "voluntary." Even so, the amounts raised never remotely paid for the billions of marks' worth of munitions shot off by the German army. (If you build a lathe, you can use it over and over; if you fire an artillery shell, it's gone.) The government's response was to print more money, the easiest way in the world of driving up inflation. By the end of the war the amount of paper money in circulation in Germany was six times that available in 1913.

During the war, the government had introduced rationing and closed currency exchanges with the Allies. Those steps hid the inflation from the public. Nevertheless, by November 1918, the German currency had fallen by half in the neutral countries.

It was Germany's alleged failure to pay anything close to that sum that brought about the 1923 crisis over the Ruhr.

For the majority of Germans, hyperinflation was devastating. A few figures make the point. By September 1929, the average factory worker had lost 30 percent of his 1913 income. A pensioner who in 1913 had been able to invest 100,000 marks found that his account was worth about 100 marks 10 years later.

Bet You Didn't Know

A widow who just before the war had rented out rooms in her house found that a decade later the cost of replacing a pane of broken glass was more than all the rent being received: The government had stabilized the level of rents.

By the autumn of 1923, hyperinflation hung over Germany like a thick, dark cloud. Especially with the government supporting the Ruhr workers, whom the French had rendered unemployed, the shaky German economy disintegrated so rapidly that in November 1923, the dollar was quoted at 4.2 trillion marks. Internally, the currency was so worthless that people would go to grocery stores with wheelbarrows full of paper currency, only to find that they did not have enough to buy the needed food. People collected their wages in paper money and stuffed the bills into sacks and washing baskets. Citizens even sold bills as waste paper. Paper money, however, was not as valuable as old rags.

The Working and Middle Classes Suffer Most

Hyperinflation was tough on the working class, but in a sense it was even tougher on the middle class, whose members found their savings wiped out. At least the workers had not expected much from life. Throughout the middle class, however—in the families of doctors, lawyers, professors, editors, stockbrokers, insurance executives, and the like—the sudden loss of status was humiliating. Abandoning the money economy, city dwellers began to barter, exchanging prized possessions for the necessities of life.

Stories were rife of peasant huts resplendent with grand pianos and elegant furniture, handed over by impoverished professionals from the cities for a chicken or a dozen eggs. It seems little wonder that the hitherto "respectable" members of the urban middle classes began to look for saviors—and scapegoats.

Hyperinflation Spells Profit for a Select Few

Not everyone was a loser, though. Exporters experienced a boom of unprecedented proportions: With the German currency valued so low, and hence with their prices at rock-bottom, they could undercut competitors abroad with ease. Those who owned physical assets, such as land, which rose fiercely in value, were newly rich. So were those in possession of foreign currencies. Speculators with dollars, pounds, francs, and so on swooped in, buying up great tracts of land, apartment blocks, and individual houses, all in the expectation (quite true, as things turned out) that when the German economy returned to sanity these properties would be worth many times their purchase prices.

Bet You Didn't Know

Unlike those who did not stand to inherit huge Prussian estates, most of the German officer corps, like other bureaucrats, had to exist on fixed salaries, incomes made negligible by the hyperinflation.

Who were these speculators? They were a mixed bag of foreigners and Germans. Some of those Germans were Jews. None of this speculation was going to endear those who became wealthy to those who had had to sell their properties. But Nazi propaganda would portray the speculation as engineered exclusively by Jews, which was a gross exaggeration.

Nonetheless, the hyperinflation, which lasted through 1923, caused bitter resentment. And in a Germany already profoundly anti-Semitic, the bitterness focused, even if unfairly, upon Jews.

We should keep in mind that nowhere was the anti-Semitism more pronounced than in the ranks of the German military. The German officer corps, like so many civilians, resented those who had so reduced its role and position at Versailles.

By curtailing industrial production, the Ruhr crisis worsened the inflation that was already besetting the German economy. The aggravated inflation in turn destroyed the fabric of Weimar society and prepared the way for the rise of Nazi Germany.

The Role of the Army

Although the Treaty of Versailles had reduced the German army to a shadow of its former self, its postwar commander, General Hans von Seeckt, had done his best to adapt to circumstances. Recognizing that a 100,000-man force could not defend Germany from *any* of its neighbors, he had turned it into a *Führerheer*, or an "army of leaders."

All soldiers were required to serve long terms and to feel a strong sense of dedication, as if the army were a religious order. Because the treaty had abolished the pre-war military schools, the army itself became one large military training organization. Each service branch (infantry, cavalry, artillery, and engineers) prepared officer candidates for commission. Noncommissioned personnel received training within the normal activities of troop units. The effectiveness of von Seeckt's efforts would become clear during Germany's rearmament in the 1930s and its string of victories in the first years of the Second World War.

Terms and Translations

Let's take the last part of *Führerheer* first. *Heer,* like the English *horde,* means a "multitude," a "host," hence an "army." Now, you think of *Führer* in the context of Hitler. But it's a noun, derived from the verb *führen,* which means "to drive, guide, or lead." So its use is much broader than Hitler.

But what really held the army together, a rum one though it was, was its ideology. The officers corps was devoted to the monarchy. In 1918, they had been released from their oath to the kaiser and they then had sworn oaths to the Weimar Republic. But they still believed that a monarchy was the best form of government for Germany and they did not give their complete loyalty to the republic.

The officers were looking for a leader. And when, in the wake of the Munich beer hall putsch, Hitler was put on trial for treason, they began to see him as such a leader; for Hitler tried to overthrow a government that the officer corps saw as treasonous.

The Attempted Putsch

By early 1923, Hitler had come to see the virtue of some kind of alliance with the army. The Ruhr crisis and the hyperinflation were tearing Germany apart. He had reason to believe, furthermore, that in Saxony and Thuringia, provinces to the north of Bavaria, Communists were on the verge of staging insurrections. Hitler's hope, therefore, was that if he could pull off a daring deed he could get the support of army groups in central and northern Germany and establish a national military dictatorship.

To bring his deed about, he would use the paramilitary segment of the Nazi Party, known as the *Sturmabteilung,* or SA, Storm Troopers, or just plain "Brownshirts."

Who were these Storm Troopers? Almost to a person they were not members of the regular army. On the whole they were youths from lower-class, impoverished

Terms and Translations

Let's break down the term *Sturmabteiling*. *Sturm*, obviously, is "storm." *Ab* conveys the sense of "down" or "away from." *Teil* means "a part" or "a portion"; *teilung* becomes "division" or "separation." So *abteilung* is a "compartment" or a "department." The Sturmabteiling, abbreviated to "SA," was the department of the Nazi Party that would storm a citadel. In imitation of Mussolini's Blackshirts, they donned brown uniforms.

backgrounds. They had grown up in violent families and they themselves were violent. Frequently, as adolescents, they were gang members. They were young thugs.

But they were thugs of a distinct sort. They loved to swagger around in their uniforms, uniforms with German imperial symbols on the collars and swastikas and death skulls on the caps. Born followers, they craved strong leadership. They readily fell under Hitler's spell and they were the backbone of Hitler's attempt to overthrow the Bavarian government.

When the Nazi Party held its annual congress in Munich in 1923, Hitler put his Storm Troopers on display. They marched about holding up swastika flags and showing off their martial discipline. They greatly bolstered his confidence.

So did support from General von Seeckt and Hugo Stinnes, leader of right-wing industrialists. At the height of the hyperinflation, Stinnes made the notorious statement: "We [the industrialists] must have the courage to say to the people, for the present and for some time to come, you will have to work overtime without any payment." When von Seeckt and Stinnes engineered Hitler's appointment as political leader of the *Kampfbund* (*Bund* is a cognate of the English word *bound*, so *Kampfbund* meant people "bound together" or "organized for struggle," a confederation of Bavarian veterans and paramilitary units), Hitler thought himself on the threshold of major success.

But Hitler was going to have to wait. Somehow or other the Weimar government actually did something: It stepped into Saxony and Thuringia and stopped the left-wingers from taking over. Then the Allies pressured the government to do something about the right-wingers in Bavaria. Even the top brass in the army, despite their own right-wing leanings, got nervous. Apparently they were afraid of French intervention. In any case, von Seeckt warned Hitler against taking illegal action.

Now the plot really thickened. Ritter von Kahr, head of the Bavarian provincial government and a right-winger himself, told Hitler that if the kampfbund tried to seize control in Munich, he would use the provincial army to stop them. Von Kahr also informed Hitler that any march on Berlin was forbidden..

All this was too much for Hitler. On the night of November 8, 1923, von Kahr was scheduled to speak at a Munich beer hall called the *Bürgerbräuhaus;* several of the provincial ministers were going to be present. When night fell, SA troopers surrounded the beer hall while Hitler strode inside. When he reached the speaker's platform, he pulled out a pistol, fired it toward the ceiling, and proclaimed: "The national revolution has begun!"

Pointing the pistol at von Kahr, Hitler demanded permission for the march on Berlin. To save his life, von Kahr gave his approval. Hitler and his followers were overjoyed.

In the morning, however, Hitler's fortunes took a turn for the worse. The police army united and were up early, guarding the city hall. Von Kahr then rescinded his approval for the Berlin march.

When Hitler, staying in the eastern suburbs of Munich, heard the news, he was dismayed. But with him was General Erich von Ludendorff, one of Germany's wartime commanders. Hitler let Ludendorff convince him that all was not lost. So with Hitler and Ludendorff in the lead, a column of 3,000 Storm Troopers and other Nazis formed a parade, crossed the Isar River, and marched to the *Feldherrnhalle*, Soldiers' Hall, Munich's major monument to German military might.

When the marchers reached the building, they found a row of policemen guarding the entryway. For a moment the column paused. But Ludendorff walked forward and those behind him followed in his steps.

At that moment, the police opened fire. The shooting lasted a full minute and it left 14 Nazis dead and many wounded. Those still upright fled the scene. Diving for cover, Hitler had dislocated a shoulder and an automobile spirited him away.

> **Bet You Didn't Know**
>
> Have you read any of the Janet Evanovitch's comic novels set in Trenton, New Jersey? She refers to the city as the "Burg." And a hamburger is named for Hamburg, the German city on the Ham.

> **Supporting Actors**
>
> Hermann Göring, the ace aviator, was with the group, and he received a bullet wound in the thigh. Carried into a nearby bank, he received first aid from the manager who happened to be Jewish.

Hitler in Jail

A few hours after the shooting, during the evening, three Munich police officers knocked at the door of the Hanfstängl residence in the eastern suburbs. Asking permission to search the house, they found Hitler in a sitting room, wearing pajamas and a bathrobe. Upon seeing the officers, he broke into a tirade against the Bavarian government and all its officials. Then, abruptly, he submitted to arrest.

After arraignment, a police automobile drove Hitler to the Landsberg prison, some 40 miles west of Munich. Throughout the trip, Hitler was silent, except to ask of the fate of Ludendorff (because of the general's prestige, the authorities had let him go). And before midnight, Hitler was in a cell, with only the bare walls and ceiling for company.

Learning of Hitler's failure at Munich, Arthur Möller van den Bruck, a political writer, commented: "There are many things that can be said against Hitler. But one thing one will always be able to say: He was a fanatic for Germany. … Hitler was wrecked by his proletarian primitivism. He did not understand how to give his National Socialism any intellectual basis. He was passion incarnate, but entirely without measure or sense of proportion."

Others, too, were speaking of Hitler in the past tense. His career seemed to be at an end. Within days of Hitler's arrest, however, in the Munich underground a particular announcement was being passed from hand to hand:

> The first period of the national revolution is over. Our highly revered *Führer*, has again bled for the German people. The most shameful treachery that the world has ever seen has victimized him and the German people. Through Hitler's blood and the steel directed against our comrades in Munich by the hands of traitors the patriotic Battle Leagues are welded together for better or worse.

The Least You Need to Know

- The Weimar Republic may have looked like a legitimate government, as the British government was legitimate, but it was shaky from the start, lacking almost all public support.

- Germans of all political persuasions saw the French occupation of the Ruhr valley as humiliating. Even worse than that humiliation, the hyperinflation of the early 1920s ripped German society apart, leading the usually conservative middle classes looking for radical solutions.

- Although the army looked with disfavor upon illegal coup attempts against governmental units, its officers were deeply patriotic and saw in Hitler the savior they thought that Germany needed.

- The failure of Hitler's Putsch of 1923 and his imprisonment gave him the opportunity to rethink the next phase of his revolution.

Hitler's Years of Struggle: 1923–1929

In This Chapter

- ◆ Hitler's time in prison and the writing of his autobiography, *Mein Kampf*

- ◆ Hitler's preparation to take power by persuading the masses

- ◆ Hitler reestablishes the roots of the Nazi Party by offering hope to the farmers of Schleswig-Holstein

- ◆ Hitler's attempt to gain wider acceptance with the middle class

- ◆ The Great Depression breathes new life into the Nazi Party

In September 1923, the German government appointed a committee to seek a way out of the financial chaos produced by the hyperinflation. As a result of the work of this committee, a currency reform was initiated. On November 15, 1923, a new mark was established, the so-called *Rentenmark*. *Rente* in German means income or profit, and the Rentenmark was backed by land values. One Rentenmark was equal to 4.2 trillion old marks. This stabilization of the German currency introduced a period of political consolidation and comparative prosperity.

Germany joined the League of Nations. And, as foreign minister, Gustav Stresemann (1878–1929) slowly regained confidence for Germany at the international conference table.

But in 1929 the Great Depression set in. It severely jeopardized the economic life of all the European nations and even of Japan, Canada, and the United States. In a country like Germany, where the economy was already so shaky, the collapse assumed catastrophic proportions. A widespread wave of unemployment quickly wiped out the recovery made between 1924 and 1929.

As we have seen, many Germans had thought that the failure of Hitler's beer hall *Putsch* in Munich spelled the end to any Nazi hopes for power. The Great Depression, though, set the Nazi star rising again.

Those who had written Hitler off grossly underestimated the strength of his will and—what many to this day negate—the magnitude of his political skills.

Hitler's Trial and Imprisonment

The town of Landsberg looked much as it had in medieval times. Steep woods surrounded it and its ancient fortress walls still stood. An old wooden bridge across the Lech River led to the prison, a group of gray-white buildings encircled by tall stone walls. Hitler's cell, in the section reserved for political prisoners, was actually more spacious than the tiny rooms where he had lived before. The narrow iron bed had a comfortable mattress and the double-barred window afforded a view of trees and shrubbery outside. The cell also came equipped with a writing desk and chair.

After suffering from depression for several days, Hitler used the chair and desk to put down some thoughts. He had made a mistake, he realized. He had tried to copy Mussolini. If his movement were to succeed, he had to find a German way. That success could only be based on his unique connection with the German people, what he believed was the magic of his oratory.

Finally put on trial for treason, Hitler put that oratory to use. He used the courtroom in Munich as a political platform. On his final day before the jury, he proclaimed:

> The army which we have formed grows from day to day; from hour to hour it grows more rapidly. Even now I have the proud hope that one day the hour is coming when these raw recruits will become battalions, when the battalions will become regiments and the regiments divisions, when the old cockade will be raised from the mire, when the old banners will once again wave before us; and then reconciliation will come in that eternal last Court of Judgment—the Court of God—before which we are ready to take our stand. Then from our bones,

from our graves will sound the voice of that tribunal which alone has the right to sit in judgment upon us. For gentlemen [Hitler was addressing himself to the jury], it is not you who pronounce judgment upon us, it is the eternal court of history which will make its pronouncement upon the charge which is brought against us.

The court found Hitler guilty as charged, but the sentencing was lenient. Hitler could have been deported to Austria, but the judge refused to take that step. "Hitler is German-Austrian," his judgment read. "In the opinion of the court a man who thinks and feels as German as Hitler, a man who voluntarily served four and a half years in the German army during the war, who earned high war decorations for bravery in the face of the enemy, who was wounded and whose health was impaired … should not be subjected to the Republic Protection Law [and thus deported]."

The court apparently valued Hitler's patriotism and so sentenced him to a year in the relative comfort of the Landsberg prison. In confinement, Hitler and other political prisoners had plenty of time to exercise in the prison garden, have dinner (usually a one-pot meal served at noon) together in the common room, tea or coffee at four, and easy access to beer or wine. Lights went out at 10 P.M.

Hitler put on weight in prison; nationalist organizations and admirers throughout Bavaria inundated him with packages of food. He also read books in the prison library, received the Munich newspapers, and heard reports of politics within the Nazi Party.

With Hitler absent, the Nazis rapidly disintegrated into warring factions, each claiming to uphold the "true values of the Hitler movement." Some of the Nazis saw themselves as out-and-out left-wing socialists; others in the ultra-right-wing focused on anti-Semitism.

In his prison cell, Hitler refused to mediate or give his approval to any one faction. This neutrality let him maintain his image as the Nazis' natural leader. By staying out of the squabbles, he also had time to compose his propagandistic and political autobiography, *Mein Kampf.*

Mein Kampf

Mein Kampf was a mix of Nazi history, theoretical doctrine, and street-smarts. Its style was almost illiterate. Hitler, after all, was largely unschooled.

He was, however, shrewd. Public opinion, he asserted, could be swayed easily. He wrote that crowds were like blank pieces of paper, on which the artistic orator could draw whatever he wished. Hitler went on to describe the proper use of gestures, symbols, and stage-effects, which he had learned about on the streets of Vienna. He was describing the methods by which he would motivate the masses.

Hitler then inveighed against the Jews. Jewish influence in Germany, he deemed, had led to the defeat in 1918. The Jews he called the source of all degeneracy, with their own special link to Marxism. Hitler stood for the purification of the German race, the purging of alien elements from its bloodstream, and the expropriation and banishment of the Jews as parasites and the seducers of honest German working people. This was why he founded the Nazi Party; Hitler intended to take German property back from the Jews and then to get the Jews out of Germany.

Terms and Translations

The word Hitler used for living space was **Lebensraum**. **Raum** means "room." **Leben** is "life." Those consonants are called labials. German and English have lots of similarities like that.

There was more. He also wrote that once under Nazi leadership the German people had to reestablish their supremacy in Europe, and then acquire much-needed *lebenstraum* (living space) in the east. Where in the east? Hitler wasn't entirely clear. But he seemed to have in mind the vast territories of Poland, Russia, and Ukraine. Of course there were Slavic people living there already, but this didn't matter to Hitler. The land to the east, he insisted, was rightfully German: Germany's birthright.

How to claim that birthright? By force, of course; but before Germany could launch a military drive toward the east, such action must have the support of the German people. Here's where propaganda came in. As Hitler pointed out, he had made himself a master of propaganda. Its appeal must be to emotion, not to reason. Its aim was to woo the stupid and unthinking masses, to hypnotize them into fulfilling their own destiny in the east.

All this may sound like a lot of drivel, but in one way at least it was quite interesting. As a veteran of the fighting in the fields of Flanders, Hitler had come out of the war regarding France as Germany's main enemy. But now, in his prison cell, he changed his mind. He was very explicit. "We must take up where we broke off 600 years ago," Hitler wrote. "We must stop the endless German movement to the south and west and turn our gaze upward toward the land to the east."

But who, besides the Slavic people, lived to the east? Jews. Russia, Hitler charged, had fallen "under the yoke of the Jew." God had chosen Germany to bring about the conquest of that vast, Jew-controlled territory. So right there, in *Mein Kampf*, was the idea that Germany would extend the Holocaust as far as it could into Poland and the Soviet Union.

Bet You Didn't Know

Once out of prison, Hitler wrote a second volume, *The National Socialist Movement*. It pretty much reiterated the themes of the first. Before 1930, sales of *Mein Kampf* were slight: 23,000 of Volume I and 13,000 of Volume II. By the end of 1933, the year Hitler became chancellor, however, 1.5 million copies had been sold, and during Hitler's lifetime, total sales were somewhere between 8 and 9 million copies. Hitler became a rich man.

Hitler's time in prison served him well. Had he just gone on making speeches, he might have worn himself out. But in prison, he rested, ate well, and, most importantly, became something of a martyr. He was released in late 1924 and immediately set about rebuilding the Nazi Party.

Rebuilding the Party

Without question, Hitler had good (ghoulish, yes, but good) political instincts. When he was released from prison on December 19, 1924 (the Bavarian Supreme Court had demanded that he be set free), he was met at the gate by Adolph Müller, his printer, and Heinrich Hoffmann, a Nazi photographer. They were driving a big touring car. Because the day was raw and gray, the canvas top was locked shut. As they sped toward Munich, Hoffmann asked what Hitler intended to do now. The answer was, "I shall start again, from the beginning."

That was not quite true. Although his influence had not reached much beyond Bavaria, Hitler still enjoyed a large coterie of followers in southern Germany. What he probably meant in his reply to Hoffmann was that he had to strengthen the Bavarian base before moving ahead.

So back in Munich, Hitler refused to take sides with any of the Nazi factions. He would be the leader, holding himself above the fray. And, of course, he would dramatize himself as that leader.

He's Back Again!

Hitler's first major speech after his release was set for February 27, 1925. Significantly, it took place in the Bürgerbräuhaus, the site of his failed coup.

He had not lost his touch. Delivered amid a frenzy of excitement, his speech expertly rallied all groups within the party around his leadership. He stated again his faith in the "inviolable principles of National Socialism"; he denounced Marxism and the Jews; and this time he demanded that the party membership grant him dictatorial powers.

By late March 1925, Hitler had received oaths of loyalty from almost all the Bavarian Nazis. Now he was truly the Führer, at least on the provincial level. As tokens of his new power and prestige, in the spring of 1925 Hitler acquired two possessions, the sorts of things dear to the hearts of Germans. First, he somehow got hold of a new red Mercedes; he spent many hours touring the Bavarian countryside with selected aides. And second, he set up personal headquarters in the mountain village of Berchtesgaden. The mountain house was rustic, but its windows afforded spectacular views. Hitler spent still more hours wearing *lederhosen* (leather shorts) and hiking through the hills.

While at Berchtesgaden, Hitler also acquired the services of a new secretary, Josef Goebbels. Son of a middle-class Catholic family from the valley of the Rhine, Goebbels had won a doctorate from Heidelberg University. His fields had been literature and drama. Sharp-faced and dark of complexion, Goebbels was a small man, just over five feet tall and weighing not much more than 100 pounds. As a child he had been wracked by infantile paralysis, a disease that had left him with a twisted foot. Because of his deformity, he had not been able to perform military service.

Supporting Actors

Why did Goebbels, a cultured Catholic, hook up with the loutish Nazis, who would attack the Catholic Church? We can only speculate.

But Goebbels' special talents more than made up for his physical deformities. He was a gifted writer and on the lecture platform his dark eyes, expressive hands, and resonant baritone voice made him an appealing figure.

He was also careful never to upstage Hitler. But as an educated man from the middle reaches of Germany, he did have an advantage over Hitler: He could speak *Hochdeutch*, High German, the lingo of the northern plains.

Even so, Hitler and Goebbels were in for a tough time in northern Germany. Largely Protestant northern Germany had a long history of antagonism to the largely Catholic south. In the northern stretches of the Rhine and over into Prussia, furthermore, even where people had some sympathy for Nationalism Socialism, many were attracted to the fighting qualities of the leftists. Northern Germany was the land of cities, where inflation had left the middle classes feeling so uprooted. There urbanites had little use for the peasant guttersnipe from Austria, Hitler.

Hitler Sets the Stage to Gain Power

Hitler, however, could bide his time: Prison had given him a sense of patience. In the presidential election of 1925, instead of going for a Karl Jarres, a compromise candidate between northern and southern Nazis, Hitler endorsed General Ludendorff. To the northerners, this step made Hitler seem even more reactionary than before. But, as he had suspected and hoped, the general ran a hopeless campaign and lost dismally. With Ludendorff humiliated, Hitler's claim to leadership of the far right in Bavaria was strengthened.

But he was far from strong enough to seize national power. From the mid-1920s onward, the German economy gradually stabilized. Mainly because of loans from the United States, Germany enjoyed a period of economic growth. Real wages (as opposed to inflationary ones) went up and unemployment went down. And with the election in 1925 to the presidency of the other famed general from the war, Paul von Hindenburg, the Weimar Republic at last took steps toward becoming a genuinely legitimate government.

So what appeared to be the tide of history was moving against Hitler. Hitler used this period to perfect his oratory. He rehearsed his speeches before a full-length mirror and practiced hand movements by the hour. Once on stage he appealed to audiences with vivid language. An actor of brilliance, he could switch from humor to sentiment to invective at will. He was the consummate poster boy for showmanship.

An actor, of course, needs a stage, and through contributions to the party, Hitler had bought, or rented, a most impressive political theater: the party's official residence on an elegant Munich street. Visitors had no trouble spotting the building. A huge red banner billowed from the rooftop. Beneath a lintel, a horizontal beam emblazoned with the words in Gothic script, "Germany Awake," were two heavy bronze doors. Two young sentries in black breeches and brown shirts stood guard. Inside, a third sentry gave a Nazi salute and checked all papers. From the lobby, a magnificent staircase rose to the showpiece of the edifice, the Party Senate Chamber. There, two dozen red leather chairs set in a semicircle faced the Führer's throne. All around the walls hung commemorative tablets that gave the names of those who had died in the beer hall putsch. They were the first Nazi martyrs. Invoking their names, Hitler would enter the room, handing down his dictates from on high. The throne was Hitler's pulpit and the chamber was the auditorium of the Hitler theater.

But Hitler's mastery of the theater was never an end in itself. Hitler wanted power, national power, and to get it he adopted a new strategy. He sent Goebbels into Berlin to sell the Führer Principle in the old Prussian capital.

Into the Cities

On October 1926, Josef Goebbels took over the leadership of the Berlin branch of the Nazi Party. The Berlin group was thoroughly reactionary. But its structure was loose and it had little support among members of the working class. So Goebbels organized a united front with two other right-wing paramilitary groups in Berlin, the *Stahlhelm* (Steel Helmet) and the *Wehrwolf* (the German word for werewolf is *Werwolf*. *Wehr* means "weapon").

Goebbels's efforts came to nothing. The Berliners simply did not wish to cooperate with these people from the hinterland.

Terms and Translations

The term *Sturmabteilung,* or Storm Division, may sound innocuously bureaucratic. It was anything but: It stood for thugs in uniform.

Hitler, however, still wanted to take Berlin; he had really never given up that dream. So in November 1926, he placed Franz von Pfeffer in charge of the SA. Pfeffer's job was to turn the thugs and street brawlers into a disciplined and useful force. Pfeffer, though, did not obtain results. The Storm Troopers resisted any and all efforts to reduce their independence—Hitler had feared that they might turn against him—and the Führer had to make a personal appeal for the group's loyalty.

That done, in the spring of 1927, Hitler ordered SA units to attack his opponents in Berlin. By May, however, he stood defeated. After weeks of provocations and bloody street fights, the Berlin police succeeded in evicting the whole of the Nazi Berlin apparatus.

Hitler and the Nazi Party were heading down a dead-end road. Hitler had suffered the worst of two worlds. He had opposed working class socialists and neglected his support within the dispossessed middle class. Like many a politician elsewhere, after the failure in Berlin he began to hear to usual query: "What have you done for us lately?"

In Bavaria, the original loyalists were drifting away. Revenues were dropping. And when Hitler approached businessmen for renewed financial support, he was told bluntly that the socialism aspect of national socialism would have to go.

By 1927, Hitler's movement faced extinction. He had brilliantly forged a coalition of Bavarian workers, professionals, and businessmen. He had spoken to their needs and desires. And he had projected the image of a political winner.

Then he lost. And we probably would never have heard of him again had it not been for the plight of farmers in Schleswig-Holstein.

The Farmers of Schleswig-Holstein

Yes, Holstein cows came from Holstein. That northern region, over which Bismarck had won his first military victory, was dairy country. There Hitler calculated that he, too, could enjoy his first victory.

Even before the onset of the Great Depression in 1929, the agricultural sectors of all the western economies had suffered from their own, what we might call minor, depressions. Minor but real. In general, agriculture had become so efficient that the supplies of food exceeded the demand. So market prices for farmers had hit new lows. In particular, in Schleswig-Holstein, the collapse of farmers' incomes had coincided with the outbreak of foot-and-mouth disease. Dairy farmers were unable to sell their milk.

The hyperinflation had already wiped out most of the rural banks. And it had left most of the farmers deeply in debt.

Where could the farmers turn? They could go to the large commercial banks, but these institutions charged high rates of interest. So by the late 1920s, the farmers of Schleswig-Holstein were at their wit's end. They and their families faced poverty and eviction.

To whom could the farmers turn? The Nazi Party.

Earlier, the peasants of the region had placed their faith in a group called the Farmer's League. The League had pretended to be the farmers' friend. But it really had been a tool of big business, which was all for free trade. But free trade, in this case meaning food imports from Poland and Denmark, had flooded the German market, aggravating the problems of the farmers of Schleswig-Holstein.

In the plight of those northern farmers, Hitler saw his opening. Rushing into the region, Nazis made appeals to the "little man," persuading the farmers that their problems lay in the machinations of Germany's Jewish financiers.

Modern Day Parallels

Most professional economists argue the virtues of free trade. Some contend that with free trade everyone worldwide becomes as prosperous as is possible. Perhaps. But free trade also means that someone loses out in the economic competition. In this case, those who lost were the farmers of Schleswig-Holstein. Embittered at losing their jobs, they were ripe for conversion to the Nazi cause.

Modern Day Parallels

Does Hitler's strategy of helping the "little man" sound familiar? It should. Faced with their own economic woes, many American farmers of the late nineteenth and early twentieth centuries—the Populists—looking for scapegoats, blamed what they saw as the doings of Jews on Wall Street.

In a way, the Nazis were getting it right at last. Their talk of doom and destruction, their offer of simplistic solutions to complicated problems, and their anti-Semitism all proved irresistible to rural audiences. Schleswig-Holstein proved that the Nazis could appeal to people beyond Bavaria after all.

The Way Forward

Hitler and his colleagues were indeed looking beyond Munich. Offsetting the Nazi Party's still dismal showing in the cities, in the Reichstag election of May 1928, it made substantial gains in Schleswig-Holstein, and in the rural areas of Hannover, Upper Franconia, and Nuremberg. As they analyzed the voting patterns, the Nazi leaders all but abandoned the workers in the cities, directing their appeals to farmers and small shopkeepers—people who were already anti-Semitic. By and large, these were the most conservative-minded people in Germany. So Nazi propaganda conjured up a mythical golden age of the past.

Supporting Actors

Paradoxically, Hitler, Goebbels, and others combined backward views with modern techniques. In an era before television and even widespread use of radio, propagandists in the Munich headquarters drew sophisticated graphs of Germany, correlating relationships among economic problems, membership growth, and patterns of political loyalty. When elections were in the offing, they would then select promising regions, blanketing them with rallies, flags, and speeches.

All this seemed so reasonable. Those people who showed up at the mass meetings would be invited for discussions in the village pubs and invited to join the party. The Nazis actually appeared respectable.

A New Respectability

The party's electoral base in Hitler's judgment was still too narrow to let him wield national power. He especially wanted to broaden the appeal to those who were most likely to vote, the middle-class suburbanites.

So in 1929, the fifteenth anniversary of the outbreak of the First World War, Hitler staged a huge Nazi rally in a stadium at Nuremberg. The stadium was decorated with all the usual swastikas and red, white, and black bunting; and Hitler engaged in his usual anti-Semitic ranting.

But this time there was a difference. Hitler shared the platform with leaders of veterans' associations and, much to the horror of lower-class Nazis, prominent businessmen. He also put on display Alfred Hugenberg, a press lord who controlled some 500 newspapers.

Hitler also built support by opposing the so-called Young Plan. Germany had been paying its reparations on schedule. But officials in Washington and financiers in New York believed that Germany could be a rich market for American goods only if the burden of reparations were lessened. Under the Young Plan, named for the American banker Owen D. Young, the American government offered to scale down those reparations. Most Germans, however, believed that they should not have to pay anything at all. In espousing their view, Hitler aligned himself for the first time with mainstream opinion.

The Breakthrough

By 1929, the Nazi Party had scored a series of successes in local and regional elections. All the same, Hitler's party was rooted in the small towns and villages, unable to make it on the national scene.

But then an event occurred which made all the difference. In October 1929, the New York Stock Exchange collapsed. The effect on Germany was almost immediate. On October 31, the *Beamtenbank* (the Official Bank), one of Germany's biggest financial firms, failed. Unemployment, which in August had dropped to 1.4 million, by December skyrocketed to 3 million.

The Great Depression was underway in Germany. For Hitler and the Nazi Party, it made all the difference.

The Least You Need to Know

- ◆ Hitler's time in prison gave him an opportunity to rethink his line of propaganda and to pose as a martyr.

- ◆ Upon his release from prison, Hitler worked to stop the factional warfare in party ranks and establish his dictatorial control over it.

- ◆ So far, the Nazi Party was distinctly a minor political party, appealing largely to conservatives in the villages and small towns.

- ◆ Hitler tried to broaden his base of support by donning an air of respectability. This step did help fill the party coffers. By no means, though, were the Nazis a force on the national level.

Chapter 10

The Great Depression: 1929–1932

In This Chapter

- ◆ How the Nazi Party uses propaganda to win public support during the even tougher times of the depression
- ◆ The formation of the SS to combat the dissention in the SA
- ◆ Nazi attacks on the Weimar Republic
- ◆ The last hour of the march
- ◆ The Nazi regime's loss of ground against the Communists

Early in 1930, a 21-year-old law student and son of a Lutheran pastor, a young man who had rebelled against his middle-class upbringing, become a Storm Trooper, and fought bloody street battles in Berlin against the Communists, wrote a poem. He titled it, "Raise High the Flag!" He had the swastika in mind.

Around the time he penned the verse, he met and fell in love with a former prostitute and moved into her apartment. Trying to eject the couple, who in her eyes were living in sin, the landlady sought help from the Communists. At her request, a gang of Reds burst into the flat and shot the young man dead.

When Goebbels learned about the incident, he saw an opportunity to transform the young man into a working-class Jesus. "Leaving home and mother," Goebbels wrote, "he took to living among those who scorned and spit on him. Out there, in a proletarian section [of Berlin], in a tenement attic he proceeded to build his young, modest life. A socialist Christ! One who appealed to others through his deeds!"

Goebbels soon saw to it that the young man's poem was set to music. Sung first by a huge chorus at a Nazi rally in the Berlin *Sportpalast*, the words went:

> Hold high the banner! Close the hard ranks serried!
> SA marches on with sturdy stride.
> Comrades, by the Red Front and Reaction killed, are buried,
> But march with us in image at our side.
> Gangway! Gangway now for the Brown Battalions!
> For the Storm Trooper clear roads over the land!
> The Swastika gives hope to our millions,
> The day for freedom and bread is at hand.
> The trumpet blows its shrill and final blast!
> Prepared for war and battle here we stand.
> Soon Hitler's banners will wave unchecked at last,
> The end of German slavery in our land!

The young man's name was Horst Wessel. The "Horst Wessel Song (*Lied*)" became the marching music of the Nazi Party. Goebbels's making the youth a martyr to the Nazi cause was typical of his tricks of propaganda. With the coming of the Great Depression, Hitler and Goebbels saw their main chance to identify themselves as the saviors of the German nation.

Unemployment

The German people unquestionably were looking for salvation—anything to free them from the scourge of joblessness. With the coming of the Great Depression, millions of Germans were out of work. Having no income and depleting whatever savings they had, they could only make weekly visits to government offices to pick up compensation cards.

These cards were in effect food stamps. But they barely covered dietary needs. So all over Germany, purchasing power was reduced. And unable to sell their goods, business firms cut back on their investments, throwing even more people out of work. Unemployment grew in a vicious downward cycle.

As in the United States at the time, unemployment produced hopelessness and hate. But unlike America then, Germany became a battlefield.

Bet You Didn't Know

Are you familiar with the musical Caberet? *It was based on a book called* Berlin Stories: I Am a Camera, *by the English author Christopher Isherwood (Random House, 1952). He was in Berlin in the early 1930s. The city, he wrote, "was in a state of civil war. Hate exploded without warning, out of nowhere, at street corners, in restaurants, cinemas, dance halls, swimming baths; at midnight, after breakfast, in the middle of the afternoon. Knives were whipped out, blows were dealt with spiked rings, beer mugs, chair legs or leaded clubs; bullets slashed the advertisements on the poster columns, rebounded from the iron roofs of latrines."*

Anger was everywhere. Shop owners who had lost their businesses railed against the big department stores. People without jobs loathed the bosses. University graduates who had hoped to become civil servants turned their wrath against the government. Facing low prices and required to pay high taxes, peasants despised city-dwellers; unemployed persons in the cities envied the peasants for their crops. Peasants and laborers both often had to live in tar-paper shacks. Beggars haunted street corners everywhere.

How many Germans were unemployed? Of a total population of roughly 50 million, eventually 6 million were registered as being without work. But that number was deceptive. Millions of other Germans had part-time work and more still were too proud to register as being jobless. Whatever the exact numbers, because of the shakiness of its economy, the Great Depression hit Germany harder than any other country.

For Freedom and Bread and a New Election

To those hit by the economic collapse, one thing seemed clear: The Weimar Republic would not or could not solve the problem. And Hitler offered an alternative. In his speeches, he continued his anti-Communist, anti-Semitic tirades, and he was outspoken in his denunciations of the Versailles Treaty. But in 1930 what mattered most was his new campaign slogan: "For Freedom and Bread."

The first test of Hitler's slogan came in September 1930. That month, Heinrich Brüning, the German chancellor, called a general election. Why did Brüning call for an election? He didn't have to yet and it's not entirely clear just why he did so. But General Paul von Hindenburg had appointed Brüning to the chancellorship (under the

Weimar constitution the president had that power), and he probably thought that by winning at the polls in his own right he could solidify his power.

> ### Bet You Didn't Know
>
> In the American political system, a presidential election takes place every four years, no matter what. But in Britain, which has a parliamentary system, the prime minister may call for an election at any time (within five years). In this regard, the Weimar Republic resembled the British model: There was a president (General von Hindenburg), who like the British monarch was head of state, and there was the chancellor, who like the British prime minister headed the legislature. So the chancellor could call an election.

Brüning's position was actually quite shaky. Like President Herbert Hoover in the United States, he had followed a policy of deflation. This was orthodox economic thinking at the time. If you're faced with a recession or a depression, cut government spending. Cut government jobs. It makes sense, doesn't it? As it turned out, it didn't make sense. Laying off public employees only aggravated unemployment. It may have lowered prices—that's deflation—but when prices fell, businesses had to lower their costs, which resulted in layoffs.

So Brüning's economics only made things worse. Most Germans didn't understand all this (nor did most Americans at the time). They just knew that they were unemployed, and they blamed their plight on Brüning.

Not surprisingly, the election only reflected the widespread animosity toward Brüning. The numbers told the tale. In the election of May 1928, the Nazis had polled a mere 3.6 percent of the total votes cast. Now, in September 1931, they racked up 18.3 percent and gained 107 seats, making their party the second largest in the *Reichstag* (the German parliament)

But what was stunning about the Nazi victory was where it took place. In Wedding, a working class neighborhood in Berlin, the Nazis won 9 percent of the vote. In middle-class Steglitz they got 26 percent and in Zehlendorf, a wealthy quarter, they reached nearly 18 percent. The Nazis had improved their standing in all social classes, and they were no longer a party of just the countryside.

This only meant that the Nazi Party had a much more diverse constituency than before. The Nazis couldn't pitch their propaganda to just the conservative farmers. In fact, while party officials in rural Saxony expressed opposition to labor strikes, Nazis in Berlin sided with metal workers who had indeed gone out on strike. Despite the victory at the polls, the Nazi Party seemed on the verge of breaking apart into feuding factions.

The Storm Trooper Rebellion

The threat of disintegration became real. Soon after the general election, the Berlin Storm Troopers announced that they were no longer going to protect party meetings. The reasons for the rebellion ran deep. Ordinary Storm Troopers had come to resent the lifestyles of the Nazi rich and famous. They also distrusted the way Hitler and other leaders had been courting big business and the old Prussian aristocracy. And they had come to feel like outsiders in their own party.

In response, in the autumn of 1931, Hitler went to Berlin. There he got rid of Franz von Pfeffer, the head of the SA, and put himself directly in charge of the organization. Hitler continued to live modestly, giving him the ability to defuse the complaints about lavish living.

Because Hitler was always busy, he could not devote all of his time to Storm Trooper problems. So he turned over day-to-day management to Ernst Röhm. A former officer, Röhm had played a leading part in the beer hall *putsch*; his current assignment was to assure the SA rank-and-file that when the Nazis finally enjoyed national power, they would get their share of the spoils.

These steps were only partly successful. Some of the members were satisfied. But overall satisfaction plummeted when, to show voters that his party would act legally, Hitler ordered SA united to stop their street fighting. Now the Storm Troopers engaged in a resistance so serious that many of them converted to the Communist Party.

That was too much for Hitler. While Hermann Göring purged the SA of dissidents, Hitler temporarily dissolved the organization. He cut the SA budget and refused permission for it to recruit new members. And he began to replace it with a new organization, the *Schutzstaffel* (Defense Echelon), or SS.

The SS actually had come into existence in 1925 as a small part of the SA; its function had been to provide protection at party rallies. But it was a distinctly minor part of the Nazi security apparatus.

Bet You Didn't Know

Totalitarian countries, such as Nazi Germany, the Soviet Union, and Communist China under Chairman Mao Zedong, rest on a foundation of violence. But violence begets violence. To stay in power, the leaders often hurl new groups of supporters against old ones. But trust is rare. So the purges start all over again.

Terms and Translations

Schutzstaffel. Schutz means "shelter" or "refuge"; *staffel* is "step," "stage," "degree," and by extension, "echelon"; so the SS was the Protection Detachment.

The Roles of Heinrich Himmler and Reinhard Heydrich

In 1929, that status began to change. Hitler had turned leadership of the SS over to Heinrich Himmler. Himmler had the receding hairline, eyeglasses, tiny clipped mustache, and slightly receding chin that you might expect of a schoolteacher. And he had come from a respectable, academic family: His father held a professorship at the University of Munich. And Heinrich had been a studious child. Although not brilliant, he did solid work at school (unlike Hitler). He was especially drawn to mathematics, Latin, and Greek—subjects that followed clear sets of rules. He went on to study at his father's university, specializing in biology and chemistry. Again, the rules—he loved rules.

Appropriately enough, in the chaotic years that followed the First World War, Heinrich found work as a filing clerk. Once he hooked up with the Nazis, and then took over the SS, he became a master of the dossier. He kept dossiers on everyone (probably even on Hitler). To maintain his files, he took on as his assistant one Reinhard Heydrich, a blond, long-faced, blue-eyed spy.

Heydrich's own agents found out that Röhm, head of the now rival SA, was a homosexual. Himmler filed the information away for future use.

Goebbels's Propaganda

But Himmler's dossiers were only one part of Hitler's overall thrust. The Führer was bound and determined to bring the Nazi movement under his personal and exclusive control. So while he was replacing the SA with the SS (which, by the way—and this reflected Himmler's own background—was by and large a middle-class organization), he made Goebbels the undisputed head propagandist. Under Goebbels's command, Nazi propaganda became highly centralized. Nazis in local cities and towns were strictly forbidden to launch their own propaganda campaigns. From party headquarters, now in Berlin, Goebbels directed even the size and color of posters and leaflets. Anyone who deviated from Goebbels's directives was purged from the party.

No one says that you can't borrow from the enemy. Over in the Soviet Union, the fount of communism that Hitler hated so much, Vladimir Lenin had developed the principle of democratic centralism. The idea was that there could be discussion before a

> **Modern Day Parallels**
>
> The Nazi Party wasn't an ordinary political party, as we know parties in America to be—big, loose-knit, with lots of differing voices and opinions. Hitler knew what he was doing. He was creating an organization that was much more like an elite army corps than a normal political party.

decision was reached, but then no more dissent. Lenin's purpose had been to develop a disciplined unit that could obey orders unquestioningly and, united, move against the institutions of the state.

Hitler took the principle one step further. There was to be no discussion *before* the decisions. But the goal was the same as Lenin's. Hitler wanted a phalanx with which he could destroy the Weimar Republic.

Nazi Attacks on the Weimar Republic

In the 1931 election, Hitler had campaigned as if he were an ordinary politician, intent on working within the political system for change. That was the image he projected: He pretended that once in power he would maintain the Weimar constitution.

In reality, he was getting ready to overthrow that constitution. The German word for what he was really up to was a *Gleichschaltung*, usually translated as "coordination."

Terms and Translations

Gleichschaltung is one of those German words that drive English-speaking people crazy. It looks so pompous, so abstract, so Teutonic. But let's break it down. The first part of the word is **Gleich**. For a moment, forget the *G*. What does **leich** sound like in English? Get it? *Ei* in German is pronounced like the *i* in *like*. So **gleich** means "like," "alike," or "same." The other part of our word is not obvious. The verb **schalten** means "govern" or "rule." So *Gleichschaltung* means political coordination, bringing into line, and even eliminating political opponents.

Hitler talked about "coordination," but what he was really up to was the elimination of his political opponents. What opponents? The trade unions, religious organizations, universities—groups that might organize against the regime.

Hitler's political acumen was acute. At that time in Germany, as in America now, poorer people didn't play a role in politics. In Germany, it was the middle class that voted. So Hitler set out to penetrate the interest groups that represented the German middle class. The Nazis began to flood the membership of such groups with party members and to replace independent spokesmen with dedicated Nazis.

The most effective campaign of Gleichshaltung was organized by a Nazi official named Walter Darré. He headed a so-called Agricultural Office. Its agents infiltrated themselves into the *Landbund* (Country Union) and in a short time turned it into an instrument of Nazi propaganda. The Nazis even organized their own interest groups. On behalf of mom-and-pop establishments, the Militant Association of Retailers mounted a campaign against the large department stores, accusing them of being run exclusively by Jews. Nazis worked with foresters, demanding that they be given higher wages.

Modern Day Parallels

An *interest group* is an organization of people who share certain attitudes and goals and who try to shape public opinion, support candidates in office, and influence the decisions of governmental officials. Washington is full of such groups: the Sierra Club, the National Rifle Association, the Teamsters, and so on. Germany was similar. It had interest groups representing doctors, various industries, public employees, and so on. As in America now, in Germany then, you could join such groups if you wanted to. You paid your dues and you were in. The Nazis took full advantage of that openness.

By the second half of 1931, Nazi cell groups had slipped into every institution of the Weimar Republic, including the civil service, the schools, and the military. Himmler the file-collector even reached into the police forces of Bavaria and Berlin.

The middle of October 1931, produced an overwhelming display of Nazi might. On the eleventh of the month, at Harzburg in central Germany, Hitler joined with other nationalistic right-wingers for a protest against the Brüning ministry. Hindenburg was present. A towering man from the old Prussian aristocracy, he looked down on Hitler with disdain. Insulted, Hitler left the parade reviewing stand. A week later, in nearby Braunschweig (Brunswick), the Nazis staged an immense rally. One hundred thousand Nazi members marched: The numbers alone made it seem likely that Hitler commanded enough force to topple the Weimar Republic.

The Nazis continued to do well in local elections and their membership rolls exploded. In December, Hitler told another huge rally: "The movement is approaching the last hour of the march!" He predicted that 1932 would be "the first year of the Third Reich."

The Last Hour of the March

Now we are coming to the all-important question of how Hitler finally rose to power. Consider his position at the end of 1931. The Nazi Party had made considerable gains at the polls but it was still a minority party. Hitler had no assurance that he could rise to the top through further elections. Nor did he dare to attempt a *coup d'état* (a sudden, violent overthrow of the government). He had learned from his time in the Landsberg prison that if he acted in unconstitutional ways—outwardly unconstitutional—the army would turn against him. However conservative, the old officers corps regarded him as a guttersnipe. Hitler had taken to heart the lesson of 1923.

So he resolved to play the game of back-room intrigue. Here Hitler proved himself the master tactician.

Hitler Uses Hindenburg

The game began in January, 1932. Now remember: General Paul von Hindenburg, one of the German commanders in the First World War, was the president of the Weimar Republic. He had been duly elected as such. And he had the authority to appoint the chancellor. But Hindenburg was an aged figure, perhaps not senile but no longer vigorous. He was also susceptible to bribery.

Already an honored officer, Hindenburg was now part of the nobility. And in a presidential office in Berlin that had come to look like a royal court, the general saw himself as the proper successor to Kaiser Wilhelm II. Hindenburg surrounded himself with flattering courtiers from the Junker class and the officer corps. One of the latter was the new commander of the army, General Kurt von Schleicher.

Bet You Didn't Know

In commemoration of his eightieth birthday, back in 1927, a group of landowners and industrialists had given Hindenburg a huge estate in Prussia.

In 1930, Schleicher had gone to Hindenburg and recommended Brüning as chancellor. The idea had appealed to Hindenburg. Although not a clever politician, Brüning was an honest civil servant who cherished the ancient conservative values of old Germany and who loathed the upstart demagoguery of Hitler and the Nazis. As did Hindenburg, Brüning feared the Nazis and tried to suppress them. Among other measures, Brüning forbade the Storm Troopers to march in their brown shirts.

At the same time and without Brüning's knowledge, however, General Schleicher was urging Hindenburg and the defense minister not to take steps against the Nazis. They were, after all, anti-Communist and they could provide the army, still restricted in size by the Versailles Treaty, with a useful reserve militia. Schleicher wanted to integrate the Nazis into the traditional German institutions. He figured that it was better to have the Nazis inside the tent glaring out than outside the tent glaring in.

General Schleicher Conspires Against Brüning

In January 1932, Hitler, in Munich, received a telegram inviting him to Berlin. He would conduct talks with Brüning and Schleicher over extending Hindenburg's seven-year presidential term.

Upon receiving the invitation, Hitler gloated to his subordinates seated before him in the Munich headquarters. "Now I have them in my pocket," he said. "They have recognized me as a partner in their negotiations."

Now Hitler proved his skill as a tactician. Once he was in Berlin, Brüning offered him a deal. If Hitler would go along with the extension of Hindenburg's term, he, Brüning, would step down and urge Hindenburg to make Hitler chancellor. Wasn't that what Hitler really wanted? Hitler turned the offer down cold.

Many thought that Hitler had made a poor decision. Without the extension of his term, the elderly Hindenburg ran again and on April 10, 1932, won reelection by a solid margin. Three days later, Brüning announced a ban on all SA and SS activities. He would enforce the ban by turning the police and the army against Hitler's legions.

But Brüning did not seem aware of what was going on around him. Behind his back again, General Schleicher was conspiring against him. Not long before, Chancellor Brüning had proposed letting unemployed farm workers live on a deserted estate in Prussia. Schleicher's trick was to get a group of Prussian landlords to visit Hindenburg on his own estate and to denounce Brüning as an "agrarian bolshevist." This was too much for the old field marshal Hindenburg. On May 29, 1932, he announced that he had fired Brüning.

Now the chancellorship was open and General Schleicher knew who he wanted to fill it: Franz von Papen. Von Papen was descended from the Prussian aristocracy, he had family ties to big business, and he was a smooth flatterer—just the kind to appeal to Hindenburg.

General Schleicher and Hitler Strike a Deal

The palace intrigues, however, went on. On the very day of Brüning's dismissal, Schleicher and Hitler struck a deal. Hitler would go along with von Papen as chancellor on the condition that the government lift its ban on the SA and the SS. The deal was done. Hindenburg accepted von Papen, and at the end of June von Papen in turn lifted the ban.

At that point, as Hitler had planned, violence erupted, especially in and around Berlin. Throughout the capital, Communists and Nazis, each provoking the other, engaged in pitched battles. The streets ran red with blood, and in July alone 86 people died in the fighting.

All that was bad enough. But remember: The German Empire under Bismarck had been a federation; the various *länder* or states had their own areas of authority; this was also the case in the Weimar Republic. And despite all the conservative landowners, Prussia had been using its powers to give a measure of protection to the workers and their left-wing organizations. But on July 29, 1932, von Papen used the emergency powers of the chancellor's office to abolish the Prussian government. For all practical purposes, the Weimar Republic was dead.

Hitler's Setback

In July, nonetheless, Germany did hold elections to the Reichstag. This time, although they did not win a majority, the Nazis emerged with more seats than any other party. Hitler accordingly went to Schleicher and Hindenburg with hard-line proposals. He would accept Schleicher as defense minister. But he wanted the chancellorship for himself and Nazis in the most important cabinet positions. Having made his demands, Hitler retired to the mountain air at Berchtesgaden to await the response.

When he was summoned to the presidential palace in Berlin, however, he was in for a shock. Refusing to dismiss von Papen, Hindenburg offered Hitler only the vice chancellorship. The indignant Hitler turned the offer down flat.

Just as Hitler had hoped, no party in the Reichstag made up a majority and the rift between the right-wing and left-wing members in that body ran so deep that no one could form a coalition government. Von Papen had no choice but to call for a new election.

This time, however, the Nazis suffered a setback. In the November 1932 general election, their percentage of the vote fell from 37.3 percent to 33.1 percent. Many observers thought that the Nazi appeal to the voters had peaked.

But the election also brought forth another set of numbers. While the Nazis lost two million votes, the Communists gained almost six million. And the combined Social Democratic and Communist votes came to 13,228,000 as compared to the Nazi sum of 14,696,000. So while the Nazis remained the largest party in the Reichstag, the existence of several minor parties kept them from having a majority. So the working-class parties were still in a strong position.

Within a year, however, the trade unions and other organizations built by three generations of German workers were smashed to pieces; most of the leftist intellectuals were either behind the barbed-wire of concentration camps or out of Germany in exile. And Hitler along with his Nazi Party held the country in their grip, already creating the totalitarian state. As the depression wore on, the Nazis gained electoral strength. That strength, however was not enough to give them the overall control they wanted. The next chapter explains how Hitler finally emerged in power.

The Least You Need to Know

- In the background of Hitler's rise to power was the Great Depression and the ensuing unemployment in Germany. The rate of joblessness in the Weimar Republic was probably higher than anywhere else in the world. Desperate, many people looked to the Communists for a solution; others longed for Nazi rule.

- Hitler's Storm Troopers often resented the privileges of high-ranking Nazis and thus reflected the mood of the country at large. He could deal with them only by enlarging the powers of the SS, which emerged as a rival organization.

- Hitler demonstrated his organizational genius by infiltrating Nazis into the institutions of the state, ostensibly coordinating them but in reality undermining their functioning under the Weimar Republic.

- The Weimar Republic was dead even before Hitler took power.

The Nazi Seizure of Power: 1933

In This Chapter

- ◆ Hitler's rise to chancellor

- ◆ Hitler's hidden agenda to divide and conquer the left and destroy the *Reichstag* (parliament)

- ◆ How Hitler uses the Reichstag fire to get rid of the Communists

- ◆ The last election and how it puts Hitler in a position of total power

- ◆ The Potsdam ceremony, a propaganda scheme to celebrate the union of old greatness and new strength

On March 9, 1933, Storm Troopers broke into the Munich offices of a newspaper called *Der Gerade Weg* (*The Right Way*) and arrested the editor, Fritz Gerlich. Born a Protestant in the north but raised in heavily Catholic Bavaria, and thus somewhat of an outsider, Gerlich had received a doctorate in history. Then he had turned to journalism. At some point in the early 1920s, he had covered Hitler and become the future Führer's bitter enemy.

By 1933, convinced that Hitler was about to seize ultimate power and lead Germany down the road to hell, Gerlich let it be known that he was going to stop his enemy. He was going to publish the exposé of exposés.

What went into the exposé we can't know. Maybe Gerlich was going to accuse Hitler of having had a sexual affair with his (Hitler's) half-niece, Geli Raubal, and then ordering her murdered. Maybe Gerlich was going to reveal that Hitler and the Nazis had received funding from foreign sources, including the American automobile manufacturer Henry Ford. Or maybe the editor had uncovered information about the Reichstag fire—proof that the Nazis had torched the building and put the blame for the blaze on the Communists. But we don't know the truth because when the Nazis crashed into Gerlich's office, they ripped the story from the presses, smashed the typeface, and destroyed every shred of the exposé.

But this we do know. Gerlich was arrested and shipped to the Nazi concentration camp at Dachau, just north of Munich. There, a year later, during what was called the "Night of the Long Knives," Nazis dragged him from his cell and shot him through the head. By way of notifying his widow, they sent her Gerlich's steel-rimmed eyeglasses, spattered with blood.

Hitler's Appointment to Chancellor

Nazi Germany was born in blood. Other countries, of course, have had their share of bloodshed. Think of the French Revolution and the American Civil War: Heads rolled onto the streets of Paris and, among other struggles, the Battle of Gettysburg was gruesome almost without precedent. But France and the United States already existed as long-formed nations: Both northerners and southerners in the American Civil War traced their national identities to the centuries of English history. This was not the case with Nazi Germany.

Remember that the German Empire had been built on the military triumphs of Prussia, and the Weimar Republic had been practically imposed on Germany by the Allies after the First World War. The two regimes that preceded the Nazis had been founded in violence. So was Nazi Germany.

Sometimes we wonder why Nazi Germany wasn't more like the West. Germany had culture. But the closest uprisings to the Nazi rise to power (that we have experienced in the West) were the Russian and Chinese Revolutions of 1917 and 1949. They, too, were steeped in killing; they, too, created reigns of terror and instituted totalitarian governments; and they, too, made the claim that they were overturning the injustices of the past.

The difference was that Hitler's revolution was a revolution not from the left but rather from the right. Let's think back to Bismarck: Once again, he's often been called the White Revolutionary (as opposed to a Red Revolutionary), a conservative who revolted against the established European international order. As blood-soaked as he was, Hitler fell into Bismarck's tradition: Trying to establish a new world order—although a conservative one.

Thus, only two weeks after the November 1932 general elections, leading industrialists such as Fritz Thyssen, the steel magnate, and Alfried Krupp, the munitions-maker, wrote a letter to President von Hindenburg. They laid down the law: They demanded that he create an authoritarian nationalist regime based on mass support. Even before Hitler completed his rise to power, they wanted in effect a Nazi state.

> **Supporting Actors**
>
> The letter to President von Hindenburg read: "We recognize in the national movement which has penetrated our people the beginning of an era, which through the overcoming of class contrasts, creates the essential basis for a rebirth of the German economy."
>
> This letter was introduced as evidence at the Nuremberg trials.

Translation? The big industrialists wanted the German government to crush the labor movement and believed that Hitler was the one to do it. They wanted Hindenburg to get rid of Schleicher and von Papen and to make Hitler chancellor.

Neither Schleicher nor von Papen wanted to step aside. The backstage maneuvering went on. Then, on December 1, 1932, Schleicher got old Hindenburg to appoint him chancellor. How did he do it? Blackmail. He threatened to make public a government report about how land-owning Prussian aristocrats had been bilking the state for funds. Schleicher showed that Hindenburg himself would be implicated in the scandal.

The Schleicher appointment gave Hitler his opening. He met secretly with the resentful von Papen in the home of a Berlin banker. A few of the top industrialists were also present. Just who said what and to whom is unclear. By the end of the meeting, though, the Nazi Party's debts were paid off. On January 5, Goebbels noted in his diary: "The present government knows that this is the end for them."

Goebbels was right. As chancellor, Schleicher suddenly began working with the labor movement; big business was outraged. Pressured by the industrialists, who may have promised to bury any charge against the aged general, Hindenburg on January 30, 1933, summoned Hitler to the presidential palace. When he emerged from Hindenburg's office, Adolf Hitler was the chancellor of Germany.

But he did not yet hold all the power. He was chancellor by the grace of Hindenburg. And most of the cabinet members had held their posts under von Papen and Schleicher. They had made up a cabinet of barons who thought they could control Hitler. Their strategy was simple: If they seemed populist enough, they could make an alliance with the left.

Little did they realize that Hitler would use the government itself to suppress the left.

The Position of the Left

It is worth repeating: In the elections of 1932, the combined vote of the Communist and Social Democratic parties was almost equal to that of the Nazis and another, much smaller, party, the German Nationalists. In terms of numbers, the working-class parties were almost as strong as their enemies on the right. And given the organizational know-how of the trade unions, in existence for decades, you would think that the left in Germany could have defended itself against the right.

Yet it was not meant to be. By the end of 1933, the left was crushed. Why?

The left in Weimar Germany consisted primarily of the Social Democrats and the Communists. As the name suggests, the Social Democratic Party was an avid supporter (just about the only supporter in Germany) of democracy. It was also the party of the trade unions. True to their Leninist heritage, however, the Communists despised the unions. Vladimir Lenin, the founder of the Soviet Union, had argued that organized labor was just a big sell-out; that as soon as union members got wage increases and better working and living conditions, they would abandon the cause of the revolution. And Ernst Thälmann, the German Communist leader, held that "There is no difference between a fascist dictatorship and a bourgeois dictatorship." He even preferred the Nazis to the Social Democrats. Under Nazi rule, the Reds at least would know clearly who the enemy was. So the leftist parties in Germany were by no means united.

In the background of Hitler's electoral victory was the rift on the left. Don't forget that despite previous financial difficulties, the Nazis got financing from big business. And the Communists appealed mainly to those hardest hit by the Great Depression—the unemployed, those without funds.

While election figures showed a rough balance between the forces of the left and the right, they hid profound imbalances. The left was divided and poor; the right was united and rich. And Hitler had a special advantage: Once he was chancellor, he could use the power of the state against his opponents.

Hitler's Big Moves

No sooner had Hitler received his appointment as chancellor, on January 30, 1933, than the jackboots of the Storm Troopers and Himmler's SS units were heard assembling in Berlin's parks and gardens. The Nazis were preparing for a triumphal march through the Brandenburg Gate and down the Wilhelmstrasse. Confident of Hitler's ultimate victory, the marchers appeared first in huge numbers in front of the Communist Party headquarters. The Nazis were gloating.

They had good reason to gloat, for Hitler had completely outmaneuvered President Hindenburg. The old field marshal had made Hitler chancellor on the condition that he could put together a majority in the Reichstag. Taken together the Nazis and the Nationalists did not make up that majority. Hitler might have got his majority by forming an alliance with the Catholic Center Party. But he didn't want them and they didn't want him.

So Hitler asked Hindenburg to dissolve the Reichstag and call a new election. Hindenburg, by this point senile and a tool in Hitler's hands, complied. He signed the necessary decree and the new elections were scheduled for March 5, 1933.

Goebbels was overjoyed. "Now it will be easy," he wrote in his diary on February 3, "to carry on the fight, for we can call on all the resources of the state. Radio and press are at our disposal. We shall stage a masterpiece of propaganda. And this time, naturally, there is no lack of money!"

The New Regime's Financial Resources

The money was indeed plentiful. With the new regime committed to crushing the labor unions, prominent business people were already inclined to fork out money. To make sure they did so, Hitler called them into Göring's office. (Göring had been made president of the Reichstag.) He launched into a long speech. "Private enterprise," Hitler claimed, "cannot be maintained in the age of democracy; it is conceivable only if the people have a sound idea of authority and personality. … All the worldly goods we possess we owe to the struggle of the chosen. … We must not forget that all the benefits of culture must be introduced more or less with the iron fist."

Hitler went on: He pledged the "elimination" of the Socialist and Communist "menace." Then he finished:

"We stand before the last election," he told the gathered businessmen. It would be Germany's last election in a decade, maybe even in a century. And no matter how the election turned out, "there will be no retreat." If he lost the election, Hitler would remain in power "by other means."

Göring added a practical point. "Those circles not taking part in the political battle should at least," he stated, "make the financial sacrifices necessary at this time."

The businessmen present coughed up three million marks.

Justifying the Regime

Even so, Hitler and his aides wanted their takeover of power to seem legitimate. On January 31, 1933, the day after Hitler became chancellor, Goebbels had confided to his diary:

> In a conference with the Führer we lay down the line for the fight against the Reds. For the moment we shall abstain from direct counter-measures. The Bolshevik attempt at revolution must first burst into flame. At the proper moment we shall strike.

Goebbels wanted a clear justification for taking action against the left.

Hoping to provoke the Communists into violence, Hitler soon persuaded Hindenburg to issue a decree that suppressed all civil liberties. The order restricted freedom of speech and the press; it outlawed assembly in public places except by permission. It allowed the police to read private letters and other papers. And it permitted what the American Constitution forbade: "unreasonable searches and seizures."

Modern Day Parallels

The First Amendment to the U.S. Constitution reads: "Congress shall make no law respecting an establishment of religion, or prohibiting the free exercise thereof; or abridging the freedom of speech, or of the press; of the right of the people peaceably to assemble, and to petition the government for a redress of grievances."

The Fourth Amendment reads: "The right of the people to be secure in their persons, houses, papers, and effects, against unreasonable searches and seizures, shall not be violated, and no warrants shall issue, but upon probable cause …"

And the Nazi treatment of such rights? As we have seen, the constitution of the Weimar Republic had been largely modeled on that of the United States. Now, with Hindenburg's Hitler-induced edict, all of that was gone.

Pursuant (as the lawyers say) to this edict, German authorities under Hitler censored the Communist press and broke up Communist meetings. Cooperating with the officials, Nazi thugs disbanded Social Democratic rallies and smashed their printing presses. Even the Catholic Center Party came on bad times. Nazis beat up a Catholic leader when he tried to speak to his followers. Even Heinrich Brüning, the former chancellor who belonged to the Center Party, was obliged to seek protection.

Though the Nazi Party was literally beating down the other parties, the left had not erupted as Hitler hoped. So if a leftist uprising did not exist, could it be invented?

Might there not be something sensational that would get the electorate to vote for the Nazis in March? Something like a fire?

> **Bet You Didn't Know**
>
> On February 22, Göring put together an auxiliary police unit to help suppress all organizations hostile to the state. Four fifths of its membership came directly from SA and SS forces. These Nazi paramilitaries killed at least 51 people and injured hundreds, perhaps thousands, more.

The Reichstag Fire

On the night of February 27, von Papen, now reduced to being vice chancellor, was dining with President von Hindenburg at a downtown Berlin club. "Suddenly," von Papen wrote, "we noticed a red glow through the windows and heard sounds of shouting in the street. One of the servants came hurrying up to me and whispered: 'The Reichstag is on fire!' which I repeated to the president. He got up and from the window we could see the dome of the Reichstag looking as though it were illuminated by searchlights. Every now and again a burst of flame and a swirl of smoke blurred the outline."

Asking a driver to take Hindenburg home, von Papen left the club to see the burning edifice more closely. In the meantime, Hitler and Goebbels, who also had been having dinner together, were in an automobile, hurtling "at 60 miles an hour toward the scene of the crime," as Goebbels said. He did not refer to the fire as accidental because he fully intended to blame the blaze on the Communists.

When Hitler and Goebbels reached the scene, Göring was already there. Having put on much weight since his days as a pilot, he was sweating and out of breath. His lack of conditioning, though, didn't stop him from yelling, "This is the beginning of the Communist revolution! We must not wait a minute! We must show no mercy! Every Communist official must be shot, wherever he is found! Every Communist deputy must this very night be strung up!"

Moments later, Nazi agents were breaking down the front doors of known Communist leaders and trucking them off to concentration camps. And the next day, Nazi newspapers were blaming the fire on a Dutch Communist, Marinus van der Lubbe, who happened to be living in Berlin.

The Reichstag fire.

(Culver Pictures)

Van der Lubbe was indeed an arsonist. And somehow he had made his way into the Reichstag building and set off a few small fires. Yet he was desperately poor and could not possibly have afforded the equipment and fuel necessary to ignite a blaze the size of the Reichstag fire. Besides, he was mentally disabled: He could not defend himself in a court of law.

For the Nazis he was the perfect stooge. Quickly arrested, he was tried for arson and found guilty.

> **Supporting Actors**
>
> The last German election before the end of the Second World War took place on March 5, 1933. Only the day before, Franklin D. Roosevelt had taken the oath of office of president of the United States. Although no one probably realized it at the time, FDR would be Hitler's nemesis.

What had really happened? This is hard to determine. Whoever set the fire—it may have been the Communists or, just as likely, it may have been the Nazis looking for a pretext to persecute the Reds—this much is certain. On the day after the fire, Hitler prevailed on Hindenburg not only to abolish civil liberties *but also* to take over all authority from the federal states *and* to decree the death penalty for anyone guilty of "serious disturbances of the peace."

Hitler thus hoped to frighten the German people into casting their ballots for the Nazi Party. And by way of reinforcing Hitler's threat, Göring on March 3, just two days before the elections, spoke at Frankfurt. He declared:

> Fellow Germans, my measures will not be crippled by any judicial thinking. ...
> I don't have to worry about justice; my mission is only to destroy and exterminate, nothing more! ... Certainly, I shall use the power of the state and the
> police to the utmost ... [This is] a struggle to the death, in which my fist will
> grasp [Communist] necks; I shall lead with the Brownshirts.

The Last Election

Despite the intimidation, the March election didn't give Hitler the support he
wanted. With 17,277,180 votes, the Nazi Party secured only 44 percent of the total.
When combined with the Nationalist Party votes, this figure translated into a slight
majority of seats in the *Reichstag*.

With a majority that slender, Hitler could carry out the routine operations of government. But he wanted more, much more. He knew what to do. Nazi thugs threw most
of the Communist and Social Democratic deputies in jail. Hitler now had an overwhelming majority.

What to do with that majority? On March 24, when the remaining members of the
Reichstag gathered in the Kroll Opera House, Hitler gave the opening speech, introducing the "Enabling Bill." The measure was the ultimate *Gleichshaltung* (coordination). It provided that the Reichstag would turn
over all its functions to Hitler.

With SS and SA men ringing the opera house
outside and thronging the corridors inside, any
remaining opposition vanished. The Catholic
Center Party voted for the legislation and then
passed out of existence.

Germany was no longer a parliamentary
democracy. It was a dictatorship.

> ### Modern Day Parallels
>
> Imagine this: One party or the
> other, Republican or Democratic,
> gains a slight majority in the
> American Congress and then
> bumps off the opposition. It's
> never happened here, but it's
> exactly what Hitler did.

The Potsdam Ceremony

Always the dramatist, Hitler wanted to seal his triumph with a ceremony of investiture. Goebbels arranged for Hindenburg to go to Potsdam and give his blessing to
the new Nazi regime. Göring and Goebbels sat in the front row of the spectators; a
few First World War military chiefs were in the background.

The show took place at Potsdam, the site of the principal palace of Kaiser Wilhelm II. In particular it took place in the Garrison Church at Potsdam. The bones of Frederick the Great, the famous Prussian monarch of the eighteenth century, were buried here; the Hohenzollern kings had worshipped their Lutheran God; and Hindenburg, as a young officer in 1866, when Bismarck defeated Austria, had come here to celebrate the beginning of Germany's unification. Hitler wanted to legitimize his new regime by linking it to the memories of the triumphs of the German past.

Even the date of the ceremony, March 21, 1933, had its symbolic significance. It was the date on which, in 1871, Bismarck had first opened the all-German Reichstag.

At the start of the ceremony, flanked by Hitler, who was wearing a morning coat and striped trousers (a far cry from the time when in Vienna he had had to sell his clothes to eat), Hindenburg marched down the nave of the church. Decked out in his gray field marshal's uniform and carrying his spiked helmet in one hand, the old general paused below the imperial gallery and the empty pew of Kaiser Wilhelm II. He snapped off a salute.

Then he reached the altar, turned, and gave a brief homily, consecrating the Nazi regime:

> May the old spirit of this celebrated shrine permeate the generation of today, may it liberate us from selfishness and party strife and bring us together in national self-consciousness to bless a proud and free Germany, united in herself.

Hitler responded in kind:

> Neither the kaiser nor the government nor the nation wanted the war. It was only the collapse of the nation which compelled a weakened race to take upon itself, against its most sacred convictions, the guilt for this war.

Having gone to the altar himself, Hitler looked down on Hindenburg, who had taken a seat in the front pew. Hitler addressed the old man directly:

> By a unique upheaval in the last few weeks our national honor has been restored and, thanks to your understanding, *Herr Generalfeldmarschall*, the union between the symbols of the old greatness and the new strength has been celebrated. We pay you homage. A protective providence places you over the new forces of our nation.

After uttering these words, Hitler stepped down from the altar, bowed to Hindenburg, and shook his hand. Hitler himself was shaking with emotion.

During the ceremony, in a church filled with Nazi banners and swastikas, movie cameras were constantly whirring. Goebbels had put them in place along with microphones so that he could bring to Germans (in their movie theaters) pictures of Hitler uniting the old and the new.

But, of course, the show inside the Garrison Church at Potsdam was more than a cinematic event. This was the moment in which Hitler proclaimed the creation of the Third Reich, supposed to endure for 1,000 years. Nazi Germany had now come into existence.

Hindenburg's death on August 2, 1934, came almost as a footnote. On that day, Hitler passed a law that combined the offices of chancellor and president. Because the president of Germany was legally the commander in chief of the armed forces, Hitler was now the complete master of Germany. And Germany had become a totalitarian state.

In the next part of this book, we look at the meaning of the totalitarian state.

The Least You Need to Know

- Hitler's rise to the chancellorship of Germany was by no means an accident of nature. He enjoyed the support of his own paramilitary units as well as the financial and political help of Germany's most prominent industrialists. They thought he would be their tool. How wrong they were!

- Once chancellor, Hitler moved quickly against the Social Democrats and Communists. A deep ideological rift separated those two groups. Hitler took full advantage of the split to weaken them both. His was an old strategy that Bismarck had used against his various enemies: Divide and conquer.

- The most dramatic episode of Hitler's rise to power in 1933 was the Reichstag fire. Who set the blaze remains unknown, but the probability is that the perpetrators were the Nazis. In any event, the Nazis used the conflagration as a pretext to use the organs of the German state to persecute the parties of the left.

- In Germany's last election until well after the end of World War II, held in early March 1933, the Nazis blatantly used terror and intimidation against the parties on the left. The election nonetheless didn't give Hitler the parliamentary majority he needed to set up his absolute rule. Therefore, he ordered his Nazi minions to arrest and even murder enough of the opposition deputies in the Reichstag to give him what he wanted: an overwhelming majority.

◆ Hitler's Enabling Act enabled him to transform Germany into a totalitarian state, with all power and authority, state and federal, gathered into the hands of Hitler, the Dictator.

◆ Hitler sought to legitimatize the totalitarian state with a ceremony at Kaiser Wilhelm's chapel at Potsdam. Through that ceremony, Hitler tried to persuade the German people that he was merely the inheritor of the policies of old. But there was no mistake about it: He had inaugurated the Third Reich, the new totalitarian state called Nazi Germany.

Part 3

The Nazi State

Nazi Germany gave us a big, ungainly word, yet one that we still use: totalitarianism. We may even throw it around too loosely, applying it to a lot of foreign leaders whom we don't like. But here's what it meant in the context of Nazi Germany: the destruction of all persons and groups that could challenge Hitler's supremacy. This destruction singled out not only Jews but also most intellectuals, the Communists and the Socialists, the labor unions, the Catholic Church, parts of the Lutheran ministry, and even elements of the Nazi movement itself. Nazism was a revolution, and revolutions tend to devour their own. Revolutions also tend to spread into other countries. Here you'll see Hitler taking his first steps toward European conquest.

12

Consolidation of Power: 1933–1934

In This Chapter

- ◆ Hitler's silencing of all opposing institutions
- ◆ Hitler's revenge on the SA and SS officials who betrayed him
- ◆ Two new weapons of mass destruction: concentration camps and the Gestapo
- ◆ Anti-Semitism is taken to a new level under Hitler

There's a line in Mel Brooks's wonderful musical comedy, *The Producers*: "Somebody burned down the *Reichstag* / And can you believe it? / They made me chancellor!"

Now let's reflect on how Hitler really did become chancellor.

Why Hitler?

As I've said, Germany before the Weimar Republic had little or no experience with democracy. The democratic ideals that we in West Europe and

North America tend to take for granted simply had no traditional body of support in Germany.

Instead, there was the Prussian–German monarchy. Let's draw the contrast between this monarchy and Britain's crown. From the time of Queen Victoria onward (she took the throne in 1837), Great Britain has had constitutional monarchs. What does this mean? The royals were supposed to show up at important events, dress accordingly, and offer knighthoods to prominent people. But the British monarch had no power. Politically speaking, monarchs didn't matter. Present-day Prince Charles becoming king would make no difference in politics.

In Germany, it would have made a huge difference. Kaiser Wilhelm II held real political power (for better or worse) and the German reverence for him was not for a symbol but rather for a real person. Once he was forced into exile, someone had to replace him, and Germany in the Weimar era was a political vacuum.

Hitler filled that vacuum. Why Hitler? Though Hitler started life as a nobody and lived much of his young adulthood as a bum, he was an Austrian, and his native dialect was similar to the dialect in Munich. As noted previously, Hitler was gradually able to pull together a coterie of supporters during bad times in Germany. He did so by appealing to Germans' vilest instincts.

Bet You Didn't Know

Does the fact that Hitler was able to create so much support mean that all Germans were vile? In 1996, Daniel Jonah Goldhagen, a young professor at Harvard, published a brilliant and controversial book called *Hitler's Willing Executioners* (Knopf, 1996). In it he implied that German culture was "pregnant with murder." Germans followed Hitler in perpetrating the Holocaust because "they wanted to." But the Holocaust came after Hitler was in power. (The subject will be introduced in this chapter.) Before he rose to power, plenty of Germans didn't subscribe to his racist rhetoric. Many of them went into exile or worse.

Hitler's appeal was broader than his anti-Semitic platform. He presented himself as an artist making the claim that he wasn't a politician. Does that sound familiar? How many times have you heard Americans running for office say that they aren't politicians? Or that they aren't Washington insiders? We Americans don't like politicians. The same was true of Weimar Germany: Politicians were associated with signing the hated Versailles Treaty.

Now let's push this point a bit further. What other prominent person in Germany had not been a politician? Kaiser Wilhelm II. If you can find it, you might browse through another brilliant book, this one by Robert G. L. Waite, called *Kaiser and Führer*. Despite obvious differences in their family backgrounds and educations, Waite shows that Wilhelm and Hitler were much alike. Both had lousy childhoods. Both had suffered self-doubt and yet called themselves all-powerful. Both considered themselves honest, yet lied constantly in matters great and small. Both were unbelievably self-centered and numbed those around them with endless talk about themselves. Both were racists and anti-Semites. Both, curiously enough, were artists. Both, most important, had visions of a Germany occupying its "rightful" place in the world.

Adolf Hitler, in short, offered himself up as a new version of Kaiser Wilhelm II. In most of his policies, in fact, once he was in power he was much in the tradition of Bismarck and Wilhelm, at home and abroad. Unfortunately, though, for the 50,000,000 or so persons who died in the Second World War, Hitler went further than either of them would have ever dared. Unlike Bismarck and Wilhelm, Hitler had no sense of restraint.

The Collapse of Previous Institutions

There's a strange contrast between America and Germany. Even after all the bloodshed of the U.S. Civil War, the former Confederacy persisted in trying to preserve its states' rights. In Germany, however, once Hitler was in charge, all those independent states we met in Chapter 1 just caved in, giving up all claims to independence. Two weeks before the Enabling Act went into being, Bavaria accepted Nazi leadership. All the other states soon received Nazi governors. They had the power to get rid of the old local governments and to replace them with ones favored by Hitler. The same was true of judges and lower state officials. The state governments became merely administrative bodies of the Third Reich. The *federalism* of the Germany of old simply disappeared.

> **Terms and Translations**
>
> **Federalism** is a political system in which the legal power of government is divided between a central or national government and smaller units of state of provincial government, usually under the authority of a written constitution. The United States and Canada are federations.

The centralization did not stop with the states. Non-Nazi political parties also soon disappeared. The regime quickly suppressed the Communists—interestingly enough, with the help of the Social Democrats. Hoping to appease Hitler, they denounced the Reds, often passing along to the authorities names and addresses of those to be arrested. Then the Nazi regime turned on the Social Democrats, denouncing them as subversives disloyal to the state. The Catholic Center Party suffered the same fate. The Catholics had once been Bismarck's most effective enemies, and if any party had supported the Weimar Republic it was the Catholic Center Party. On July 4, 1933, the party was outlawed—which didn't stop the pope from signing a concordat, or peace treaty, with Hitler two weeks later.

> ### Bet You Didn't Know
>
> Inside Germany, the Catholic Church itself soon became a victim of persecution; many Catholics developed an almost instinctive empathy with the plight of the Jews. Yet the Vatican notoriously helped prevent Jews from getting out of Germany.

> ### Modern Day Parallels
>
> A **totalitarian state** or dictatorship consists of an ideology, a single party typically led by one man, a terroristic police force, a monopoly of communications and weapons, and a centrally directed economy. Are there examples other than Nazi Germany? Sure—the former Soviet Union and the People's Republic of China under Mao Zedong are two.

Then there was that other right-wing party, the German Nationalists. This was just a small group, but it had had close ties to Hindenburg, the army, and the landowners. It had also helped Hitler in his rise to power. Out it went. On June 21, 1933, police agents and SA troops took over Nationalist Party offices all over Germany.

By the middle of July of 1933, only one political party existed in the Third Reich. An edict declared: "The National Socialist German Workers' Party constitutes the only political party in Germany."

The trade unions went the same way. Back in the early 1920s, as we have seen, a strike by the workers prevented a right-wing takeover of the government in Berlin. With Hitler in power, however, there was no similar resistance. On May 2, police agents and SA troops—the usual suspects—moved in on trade union headquarters, destroyed the papers, stole the money, and packed the leaders off to jail.

By the middle of 1934, Hitler had gone a long way toward establishing a *totalitarian state*. But not all the way.

Hitler and his comrades had crushed the left. But there was still the right. Allied with big business, the old Prussian powers—the generals and the aristocrats—were still a formidable force, by no means under Hitler's control. He still needed them as much as they needed him. A political pragmatist despite the belligerence of his speeches, Hitler's inclination was to maintain his alliance with the right. The right was the fount of his power.

Supporting Actors

The purge didn't stop with private organizations. Government bureaucrats who bore the slightest taint of disloyalty to Hitler were ousted from their posts and replaced by Nazi Party members, regardless of qualifications. A case in point: The *Reichsbank* was Germany's central bank, roughly the equivalent of America's Federal Reserve; its president, Dr. Hans Luther, a cautious and highly respected economist, had stayed out of politics. So he had to go, dispatched by Hitler as the ambassador to the United States. In his place came Dr. Hjalmar Schacht, also an economist, but one known primarily for his groveling obeisance to Hitler.

The Night of the Long Knives

Ernst Röhm, head of the SA, saw things differently than Hitler. The SA, remember, was made up of riff-raff, toughs from the lower classes who thought that the Nazi revolution was aimed against their social superiors. The conflict between Hitler, who knew where the power lay and how to sidle up to it, and Röhm, who saw himself as a kind of vanguard of the proletariat, was building to a climax.

The Röhm–Hitler Conflict

In June 1934, Röhm, who by that point presided over roughly two million Storm Troopers, made his position public:

> One victory on the road of German revolution has been won. ... The SA, however, who bear the great responsibility of having set the German revolution rolling, will not allow it to be betrayed at the halfway mark. ... If the Philistines believe that the national revolution has lasted too long ... it is indeed high time that the national revolution should end and become a National Socialist one. ... We shall continue our fight—with them or without them. We are the incorruptible guarantors of the fulfillment of the German revolution.

Can you imagine the effect that speech had on Hitler? Röhm was practically accusing the Führer of betraying the cause, selling out to the right!

The conflict between Röhm and Hitler took on an aspect of personal tragedy. The two men had been very close (just how close had long been a subject of considerable speculation). Of all in the Nazi entourage, Röhm alone had the privilege of addressing Hitler with the familiar *du*.

The former closeness of Hitler and Röhm made their separation even more bitter. However, 1933 came and went without a public rupture. Hitler even wrote to Röhm:

> At the close of the year of the National Socialist Revolution, I feel compelled to thank you, my dear Ernst Röhm, for the imperishable services which you have rendered to the National Socialist movement and the German people, and to assure you how very grateful I am to fate that I am able to call on such men as you my friends and fellow combatants.
>
> In true friendship and grateful regard,
>
> Your Adolf Hitler

Published in the Nazi daily newspaper, the *Völkischer Beobachter* (*The People's Observer*), the letter used the *du* form of address. Talk about a kiss of death!

Röhm Seals His Fate

Perhaps Röhm didn't see what was coming. He certainly took a step that sealed his fate. In February 1934, he presented the Nazi cabinet with a memorandum proposing that the SA be renamed the "People's Army"—a term that sounded like a Communist usage—and that he be made minister of defense. In effect he was urging that he be put in charge of the regular army and that it be merged with the SA.

If Röhm thought that the officer corps would accept all this, he was fooling himself. The brass of the military had sworn allegiance to the Weimar Republic with the greatest reluctance. Now were they supposed to be loyal to a bunch of street thugs? Especially when they suspected Röhm of leftist leanings?

And there was something else. As Himmler had discovered, Röhm was a homosexual, and the generals learned (Himmler made sure they learned it) that most of the top SA officials were also gay. As one general put it later to the Nuremberg court, "Rearmament was too difficult a business to permit the participation of peculators, drunkards, and homosexuals."

Did the generals think any more highly of Hitler? Most likely not. But Hitler gave them no choice but to accept his leadership. And the army prodded Hitler into action.

The Purge on the Night of the Long Knives

The action came at the end of June 1934. Himmler's agents tracked Röhm and other SA leaders to a hotel by a lake outside Munich. Shortly after dawn on June 30, Hitler and a group of loyal Nazis barged into the establishment. Two of the SA men were in bed together: Hitler summarily ordered them taken to the courtyard outside and shot to death. Then he woke up Röhm, gave him a dressing gown, and had him sent to the Stadelheim prison in Munich. A pistol was lying on a table in the cell. Röhm refused to use it. Then two police officers entered the cell and killed him with their revolvers.

In the meantime, in Berlin, Göring and Himmler were carrying out other aspects of the purge. Lined up against a wall in a military school, some 150 SA officers lost their lives to a firing squad.

Early the same morning, a squadron of SS men in civilian clothes rang the doorbell at the villa of General von Schleicher on the outskirts of the capital. Von Schleicher had been the one to maneuver against Hitler. When he opened the door, they murdered him. Gregor Strasser, an old rival of Hitler in the Nazi Party, also lost his life. Placed under house arrest, von Papen alone among Hitler's rivals survived the Night of the Long Knives.

How did the rest of the world react to this purge? It reacted with a feeling of horror.

Bet You Didn't Know

The "Night of the Long Knives" was a grisly act of revenge ordered by Hitler, Himmler, and Göring on June 30, 1934, partly against Ernst Röhm and the leadership of the SA but also against just about everyone who had tried to stop Hitler's rise to power in 1932 and 1933. The highest-ranking of the victims was General Kurt von Schleicher, who had served briefly as chancellor. At the time of the purge, however, von Schleicher was out of power. The greatest danger to the Nazi regime at the time was the SA. It consisted of some two million troops and Röhm had been ambitious to turn it into Germany's principle army, over which he, and not Hitler, would exert control. The "Night of the Long Knives" (a term adopted by the Nazis themselves), thus, was the result of a deadly struggle for supreme power in Germany.

The German Army After the Purge

Now let's put the purge in perspective. Hitler, Himmler, and Göring had rid themselves of their major enemies. And, while not participating in the killing, the military had looked the other way: It had let the unholy triumvirate eliminate a direct threat to the primacy of the army on the German scene. Ever since Bismarck, the German army had been practically a state within the state: a law unto itself, facing few if any challenges to its budgetary demands. So with the Night of the Long Knives, the army was back in its old position of power—or so it seemed.

The generals had good reason to be smug. In a speech delivered on July 13, 1934, Hitler stated that the army was to remain "the sole bearer of arms."

The generals, however, had not looked closely enough at what Hitler and other top Nazis were doing. Instead, they had developed and expanded two new instruments of power, the SS and the Gestapo.

The New Instruments of Power

Believe it or not, the Nazis did not originate the concentration camp. The British started that little number. During the Boer War, fought on the veld of South Africa between 1899 and 1902, General Herbert Horatio Kitchener came up with the idea of rounding up the wives and children of his enemies, the Boer guerrillas, and incarcerating them in huge barbed-wire compounds guarded by tall watchtowers. Given the poor food and lack of sanitation, thousands of people died in these camps. Kitchener got the nickname "The Butcher of the Veld" and was condemned throughout the European continent. Ironically, the loudest protests came from Germany.

But the Nazis were quick to adopt the idea. Within days of the takeover of power, Hermann Göring, whom Hitler had appointed Minister of the Interior for Prussia, was the originator of the first Nazi concentration camps. This was at the end of February 1933, and the purpose was to aide the regime in suppressing civil liberties.

Heinrich Himmler.

(U.S. Holocaust Memorial Museum)

Experimental Camp Dachau

But it was Himmler who expanded on the idea. As president of the Munich Police (those guys loved their titles as well as their uniforms) on March 21, 1933, he announced the opening of an "experimental" concentration camp at Dachau. It would hold 5,000 prisoners.

Reichsführer-SS Himmler as always thought in chilling terms. People arrested and put in the camps were there on the basis of "protective custody." The Nazi regime was to be protected from "racial traitors and Bolshevik agitators," people who in Himmler's judgment might interrupt the efficient workings of the state.

Terms and Translations

"Based on Article I of the 'Decree of the *Reich* President for the Protection of People and State' of February 28, 1933, you are taken into protective custody in the interest of public security and order. Reason: suspicion of activities inimical to the state." Note the word *suspicion*. In the western democracies, a person arrested may not be detained indefinitely on the basis of suspicion. Sooner or later, the authorities must plea-bargain or put the suspect on trial. This obviously was not the case under Himmler: Suspicion was enough to arrest.

Hitler's Henchmen and the Gestapo

For Himmler, however, the mere imprisonment of suspects was not enough. In an SS order issued in April 1933, he stated: "A great deal of potentially useful information can be extracted from suspects. Even if suspicion of treasonable activities proves to be unfounded they can often be persuaded to give information that will lead to other suspects. Such information is usually readily given under duress, threat, or promise of release."

Himmler's underlings, such as Adolf Eichmann, at Dachau were given carte blanche to interpret his instructions however they wished. They often obtained information by flogging their victims. Those who still resisted were often shot to death or hanged.

But who put the inmates in the concentration camps in the first place? Answer: the *Gestapo*.

Unlike the SA and the SS, the Gestapo was not created until the Nazis had come into power. Operating originally in Prussia, it got its name after Göring had purged the state police,

Terms and Translations

Gestapo was short for *GEheime STAatsPOlizei*—Secret State Police.

putting Nazi supporters in all posts. These persons were the core of the new Gestapo. Its headquarters were established at 8 Prinz-Albrecht Strasse in Berlin, a building that soon became notorious as the Gestapo's chief interrogation center.

Göring became ever more involved in plans to build up a German air force, and control of the Gestapo soon passed into the hands of Himmler. It also became a nationwide institution. Under Himmler, the Gestapo became involved in every aspect of terror as practiced by the Nazis. In time this meant the maltreatment of prisoners of war, the operation of slave labor programs, excesses in the administration of occupied territories, brutalities and murders in the concentration camps, and the persecution and extermination of the Jews.

Hitler's War on the Jews

Many of these crimes did not take place, or at least not in any major way, until the coming of the Second World War. Right from the start, nonetheless, the Gestapo waged war on the Jews.

Since the end of the Second World War, historians, especially in Germany, have examined Nazi Germany. Many debates have surfaced; some Hitler interpreters have argued that his primary motivation was the quest for power. In this school of thought, ideology for Hitler was nothing more than a tool to be used or discarded as the political situation required. Therefore, such historians contend, he may not have been sincere in his denunciations of the Jews.

Who can peer into Hitler's brain? We don't have to. He unleashed the Gestapo against the Jews long before the advent of the Second World War. Perhaps the coming of the war helps explain the Gestapo's torture of captured prisoners. But it does not account for Hitler's use of the Gestapo as a weapon against the Jews.

Anti-Semitism

We've got to start with an overview of German anti-Semitism. Anti-Semitism had been endemic throughout Europe for centuries. Some countries such as Holland, to be sure, had been relatively tolerant. But if you were to look back over the four decades or so that preceded the Nazi takeover of power, you would think that anti-Semitism was the most virulent in France. In 1895, a Jewish French army officer named Alfred Dreyfus was tried and found guilty of treason. Four years later he was tried again with the same results. Then, in 1906, as a result of intense political pressure from the left, the government acquitted him. But for a decade, the government had wrongfully imprisoned Dreyfus because he was Jewish. And then there was Russia, with a centuries' long history of anti-Jewish pogroms.

But the Holocaust started in Germany. Why?

Let's think back to the rise of German nationalism: That nationalism had arisen from the Napoleonic wars. When the armies of Napoleon crossed the territories of the many Germanies, they brought with them the ideals of the French Revolution, especially liberty and equality. In practice that meant the liberation of Jews, particularly in cities like Frankfurt, that previously had kept them restricted to ghettoes. To many Germans, therefore, Jews were the beneficiaries of the French occupation: Jews became defined as the enemies of the German nationalistic spirit.

In the course of the nineteenth century, German public opinion became more liberal. But as we know from debates over globalization now, free trade always leaves somebody out. And with the economic unification that reached its peak with Bismarck, many Germans—farmers, artisans, small businessman, and the like—began to blame their reduced status on the Jewish financiers. That view was unfair: There were Gentile financiers, too. But as we know from America's own paranoid traditions, populism often looks to foreign devils as the sources of trouble. And in a Germany that was largely Christian, Jews did appear to be those foreign devils.

In the Bismarck period there was no Holocaust, but there was plenty of anti-foreign feelings aimed against the Slavs and the Jews. Bookstores were full of anti-Semitic tracts.

Then came the First World War: This was the catalyst of the explosion to come. By the middle of 1916, the war was going badly. Many young men had died or were wounded at the front, hardships were mounting at home, and the government produced no victories that could make up for the sacrifices. What was going wrong? People couldn't blame Kaiser Wilhelm II and his top generals; that wasn't the German way. Nor could anyone accuse the soldiers who were fighting so valiantly. So guess who began to come under attack? Those apparent foreign devils, the Jews.

Once the war was over and Germany had to face defeat, anti-Semitism became rife. Newspapers and books demanded the exclusion of Jews from public life. State and national legislators regularly introduced anti-Semitic bills. And a booklet called the *Protocols of the Elders of Zion*, a forgery purporting to be a Jewish plot to take over Germany, received wide attention.

Bet You Didn't Know

Orators everywhere repeated the mantra: "*Deutschland erwache, Juda verrecke.*" "Germany awakes, Judea kicks the bucket."

Anti-Jewish Legislation

Germany by the late 1920s and early 1930s was filled with hate, paranoia, and a sense that Jews had caused every one of the nation's misfortunes. If only Germany could rid itself of the Jews, much popular thinking went, then all would be well.

From the very outset, Hitler intended to make the Jews "kick the bucket." On April 7, 1933, the Third Reich promulgated its first anti-Jewish law. Titled "Law for the Restoration of the Professional Civil Service," the measure forced the retirement from governmental posts of all "non-Aryan" officials.

The war against the Jews had begun. Much more was to come.

The Least You Need to Know

◆ In the first year of Nazi rule (1933–1934), previously influential institutions such as the labor unions, the free press, and the like simply collapsed under the pressure of their Nazi opponents.

◆ In the Night of the Long Knives, Hitler, Göring, and Himmler eliminated their SA enemies. Interestingly, Goebbels took little part in this fight. Why did he not get purged? His skills as a propagandist were enormously valuable to Hitler.

◆ With the SA out of the way, the Nazi regime turned to using concentration camps and the Gestapo to eliminate any and all traces of leftism.

◆ The Third Reich instituted its war against the Jews.

Life in Nazi Germany: 1934–1936

In This Chapter

- ◆ How the Nazis transform the German culture into the Nazi German culture

- ◆ The elimination of any influences alternative to the Nazi Party, via the media, education, the courts, and even the churches

- ◆ The Nazi preparation to eradicate the Jews

Hitler and the Nazis were now in power; no group could or would challenge that power. Certainly not big business; Hitler was going to support their interests. The military? The Prussian officers may have looked down their monocles at Hitler but he held out the restoration of their one-time military eminence. Then what about ordinary Germans? With the Night of the Long Knives looming in the background, there wasn't much dissent. And Hitler certainly appealed to German patriots: He promised to free Germany from the shackles of the Versailles Treaty and to make Germany once more a great power. Hitler's was an appeal to popular pride.

So now we come to a really big question: What were the sources of Hitler's power? Big business and the army, of course, and organs of terror such as the Gestapo. But could these institutions by themselves have enabled Hitler and the Nazis to enforce their tyranny? A lot of historians have addressed these issues. And their conclusion? Hitler triumphed because the German people on the whole supported his triumph. In fact, the bulk of the German people supported Hitler's tyranny.

This raises yet another question: Did the German people on the whole know about that tyranny? The evidence is overwhelming. We now know that a vast array of information about Nazi assaults on the churches, the press, the courts, the Jews, and others deemed to be social outsiders was widely published and read by the German population. Indeed, the population helped single out suspected enemies and did so in a spirit of cooperation and patriotism.

This much has become utterly clear: Hitler didn't do it alone. But he did mobilize the masses to do his bidding. He and his cohorts did so with undeniable brilliance.

German Culture During Nazi Rule

Once in power, the Nazis lost no time in wooing the public with glittering showmanship. Central to that political theater was a dazzling mythology that even included a calendar of feast days. These swastika-draped occasions coincided—by no accident—with traditional, even medieval German holidays. The Nazi propaganda machine wove together Christian and pagan rituals, liturgies in which the deity was Adolf Hitler.

Hitler's birthday, May 20, was celebrated nationwide with daytime displays in shop windows of his picture wreathed as if it were an icon, and nighttime torchlight ceremonies—fire being an ancient pre-Christian symbol. May Day became an occasion for more torchlight parades and swastika displays. The summer solstice, June 22, another Teutonic holiday, saw more of the same. All the displays of fire evoked the principle of life—German life—and by implication, death to others.

Other celebrations reinforced the propagandistic union of the ancient and the modern. At Stralau, a town near the Baltic, with swastikas draping the front of the municipal hall, a man dressed in Nordiclike skins and carrying a trident each year marched down the steps. Following him were young women dressed like sea nymphs, and behind them came other young women in peasant dirndls, full-skirted dresses with tight bodices. The ceremony revived an ancient folk festival that honored a year's success in catching fish.

Every year on the anniversary of the failed 1923 Munich *Putsch* (the uprising), Hitler flew to the city to give a celebratory speech in the beer hall.

But the greatest ceremony of all took place annually at Nuremberg (Nürnberg) on the northern edge of the Bavarian Alps. The festival—for the Nazi Party—took place in late September, at the time of the autumn equinox with its promise of snowfall in those beautiful mountains. The Nuremberg show lasted a week. After Hitler opened the ceremonies with one of his grandiose speeches, various extravaganzas followed: Worker's Day, in which Nazis drilled with polished shovels; Hitler Youth Day, featuring marches by uniformed teenagers; Party Leaders' Day, with parades of 150,000 marchers; Army Day, with mock battles fought with weapons that were becoming plentiful; and, above all, Closing Day, with flags, banners, brass bands, torches, and hundreds of thousands of uniformed Nazis marching in perfect unison past Hitler's reviewing stand.

These rituals were profoundly seductive: The Nazi regime was trying to consolidate its conquest with irresistible cultural glamour. It was also trying to eliminate all possible sources of dissent from its rule.

Burning of Literature

About four and a half months after Hitler became chancellor, his propaganda chief, Goebbels, used a torchlit parade for a most special purpose. At midnight on May 10, 1933, thousands of students trooped to a square at the end of *Under den Linden*, facing the University of Berlin. They were carrying textbooks with them and with those tomes they made a stack and set it on fire. With Goebbels looking on approvingly, the students made the fire blaze high by hurling in classics of German literature, including the novels of Thomas Mann, Stefan Zweig (the Viennese writer who had observed the first reaction of his government to the assassinations in Sarajevo), and Erich Maria Remarque (author of the worldwide best-selling antiwar novel *All Quiet on the Western Front* [*Am Westen Nichts Neues*])

Goebbels had majored in literature and he knew what he was doing. He directed the students to next pitch in classics from beyond the frontiers: Proust, Zola, Freud, H. G. Wells, Helen Keller, Upton Sinclair, and Jack

> **Modern Day Parallels**
>
> Lots of American college students from time to time would love to burn their books. The frustrations of student life can be great. But imagine a campus on which students raid the library and throw hundreds or thousands of the works kept there into a bonfire. They would be destroying much of their own culture. It doesn't happen here, but it did over and over in Nazi Germany.

London. Under Goebbels's guidance, the students were expressing contempt for modern literature altogether.

Nazification of German Culture

The Nazi regime banned all forms of modernity in art and drama. Before production, every book or play had to go to a censor for approval. In music, Bach, Beethoven, and Brahms were okay. The works of Felix Mendelssohn, who had been born into a Jewish family but converted to Christianity, were banned. Not even converts "need apply." All Jewish composers, in fact, were outlawed. But who substituted for them? Richard Wagner.

The lush harmonies and soaring melodies of the Wagnerian operas, with their evocations of a mythological Teutonic past, were perfect as idealizations of Nazi rule.

What was going on was the Nazification of German culture. Many people have wondered: How could so cultured a people as the Germans have accepted Nazi rule? Part of the answer at least is that the Nazis obliterated much of that culture just as they tried to obliterate the Christian religion.

The Nazis and the Churches

Christianity, of course, was part of the German tradition. But churches from time to time have defied temporal authority. The Nazis were not about to countenance any such defiance.

The Nazi war against Christianity started slowly. Hitler himself had been born a Catholic. And although in *Mein Kampf* he had made disparaging remarks about Rome, in a speech given on March 23, 1933, he had praised Christianity as essential "for safeguarding the soul of the German people." Four months later, Berlin even entered into a concordat with the Vatican, promising that in Germany the Catholic Church could "regulate her own affairs."

The Nazis broke the agreement. Or at least church-state relations disintegrated badly. In an effort to ensure the racial "purity" of the German people, the regime passed a sterilization law. Many women who were Jewish, or of "low moral repute," or apparently mentally slow, were rendered unable to produce children. To Catholics, with their right-to-life stance, the measure was grossly offensive. Their protests, in turn, triggered reprisals. For example, one of the people murdered during the Night of the Long Knives was Erich Klausener, leader of the Catholic Action League. The regime began to arrest priests and nuns, charging them with false accusations such as "immorality" or "smuggling foreign currency." Catholic magazines and newsletters were censored; Nazi agents even violated the sanctity of the confessional.

Bet You Didn't Know

Early in 1960, a movie called *Counterfeit Traitor* reached the cinemas. It starred William Holden and Lillie Palmer and was based on a true story. Holden played the role of an American businessman based in neutral Sweden during the Second World War. While pretending to be neutral himself, he did business in Nazi Germany, and in the course of his many trips to the *Reich* gathered valuable military intelligence that he passed along to the United States embassy in Stockholm. Palmer played his lover and contact in Germany (in real life she was an Austrian actress). But she realized that the information she was giving him enabled Allied bombers to kill scores of German children. A staunch Catholic and conscience-stricken by her actions, she went to a church to confess. Sitting in the confessional booth, she told all to the priest. Only the priest wasn't a priest. As she peered closely through the little window, she saw in profile the face of a Gestapo agent she had met.

Lillie Palmer's character did not survive, and the Holden character just about fell apart. It was a great flick. And it was the sort of trick the Nazis really used.

Catholicism

By 1937, the Catholic clergy in Germany had had it. After they had reported the Nazi misdeeds to the Vatican, Pope Pius XI issued a papal bull titled *Mit Brennender Sorge*. The Vatican accused the Nazis of violating the concordat. The Vatican formally accused Hitler and his gang of "suspicion, discord, calumny, of secret and open fundamental hostility to Christ and His Church."

Terms and Translations

Let's break down **Mit Brennender Sorge. Mit** is easy; it means "with." For the verb **brennen,** take the English verb *burn* and reverse the *u* and the *r*. You get "brun." This is close to *brennen*. At some point, when the German-speaking Saxons shipped over to the British Isles, there supposedly occurred something called the "great vowel shift." *Brennen* means "to burn." For the word **sorge** the connection to English is the word *sorrow*. In German and English the first three letters are the same. How the *ge* in the German became the "row" in English, who knows. Regardless, *Mit Brennender Sorge* translates as "With Burning Sorrow," a pretty tough statement about the Nazi regime.

Although he had issued *Mit Brennender Sorge*, Pius XI would prove, shall we say, less than cooperative with Jews trying to escape the clutches of the Third Reich. But the Catholic Church does defend its own. *Mit Brennender Sorge* was practically a declaration of war from the Vatican against Nazi Germany.

Protestantism

What about the German Protestants? Their history was significant. Although splintered into many sects by the twentieth century, as was the case in the United States, their dominant denomination was Lutheran. The founder, Martin Luther, may have broken with the Catholic Church over its corruption, but he had left his own dubious legacy. He was violently anti-Semitic—at one point Luther urged of the Jews that "their synagogues and schools be set on fire, that their houses be broken up and destroyed, and they be put under a roof or stable like the gypsies, in misery and captivity as they incessantly lament and complain to God about us"—and he preached the doctrine of obedience to the state. So it is little wonder that when Hitler came to power, most of the Lutherans opened their arms in welcome.

In particular, Pastor Martin Niemöller, the leading Lutheran cleric, was overjoyed with the ascent of the Nazis. A submarine commander in the First World War, Niemöller had seen the Weimar period as "years of darkness." He thus welcomed the Nazis as bringing about a "national revival."

He certainly was in for a big surprise. Hitler appointed a supporter, a Chaplain Müller to the post of Reich Bishop. (How's that for separation of church and state?) Müller in turn oversaw the folding of the Protestant churches into the regime itself. Church congregations were required to pledge "One People, One Reich, One Faith."

After a year of this, Niemöller had had enough. Breaking away from the now-state-controlled Lutheran Church, in May 1934, he founded an alternative denomination, the "Confessional Church." Niemöller and his colleagues began to use their pulpits to denounce the regime.

The result was inevitable: by the end of 1935, Nazi agents had arrested several hundred pastors of the Confessional Church. A leader in the anti-Hitler opposition, Niemöller on June 27, 1937, preached his last sermon in the Third Reich. Probably aware of what was to come, he declared:

> We have no more thought of using our own powers to escape the arm of the authorities than had the Apostles of old. No more are we ready to keep silent at man's behest when God commands us to speak. For it is, and must remain, the case that we must obey God rather than man.

Pastor Niemöller was arrested at the beginning of July, and was confined to a cell in a prison in Berlin. He ended up in Dachau, where he somehow survived until the Second World War ended.

We should not let these events deceive us. For the vast majority of Germany, Catholic or Protestant, the loss of freedom of religion did not matter much. If they wanted to, they could still go to services, listen to the familiar dogmas, and sing the familiar hymns. What turned them on were the glories of Nazism, as reported to them in the state-controlled press.

The Media

This author is far too young to have lived in Nazi Germany, but he has lived in another totalitarian country, the People's Republic of China, and it was amazing to see firsthand how state control of the media works. Movies were wholly propagandistic, denouncing the West as imperialistic and excoriating the enemies, real or supposed, of the state. The radio was the same. And the newspapers served primarily to give readers slogans of the day.

Nazi Germany was much the same. Newspapers and films remained in private hands but Goebbels's Ministry of Propaganda and the Chamber of Films, a governmental entity, oversaw every aspect of what reached the public. Freedom of the press in Nazi Germany was simply nonexistent. Editors occupied their posts on the basis of their racial purity and slavishly printed each day's news stories as dictated from Berlin.

The movie industry was no different, except that films could produce results visually more spectacular than anything in the papers. Hitler's favorite motion picture director was a gorgeous woman named Leni Riefenstahl. Her specialty was the documentary film. She produced a feature-length portrayal of the 1934 Nazi Party rally at Nuremberg. With cameras placed on airplanes, flagpoles, and cranes, she captured Hitler's dramatic entrance into the Luitpolt Arena. Her soundtrack carried the strains of Richard Wagner.

Tightly regulated, the media in Nazi Germany served one purpose alone: the glorification of Hitler and the Third Reich. Such also became the purpose of education.

Education

Hitler had been an educational drop-out as well as a reject from the academy in Vienna; he had little love for the public schools or the universities. His contempt for professors and the academic life ran like a red thread through the pages of *Mein Kampf*. Indeed, he had little use for any form of conventional education in which the purpose is the discovery of truth.

He and his cohorts, rather, saw education as a means of molding the loyalty of the young to the Nazi regime. In a speech given in November 1933, Hitler stated: "When an opponent declares, 'I will not come over to your side,' I calmly say, 'Your child belongs to us already. ... What are you? You will pass on. Your descendants, however, now stand in the new camp. In a short time they will know nothing else but this new community." And on May 1, 1937, Hitler boasted: "This new *Reich* will give its youth to no one, but itself will take youth and give to youth its own education and its own upbringing!"

The regime lost no time Nazifying the schools and the universities. Old textbooks went out and *Mein Kampf* became the heart of the curriculum. Teachers and professors had to join the National Socialist Teachers' League; according to a new statute, the League was "responsible for the execution of the political coordination of all teachers in accordance with the National Socialist doctrine." Schoolteachers could get jobs only if they had served in the SA, the SS, or the Hitler Youth, and even then had to be vetted for their ideological "reliability." Secret police agents penetrated the schools to ferret out any signs of disloyalty. The National Socialist Association of University Lecturers, an organization run not by academics but rather by party hacks, made sure that the professors whom Hitler so loathed did not depart from the party line.

The effect of party control over the schools and universities was disastrous. Needless to say, Jews were expelled from all teaching positions. (The plight of the Jews is discussed more at the end of this chapter.) History and literature became exaltations of a mythical Teutonic past. Something called racial science entered the curricula. Science itself became German science, so that students studied German physics and German mathematics, whatever those were. Einstein's theories were ignored and he became a nonperson, soon to go into exile.

Bet You Didn't Know

The *Hitlerjugend* oath stated: "I the presence of this blood banner, which represents our Führer, I swear to devote all my energies and my strength to the savior of our country, Adolf Hitler. I am willing and ready to give up my life for him, so help me God."

All this assumed the importance of the classroom and the laboratory in the educational process. The Nazis, however, refused to make that assumption. For them, the real education of the young people was to take place outside school and university walls. Boys were required to enter the *Hitlerjugend*, or Hitler Youth. After swearing an oath of allegiance to Hitler, members of the group would devote much of their time—time when normally they would have been in school—to camping, hiking, marching, and, in fact, to military drilling.

The regime did not forget the girls. Young women were enrolled in the *Bund Deutscher Mädel* (League of German Maidens) and, like the youths, sent out to drill and march. They were to be healthy: healthy mothers to breed healthy children.

A point bears repetition: In Nazi Germany, education existed as a service to the state, not to the pursuit of truth. So it was also, not surprisingly, with the courts.

The Courts

Late in the summer of 1974, after a decision by the U.S. Supreme Court that required him to turn over White House tapes to the Watergate prosecutor, President Richard M. Nixon resigned his office. In the American system of justice, the courts are supposed to be guardians against abuses of power by those in positions of authority. That means that American courts are to be independent of the legislative and executive branches of government.

This was the case in Nazi Germany. There, Hitler *was* the law. In 1936, Dr. Hans Frank, the Nazi commissioner for justice, made this point perfectly clear: "The National Socialist ideology is the foundation of all basic laws," he told an audience of judges, "especially as explained in the party program and in the speeches of the Führer."

Frank elaborated and, even now, his words are chilling:

> There is no independence of law against National Socialism. Say to yourselves at every decision which you make: "How would the Führer decide in my place?" In every decision ask yourselves: "Is this decision compatible with the National Socialist conscience of the German people?" Then you will have a firm iron foundation which, allied with the unity of the National Socialist People's State and with your recognition of the eternal nature of the will of Adolf Hitler, will endow your own sphere of decision with the authority of the Third Reich and this for all time.

The message for all judges was plain enough: Hand down your verdicts according to the guidelines laid down by Hitler. Basically, that meant that anyone Hitler did not like should be found guilty of treason. Sometimes, to be sure, the judges got confused. In 1934, for example, a court in Berlin tried a businessman charged with bribing a government official. The evidence of guilt was clear and straightforward. The judge should have sentenced the businessman to prison. But the official in question was Göring. Somehow, on orders from on high, the case was dismissed.

That sort of thing severely reduced the prestige of Germany's court system. That is hardly surprising. In the United States we regard the courts as beacons of individual rights. Not so in Nazi Germany. As the courts faded from view, the SS began to take their place. And even in the mid- to late 1920s, the primary task of the SS was the extermination of the Jews.

The Plight of the Jews

For a time, between 1933 and 1935, the Nazi regime had concentrated on passing anti-Jewish legislation: Bundles of laws deprived Jews of their jobs, their businesses, and even their homes. But the implication of everything we have seen in this chapter—the glorification of Aryan culture, the official contempt for religion, the use of the media and the schools to inculcate some kind of Aryan ideal, and the deliberate weakening of courts that might have provided justice for minorities—all pointed in one direction. They all implied the final solution to the "Jewish problem."

The SS was to be the instrument of the final solution. A standard passage in the indoctrination of SS troops read: "The Jew is a parasite. Wherever he flourishes, the people die. Elimination of the Jew from our community is to be regarded as an emergency defense measure."

When Hitler came into power, the government itself was in charge of the Jewish question; the SS did little more than maintain the Himmler–Heydrich filing system in Munich. With the crushing of the SA, however, the dividing line between the state and the party became invisible. Himmler and Heydrich rushed in to take over the government's anti-Jewish functions.

For a time, that function may have seemed relatively benign. In 1934 and 1935, a number of officials in the SS confined themselves to discussions on how to encourage Jewish emigration.

By 1936, though, the tune of SS documents was changing. On August 28, an SS officer who at the time was Adolf Eichmann's superior at Dachau, put that new tone in writing:

> The Jew is a 100 percent enemy of National Socialism, as proven by the difference in his race and nationality. Wherever he tries to transmit his work, his influence, and his world outlook to the non-Jewish world, he discharges it in hostile ideologies, as we find it in Liberalism, especially in Freemasonry, in Marxism, and not the least in Christianity.

Look again at that last little bit. One of the alleged sins of the Jews was that they were espousing Christianity.

The document went on:

> We shall unremittingly fulfill our task, to be the guarantors of the internal security of Germany, just as the *Wehrmacht* [the army] guarantees the honor, the greatness, and the peace of the Reich from the outside. We shall take care that

never more in Germany, the heart of Europe, can the Jewish–Bolshevik revolution of subhumans be kindled internally or by emissaries from abroad. Pitilessly we shall be a merciless executioner's sword. ...

In the next chapter, we'll see Hitler's preparations for a war abroad. But let's keep in mind that, at the same time, the SS, with Hitler's full approval, was making preparations for a war at home—a war against the Jews. A lot of people have sought to defend Nazi Germany by saying that the Holocaust came about only after Germany was at war and thus was a means of national defense. The documents quoted in this chapter, however, show beyond a shadow of a doubt that the Nazis were preparing for the Holocaust well before Germany was at war.

The Least You Need to Know

- ♦ The Nazis used every available instrument—newspapers, the radio, movies, as well as parades and other such extravaganzas—to laud the ideal of Aryan racial purity.

- ♦ The Nazi Party deliberately tried and largely succeeded in eliminating or reducing any and all institutions, such as the churches, the schools, and the courts, that might have threatened the Nazi rulers with alternative centers of power and influence.

Chapter 14

The First Steps Toward Conquest: 1934–1936

In This Chapter

- ◆ How the Third Reich breaks the Versailles Treaty
- ◆ Germany's attempt to occupy the Rhineland
- ◆ The 1936 Olympic Games, Germany's propaganda tool to exhibit the superiority of the pure Aryan athlete

Up until now, the Nazi Party's control was concentrated in Germany, but we must not forget developments abroad. All the foregoing had to do with life in Nazi Germany. But we must not forget developments in the land of Hitler's birth, Austria.

The Anschluss and the Dollfuss Murder

In the earliest pages of *Mein Kampf*, Hitler had made clear that he would seek a Greater Germany, with Austria joined to the Third Reich. To carry out that goal, almost as soon as he came into power Hitler sent agents into Austria. Their task was to overthrow the government in Vienna and bring about the link. The agents had plenty of help: Hundreds of thousands of Austrians were Nazis and, citing the common ethnicity, were clamoring for what they called *Anschluss*, annexation by the Third Reich.

But not all Austrians agreed. The Austrian chancellor, Engelbert Dollfuss, wanted no part of a union with the Third Reich. Dollfuss was a tiny man—the Viennese nicknamed him "Millimetternich," after Prince Klement von Metternich, the leading statesman at the Congress of Vienna—but his determinaton was great. Outlawing both the Socialist and Nazi parties, he had set up a dictatorship modeled on that of Mussolini.

> **Terms and Translations**
>
> The verb **schliessen** means "to lock or to close." The prefix **an** carries the sense of motion toward something. So the noun **anschluss** means "union"; it can also mean "a highway" or "rail junction."

Forced underground, Austria's Nazis turned to terror. In July 1934, at just about the time of the Night of the Long Knives, they blew up a power station in Vienna. Dollfuss responded with a threat to execute any Nazi caught with explosives.

A week or so later, Dollfuss was meeting with his cabinet. Suddenly 10 Nazis, garbed in uniforms stolen from the Austrian army and police, burst into the chamber. One of them shot the chancellor in the neck and chest and two others dropped him, bleeding but still alive, on a sofa.

While the ministers were held as prisoners, the Nazis occupied the chancellery for some six hours. As they did so, Dollfuss bled to death. The time for Austria's joining the Third Reich seemed at hand.

But those who wanted such a union would have to wait. During the Nazi break-in at the Austrian chancellery, one cabinet member was absent. This was Minister of Education Kurt von Schuschnigg. When he learned what was going on, he ordered Austrian soldiers to surround the building. Inside, the gin-toting Nazis got nervous. One of them telephoned the German embassy in Vienna. A German official arrived on the scene, arranging with von Schuschnigg what he thought was a truce: The gunmen would let the other cabinet ministers go if they could have safe conduct to the German border.

It was a trap. The moment the Nazis left the chancellery, von Schuschnigg had them arrested. Soon the leaders were hanged, and von Schuschnigg became the new chancellor.

The Dollfuss murder nonetheless shocked the outside world. Headlines in New York proclaimed a "war scare." In London, the *Times* regarded the assassination as making the very word "Nazi stink in the nostrils of the world." And in Rome, Benito

Mussolini took the murder personally—at the time of the killing, Dollfuss's wife and two children had been vacationing with the Mussolini family at an Adriatic resort. After putting the widow on a plane back to Vienna, an angry Mussolini sent 50,000 Italian troops to the Brenner pass, right on Italy's frontier with Austria.

Alarmed, the German government denied that it had had anything to do with the Dollfuss murder. Hitler himself claimed that he wanted only to set German–Austrian relations on the path of peace.

In the face of Mussolini's military action, Hitler did nothing: There was no confrontation with Italy. The reason was simple: Germany was too weak to do so. But Hitler did learn a lesson from the Dollfuss affair. Germany, he believed, had to rearm (even in violation of the Versailles Treaty), and do so as soon as possible.

The Rearmament of the Third Reich

The rearmament proceeded in strict secrecy. Goebbels instructed his newspapers not to use the phrase "General Staff": The treaty had forbidden such a group even to exist. The government stopped publication of the list of its officers. And in June 1934, Admiral Erich Räder, in charge of the navy, wrote that the "Führer demands complete secrecy ..."

Secrecy about what? Hitler had ordered the construction of a new submarine fleet, and that was not all. In 1933 and 1934, the German navy began the construction of two battle cruisers: at 26,000 tons apiece, once finished they would exceed the Versailles limit by 16,000 tons. (These warships eventually would be dubbed the *Scharnhorst* and the *Gneisenau*, named for Prussian generals who took part in the defeat of Napoleon at Waterloo.) Hitler furthermore had mandated the expansion of the army by October 1, 1934, from 100,000 men to 300,000 men.

Göring, too, was busy. He had taken on the job of minister of aviation. On paper this meant building civilian airplanes. Actually, Göring was letting out contracts for war planes. And under the rubric of a group called the League for Air Sports, pilots were learning to handle military aircraft.

The Versailles Treaty had been signed only a decade and a half before. That meant that if they learned about Germany's rearmament, the Allies, and especially the French, might very well invade, just as they had done in the Ruhr.

The French had left the Ruhr in the late 1920s. With the Great Depression draining financial reserves, Paris had considered the Ruhr occupation too costly to be continued.

But French spies remained in the region and their secret reports to Paris must have raised alarms. For the great factories of the Ruhr Valley were as busy as they had been before the First World War. After 1919, the Western Allies had ordered Krupp, the mighty munitions maker, to get out of gun-making. The Krupp managers disobeyed the order. Later, once war had enveloped Europe once again, Gustav Krupp, the owner, bragged that "the basic principle of armament and turret design for tanks had already been worked out in 1926. ... Of the guns being used in 1939 to 1941, the most important ones were already fully complete in 1933."

Much the same was true of I. G. Farben, the chemical giant. During the First World War, Farben scientists had figured out how to make synthetic nitrates, vital ingredients of explosives; the British blockade had shut off shipments of mined nitrates from Chile. The Allies had prohibited Farben from reentering the synthetic business.

So much for the Allies. Germany's national defense called for huge supplies of oil and rubber. As early as the mid-1920s, Farben had figured out how to make gasoline from coal. Later it discovered that coal and other raw materials that abounded in Germany could yield artificial rubber.

During the First World War, the British embargo had really crippled the German war machine. Now, with regard to both oil and rubber, Germany was self-sufficient. That left one ingredient to go: iron ore. Germany had no significant iron deposits: The Reich had to import the ore from Swedish mines through Narvik, a port in northern Norway. Hitler would solve the problem of depending on iron imports: He invaded Norway.

> **Bet You Didn't Know**
>
> Were Germany's top leaders familiar with the doctrines of John Maynard Keynes, the British economist? Keynes had diagnosed the depression as a case of shrunken consumption. His remedy was massive spending by the biggest consumer of all, government. Hitler, Himmler, and the gang probably knew nothing of Keynes. Unwittingly or not, though, they put Keynesianism into practice. Deficit spending for the purpose of rearming the *Reich* produced jobs, thousands of them; by the mid-1930s joblessness in Germany was gone.

Allied Responses to Germany's Rearmament

Early in 1934, the Reich Defense Council had sent out contracts to more than 200,000 munitions plants. The hope was that these plants could operate in secret. But secrecy became hopeless. By the end of the year, the Allies were fully aware of what Germany was doing.

But the British and the French differed on what to do. London was prepared to accept Germany's rearmament as a *fait accompli*—an accomplished fact that no one could do anything about. In the spring of 1934, the British foreign secretary, Sir John Simon, even proposed an arms parity treaty to Germany. The French were aghast. The treaty did not come into existence (although Germany and Great Britain did sign a naval limitation treaty).

But Hitler saw in the British attitude a chance to score a diplomatic victory. In January 1935, voters in the Saar, that little coal-rich corner of the Ruhr Valley where the Rhine turns northward, elected by a margin of 10 to 1 to return to the Reich. Hitler used the occasion to state publicly that he would make no claims to Alsace and Lorraine. Bismarck had taken those territories, Versailles had given them back to France, and so Hitler was relinquishing a claim to what he didn't have anyway. But his pledge created a sense of relief, at least in London.

Hitler's "Peace"

Hitler's moment had come. On March 16, 1935, he formally announced the creation of an army of half a million men. He was openly defying the military restrictions of the Treaty of Versailles. But, he said, Germany was not looking for war. And in a May 21 speech to the *Reichstag* (meeting in its restored building) he underlined his peaceful intentions. Following is the heart of that speech:

> The blood shed on the European continent in the course of the last 300 years bears no proportion to the national result of the events. In the end France has remained France, Germany Germany, Poland Poland, and Italy Italy. What dynastic egotism, political passion, and patriotic blindness have attained in the way of apparently far-reaching political changes by shedding rivers of blood has, as regards national feeling, done no more than touched the skin of the nations. It has not substantially altered their fundamental characters. If these states had applied merely a fraction of their sacrifices to wiser purposes the success would certainly have been greater and more permanent. ... National Socialist Germany wants peace because of its fundamental convictions. And it wants peace also owing to the realization of the simple primitive fact that no war would be likely essentially to alter the distress in Europe. ... The principal effect of every war is to destroy the flower of the nation. ... Germany needs peace and desires peace. ...

Did Hitler believe this? Was he sincere? Who can say? But the cold, hard fact is that if Hitler wanted to avoid a war, he took steps that could not have been better calculated to produce a war. The first of those steps came the following winter.

The Versailles Treaty, let's recall, not only had mandated Germany's disarmament but also had separated East Prussia from Germany proper, forbidding a union of Germany and Austria, and the demilitarizing the Rhineland.

In the thinking of most Germans, and not just Hitler, the Rhineland had a special significance: It was the region that historically France had used to weaken Germany.

Hitler's action was immensely popular in the Third Reich. He wanted the Rhineland under his complete authority.

The Occupation of the Rhineland

In April 1935, Jean Dobler, the French consul in Cologne (Köln) noticed that everywhere he walked or drove, through the narrow medieval streets of the city, high along the banks of the Rhine, or out into the fertile German countryside, he saw swarms of men erecting barracks, building depots, and laying out airfields. All this was just what the Rhineland would need to shelter a German force of occupation.

Back in the consulate, Dobler fired off two cables to Paris, warning his government of the developments. He received no acknowledgement.

On November 21, 1935, officials in the French embassy in Berlin were frowning with puzzlement. The French ambassador, André François-Poncet, had just rushed in from a session with Hitler. Entering his private office, the ambassador left the strictest orders that he was not to be disturbed.

Obviously, the officials remarked, the ambassador was greatly alarmed. Was it something Hitler had said?

It was. Hitler had launched into a tirade against the recently signed Franco–Soviet Pact: The French and the Russians had agreed, in principle at least, to resurrect the old pre–First World War alliance aimed against Germany. Here, in Hitler's eyes at least, was the old encirclement that Kaiser Wilhelm II had seen as so threatening. Like Wilhelm, Hitler had intimated that he was going to take preemptive action.

Ensconced in his office, François-Poncet cabled Paris with a warning. Like Consul Dobler, however, he received no indication that Paris would act.

Weeks passed. On the last day of 1935, in a black and bitter mood, the ambassador repeated his message. Once again, silence.

François-Poncet's Plea for Peace

On March 2, 1936, François-Poncet motored again to Hitler's chancellery. He wanted to plead for peace. SS guards outside Hitler's office requested that he wait in the antechamber. The Führer, they explained, was in an urgent meeting.

Suddenly the door of Hitler's office flew open and through it stepped a figure familiar to the French ambassador: General Werner von Blomberg, the German chief of staff. He was obviously upset. Then the French ambassador gained admission into Hitler's inner sanctum. France had no intention of attacking Germany, François-Poncet began to say—but Hitler cut him short. The Franco–Soviet Pact, he screamed, was criminal, a grave menace to Germany.

François-Poncet thought it useless to stay and rose from his chair. He tried once more: France wants peace, he said, not war. He put on his coat. But then he paused. Hitler had spoken his name.

All smiles and charm now, Hitler had one small favor to ask: Would the French ambassador keep his visit a secret for just a few days?

François-Poncet soon learned why Hitler had made such a peculiar request. General von Blomberg had gone straight to his senior generals with the Führer's orders to mobilize the troops.

The French Sit Idly By ...

Five days later, on March 7, 1936, on the pretext that France was about to attack, the German army was to march into the Rhineland. The generals protested. Surely, they argued, the *Wehrmacht* (the army) was still too weak to risk a war. Yes, von Blomberg admitted, it was a considerable gamble. But he would send only a token force into the Rhineland, and if the French counterattacked, he would retreat immediately.

So it was that, on the chilly, misty morning of March 7, 1936, helmeted and gray-coated German troops marched across the *Hohenzollern* Bridge over the Rhine. Even the name of the bridge, that of the family of the exiled Kaiser Wilhelm II, was in keeping with Hitler's use of symbols But the march was more than symbolic. In utter violation of the Versailles Treaty, Hitler was putting his guns and his men directly on the border of France.

Von Blomberg did not have to retreat. On the morning of the occupation, the French ambassador to London scurried to No. 10 Downing Street, only to find that Prime Minister Stanley Baldwin and the rest of the British cabinet had scattered for a week-end in the countryside. Then, at a dinner party the next week, Baldwin told Pierre

Flandin, the French foreign minister, that "if there is even one chance in a hundred that war would follow [a counterattack by France in the Rhineland] I have not the right to commit England. England is simply not in a state to go to war." He was leaving the job to France and France did not move.

The French, to be sure, did a good deal of talking. They conferred with each other, they negotiated with their allies, and they orated in the chambers of the League of Nations. But when the three battalions of Germans marched into the Rhineland, the French failed to act. Had they done so, Hitler later admitted, "we would have had to withdraw with our tails between our legs."

War did not break out, not then in 1936. The Third Reich nonetheless celebrated the occupation of the Rhineland as if it had been a great victory. As if to demonstrate that Germany was once again a great power, Berlin staged the 1936 Olympic Games. There was considerable prestige attached to hosting the Olympics. But the Olympics also would show—to Hitler surely they would show—the racial superiority of Germany's Aryan athletes.

The Nazi Olympics: Symbol of Virility

As athletes from around the world gathered in Berlin in the summer of 1936 for the XIth Olympiad of the modern era, the rulers of the Third Reich were nervous. Much of their propaganda had stressed the superiority of "pure" Germans in all aspects of life, including sports. Since the first modern games, held in 1896, however, the dominant national group had been the Americans. The leadership in Berlin could have explained that fact away by pointing to the large size of the population of the United States and to the large part of that population descended from Germany. By 1936, however, many on the United States team were African Americans.

To Nazi ideologists, black people were subhuman. What if they would walk away with large numbers of medals? How could that be explained away?

Or maybe it didn't have to be explained away. Perhaps, if those dark-skinned Americans won too many events, the Germans could rig the scoring systems to deprive them of their earned rewards. Would the Nazis pollute the Olympics, as they had polluted everything else in Germany? Sure.

The Olympic Setting

The Nazis were determined to use the Olympics as propaganda, perhaps the ultimate form of propaganda, intended to legitimatize the Nazi regime in the eyes of the people. Back in February 1935, the government had opened the Olympic Exhibition in the German museum in Berlin. The exhibit put on display photographs of Germany's most noted athletes as well as models of the yet-to-be-erected Olympic Stadium, the Olympic Village, and other such facilities. On view were also photographs of the ruins of the Olympic Stadium in ancient Greece and plaster models of supposed Greek athletes.

Germans for generations had venerated the Greeks as the master race of classical antiquity. The regime, therefore, was creating a direct visual link between the ancient Hellenes and the modern Germans—both superior people.

Remaining in Berlin for several weeks, the exposition traveled to all the other major cities. So well before the opening of the games, urbanites could share in the impending excitement.

True to their origins, the Nazis also made special efforts to spread the excitement into the rural regions. Throughout the winter and spring of 1936, a caravan called the *Olympia-Zug* descended upon towns; this was an extraordinary event. The procession consisted of four huge Mercedes-Benz trucks, each flying swastikas and hauling two trailers. Arriving in a town early in the morning, the trucks would stop in the plaza, parking on the cobbled streets and under medieval gables. Workers then would stretch the trailers—built like accordions—so that townspeople could enter a series of exhibition rooms. Inside, spectators could watch movies about the Olympics and gawk at the copies of classical artifacts.

> **Terms and Translations**
>
> **Olympia-Zug.** As in the English word *tug*, **zug** has to do with pulling or hauling. So it can refer to a train or a truck; the **Olympia-Zug** was a caravan of trucks.

Admission to the expositions was free, for the government did not want to leave anyone out, and the caravan was universally a hit. It usually stayed in the same town for three days. This was in an era before television, of course, and even before the widespread use of radios, and so the locals had never seen anything like it. The *Zug* tugged its trailers all over Germany, all the way from the North Sea to the Bavarian Alps.

The message was always the same: The Olympiad of 1936 in Berlin was going to put on display (for all the world to see) the virility of the German people. Every German was invited to witness the games.

The Olympic Complex

In Berlin itself, the construction of the Olympic complex was proceeding rapidly. Located on the western edge of the German capital, the stadium was the largest that had been built anywhere. Even so, it occupied no more than one twentieth of the area of the total complex. Surrounding the stadium was a huge array of practice fields, racetracks, parking lots, dormitories for the athletes, and even a new subway station.

Connecting the compound to Berlin itself was also a special boulevard, called the *Via Triumphalis* (Triumphal Way): The Nazis were trumpeting what they claimed to be Germany's derivation from the Roman Empire.

The avenue ran almost 10 miles from the kaiser's palace and the *Lustgarten* (Pleasure Park) along *Unter den Linden* (Under the Linden Trees) and through the *Brandenburger Tor* (Gate) straight out to the western suburbs. Swastikas lined every yard of the boulevard.

The Olympic procession marched along this boulevard. And when the athletes reached the front gate of the stadium, over which hung the five interlocking circles of the Olympic banner, members of a German brass band stood behind their music stands to intone the official welcome.

The German Caesar

The Olympiad was scheduled to open on July 31, 1936. At first, however, the rituals had nothing to do with sports. Josef Goebbels had seen the Olympics as a chance to stage the greatest Nazi show yet seen, and the star of the show was Adolf Hitler.

Garbed in the brown uniform of a Storm Trooper and wearing high leather boots, Hitler left the chancellery that day in an open touring car. Behind him followed a long row of Mercedes convertibles that bore various dignitaries, politicians, and Olympic officials. The column moved slowly along the *Via Triumphalis;* some 40,000 Nazi guardsmen held back the crowd that lined the boulevard 20 to 30 people deep.

When the procession reached the stadium, Hitler stepped down from his automobile, greeted the rows of assembled athletes, who were standing at attention, and then walked alone through the Marathon Gate. As he emerged into the stadium, facing the huge crowd of spectators, a fanfare of 30 trumpets announced his arrival. As he took his seat of honor, Richard Strauss, the aged composer, conducted an immense orchestra and a chorus of 3,000 voices in performing "*Deutschland über alles,*" the "*Horst Wessel Lied*" (the "Horst Wessel Song"), and a version of the "Olympic Hymn," composed by Strauss himself.

The music stopped. Approaching Hitler's booth, a small girl, blond and wearing a blue dress, handed the Führer a bouquet of flowers. Seated in the stadium, a multitude of 100,000 persons sighed tenderly: Hitler, after all, was known for his love of children.

A huge bell announced the start of the parade of the athletes. As always it was a colorful event. Some details, however, were out of the ordinary. Passing below the Führer's booth, the Austrian team gave the Nazi salute; the crown cheered loudly. To the surprise of almost everyone, the Bulgarians goose-stepped by. The French gave a salute that looked like the Nazi one, although they claimed later that it was the raised Olympic salute. The British did not lift their eyes to the "Tribune of Honor" and got booed.

Last in the alphabetical list of the foreign teams was the *Vereinigten Staaten*, the United States. On passing below the booth, all the previous groups had lowered their national flags. The Americans refused to do so.

Hitler didn't have time to put on one of his rages. Just as the undipped American flag passed beneath his reviewing stand, the German team, striding eight abreast, emerged from the Marathon Gate. They were uniformed in white and all wore yachting caps—perhaps in tribute to the yacht-loving Kaiser Wilhelm II. As they marched onto the track, the musicians under Richard Strauss' baton again performed "Deutschland" and the "Horst Wessel" song. As the German team reached a point on the track directly below Hitler's booth, the entire body of spectators rose from their stadium seats, gave the "Heil Hitler" salute, and held until the German team had taken its place at the far end of the field.

The spectacle had been staged as a homage to Hitler, sometimes by this point called the German Caesar. The word *kaiser* was derived from Caesar. The Berlin Olympiad opened as a salute to the new German monarch.

Standing in his booth, Hitler walked to a microphone. For once, he had no speech to make. He simply declared: "I announce as opened the Games of Berlin, celebrating the 11th Olympiad in the modern era."

Let the Games Begin

After the opening ceremonies, Germans were confident that their athletes were going to overwhelm all others, even the mighty Americans. Some of the German athletes, to be sure, did superbly well, helped by Germany's rigging of some of the scoring. Even the American point tabulation put Germany in first place overall.

For Hitler, though, such rankings were not enough. He wanted the athletes of the Reich to demonstrate their superiority to those of "lesser" races. Much to Hitler's consternation, the star of the 1936 Olympics was an African American student from Ohio State University, Jesse Owens. During the track and field competitions, held between August 2 and August 9, 1936, Owens swept to victory in every event he entered.

Such success was too much for Hitler. As the one who presided over the Berlin games, the Führer had personally awarded the medals and shaken the hands of the winners. But not the hand of Jesse Owens. Hitler snubbed the true hero of the 1936 Berlin Olympics. Untroubled, he next set out to annex Austria.

The Least You Need to Know

♦ Hitler's first step in regaining Germany's former rank as a great power was that of rearmament. The Versailles Treaty had demanded that Germany's military force remain small, but, believing correctly that the British and the French in the 1930s would not enforce the treaty, he proceeded to rebuild the armed forces.

♦ The occupation of the Rhineland, carried out in 1936, was also a violation of the treaty. Hitler again calculated rightly that the Allies would stand aside.

♦ The Olympic Games, held in Berlin in the summer of 1936, were intended—at least by the Nazi regime—to demonstrate the physical superiority of the "pure" Aryan "race." On the whole, the Germans did field the best team. But through his own victories, Jesse Owens, an African American, shattered the Nazi race theories.

Chapter 15

The Annexation of Austria: 1936–1938

In This Chapter

♦ Germany's involvement in the Spanish Civil War and its newfound air-strike capabilities

♦ Written accounts of Hitler's intentions to take over Austria

♦ Austria's fall to Nazi Germany

♦ The union of Hitler's homeland with Germany

♦ *Kristallnacht*, Hitler's revenge against the Jews

In a sense, 1936 was a pivotal year. With Germany's rearmament, the occupation of the Rhineland, and the display of Teutonic virility at the Olympic Games, we might say that the post-war (First World War) period was over. We might also say that the pre-war (Second World War) period had begun. The Rhineland invasion had been peaceful. But Hitler chose to intervene militarily in the Spanish Civil War, and that intervention was anything but peaceful. It also revealed the appalling violence of which Nazi Germany was capable.

Dress Rehearsal in Spain

The Spanish Civil War (1936–1939) may seem remote from the subject of Nazi Germany. But it led to an understanding between Nazi Germany and Fascist Italy, an *entente* that led directly to Hitler's annexation of Austria. So let's take a quick look at the causes and consequences of the conflict in Spain.

Pre–Civil War Conflict in Spain

Back in 1931, a quick revolution in Spain tossed Alfonso XIII off the throne and brought about the establishment of a democratic Spanish Republic. That republic, however, was even weaker than its relative in Weimar. Below the seemingly peaceful surface, great tensions erupted. Catalan, the region around Barcelona, demanded its independence, and even though the government in Madrid granted some local freedom, the freedom drive continued. The peasants wanted their own land, and the government broke up some of the larger estates, although not enough to satisfy the peasants. At the same time, the great landowners were outraged and swore revenge against the leaders of the country. The government also represented the many Spaniards who were anti-Catholic, while the landowners were adherents of the Church.

In 1933, then, the government fell into the hands of the landowners, the Catholic clergy, and their conservative allies. They overturned the land reforms, crushed strikes among coal miners, and brutally repressed the Catalan independence movement.

February 1936 saw a general election in Spain. The polling pitted against each other the two sides of the Spanish split: on the left, republicans, socialists, anarchists, and Communists all joined in what was called a Popular Front; on the right, monarchists, clerics, army officers, and landowners, who together were known as the Falangists or Spanish Fascists. The Popular Front won the election.

That victory was wholly unacceptable to the Falangists. Shortly after the election results were known, certain officers associated with the right plotted a takeover of the government. Their leader was a general named Francisco Franco.

Spaniards Say "*No Pasaran*" to Francisco Franco

A De Havilland Dragon–Rapide, a light airplane, had been parked for several days at an airstrip in the Canary Islands, just off the southwestern tip of Morocco. Its papers indicated that it had been chartered by some British tourists who were on vacation. Early in the afternoon of July 18, 1936, however, and much to the surprise of the English pilot, three Spanish men, dressed in civilian suits, came aboard and ordered him to fly to Spanish Morocco, immediately south of Morocco. The destination was Tetuán, the Spanish colonial capital.

Cecil Bebb, the pilot, was in for another surprise. Once over land and nearing Tetuán, he was told to fly low enough to let his passengers get a good look at a group of men gathered on the runway. Then, realizing that those below were friendly, one of the men, obviously the leader, had the pilot land. While the airplane was taxiing to a stop, the man who was the leader changed from his suit into the khaki uniform of a Spanish general. He was Francisco Franco and he stepped out of the plane to a flourish of salutes from those by the runway.

Bet You Didn't Know

Franco had arrived to lead some 24,000 Spanish troops on a march to overthrow the Spanish Republic. Thus began the Spanish Civil War.

Faced with the rebellion, the republican government in Madrid tried to purchase weapons abroad. Neither Paris nor London, however, was willing to authorize such sales: The French and British governments feared that the civil war in Spain would spread into a wider war in Europe. In fact, at the request of the British and the French, 27 other governments, including that of the United States, laid embargoes on weapons sales to Spain and refused to take sides in the conflict.

The policy of nonintervention, however, was a farce. Three countries (the Soviet Union, Fascist Italy, and Nazi Germany) all sent military equipment to Spain. The Soviets sided with the Loyalists, that is, supporters of the government; Germany and Italy aligned themselves with the Franco-led rebels.

For about a year, even with German help, Franco's rebels failed to make much headway. They eventually ringed Madrid with a siege while German bombers dropped their loads on the city. The explosions, however, did not cause the morale of the capital to fold. Quite the contrary. The determination of the Madrid residents to hold on only stiffened. Their resolve was reflected in the slogan, "No Pasaran!" (They shall not pass!).

The city dwellers heard those words chanted regularly over the radio by Dolores Ibarruri, called *La Pasionaria*, "the impassioned one." Once a staunch Catholic, she had become a Communist. Spanish workers viewed her as a revolutionary saint. She was the real inspiration of Madrid's resistance.

The Raid on Guernica

By the end of March 1937, Franco realized that to conquer Spain he would need to do something new. He turned to his German advisers for their thoughts. Those thoughts were simple: Starve Madrid into submission. Undoubtedly, the German officers in Spain remembered well the effects on their own country of the British naval blockade in the First World War. Take the farmlands! Take the coal and iron mines in the north, up in Basque territory! If you can't overrun Madrid yet, go after Bilbao, up on the Bay of Biscay! Bilbao was a major industrial center. Take Durango! Durango also was a northern industrial city. Let us—the Germans—use those cities as test sites for a new technique of warfare that we have developed, the combined use of incendiary and high-explosive bombs!

Franco went north. As he did so, a German air unit called the Condor Legion followed along. It hit Bilbao and Durango. Then, for no reasons of military necessity, the Condor Legion unloaded on Guernica.

About 18 miles east of Bilbao, Guernica was a town of some 7,000 inhabitants. Isolated for centuries by the mountains of northern Spain, it was the cultural and religious center of the Basque region. Full of churches and convents, the town centered on a large plaza, a gathering place formed by a railroad station, a hotel, a public school, and the municipal hall. Right in the middle of the plaza stood the sacred oak of Guernica, a symbol of Basque independence. Early in 1937, the tree bloomed. Some of the town's people thought it a bad omen. They were right.

At 4 P.M. on April 26, 1937, two nuns went up into a church in the center of the town and began to pull the bell. They called down, *"Aviones! Aviones!"* (Airplanes! Airplanes!) Sure enough, in just a moment bombers from the Condor Legion were overhead. Bombs fell into the plaza in front of the railway station. Wrote one survivor, "A group of women and children were lifted high into the air, maybe 20 feet or so, and they started to break up. Legs, arms, heads, and bits and pieces flying everywhere."

Before nightfall, eight more waves of planes from the Condor Legion showed up in the sky over Guernica. By the time they left, roughly 2,000 persons were dead and all the buildings around the plaza lay smashed to bits.

In Berlin, Hitler knew that he had a public relations disaster on his hands; Berlin sent the Condor Legion strict orders to shut up about the attack.

The news got out anyway. Although Franco's propagandists claimed that the town had been destroyed by retreating Loyalist troops, foreign sympathizers of the Spanish republic, charged Franco with war crimes. And in Paris, a Spanish artist named Pablo Picasso painted *Guernica*, a classic antiwar statement.

For Hitler, however, the raid on Guernica had a positive effect. Up to that point, Mussolini had regarded Hitler with a mixture of pity and contempt: He had seen the Führer as a clownish upstart, not to be taken altogether seriously. Now, though, *Il Duce*, "The Leader," as Mussolini called himself, began to feel the tremors of fear.

As we have seen in Chapter 14, Mussolini reacted with rage to the Dollfuss murder. He felt close to the Dollfuss family and, just as important, he regarded Austria as lying within Italy's sphere of influence. Remember: During its wars of unification in the 1860s, Italy had expelled the Austrians from Lombardy and Venetia; then, with the Paris peace talks of 1919, Italy had acquired Trieste, which had been the major Austro–Hungarian port on the Adriatic. Like a lot of other Italians, Mussolini had thought of Austria as almost an Italian colony.

But not after Guernica. Despite his imperial pretences, Mussolini knew that in battle Italy would be no match for Germany. If Hitler wanted Austria, Mussolini would let it be known, he could have it.

The Hossbach Memorandum

So now, well before the advent of the Second World War, we come to Nazi Germany's first advance beyond the country's traditional borders. And we have to face the question: What was Hitler really after?

On the afternoon of November 5, 1937, six officials were summoned for a secret meeting in Hitler's office at the Chancellery. In attendance were Field Marshal Werner von Blomberg, commander in chief of the German army; General Werner von Fritsch; Chief Admiral Erich Räder; Hermann Göring, head of the *Luftwaffe* (the air force); and Baron Konstantin von Neurath, the foreign minister. The five men represented respectively the army, the navy, the air force, and the diplomatic corps. The sixth man was a Colonel Friedrich Hossbach. A staff officer assigned to Hitler, his function at the meeting was to take notes.

Seated at a big round table, Hitler as usual did most of the talking. He began by harping as of old on Germany's need for *Lebensraum*, "living space." But expansion where? For a while he talked about overseas colonies. But these, he thought, might be too expensive to acquire and maintain. So expansion—a necessity—would have to take place in Europe.

Where in Europe? In countries right next to the Reich. He mentioned Austria and Czechoslovakia. Close by, those countries would be sources of food for Nazi Germany and they would offer space for emigration, once Austria and Czechoslovakia had been cleared of racial "undesirables."

But there was a problem. "Germany," according to the Hossbach memorandum of the meeting, "had to reckon with two hate-inspired antagonists, Britain and France. … Germany's problem could only be solved by means of force and this was never without risk." Hitler added that to both London and Paris "a strong German colossus in the center of Europe would be intolerable."

Some of the men around the table were shocked. If Hitler was talking about going to war, a few at least believed, he was putting Germany on the road to disaster. Fritsch pointed out that the Czechoslovakian defenses were potent indeed. Blomberg contended that France was superior to Germany militarily even if Paris took on Italy at the same time. And Neurath saw no great likelihood of a war between France and Italy.

The meeting lasted until after dark. Waving the doubts aside, Hitler ended with the comment that he might move "as early as 1938." That, the men in the room realized, would be only a few months away.

Those who had raised doubts were in for rude surprises. Within three months of the meeting, Blomberg, Fritsch, and Neurath were all out of office. Neurath's replacement as foreign minister was Joachim von Ribbentrop (in this case the "von" was phony), whose qualifications for the job were that he had been a champagne salesman, could speak several languages, and was Hitler's utter toady.

The removal of Blomberg, Fritsch, and Neurath took Hitler three months. Blomberg, for example, was popular in the army and Hitler could not get rid of him until Gesta-po spies discovered that the general, a widower, in early 1938 married a young woman who had been a prostitute. The Gestapo framed Fritsch on a charge of homosexuality. He demanded a trial and for once a Nazi court handed down a verdict of innocent. By then, however, Hitler had forced the general's resignation.

With the three dissenters from the November 1937 meeting out of the way, Hitler on February 4, 1938, had a decree broadcast by radio throughout the Third Reich. It stated: "From now on I personally take over the command of all the armed forces."

Consider Hitler's position at that moment: He must have thought he was on the top of the world. He had long since crushed the German left. He had made a mockery of those institutions, the press, the schools, and the courts, that in the Western democracies often stood independent of state power. Many Germans still attended their churches, although hundreds of Protestant clergy, who had refused to remove crosses from their churches or to renounce the divinity of Jesus, were without jobs or in jail. In the Catholic south, anti-Nazi priests had been jailed on charges of pederasty. As we know in America today, sometimes such charges are valid. In Nazi Germany, however, they were attached only to those who opposed the regime.

Strikes and labor walkouts were strictly forbidden. But then the workers were relatively content. Hitler, the would-be architect, had authorized all sorts of public works projects; those, plus rearmament, provided jobs, jobs a-plenty.

Hitler, in short, was in command of the home front. Abroad, as we know from the Hossbach memorandum, he worried about France and Great Britain. But he was confident that neither of those powers regarded Austria as an area of serious interest.

Hitler's Threats Against Austria

All through 1937, Austria's Nazis, with money and encouragement from Berlin, renewed their terrorizing tactics. Bombs went off all over the country and violent demonstrations gave rise to the rumor that the Nazis were planning to kill the new chancellor, Kurt von Schuschnigg, as they had murdered Dollfuss, his predecessor.

Against this background of intimidation, Hitler ordered the head of the government of Austria, to meet with him in the Alpine retreat at Berchtesgaden. The session took place on February 12, 1938.

When they met in the frosty mountain air, Schuschnigg, the possessor of upper-class Austrian politeness, commented eloquently on the beauty of the view. But Hitler was not of an upper-class Austrian background. Pointedly, he interrupted, saying that he wasn't there to discuss scenery. Then the Führer launched into a tirade:

> You have done everything to avoid a friendly policy. … The whole history of Austria is just one long act of high treason. That was so in the past and is no better today. This historical paradox must now reach its overdue end. And I can tell you right now, Herr Schuschnigg, that I am absolutely determined to make an end of all this. The German Reich is one of the great powers, and nobody will raise his voice if it settles its border problems.

Hitler was talking about annexing Austria. Schuschnigg was taken aback, asking just when Austria had been so treasonous.

Hitler ignored the question. Resuming his tirade, he proclaimed: "I have a historic mission, and this mission I will fulfill because Providence has destined me to do so. … Who is not with me will be crushed … I have chosen the most difficult road that any German ever took; I have made the greatest achievements in the history of Germany, greater than any other German. And not by force, mind you. I am carried along by the love of my people …"

Saying that he was willing to accept all that, Schuschnigg offered to reach an understanding. But an understanding was not what Hitler had in mind:

Listen, you don't really think you can move a single stone in Austria without my hearing about it the next day, do you? ... I have only to give an order, and in one single night all your ridiculous defense mechanisms will be blown to bits. You don't seriously believe that you can stop me for half an hour, do you? ... I would very much like to save Austria from such a fate, because such an action would mean blood. After the army, my SS, and the Austrian Legion [Austrian Nazis] would move in, nobody could stop their just revenge—not even I.

Hitler then laid out specific demands: In fulfilling them, Austria in effect would be giving up its sovereignty. The Austrian Nazi Party, which was outlawed (at least on paper), must be made legal. Arthur Seyss-Inquart, an Austrian attorney who was already state councilor in the Austrian cabinet (the position was roughly equivalent to attorney general), was to be made minister of the interior, in charge of all law enforcement. Nazis were to head up the ministries of defense and finance.

Hitler wanted it all. In Austria, Nazis would control the courts, the police, the army, the navy, and the money. What else was left? That was Schuschnigg's question, only he didn't dare ask it. Instead, completely browbeaten, he signed a piece of paper agreeing to everything.

Austria's "Resistance"

Back in Vienna, however, Chancellor Schuschnigg decided to stand up to Hitler. On February 24, 1938, in a speech to the Austrian parliament (it was called the *Bundestag* and—we must make no mistake about this—its members were loyal supporters of a one-party, dictatorial regime), he declared: "Thus far and no farther!" Austria, he proclaimed, would never give up its independence. He ended with a stirring chant: "Red-White-Red [the Austrian national colors] until we're dead!"

Terms and Translations

Red, in German, is *rot;* dead is *tot.* So Schuschnigg's "red-dead" rhyme worked in German as well as in English.

The response to the speech? That very day, in Graz, a town in southern Austria almost at the border of Yugoslavia, a huge crowd of Nazis marched into the square, pulled down the red-white-red Austrian flag, and ran up the German swastika.

Normal governance in Austria began to collapse. As minister of the interior, Seyss-Inquart, the first of the major collaborators, did nothing to quell further Nazi demonstrations. Alarmed, lots of Austrians pulled their money out of the banks and made plans to flee the country. Tourists suddenly stopped coming; from New York, Arturo Toscanini, the famed conductor, cabled that "because of political developments in

Austria," he would not appear at the Salzburg Festival; each summer the festival drew tens of thousands of visitors. Foreign firms withdrew their investments. Suddenly, lots of people in Austria were out of work. Austria stood on the brink of economic disaster. And all the while the Nazis were marching in the streets.

Supporting Actors

Desperate, Schuschnigg did something that played right into Hitler's hands. As chancellor, he had sworn to defend Austria's sovereignty. But that did not mean he was a left-winger. Quite the contrary. Assuming power after the murder of Dollfuss, von Schuschnigg had clapped lots of left-wingers, workers, trade union leaders, strikers, and Social Democrats, in jail. Like Hitler, he believed in authoritarian, one-party, right-wing rule. On March 4, however, he let the leftists out of their cells.

Now the streets of Vienna and other cities were full of leftists, eager and willing do battle with the Nazis. What they wanted in turn from the chancellor was a chance to reform their own, Social Democratic, political party and run candidates for seats in the parliament. Believing that he had no choice, Schuschnigg scheduled a nationwide election to be held on March 13.

Hitler Moves

When Hitler heard news of the election plan, he flew into a rage. For what happened as a result of that rage, we have an entry from the diary of General Alfried von Jodl, chief of operations in the German army: "Führer is determined not to tolerate [the Austrian election]. The same night, March 9 to 10, he calls for Göring. General v. Reichenau is called back from Cairo Olympic Committee, General v. Schobert [commander of the military district on the Austrian border] is ordered to come ..." Hitler was gathering his top generals in preparation for action.

The next morning, March 10, Hitler told them of his decision. He was going to launch a military occupation of Austria.

Certain that France and Great Britain would do nothing to stop him, Hitler saw only one question: How would Mussolini react? A telephone call from Philip of Hesse, a German prince who had married a daughter of the late king of Italy, provided the answer. Mussolini did not object at all.

Over the wire Hitler almost gushed: "Please tell Mussolini I will never forget him for this ... Never, never, never ... I shall stick with him whatever may happen, even if the whole world gangs up on him."

The Nazi Invasion of Austria

At 5:30 A.M., March 11, 1938, Schuschnigg's bedside telephone rang. On the line was his chief of police. The officer reported that the Austrian–German border at Salzburg had just been closed. Dressing quickly, the chancellor rushed to his office. There he learned from intelligence reports that German units in the Bavarian military district had mobilized. Their destination, presumably, was Austria.

At about 10 A.M., Schussnigg had a visitor, his own minister of the interior, Seyss-Inquart. The latter produced an ultimatum from Berlin. Schuschnigg must resign and cancel the election. He had until noon to telephone Göring, saying that he had taken these steps. Otherwise Germany would invade.

Time was short. The chancellor made some quick inquiries. Could he throw a police cordon around Vienna? The answer came back: So many of the policemen were Nazis that members of a cordon would welcome the invaders. Could he make an appeal to world opinion? From the foreign ministry, also under Nazi control, came the sneering news that Mussolini would not lift a finger—nor would the British and the French. And Stalin would do nothing to help his own leftist allies in Vienna.

So that was that. At about 4 P.M., Schuschnigg canceled the voting and resigned. But he had missed the ultimatum's deadline. So Germany invaded anyway.

The invasion was not much of an invasion. When the German troops crossed the frontier at Salzburg on Saturday, March 12, the townspeople welcomed them with flowers and Nazi flags. A group of locals tore down the border station that had separated the two countries. And later in the day, when Hitler's Mercedes limousine entered Austria, heading along the country road toward Vienna, peasants by the roadsides scooped up pieces of earth the tires had touched.

When Hitler reached Vienna in the late afternoon, he made the inevitable speech. "I believe," he claimed, "that it was God's will to send a boy from here into the Reich, to let him grow up, to raise him to be the leader of the nation so as to enable him to lead back his homeland into the Reich." Almost immediately, Hitler banned the use of the word *österreich*, Austria. Austria was now officially part of the Third Reich.

Austria Under the Nazis

Wholly submerged into Germany—a plebiscite taken shortly after the Anschluss (the Union) had 99 percent of the Austrians voting for such unity, surprise! surprise!—Austria as a country ceased to exist. For a short time, the Germans called it *Ostmark* (East boundary or frontier, as when you mark something off), but even that sounded too dignified for a noncountry. So they simply referred to Austria by its various *Gaue* (districts), such as Salzburg or the Tyrol. Vienna became just a regional administrative center, indeed an increasingly shabby, down-at-the-heels city.

Socialists and Communists were publicly whipped. Jews were made to scrub the streets and clean latrines. Kurt von Schuschnigg ended up in the concentration camp at Dachau, not to be freed until the arrival of American troops in 1945.

Overseeing the former chancellor's arrest and shipment to Dachau was Reinhard Heydrich, the number two man in Himmler's SS. Over the course of the next two years, Vienna would see a good deal of Heydrich. For the Holocaust, in which Heydrich would play a major part, was now truly underway.

Bet You Didn't Know

Hitler was allowing Vienna to rot away. It was his revenge for the way he had been treated, or thought he had been treated, during his earlier years as a bum in the city.

Kristallnacht

On November 7, 1938, Herschel Grynszpan, an unemployed, 17-year-old Polish Jew living in Paris, entered the German embassy and shot to death one of the officials working there. The youth's motivation, he said, was revenge for the way Nazi Germany was treating his fellow Jews. When word of the assassination reached Berlin, the infuriated Hitler ordered the worst *pogram* in Germany to that date.

Hitler ordered the punishment of all German Jews and it is fair to say that most Gentile Germans responded with eagerness. Within just three days of Grynszpan's confession, vandals systematically hit synagogues and Jewish stores and homes.

Because of the shards from broken windows that littered the streets, the orgy came to be known as *Kristallnacht*, or Crystal Night. Ninety-one Jews were killed, 20,000 were arrested, and a fine leveled against all German Jews came to one million marks. And when Jews tried to collect insurance for all the damage, the Nazis confiscated the payments. After all, went the official excuse, if the Jews hadn't been there, nothing would have happened.

Terms and Translations

Pogrom is a Russian word meaning "like thunder." It is an organized and often officially sanctioned massacre or persecution of a minority group, especially against the Jews.

The next step in Hitler's plan was Czechoslovakia. Like Austria, Czechoslovakia had a German-speaking population. Unlike Austria, however, that population was a minority. Thus, with the impending annexation of all Czechoslovakia, Hitler could no longer claim that he was simply trying to unify German-speaking peoples.

The Least You Need to Know

- The horrors of the Spanish Civil War may seem a bit removed from the subject of Nazi Germany. But they weren't really: At Guernica, Nazi bombers inflicted hideous, and wholly uncalled for, suffering.

- As the Hossbach memorandum, eventually captured by the Allies, revealed, Hitler after the Rhineland occupation was definitely planning conquests in Central and Eastern Europe.

- The first step in that drive was to be the annexation of Austria. Upon that bloodless conquest, Austria as such ceased to exist. Its nonstatus as a country, however, hardly stopped the Nazi persecution of the Jews.

Chapter 16

The Destruction of Czechoslovakia: 1938–1939

In This Chapter

◆ Sudeten Germans' push to become part of Germany

◆ Great Britain's appeasement in an attempt to secure peace

◆ The Nazi invasion of Bohemia and Moravia

◆ The Germans take control over the fate of the Jews

◆ Great Britain's formal announcement to defend Poland if Germany invades

Czechoslovakia was shaped somewhat like a fish. The narrow tail, the region called Slovakia, was on the east, bordered by Poland, Hungary, and a swatch of Romania. Where on the map we might imagine the gills was what is now the Czech Republic, and its capital, Prague; Hungary and Austria lay to the south. The head of the fish, the Sudetenland, nuzzled into the side of Germany, so that Dresden was above and Munich below.

Because of its proximity to Germany, German speakers largely inhabited this last part of Czechoslovakia, forested and mountainous. When the

Versailles Treaty created this multi-ethnic country, it forbade the unification of the Sudetenland with Germany. But when Austria was joined to the Reich, a clamor went up among the Sudeten Germans: Why can't we do the same? Hitler thought it was a good question. And that's where a whole lot of trouble began.

Map of Czechoslovakia.

(Eric Stevens)

The Sudeten Drive for Unification with Germany

Hitler realized that an attempt to annex Czechoslovakia could lead to trouble. Austria had been one thing, just a little country that no one cared much about except to visit as tourists. Czechoslovakia was different. The Allies had designed Czechoslovakia as a barrier against Soviet *and* German expansion: As we heard Hitler say in the last chapter, the last thing the British and the French wanted was a German superpower in the center of Europe. Yet Hitler was determined to capture the Sudetenland, if not all Czechoslovakia. What he needed was a very good pretext.

And sometimes a good pretext is not hard to find. Early in the morning of September 13, 1938, a pair of Czech policemen on bicycles rode through Eger, a town in the Sudetenland, and stopped outside the Victoria Hotel. While one rang the doorbell, the other pulled a piece of paper from his pocket. The document was a search warrant. A Czech judge had learned that the hotel was the headquarters of the Sudeten Nazi Party and that it contained a cache of illegal weapons. The two police-men were supposed to investigate.

They did not get very far. While they were waiting for someone to open the door, a bullet fired from a window above hit one of the officers, killing him almost instantly. The other tried to escape on his bicycle, but was too frightened to mount it, and so ran around a corner. Soon he reported the incident to his police headquarters.

Shortly afterward, two Czech motorcycles, followed by a squadron of armored cars, descended on the Victoria Hotel. As they pulled up to the front, shells from the armored cars smashed in through the hotel's second-story windows. A Czech officer with a megaphone called out, demanding that those inside surrender immediately. By way of an answer, those inside returned fire; someone up there tossed down a hand grenade, which killed one of the Czechs.

Czech army units showed up. Mortar specialists took careful aim and demolished the roof of the hotel. Those inside kept up their return fire, which continued until noon. Only then did a white flag of surrender emerge from one of the windows.

When the fracas was over, the Czechs entered the building. In the rooms up stairs, eight men were dead, all of them Sudeten Nazis. There were two survivors. One was the rifleman who early in the morning had killed the Czech cyclist. The other was Karl Hermann Frank, number-two man in the Sudeten Nazi Party. When the shoot-ing began, he had slipped out a back door of the hotel and, obtaining a car, had driven to nearby Asch. There he had told his chieftain what was going on. Returning to Eger, Frank surrendered. He was confident that he would not spend much time in jail.

The leader of the Sudeten Nazis to whom Frank had reported was Konrad Henlein. When Hitler became chancellor of Germany in 1933, Henlein was a gymnastics teacher; as such, he was much in tune with the Nazi emphasis on the physical fitness of youth. He also accepted the rest of the Nazi ideology, so much so that by 1935 he had organized the Sudeten branch of the party and was receiving a substantial subsidy from the German foreign office. Under Henlein's leadership, the Sudeten Nazi Party caught on with Czechoslovakia's Germans. Soon Henlein was agitating the unification of the Sudetenland with the Third Reich.

The Sudeten Germans claimed that the Czechs, who made up the majority in Czechoslovakia, discriminated against them. Although the evidence is most sketchy, this may have been true. The Slovaks made much the same claim. And it's a fact that ethnic hatreds bloomed like tropical flowers then in Central Europe (much as they have done in our time in the former Yugoslavia). Nonetheless, with subsidies from Berlin, Henlein organized and led a Nazi *fifth column* in Czechoslovakia.

On hearing the news of Eger from Karl Hermann Frank, Henlein, a pudgy-faced man who wore eyeglasses and had a deceptively mild manner, was overjoyed. "Our comrades have fallen in the battle for freedom, killed by the Czechs, but they will not be forgotten," he exclaimed to Frank. "I must inform the Führer at once. Adolf Hitler can now demonstrate to the world that Sudetens and Czechs can never live together, that it is useless to go on negotiating, that the only place for the Sudeten Germans is back home in the Reich!"

For Hitler, the Eger incident was lucky indeed. Two days later, Neville Chamberlain, the British prime minister, was scheduled to fly out of London to meet with the Führer. On both sides of the German–Czechoslovakian border, agitation for unification had been intense. To Chamberlain, as well as to the French premier, Éduard Daladier, the situation was critical. They didn't care about the woes of one ethnic group or another. They probably didn't even care about whether Czechoslovakia remained a democracy: After all, France and Great Britain had been indifferent to Franco's takeover of power in Spain. And as a means of containing Germany, the Sudetenland, the British and the French knew, was useless: For all practical purposes, it was already part of Germany.

But the rest of Czechoslovakia—that was the key to keeping Hitler and Germany out of Eastern Europe. This goes back to the old balance of power principle. For the British at least, preventing the rise of any superpower in Europe was the essential ingredient of national security. The British hadn't forgotten Napoleon. Hitler had all the potential of being a new Napoleon.

Yet Great Britain was in no position to fight a land war on the European continent. The Royal Navy was still potent, far more than the German fleet. But how was a British military force even to get to Czechoslovakia to defend that state? No way.

So Chamberlain needed to work out a compromise with Hitler. That's why Chamberlain, in the middle of September 1938, flew down to Munich to meet Hitler. A gifted politician, the British prime minister thought he could effect a settlement.

The Munich Conference and the Myth of Appeasement

The story of Chamberlain's meeting with Hitler—actually, there were two meetings, one in mid-September 1938 and the other at the end of the month—has been told over and over. It has been the tale of a British politician, a nice enough chap, flying down to Germany, meeting with an absolute thug, being scared silly, and so giving way to Hitler over the Sudeten issue on the mere paper promise of peace. Giving way in the manner that Chamberlain did has always been called the appeasement.

Here is a typical passage, written by Harold Nicolson, an English author and historian, who is also a member of Parliament: Chamberlain and an aide, Sir Horace Wilson, a member of the British cabinet, flew to Germany with "the bright faithfulness of two curates entering a pub for the first time; they did not observe the difference between a social gathering and a roughhouse; nor did they realize that the tough guys assembled did not either speak or understand their language. They imagined that they were as decent and as honorable as themselves."

Terms and Translations

The dictionary defines **appeasement** as the policy of granting concessions to potential enemies to preserve peace. When applied to Hitler and Chamberlain, the word takes on more freight than that. It conjures up the picture of a British statesman who, utterly naïve, was way out of his league.

"We should have traveled with about 50 secretaries and an imposing array of bodyguards," Sir Horace Wilson later admitted; they had only taken one secretary, a detective from Scotland Yard, and a foreign office expert on Central European affairs with them. "Instead we had this tiny delegation, and for a great power we looked puny. We didn't know any better."

They landed at the Munich airport. The British ambassador and Joachim von Ribbentrop, the German foreign minister, were waiting for them by the runway. A special train took them to a hotel at Berchtesgaden, Hitler's hideaway. After changing clothes, they started in two cars up the mountain slope. Both sides of the winding road were lined with black-uniformed, jackbooted SS troops. Wilson would remember, "thinking to myself as we climbed the mountain past all those guards, 'I wonder if we'll come out of this alive. I wonder if we will ever get down again.'"

When the cars came to a stop at the top of the mountain, Hitler was standing by the steps to the villa. Wilson recounted:

I remember I wasn't at all impressed with his uniform. He looked just like a draper's assistant. He greeted Neville Chamberlain and we all went inside for tea. The weather had changed by this time and it had begun to rain. We were taken into this large room with a great picture window which was supposed to look down on Salzburg, but all it looked down on at that moment was rain and mist. We all seated ourselves around a large table. Hitler sat next to [Neville Chamberlain], with Schmidt [the German] translator, on [Chamberlain's] right, and then Göring, Field Marshal Wilhelm] Keitel, then me and [William] Strang [the foreign office European expert] and Nevile Henderson [the British ambassador to Germany]. I was sitting right opposite Hitler, and I was glad of that. It gave me the opportunity of having a good look at him. When I was a negotiator on the Ministry of Labour, I always liked to be sitting in a position where I could take a good look at my adversary so that I could size him up and see what sort of chap he was. I looked at Hitler. I didn't like his eyes, I didn't like his mouth; in fact, there wasn't very much I did like about him.

Chamberlain and Hitler Dialog

What Chamberlain thought of Hitler is hard to say. As they opened their discussions, nonetheless, he stayed calm and to the point. Here's some of their actual dialog:

Chamberlain: This business of the Sudeten Germans isn't really our affair, you know. We are only interested in it because of Great Britain's interest in the maintenance of peace.

Hitler: How can you talk about peace when peace in Czechoslovakia has already ceased to exist? Let me make it clear once more that I am determined to solve this problem one way or the other. It can no longer be tolerated that a minor country like Czechoslovakia should treat the great 2,000-year-old Reich like an inferior.

Chamberlain: But look here. I am a practical man. How can it be arranged in a practical manner that the Sudeten Germans can be brought back into the Reich? ... Why worry about a new frontier? Why not a resettlement?

This was indeed a practical suggestion: If the Sudeten Germans thought themselves persecuted, why not welcome them into Germany itself? Hitler exploded.

Hitler: Don't you realize that whole districts in the Sudetenland have already been evacuated by the people? Ten thousand refugees are already on German soil! ... This persecution of German nationals must stop, and I am determined to put an end to it!

The argument continued for quite a while, and then Chamberlain made a considerable concession to Hitler: He was prepared, he said, to discuss with cabinet colleagues back in London whether Great Britain should accept "the separation of the Sudetenland from Czechoslovakia on the basis of self-determination." .

When the British party returned home, the cabinet acquiesced in Chamberlain's proposal. At the end of September, Chamberlain and Hitler met again outside Munich. Daladier and Mussolini were also at the conference.

Hitler's Supposed Peace

This time Hitler made a formal pledge that if he could have the Sudetenland, he would then pursue a policy of peace.

Landing again at the Heston Airport outside London, Chamberlain deboarded his airplane and held aloft a piece of paper. It was a promise of peace and it bore Hitler's signature. Later, in Ten Downing Street, the residence of the British prime minister, Chamberlain leaned out a window and said to a crowd below, "Peace is at hand!"

While Chamberlain was celebrating in London, Hitler returned to Berlin in triumph. Standing in an open Mercedes limousine, the Führer extended the Nazi salute to the huge crowds that lined every street and intersection to the chancellery. Just a few days later, on October 3, 1938, the German army moved into the Sudeten region of Czechoslovakia. Shortly afterward, Hitler made another triumphal entry, this time into Karlsbad, just across the border in the western tip of Czechoslovakia.

Now, like Austria, the Sudetenland was part of what the Nazis called Greater Germany. And Hitler had won a substantial victory. Or had he?

Britain's New Policy

We have here a bit of an historical puzzle. We have seen the British go along with the German reoccupation of the Rhineland in March 1936, the *Anschluss*, unification, with Austria in March 1938, and now the annexation of the Sudetenland in October 1938. Yet only 11 months later, when Nazi Germany (along with the Soviet Union) invaded Poland, Great Britain declared war on the Third Reich. So why the change of policy?

The usual explanation is that the members of the British government, perhaps feeling guilty over the settlement imposed on Germany by the Versailles Treaty, perhaps naïve and gullible, and perhaps even favorably inclined toward the Nazi dictatorship, appeased Hitler. But we'll get into this in just a bit. After signing the peace agreement with Chamberlain, Hitler broke his word. In the middle of March 1939, he ordered the German invasion of Bohemia and Moravia (now the Czech Republic). At that point, the "appeasers" woke up to the danger posed by Hitler's aggression. It was only then, in March 1939, that the British government resolved to take action against Hitler's expansionism.

Sometimes academic research shows us some very interesting things. A case in point is a book by Simon Newman called *March 1939: The British Guarantee to Poland* (Oxford University Press, 1977). Newman tells that, almost from the moment of Hitler's takeover of power, the British government was determined to block German expansion into Eastern Europe. After the First World War, though, Great Britain had let its military power decline and then, with Great Depression, had little money with which to rebuild. But what London could do and did do was to sign a series of economic agreements with the countries of Eastern Europe. These agreements gave such countries easy entry into the British home market; in return for that access, the Eastern European nations raised barriers against German trade and investment. London was deliberately trying to contain Nazi Germany, right from the start.

You can say that such trade agreements weren't much, and you're right: They didn't stop the spread of Germany across the whole of Eastern and Southeastern Europe. But they do show that London was trying to resist German expansion by just about all means short of war.

Despite Germany's rearmament program, its forces remained weak. When the forces of the Third Reich entered the Sudetenland, one of the German generals remarked that one determined Czech peasant with a blunderbuss probably could have stopped them. And at the same time, the British were frantically rearming themselves. The British government believed that at last it could do more than take steps short of war.

Bet You Didn't Know

Did Hitler realize the precarious nature of his situation? Probably not. When he rode in triumph into Karlsbad, he noticed a Czech fort standing on a hilltop. Offended by its presence, he ordered German artillery to blast it into ruins. Guns fired away and shells hit the fortress, but nothing happened: The fort was too solidly constructed to be knocked down by Hitler's artillery. "Well," Hitler said, "it doesn't matter if the will of the people collapses."

Hitler wholly underrated the will of the British people. Unknowingly, when in March 1939, he ordered the conquest of the Czech-speaking part of Czechoslovakia, he was signing the death warrant of Nazi Germany.

The Nazi Conquest of Czechoslovakia

On October 21, 1938, less than a month after the conclusion of his talks with Prime Minister Chamberlain, Hitler sent a top-secret directive to his top military officers. He told his leaders that the armed forces must be prepared for the following:

- Securing the frontiers of Germany

- Occupying the Memel district

- Liquidating the remainder of Czechoslovakia

Memel was a German-speaking port on the Baltic that the Versailles Treaty had taken from Germany and given to Lithuania. Its recapture (along with the corridor in Poland that separated Germany from East Prussia) would complete the reunification of the German Empire of old.

But Hitler was looking beyond the Bismarckian borders. Perhaps he thought that Eastern Europe, with the Jews expelled or dead, would provide *Lebensraum*, living space. Perhaps he believed that the oil deposits of Romania and the grain fields of Ukraine would make Germany at last self-sufficient, immune from another British naval embargo. Perhaps he was becoming megalomaniac, seeing himself as the new Napoleon—or perhaps all three. But whatever his motivation, he wanted to be ready at any time to crush Czechoslovakia.

His directive continued:

> The preparations to be made by the armed forces for this contingency [an attack of Bohemia and Moravia] will be considerably smaller in extent than those for *Fall Grün* [Case Green: the code name given to a contingency plan for a two-front war]; they must, however, guarantee a considerably higher state of preparedness since planned mobilization measures have been dispensed with. The organization, order of battle, and state of readiness of the units earmarked for that purpose are in peacetime to be so arranged for a surprise assault that Czechoslovakia herself will be deprived of all possibility of organized resistance. The object is the swift occupation of Bohemia and Moravia, and the cutting off of Slovakia.

Bet You Didn't Know

Slovakia had plenty of grievances against the Czechs, or so they claimed. Hitler's hope thus was to set Slovakia up as an "independent" country. Hungary, soon to become a German ally, was to grab off the eastern tail of the fish of Czechoslovakia.

The fall of Czechoslovakia came about with startling ease. Throughout the winter of 1939, Emil Hácha, the country's president, tried to stop the disintegration by getting rid of the leaders in Slovakia and Ruthenia, the latter being the easternmost province; in both, officials of government had been kicking up a pro-Nazi fuss. Hácha, though, didn't have the power to dismiss them. In fact, Slovakia proclaimed its independence and Hungary demanded that Prague's troops leave Ruthenia.

Desperate, Hácha and his foreign minister went to see Hitler in Berlin, pleading for mercy. The Führer showed none at all. Instead, he demanded that Hácha sign away the little that was left of his country's sovereignty.

By daybreak, March 15, 1939, German troops entered Bohemia and Moravia. Although a blizzard hit Prague that morning, people were out on the streets, going to work as usual or making last-minute preparations for the German occupation of their ancient city. The Germans were quick to arrive.

> ### Bet You Didn't Know
>
> An American diplomat, George F. Kennan, happened to be outside in Prague. At about 10 A.M., he encountered a German armored car stopped in the middle of a narrow street. Trying to find his way to the German legation, the driver had become lost. A crowd of embittered Czechs down on the street refused to tell him the way. The soldier in the turret sat huddled up against the driving snow, nervously fingering the trigger of his machine gun as he faced the group of people. The armored car moved on without incident.

That night, Hitler arrived in Prague. He announced to the world, "Czechoslovakia has ceased to exist." To underscore the magnitude of his triumph, he spent the night in Hradčany Castle, the traditional home of the kings of Bohemia.

Hitler called Bohemia a German "protectorate." The last thing the Nazis did was to protect the Jews of the country.

The Fate of the Jews in the Former Czechoslovakia

It wasn't long before Heinrich Himmler of the SS and Karl Hermann Frank, number-two Sudeten Nazi, got their hands on the "protectorate." Himmler's published rationale for what was to follow went this way:

> For a thousand years the provinces of Bohemia and Moravia formed part of the *Lebensraum* of the German people. ... Czechoslovakia showed its inherent inability to survive and has therefore now fallen a victim to actual dissolution.

The German Reich cannot tolerate continuous disturbances in these areas. ... Therefore the German Reich, in keeping with the law of self-preservation, is now resolved to intervene decisively to rebuild the foundations of a reasonable order in Central Europe.

The German Reich itself to be sure had played a major part in bringing about the disorder. But above all, the rebuilding a "reasonable order" in the former Czechoslovakia meant getting rid of the Jews.

About 120,000 Jews lived in Bohemia and Moravia. Under the Czechoslovak Republic, they had enjoyed full civic and religious freedom. While some anti-Semitism had existed, there had been little or no violence. No matter.

On June 21, 1939, Himmler issued a decree that placed all the Jews of Bohemia and Moravia under "German jurisdiction." The term may have deceived some people. But what it meant was that the Reich took unto itself to isolate the Jews and to expropriate their property without due compensation. These were the first steps toward the expulsion of the Jews from the region.

Bet You Didn't Know

Soon after Pearl Harbor, following instructions from the federal government, authorities in California, Oregon, Washington, and British Columbia took over the few properties owned by Americans of Japanese birth or descent and did so without due compensation—which is a fancy legal term for stealing. The expropriation of the property was the initial move in sending the victims to concentration camps in the inner western states. Fortunately, those jailed in the United States were not sent to gas chambers.

Where were the expelled Jews (from Bohemia and Moravia, as well as from Austria, the Sudetenland, and Germany itself) to go? Some in the German government thought that Palestine was a good idea. For a long time the Zionists had been pressing for a Jewish homeland there. But the British controlled Palestine and, out of regard for Arab opinion, were resisting further Jewish immigration into the region.

So with regard to Palestine, the British were not about to appease Nazi Germany. And with Hitler's dismemberment of Czechoslovakia, appeasement with regard to the middle of Europe, if that appeasement did really exist, came to an end.

The British Pledge to Defend Poland

At 2:52 P.M., March 31, 1939, Prime Minister Chamberlain appeared before the House of Commons; the galleries were packed and tense in anticipation. His statement was terse, very much to the point: "I now have to inform the House that … in the event of any action which clearly threatened Polish independence … His Majesty's Government would feel themselves bound at once to lend the Polish Government all support in their power. They have given the Polish government an assurance to that effect."

This is a book not about all of the Second World War but rather about Hitler and Nazi Germany. Yet the war has to be in the background, and here we have come to *the* major turning point. The British government was stating officially and for all the world to know that, if Hitler invaded Poland next, Great Britain would declare war on Nazi Germany.

The Least You Need to Know

- Seeing the success of Austria's Nazis in joining up with the Third Reich, the Sudeten Germans were clamoring to do the same. Money and agents from Germany helped stimulate the agitation.

- The old story that the British appeased Hitler at Munich, accepting the unification of the Sudetenland with Germany in exchange for Hitler's promise of peace, was a vast oversimplification, even a myth. When Hitler first rose to power, the British government was determined to prevent the emergence of a super-Germany in Central and Eastern Europe.

- As long as the states of Eastern Europe could stand up as bastions against German expansion, Great Britain did not need to go to war. But the dismemberment of Czechoslovakia proved that those barriers would tumble readily.

- London pledged formally to declare war on Germany if Hitler invaded Poland—which Hitler was planning to do.

Chapter 17

The Dark Summer: 1939

In This Chapter

♦ Hitler's quest to control Danzig and the Polish Corridor

♦ The pact between the Soviet Union and Nazi Germany, the lesser of two evils

♦ Hitler's invasion of Poland

♦ The declaration of war by the Allies

♦ The beginning of the Holocaust in Poland

Slovakia was now an "independent" country, although heavily influenced by decisions in Berlin. Moravia, Bohemia, and the Sudetenland were all provinces of the Third Reich. Helping itself to Ruthenia, the easternmost part of the former Czechoslovakia, Hungary became an ally of Nazi Germany. In April 1939, Hitler's other ally, Benito Mussolini, took over control of Albania across the Adriatic to the east. Hitler also seized Memel from Lithuania and raised demands for Danzig and the Polish Corridor. That he would drive into southeastern Europe and the Soviet Union seemed only a matter of time.

All this set off alarm bells in London and Paris. Great Britain followed its guarantee to Poland with similar ones to Romania and Greece. In the spring and summer of 1939, the British and the French tried to forge an anti-German pact with the Soviet Union. (France already had an understanding with the USSR, but that wasn't solid, and its alliance with Czechoslovakia was gone, of course.) Stalin, too, understood the German danger. But Poland and the three Baltic republics, Latvia, Estonia, and Lithuania, refused to accept the presence of Russian troops on their soil, even as a defense against Germany. Understanding their fears of Russia, the British and the French refused to put pressure on those small countries.

Stalin in turn thought the British and French to be hypocritical. After the First World War, Poland had taken more territory from Russia than the peace settlement allowed, pushing its eastern border well into Byelorussia, almost to Minsk. And the Allies had done nothing to stop the Poles. So Stalin and his comrades wondered, whose side were the British and the French really on? Weren't they willing to see the Soviet Union receive the brunt of a war with Nazi Germany? An alliance with the Soviet Union, proposed by London and Paris, did not come about.

And all the time, Hitler was making noises about Danzig and the Polish Corridor. In doing so, the Führer was taking Europe to the brink of war.

Danzig and the Polish Corridor

Danzig (now the Polish port of Gdansk) was a town of about 400,000 persons. Almost all of them were German. That was not surprising. Danzig was, as it had been for centuries, an important German trading center, once a member of the Hanseatic League. The Hanseatic League (the "*Han*" was connected to "*Handel*," the German word for trade or commerce; so in English we might refer to the great composer as George Frederick Trader) was an association of northern German and other Baltic and North Sea ports, formed for the defense of their trading interests. During its heyday, which lasted from the late thirteenth century to the end of the fifteenth century, it dominated the commercial history of Northern Europe. Even in the sixteenth and seventeenth centuries, when Poland was its nominal ruler, Danzig had been virtually an independent city, an emporium especially for grain and timber. Because the merchants of the Hanseatic League stored such supplies along the waterfronts and built their homes over the warehouses, the ports of the association all displayed high-gabled houses that rose above cobble-stoned streets. So it was with Danzig, which bore a striking physical resemblance to Amsterdam, Brussels, Lübeck, and Memel.

Such had been Danzig for centuries. With the German defeat at the end of the First World War, however, the question arose: What should be done with Danzig? At the Paris peace talks, Poland argued convincingly that it needed a corridor to the Baltic.

If the Allies were serious about having a free Poland as part of the antiaggression buffer in Eastern Europe, then that Poland had to have a way to survive. Survival rested on commerce; hence the Polish demand for the strip of land through Germany to the sea.

The Allies bought the idea. But they had no intention of turning Danzig itself over to Poland. The Allies had fought the war against Germany, but they had a high regard for German culture. Danzig had been an important German cultural center. That meant, among other things, that the houses in Danzig were swept and painted, the city government was uncorrupt, and the dockworkers skilled.

Danzig.

(Culver Pictures)

And although they accepted the idea of Polish independence, Allied leaders regarded the inhabitants of that country as dirty, uncouth, and backward.

So the peace negotiators at Paris worked out a compromise. Danzig and its suburbs would be called the Free City of Danzig, administered by a high commissioner appointed by the League of Nations.

What of the Polish Corridor? It was a strip of land that varied between 50 and 100 miles wide. At the west of the strip was Germany proper; to the east was East Prussia; at the top was Danzig. And the people who lived in the corridor were overwhelmingly German. Despite the arrangements made in Paris, they *thought* of themselves as

German, and sneered at the Poles under whose rule they now lived. To the Germans living in the corridor, the Poles were inferior intellectually, socially, and morally. These corridor-dwelling Germans could not forget that for centuries it had been the duty of the Teutonic Reich to hold back the Slavic tide from the east. Not for a moment from 1919 to 1939 had these Germans accepted the circumstance into which the peacemakers of Paris had cast them.

This next bit may sound weird but it's true. At least two British statesmen also found that circumstance troublesome. Not long after the signing of the Versailles Treaty, David Lloyd George, one of the framers of the agreement, allowed that he could not imagine any arrangement better calculated to produce another war than the corridor through Germany. And Austen Chamberlain, the older brother of Neville and a leading Conservative politician in Britain, said that the corridor wasn't worth the bones of a single British soldier.

Bet You Didn't Know

If Germans wanted to travel by land between Germany proper and East Prussia, by Polish law they could do so only in trains that were sealed with all curtains closed. Hitler himself asked a group of visiting Americans how they would like to take such a train between Texas and New Mexico with a Mexican corridor lying between. Practically all Germans, even many Jews, believed that the Reich had the right to redress the grievance.

Hitler Unnerves Colonel Josef Beck

In 1938, Hitler asked Colonel Josef Beck (the Polish foreign minister) if Warsaw would allow the Reich to lay down a six-lane *Autobahn* across the corridor. Beck's response was a blunt, "No!"

By January 1939, however, Hitler was no longer asking. This time Beck was nervous. But then came the dismemberment of Czechoslovakia and the British guarantee to Poland. Beck accepted that guarantee (he was quoted as saying), between "two flicks of my cigarette ash." Warsaw now had an assurance of safety.

Terms and Translations

Bahn in German means "path," "track," or "course." So an *autobahn* is a highway. A *bahnhof* is a train station.

Or did it? During the May 1939 celebration in Berlin of Hitler's fiftieth birthday, one of the foreign dignitaries present was Grigore Gafencu, the foreign minister of Romania. Joachim von Ribbentrop, his German counterpart, informed him that the Danzig situation was "impossible." And in a private interview with Hitler, the Führer screamed on and on about the British guarantee to Poland. Why, Hitler demanded to know, did Britain care about Danzig? Danzig and the corridor were properly German! They had been German for centuries! Great Britain, Hitler opined, was trying to encircle the Reich, to use Danzig as a pretext for going to war!

Well, that was Hitler's view. But then a lot of real trouble ensued, not necessarily instigated by the British. German newspapers carried reports of acts of Polish violence toward Germans. Remember: Populations in Eastern Europe were swirled about like a marbled cake. Lots of Germans therefore lived in Poland itself. According to the journalistic accounts, Poles set fire to German real estate firms, clubbed members of choral societies, and smashed the windows of German-owned stores.

In the middle of May, then, Storm Troopers in retaliation attacked a Polish customs post on the East Prussian border, beat up the officials, and kidnapped them. With the Polish guards removed from the scene, trucks carrying German-made weapons roared into Danzig. The citizens of Danzig were now armed.

Street orators in the port city began to demand the return to the Reich. Swastikas and banners with Nazi slogans adorned every major street.

With the crisis heating up, the Polish government turned the stove up even higher. Beck already had the guarantee from London; now, in the early summer of 1939, he got a promise from Paris: If war broke out between Germany and Poland, the French pledged, they would attack the Reich from the west. We can presume that the French thought their promise would ease things a bit. Quite the contrary, without consulting London and Paris, Colonel Beck informed the Germans in Danzig that he would meet any attempt to join Germany with force.

"You want to negotiate at the point of a bayonet," the German ambassador complained to Beck. Beck replied: "That is your method!"

Danzig Descends into Chaos

Danzig itself was descending into chaos. The few Polish students in the city and their German counterparts engaged in fistfights. University classes closed down. More weapons were smuggled into German hands in Danzig.

Then, in early June, Dr. Goebbels showed up. As a speaker he was almost as spellbinding as Hitler. "We are not gathered here today, citizens of Danzig, to decide whether this great city should return to the Reich, but *when!*" Goebbels told a huge crowd gathered in the main square. "Soon, comrades, soon! There is not much time to waste. Just like the Jewish whores who try to sneak into our beds and rob us of our manhood, so do the Poles and the British scheme to steal our land and our people. All we ask is what rightfully belongs to us. Danzig is German. It must return to Germany. … Already the Polish in Warsaw talk about claiming East Prussia and German Silesia. And don't fool yourselves, if we let them they will go farther than that. They will claim that their frontier should be on the Rhine. … But will we let them? We will not let them! We will drive them out of Danzig!"

Talk about demagoguery! In Warsaw Beck was just as bad. "We in Poland do not recognize the concept of peace at any price," he told the Polish parliament! "There is only one thing in the life of men, nations, and states which is beyond peace, and that is honor."

It was almost as if Danzig the place did not matter. The quarrel between Nazi Germany and Poland (which was every bit as nationalistic, undemocratic, and anti-Semitic as Germany) was raising Danzig to the level of principle.

The principle was the matter of the mastery of Eastern Europe. Well before the Nazis, Germany had asserted the right to that mastery; now, rearmed, Germany under Hitler seemed to be in a position to exert control. But Poland opposed any such extension of German power. What could Poland do to stop that expansion? With an army on horseback, armed with lances, Poland was mired in the Middle Ages—no match at all for German airplanes and tanks. So Poland had to rely on France and Great Britain for its defense.

Poland's Problem Maintaining a Proper Defense

Could London and Paris truly assist Poland? As events were to show very soon, the answer was, "no way." Germany in the short-run would prove unstoppable. Nonetheless, in June 1939, far away from Central Europe, there occurred an event which in the long-run would spell the doom of Nazi Germany.

So just for a couple pages, let's turn to the capital city that in time would engineer that demise: Washington, D.C.

Late in September 1938, King George VI of England, Scotland, India, etc., received a letter from President Franklin D. Roosevelt. The British monarch was planning to visit Canada in June 1939. Would he care to add the United States to his itinerary? Roosevelt asked. The king accepted the invitation almost immediately.

At exactly 11 A.M., Friday, June 8, 1939, the royal train with a blue and silver central car pulled into Washington's Union Station. In an unusual move, FDR himself had been driven to the station. Standing beside Mrs. Roosevelt on the platform, the president balanced himself on the arm of a White House aide. When the train stopped, the secretary of state, followed by King George and Queen Elizabeth (she became the Queen Mum, who died in 2002) stepped down from the car. The secretary of state, who had met the royal couple at the Canadian border, introduced them to President Roosevelt. As they shook hands all around, the Marine Band played "The Star-Spangled Banner" and "God Save the King." Then the party left the station in a procession of limousines that rode to a point of First Street, just below the Capitol Dome. Two huge American flags flew in front of the Capitol. The king, dressed in the full get-up of a British admiral, snapped off a salute—and the huge crowd of American on-lookers went wild. The motorcade then headed for the White House.

The First Lady, King George VI, the president's mother, Queen Elizabeth, and Franklin D. Roosevelt seated on the veranda of the Roosevelt home in Hyde Park, New York.

(Franklin D. Roosevelt Presidential Library)

This vignette does have a point. During an evening conversation in the mansion's library, the president and the king chatted about the "firm and trusted friendship" between Canada and the United States. We know this from the king's diary. Roosevelt indicated that he wanted access to the British base at Trinidad. From there, if the American Navy spotted a German submarine, it would fire away and worry about the consequences later.

Then came the zinger. Roosevelt promised no alliance. "If London was bombed," however, the president said to the king, "the USA would come in."

Bet You Didn't Know _____

In the course of the weekend visit, the first time a British monarch had set foot in the United States, the royal couple visited Mount Vernon (the king of England laid a wreath on the tomb of George Washington), the New York World's Fair, and the Roosevelt mansion in Hyde Park, New York, overlooking the valley of the Hudson River. At Hyde Park, the royals attended an Episcopal service at St. James's, the parish church, and, under the gaze on onlookers held back by police barriers, His Majesty ate a hot dog, drank a beer, and asked for seconds. How democratic can you get? Then the young couple returned by train to Canada.

The consequences of that promise were immense. The British government had an assurance that, if it went to war with Germany over Poland, and the war got out of hand, the United States would come in, much as it had come in 1917 and 1918. FDR's promise strengthened the British resolve to face Hitler down in Eastern Europe.

But there came a great shock. In August 1939, Nazi Germany and the Soviet Union signed a treaty of peace. Any hope that the British government may have had of encircling Germany with a 1914-like Triple Entente was shattered. For the treaty with Moscow gave Berlin a free hand in Poland.

The Nazi–Soviet Pact

Let's look at the world for a bit from the points of view of Josef Stalin in Moscow and Adolf Hitler in Berlin.

Stalin first. To him, Nazi Germany was loathsome. The Nazis had murdered or exiled thousands of his fellow Communists. The Nazis, according to propagandists in the Soviet Union, were the arch-representatives of capitalism. The Nazis, once armed, might be deadly enemies. Yet the Allies of the First World War were just as bad. In 1919, not Germany but rather America, Britain, France, Poland, and Japan had invaded Russia, trying to kill off the new Communist government before it could even get control of its country. At the peace settlement, the Allies had also sheared the Baltic states away from the old Russian Empire and had allowed Poland to expand at Russia's expense. And throughout the 1920s and 1930s, they had treated the Soviet Union as an international pariah. Only now, in 1939, were the British and the French making overtures to Moscow, trying to create a new alliance. But why? Stalin was supposed to have said that he trusted no one, not even himself. He certainly didn't trust the British and the French. He suspected, and with good reason, that they were trying to get Russia and Germany to fight each other—so that they, the British and the French, could move in and acquire the spoils. Stalin didn't trust any of the European powers: He just distrusted Germany a little less than he did France and Great Britain.

What about Hitler? He had expressed the fear that London and Paris were trying to organize Poland and Russia into a ring of allies intended to encircle Germany and then strangle it. Hitler may well have been nuts. But was this specific fear irrational? Kaiser Wilhelm II believed he confronted a similar ring. Then there was America. Like all Germans even partially in possession of their facilities, Hitler remembered vividly that the intervention of the United States in the First World War had led directly to Germany's defeat. In 1939, true, the United States was neutral. But so it had been between 1914 and 1917. And if the United States joined that encircling ring, Germany was doomed again. But perhaps Hitler could prevent that ring from coming into being. Perhaps he could split the Soviet Union off from the Anglo–Franco–Polish connection. Perhaps he could then crush Poland. And just perhaps he could defeat France—as Germany could have done in 1914 if it had not foolishly abandoned the Schlieffen Plan. (See Chapter 4 for more information.) So Hitler set out to soothe the Soviet Union. He had no love for the Soviet regime, with its Communist system and all those Jews in places of political prominence.

But we misread Hitler if we see him as just an anti-Semite ideologue. He could be as realistic as any statesman in the history of diplomacy. Granted, he would make a fatal blunder in attacking the Soviet Union two years later. In the summer of 1939, however, he had a firm grasp on German self-interest. That interest lay in driving a wedge between the Western powers and the Soviet Union.

Hitler's Telegram

On August 19, 1939, a coded telegram went out from Hitler at Berchtesgaden to the German embassy in Moscow. There, Friedrich Werner von der Schulenburg, the German ambassador, was to deliver the message (decoded and translated into Russian) to Stalin. It read:

> M. STALIN, MOSCOW:
>
> THE TENSION BETWEEN GERMANY AND POLAND HAS BECOME INTOLERABLE. IN MY OPINION IT IS DESIRABLE NOT TO LOSE ANY TIME. I THEREFORE PROPOSE THAT YOU RECEIVE MY FOREIGN MINISTER ON TUESDAY, AUGUST 22, BUT AT THE LATEST ON WEDNESDAY, AUGUST 23. I SHOULD BE GLAD TO RECEIVE YOUR EARLY ANSWER.

Bet You Didn't Know

Hitler was extraordinarily nervous the night he sent the telegram to the German Embassy. Unable to sleep, he paced up and down in front of the big plate glass window. In the middle of the night, he telephoned Göring, who was in Berlin: The government had had no response from Moscow. Dawn came, and Hitler could see the sun rise over the mountains to the east; still nothing from Moscow. The day dragged on—later Hitler said that it was the longest day of his life—and he watched the sun set over the mountains to the west. Still nothing. Outside the window all was black.

Then, at 10:50 P.M., August 21, the teletype machine in the villa made a noise. Hitler raced to read the message:

TO THE CHANCELLOR OF THE GERMAN REICH, MR. A. HITLER:

I THANK YOU FOR THE LETTER. I HOPE THAT A GERMAN-SOVIET NON-AGGRESSION PACT WILL BRING ABOUT A DECIDED TURN FOR THE BETTER IN THE POLITICAL RELATIONS BETWEEN OUR TWO COUNTRIES. THE SOVIET GOVERNMENT HAS INSTRUCTED ME TO INFORM YOU THAT THEY AGREE TO MR. VON RIBBENTROP'S ARRIVING IN MOSCOW ON AUGUST 23.

J. STALIN

The following morning, Ribbentrop, the foreign minister, flew from Berchtesgaden to Berlin, where he collected 30-some officials, photographers, and reporters. Thereafter, with a stopover in Königsberg in East Prussia, Ribbentrop, his party flew on to Moscow.

Von Ribbentrop's Meeting with Stalin and Molotov

When the Germans descended from their airplanes at the Moscow airport and reached the ground, they stood at attention. A Red Army band played the "Internationale," the Communist hymn to revolution, and the "Horst Wessel Lied," the Nazi ode to the destruction of the Communists. The visitors then passed through two rows of Soviet troops who held aloft both hammer-and-sickle flags and swastikas. A motorcade took Ribbentrop and his delegation to the Kremlin.

After luncheon in the Kremlin, Ribbentrop sat down with Stalin and Vyacheslav Molotov, the new Soviet foreign minister. Molotov was new because, as a signal of goodwill toward Berlin, Stalin had just dumped his predecessor, Maxim Litvinov, who was Jewish.

With the help of translators, the Nazi and the two Soviets easily agreed upon a nonaggression pact. Then the bargaining started. If Germany got Danzig, the corridor, and most of central Poland, what would Russia get? The answer soon became clear: The Soviets could get the rest of Poland plus the Baltic states, Finland (if they could take it), and Bessarabia, which was a Romanian province. The nonaggression pact, the conferees concurred, would be made public. The rest was to be kept secret.

Even without the unrevealed codicils, the announcement of the Nazi–Soviet agreement stunned the world. As just about all observers could see, it meant that Germany and Russia were going to divide up Eastern Europe between themselves. And that's just what happened. On September 1, 1939, while Soviet units began their lumbering moves into Finland and down the Baltic coast, Hitler's army (the *Wehrmacht*) and air force (the *Luftwaffe*) unleashed a lightning war (*Blitzkrieg*) into Poland.

The Invasion of Poland

On the morning of September 1, 1939, Hitler walked to the microphone that stood before the *Reichstag*. On a raised dais directly behind and above him sat Göring; on the wall behind Göring a huge swastika hung suspended from the talons of a sculptured eagle with its wings spread wide. And before this tableau the entire body of the Reichstag were standing at attention, right arms thrust forward in the Führer salute.

When all had sat again, Hitler made an important announcement. He was wearing a gray uniform, he pointed out, because that was the "sacred coat" of the German troops in the First World War. His wearing the gray was highly symbolic: Six hours earlier, in the pre-dawn darkness, the air, land, and sea forces of the Third Reich had begun the attack on Poland.

The first shots were fired at Danzig. Two days before, the *Schleswig-Holstein*, a training ship with the German navy, had pulled into the harbor at the old port city. The captain of the ship announced that he had come on a courtesy visit. It was not so. He and his crew had better things to do than gaze at the picturesque gabled houses of the medieval merchant-princes. Once a battleship, the *Schleswig-Holstein* was still equipped with 11-inch guns. With these, as soon as the sun rose on September 1, 1939, it blasted away at the Polish island fortress that guarded the mouth of the harbor.

Overwhelmed, the Polish garrison surrendered quickly. So did the rest of Poland. The German forces took Poland as easily as if it were a child's sandbox. Waves of high-flying bombers reduced the rear of the Polish army to shambles, destroyed Warsaw's air force as it sat on the ground, and spread terror among the civilian populations of the cities. Then came waves of *Stukas*, dive-bombers, outfitted with sirens to magnify the psychological effects of their downward sweeps upon the front lines. Following were motorcycles, troops in trucks, and the Panzers, newly designed and fast-moving German tanks.

In the face of the German advance, the roads of Poland became chaotic. Fleeing peasants, their earthly belongings piled onto wagons or wheelbarrows, their horses nervous and their few automobiles breaking down, formed endless columns of eastward-bound refugees. Joining them were their own soldiers, dazed and demoralized. All this was bad enough. But frequently, diving from behind the columns came the *Stukas*, smearing the Polish roadways with the blood of civilians.

Within two days, led by General Wilhelm von Keitel and his principal aide, General Alfred Jodl, the German invaders had brought Poland to the edge of defeat. All that remained were the mopping-up operations.

At the end of those two days, on September 3, France and Great Britain declared war on Germany. Their actions came too late to do anything for Poland.

But at least the prelude to war was over. The Second World War had begun in Europe. And something else, too, had begun: the Holocaust in Poland.

The Organization of the Holocaust

Up to this point, Nazi treatment of the Jews had been hateful and on occasion, as during the *Kristallnacht* (Crystal Night; see Chapter 15 for additional information), murderous. The regime and its local agents had forced many Jews to abandon their businesses. Jewish doctors, dentists, and lawyers were not allowed to offer their services to Aryans. Jews were obliged to carry identity cards and from October 1938 onward, all Jewish passports were stamped with the letter J. Nazi authorities had been exploring ways of encouraging Jewish emigration. But the program of systematized killing had not yet got underway.

Terms and Translations

The term **Einsatzgruppen** is a little complicated. The **gruppen** is easy: It's the plural of "group." Now as for **einsatz—ein** is "in." **Satz** comes from *setzen*, "to set." So **einsatz** means something "set in," inserted.

With the invasion of Poland, however, Nazi policy became thoroughly cold-blooded. Through his chain of command, Himmler and then Heydrich of the SS, and Hans Frank, their deputy and governor of the province of Poland, Hitler passed down one of his most notorious orders. In the wake of the German army, five *Einsatzgruppen* were to enter into Poland. The Einsatzgruppen were squads of professional killers inserted into Poland for the expressed purpose of eliminating part of the population. They were put in Poland to commit mass murder. More exactly, these death squads were to kill off tens of thousands of officials, priests, and intellectuals in an effort to deprive the Poles of their natural leaders.

In September 1939, the Einsatzgruppen did not yet target Jews as such. The squads nonetheless were part of the SS, and the SS high command soon realized that Poland, remote from the German population, would be an ideal place to build new concentration camps.

The Least You Need to Know

♦ Egged on by Hitler and the local Nazis, the Danzig crisis came to a head in the summer of 1939. That meant that despite Polish resistance, Hitler demanded the return of Danzig and the corridor to the German Reich.

♦ Hitler's major worry was that the Soviet Union might intervene on behalf of Poland. Signed in August 1939, the Nazi–Soviet treaty, however, eliminated the threat of war between Germany and Russia—for the moment.

♦ The German invasion of Poland on September 1, 1939, was the step that formally led to the start of the Second World War in Europe. It also laid the foundation for the Holocaust.

Part 4

The Rising Tide

Here you'll find a Nazi Germany seemingly unstoppable, on the road to what many feared was world conquest. Faced with the German juggernaut, smaller countries—Poland, Denmark, Norway, Holland, Luxembourg, Belgium, France, Yugoslavia, and Greece—fell like nine-pins. In the North African desert, General Erwin Rommel, the famed tank commander, appeared to be on the brink of taking control of the Suez Canal. For Rommel, however, a funny thing happened on the way to the Nile. He began to run out of gas. And by the end of 1942, he had lost the fight, squeezed out of North Africa by the advancing British and Americans. Yet that loss didn't seem to matter: Hitler had invaded the Soviet Union.

Chapter **18**

Life in the Third Reich: 1939–1940

In This Chapter

- ◆ How Germany's economy flourishes before the onset of the war
- ◆ Hitler's popularity with the masses, specifically Germany's youth
- ◆ Eugenics, the beginning of the end for the Jewish people
- ◆ The start of the Holocaust and different theories as to how it began
- ◆ The Austrian people's support of Hitler and his cause
- ◆ Germany's suffering in the name of the cause
- ◆ Germans' feelings at the beginning of the war with France and Great Britain

So much written about Hitler and Nazi Germany has to do with the Second World War. This is understandable, because the war was so dramatic. But we sometimes forget that the war wouldn't have taken place at all if Nazi Germany had not been mobilized for war. So it's worthwhile to take a look at what was going on inside Germany (and Austria) to see how the people made the war possible and how the war affected the people.

One thing seems quite certain: When the war broke out in Poland, ordinary Germans and Austrians had little or no idea what was in store for them. On September 10, 1939, William Shirer, an American foreign correspondent posted to Berlin, wrote in his diary:

> Life here is still quite normal. The operas, the theaters, the movies, all open and jammed. *Tannhäuser* and *Madame Butterfly* playing at the Opera. The Metropol, Hitler's favorite show-house, announced a new revue Wednesday. One week after the Anglo–French declaration of war the average German is beginning to wonder if it's a world war after all. He sees it this way. England and France, it is true, are formally fulfilling their obligations over Poland. For a week they have been formally at war with Germany. But has it been war, they ask? … The industrial heart of Germany lies along the Rhine close to France. From there come most of the bombs that are blowing up Poland with such deadly effect. Yet not a bomb has fallen on a Rhineland factory. "Is that war?" they ask.

The Arms of Krupp

Although it manufactures only a few weapons now, the Ruhr Valley even today is dense with industrial pollution. If you fly over the area you can see the smokestacks of the factories sticking up through the smog as if they were cathedral spires. But this is nothing new. Even back when Nazi Germany went to war, the Ruhr Valley was the healthy heart of the economy.

In that economy, no firm, or rather combination of firms, was more significant than Krupp, the arms manufacturer. The German government for a long time had allowed the formation of cartels, huge trusts designed to crush competition and fix prices. Krupp was the biggest trust of all, comparable to large computer companies in the present-day American economy.

For Krupp, as well as for the Ruhr Valley as a whole, business was booming. Contracts were plentiful because they came from the Nazi government. On a personal level, Alfred Krupp, scion of the family dynasty and head of the enterprise in 1939, had no use for Hitler. Yet he had seen in Hitler's war cries for rearmament a source of wealth worth more than rubies and emeralds. Rearmament meant contracts for Krupp, so Krupp had helped finance Hitler.

Because of a German television documentary called *Hitler's Money*, aired in 2002, we now know about how much financing Hitler received from Krupp and other big businessmen: in today's money, well over $3 billion. In return, Krupp and his colleagues made billions more for their war work.

The German economic system thus was highly corrupt (more so than the American economic system today?). Up to a point, though, the corruption was useful. It provided jobs and engendered overall prosperity. Lots of people had cars. Expensive boutiques abounded. Well-dressed city-dwellers could frequent cafés. No longer did Germany have the shabby and bedraggled look of the years of the Great Depression. In terms of public opinion, the chief beneficiary of the new prosperity was Hitler. He was seen as the savior of the German nation—and now he was the valiant victor in the war against Poland.

Hitler's Appeal to the Germans

Before the attack on Poland, quite a number of Hitler's top generals were nervous. Their forces were untried on the field of battle and with an Anglo–French declaration of war looming over their heads, they feared that they might be marching toward disaster. Hitler proved them wrong, at least in the short run.

It's hard to imagine the degree of Hitler's popularity after his victory in Poland. With that victory he had delivered everything he had promised. A lot of people say that we shouldn't think of Hitler as an ordinary politician. Indeed, in his monstrosity, he was not ordinary. But he *was* a politician. Politicians who don't deliver fall from popular favor—and Hitler had delivered.

Pretend that you are a German and meditate on this list of achievements. Just as he said he would, Hitler …

- Rose to power. As he said he would, he demolished the left.

- Started Germany down the course of rearmament and in the course of so doing, intentionally or not, he provided Germans with jobs.

- Reoccupied the Rhineland—traditionally the source of Germany's industrial might.

- Unified Germany and Austria, fulfilling part of the nationalistic dream of bringing all Germans together.

- Also brought the Sudetenland into the Reich. As he said he would, he dismembered a Czechoslovakia that, his propagandists had told the German people, posed a serious military threat.

- Recaptured Danzig and destroyed the Polish Corridor, eliminating the barrier between Germany proper and East Prussia.

- Brought those backward Poles under the German heel—providing space for German emigration and a place for getting rid of the Jews.

Hitler, Frau Morell, and Eva Braun.

(Culver Pictures)

In the process of all this, Hitler became rich, partly through the immense royalties from *Mein Kampf*, partly from the bribes he received or extorted from businessmen, and partly from simply looting the nation's treasury. With the money he lived well: He built a house in Munich for Eva Braun, his paramour; he started the reconstruction in Poznan, in Poland, of a palace originally built for Kaiser Wilhelm II; and he had his mountaintop villa at Berchtesgaden in the Bavarian Alps. We can speculate that a lot of Germans held his displays of wealth in awe, or at least that with those displays Hitler was trying to impress them.

Bet You Didn't Know

Hitler had a mistress. The daughter of lower-middle-class Bavarians who disapproved of her relationship with him, Eva Braun was a slender, blond, pretty young woman who doted on him. But Hitler usually kept her hidden away at Berchtesgaden and for a long time refused to marry her. Some relationship!

We also know from the documentary mentioned previously that Hitler spent millions, in lavish gifts and payments, to buy the loyalty of politicians and businessmen and to keep them dependent upon him. In a sense, Hitler ran a great big political machine.

But money pressed into the hands of his cronies would not have explained Hitler's popularity with the German masses. Nor would his string of victories, at home and abroad, account for the reverence offered him by the people of Germany. And his private personality, nasty, mediocre, and bizarre, doesn't tell us much about the magnetism of his popular appeal.

Why was this one-time tramp—who in his Vienna days couldn't lead anyone—now the Führer?

The answer might well be that there was a Hitler cult.

The Hitler Cult

We've seen cults in America, the Branch Davidians and others. Perhaps there was a cult of Elvis Presley. But the Branch Davidians were few in number, certainly not nationwide. And despite his huge popularity, Elvis wasn't surrounded by standard salutes and flags: He didn't run for high office. The Hitler cult, on the other hand, was widespread and it constantly embodied dramatic symbols. It was a systematic effort to endow Hitler with a public, contrived, personality—one that was elevated to the status of a demigod.

Have there been other such personality cults? Sure. Mussolini comes to mind; so does Stalin (whose successor, Nikita Khrushchev, denounced Stalin's cult of personality); and Mao Zedong, the "Great Helmsman" of the People's Republic of China. Despite the differences among German, Russian, and Chinese cultures, cults have this in common: They are mass movements; they create an image of heroic leadership; and they use propaganda, symbolism, and incantations to endow the leader with divine qualities. The cultists also present themselves as struggling against the forces of evil: for Stalin the capitalist West, and for Mao Zedong the United States.

Terms and Translations

The dictionary defines a **cult** as a system or community of religious worship and ritual, especially one focusing on a single deity, spirit, or person.

The Hitler cult began in the middle of the 1920s after Hitler's release from prison. The obligatory "Heil Hitler" and the stiff-armed salute among Nazi Party members were signs of devotion to the leader; the swastika was a pseudo-religious image. (It was derived from an ancient Buddhist symbol.)

In the 1920s, of course, the Nazi Party represented no mass movement. For those who voted for him in the early 1920s, Hitler had come to represent struggle, just as the title of *Mein Kampf* had boasted: the struggle of the "little man" against society's "big battalions"; the struggle against what so many saw as the moral decadence of the Weimar Republic; and the struggle of Germany against the outside world.

We must remember, though, that Hitler had a bit of trouble actually winning elections. So how could the Hitler cult spread as rapidly as it did throughout much of the German population?

At least three things came into play. First, given the decrepitude of the Weimar system, Hitler offered a new face; lots of Germans were prepared to give him a chance. Second, in his lightninglike thrust toward power, he proved himself a winner. And third, he put out a call for striving, commitment, and sacrifice; in the German context he was appealing to ideals.

Supporting Actors

Once Hitler was in power, it didn't hurt at all that the Nazis controlled the media. Working behind the scenes, Goebbels could present Hitler as the one and only German leader, the "Symbol of the Nation." Hitler's cluster of "virtues," his strength, determination, and vision (broadcast endlessly through all the media), were precisely what the Germans craved. So was Hitler's constant harping on the need to rid Germany of its enemies at home and abroad.

All this came to a culmination with Hitler's victory over Poland. To most Germans—or at least in the government-controlled newspapers they read—that victory was not only triumphant, it was also cost-free. The economy was strong and most people were more prosperous than ever before. And Hitler had been *right*. Like King Midas, everything he touched had turned to gold.

The future itself seemed golden. So believed the most ardent of Hitler's supporters, the youth of the nation.

The Hitler Youth

By 1939 and 1940, Germans of high school age all had been inculcated with the need to follow the Führer. After the Second World War, one former Hitler Youth explained how this indoctrination had come about:

> No one in our class ever read *Mein Kampf*. I myself only took quotations from the book. On the whole we didn't know much about Nazi ideology. Even anti-Semitism was brought in rather marginally at school—for example via Richard Wagner's essay, "The Jews in Music" … Nevertheless, we were politically programmed: to obey orders, to cultivate the soldierly "virtue" of standing to attention and saying, "Yes, Sir," and to stop thinking when the magic word "Fatherland" was uttered and Germany's honor and greatness were mentioned.

In such an educational and cultural climate, war seemed normal and violence legitimate. Hitler's victories abroad between 1936 and 1939 led Germans to take pride in a Führer who combined violent threats, claims of legal right, and risk-taking to produce success.

On the whole, they were proud of Hitler for also putting into effect the "purification" of the "Aryan race." Such "purification" included purging more people than the Jews.

Social Outcasts

You can't say that Hitler didn't think big or in terms of the long run. For Germany's welfare, self-defense, and perhaps never-ending conquests, he wanted to create a "master race." As we know, the Jews were not a part of that race. But neither were Gentile Germans who for reasons of biology were unable to play productive roles in society.

Early in 1939, Hitler authorized the murder, either by injection or deliberate starvation, of severely handicapped babies. Then, at just about the time of the signing of the Nazi–Soviet accord, he extended the program to include adults. These included not only those who were physically deformed but also those suffering from mental retardation and illnesses. In 1939, some 200,000 Germans were so afflicted. How to get rid of them? In six mental hospitals throughout Germany the regime constructed gas chambers that could induce death through the introduction of carbon monoxide. Transferred from all over the Reich, about 72,000 persons lost their lives in these hospital facilities. Only in 1941, in response to public pressure, did Hitler stop the program. He did not stop the maltreatment of the Jews.

> **Terms and Translations**
>
> **Eugenics** is the study of hereditary improvement, especially of human improvement, by genetic control. The horticultural and agricultural sciences have long known how to make new and improved varieties of plants; horse owners breed stallions and mares to produce Kentucky Derby winners. The Nazis proposed to do the same with human beings.

The Emerging Holocaust

In January 1939, only eight months before the start of the war in Poland, Hitler went before the Reichstag and made a statement that received wild approval: If "international Jewish finance inside and outside of Europe succeeds in involving the nations in another war, the result will not be the bolshevization of the earth and the victory of Judaism but the annihilation of the Jewish race in Europe." He also told the Czech foreign minister the same month that "we are going to destroy the Jews. They are not going to get away with what they did on November 11, 1918."

It's worth taking a moment to look at these statements. Some Hitler apologists—you find them here and there in British and American universities—point out that Hitler was notoriously given to wild talk and that therefore we shouldn't take these statements too seriously. These utterances, the apologists hold, don't mean that Hitler intended the Holocaust. What can we say in the face of such claims? Hitler did have loose lips. Yet as we've just seen, he turned just about all his ranting into reality. Why should we look at these statements any differently? How can we escape the conclusion that Hitler once again meant just what he said: that he was intent upon the "annihilation of the Jewish race in Europe"?

But there's something more to be said. The two passages quoted above contain a massive inner contradiction. For Hitler, the Jews both started the First World War and ended it. How or why they would have done both he somehow neglected to say. But then, surely, Hitler's language was designed for the purposes of propaganda. It had been Germany's top generals who had taken the country out of the war, but it was popular to pin the blame on the Jews. So in his conversation with the Czech foreign minister, Hitler was raising again the old slander against the Jews.

But now note: Hitler stated that if "international Jewish finance … succeeds in involving the nations in another war …" He was getting ready to blame the coming of the war in Poland on the Jews. A war that he himself was concocting could be used to justify the Holocaust.

One Author's Speculation

This is purely speculative. This author has found no documents that support the following thought, but consider this: If Hitler was so determined to see the return of Danzig and the Polish Corridor to Germany, why didn't he just take them and stop? Why the broader war with Poland? Perhaps he had a lust for conquest: but he never attacked Sweden, Switzerland, or Spain. So why Poland? It's possible that the Nazis could use that war and the sense of excitement it engendered in Germany to justify the murder of Jews—for "military reasons," of course. This certainly is what German propaganda said. So perhaps here we have the link between the Holocaust and the Second World War: That attack on Poland, which embroiled Nazi Germany with France and Great Britain, may have had as its ultimate purpose the murder of European Jews.

The Nazi Solution

This next point *is* based on hard evidence. Even while the war was taking place in Poland, Nazi leaders were developing a new "solution" to the "Jewish question."

Hitler intended (this he told associates) to turn Poland into a slave state, with its inhabitants forced to serve the master race of German settlers. The first step of this enslavement would be forcing the three million-some Polish Jews into ghettos; later they would be transferred to a reservation near Lublin, a bit southeast of Warsaw.

This was no mere plan. Only a month after the German invasion of Poland, Heinrich Himmler in his role as Reich commissioner took over the "Germanization" of Poland. This meant that Poland's Jews, or at least those west of the Soviet zone, were wholly at the mercy of the SS. Between December 1939 and February 1940, accordingly, 600,000 Jews in Danzig and the former Polish Corridor were forced from their houses and apartments, prodded into cattle trucks, and shipped into the Polish territories annexed by the Third Reich.

But the plan went awry. In captured Warsaw, Hans Frank, the Nazi official in charge, protested that he already had about 1,400,000 Jews under his jurisdiction. The addition was causing a strain on food supplies. He began to withhold food from Jews.

Bet You Didn't Know

Wherever they lived, Polish Jews were forbidden to move—the regime wanted to keep tabs on them—and required to obey a curfew, wear the yellow star, and perform slave labor in newly constructed German factories.

As onerous as these restrictions were, they did not yet amount to the Final Solution. The problem of food shortages, however, raised the fatal issue: Instead of feeding Jewish slaves in the factories of Poland, wouldn't it be better simply to kill them off?

The Austrian People and Hitler's War

Austrian reactions to the start of the war were similar to those in Germany itself. When news of the German invasion of Poland reached Vienna, people were stunned. "I heard Hitler's speech [declaring war on Poland] at the Carlton," an Austrian diplomat wrote; "the club was packed with listening guests. Everybody with grave expressions. No applause. A small crowd of people on St. Stephen's Square. Those near the loudspeakers raised their arms during the national anthem. Those standing farther away not at all. Everywhere depressed spirits. Vague hopes of a short local war. Not one trace of enthusiasm."

The mood soon changed. The stunning success of the *Blitzkrieg*, lightning war, in Poland washed the fears away in Austria and unleashed both admiration and rejoicing. Within days Austrian troops who had fought alongside German counterparts were showered with flowers, food, and cigarettes. And they were favored with more than that. "In the euphoria of reunion," an Austrian official reported, "no one was offended that formerly prevailing bourgeois morals are no longer being observed."

Few cared about the breakdown of earlier sexual morality because Austria, like Germany, had a new morality: the Hitler cult. Hitler, after all, was the local boy made good. Hitler worship was replacing Austria's traditional Catholicism.

But the traditional anti-Semitism remained and even intensified. Led by Arthur Seyss-Inquart, the Austrian Nazi whom Hitler had placed in charge in Vienna, party members throughout the country stepped up the maltreatment of the Jews. In one town, Türkenschanze, Nazi militants demanded that Jewish homes post identity plates; in another, Kettenbrücke, they had to wear the Star of David.

As in Germany, Austrian Nazis were willing to blame the Jews for any and all woes. And despite the joys of the autumn of 1939, the advent of winter brought unexpected distress.

The Winter of Discontent

Throughout Germany and Austria, the winter of 1939 to 1940 faced consumers with shortages of just about everything: milk, flour, coffee, meat, and vegetables. Foodstuffs were being routed to the military, not the civilians. The regime in Berlin responded to the shortages by imposing rationing, which only aggravated bottlenecks in production and delivery. Because of the demands of the armed forces, new shoes and clothing were also scarce.

Then, in the midst of an unseasonably cold winter, came a coal crisis. The peasants could cut trees for fuel but the city-dwellers could not. And the regime in Berlin raised taxes. That was how it had to pay for the war. Finally, inflation set in.

All this foreshadowed the hardships to come. Still, daily life went on much as usual, food allotments were adequate, and the war seemed remote. In fact, the war hardly seemed to be a war at all.

Suddenly, however, in the early spring of 1940, the war became real. The Phony War was over.

The Phony War

The Germans called it the *Sitzkrieg*, the Sitting War; the French termed it the *drôle de guerre*, the "funny war"; Neville Chamberlain used the term "twilight war." American journalists in Europe were blunter: For them it was the "Phony War."

All the terms missed the point. First of all, there was definitely a war at sea. Shortly after the start of the carving up of Poland, a German submarine sank a British liner called *Athenia;* another U-boat slipped into the harbor at Scapa Flow and sank the British battleship *Royal Oak.* The British in their turn trapped the German battleship *Graf Spee* in the waters of the Rio Plate, which joined the Atlantic at Montevideo, Uruguay, and sent it to the bottom.

But second, all sides were preparing for a real war. Although the Royal Navy was much more potent than the German fleet, as during the First World War, and although they had taken many steps toward the building of an air force, the British were frantically trying to build up their land forces. Eventually, by December 1939, London was able to place the four divisions of the British Expeditionary Force in northeastern France. Although the British officers looked upon the French troops with contempt—General Alan Brooke wrote of "men unshaven, horses ungroomed, clothes and saddlery that did not fit, vehicles dirty, and complete lack of pride in themselves and their units"—the British contingent was a mere drop in the bucket of the 100 French divisions with their famous Maginot Line.

> ### Memorable Places
>
> Named for a French minister of defense, the Maginot Line, constructed between 1930 and 1935, was a row of concrete and steel fortifications that ran all the way from Switzerland to Luxembourg along the French–German frontier. With heavy artillery encased in bombproof casements, the line was thought to be unbreachable.

The Maginot Line seemed to be unbreachable. But it stopped at Luxembourg. Why? Partly for budgetary reasons and partly because thick woods called the Ardennes Forest protected (or seemed to protect) France from Germany. But the line also did not parallel France's frontier with Belgium. The French thought they could make up for that shortcoming by placing most of their 100 divisions at the Belgian border.

The Germans had their own variant (although not so formidable) of the French fortifications, the West Wall. The British nicknamed it the Siegfried Line, a title made popular by a passage in a British music hall comedy, "We're going to hang out the washing on the Siegfried Line." It ran just inside the German frontier, facing the Maginot Line. Like its French counterpart, the Siegfried Line was defensive. It's difficult to believe, given Hitler's successes-to-come, but against the French 100 divisions, the Germans could array 23. Most of the German forces were mechanized, but repairing and refitting the tanks, armored cars, and airplanes used in the Polish campaign took time.

So by the coming of springtime 1940, the war was not yet a war at all. But Hitler had stated "that if the Allies planned to enlarge the scope of hostilities, he would beat them to the punch."

On April 9, 1940, German forces landed in neutral Denmark and Norway. Hitler had indeed beaten the Allies to the punch.

The Least You Need to Know

- Undergirding Nazi Germany's eventual successes in war was its industrial prowess. The heart of the German economic machine was the Ruhr Valley and was represented best by Krupp, the munitions maker.

- Also important for understanding Hitler's victories was his hold on the German and Austrian people. His was a cult of personality of the magnitude of Stalin's or Mao Zedong's. Hitler's appeal was especially great among the youth, molded (by the educational system) into good little Nazis.

- Not all Germans or Austrians were treated like good little Nazis. Hitler and his associates unleashed a full-fledged program of euthanasia: The widespread murder of persons who were handicapped (physically or mentally) and who thus could not contribute to the greater glories of the Third Reich.

- The persecution of the Jews, now not only in Germany but also in Czechoslovakia, Austria, and Poland, went forward. Directed by the SS, the campaign against the Jews took the form of moving them out of the way, that is, into ghettos in remote Polish towns.

- After the fall of Poland, the European enemies, Nazi Germany on one side and France and Great Britain on the other, seemed to refrain from further hostilities. This was called the Phony War. There was, however, nothing phony about it. Both sides were preparing for a wider conflict. That widened war broke out on April 9, 1940.

Blitzkrieg: 1940

In This Chapter

- ◆ Nazi Germany's atomic bomb program
- ◆ The fight to control Norway
- ◆ Hitler's revised version of the Schlieffen Plan
- ◆ Dunkirk, one of the greatest military defeats in Great Britain's history
- ◆ France's fall to Nazi Germany

During the Nuremberg trials, held from 1945 to 1946, one of the German defendants, Albert Speer, an architect by profession and designer of Germany's military production during the war, made a startling statement. When the war ended, Germany was only two years from having an atomic bomb. Then, perhaps to lighten his own sentence, he added: The delay served Germany right, because the Nazis had driven out most of her brilliant scientists, including Jewish physicists who could have brought the bomb project to an earlier completion. When Speer finished his statement, the audience in the courtroom stood and cheered him.

Talk about a brain drain! Not all the eminent personages whom the Nazis drove out were Jewish, but they certainly made up an intellectual elite rarely, if ever, matched in any country. They included the following:

- The Nobel Prize–winning and anti-Nazi novelist Thomas Mann and his wife, Katya

- Dr. Sigmund Freud and his daughter, Anna, who made their way to London

- Erich Maria Remarque, the author whose famed novel *All Quiet on the Western Front* (*Am Westen Nichts Neues*) had exposed the horrors of front-line warfare

- Erich Leinsdorf, the young conductor of the Salzburg Festival Orchestra, who landed a job conducting Wagner for the Metropolitan Opera Company

- Furniture designer Marcel Breuer and architect Walter Gropius, who in Germany had founded a school of modernist design called the *Bauhaus* (Build House)—condemned by the Nazis as decadent—and who ended up teaching at the Harvard School of Design

- Another *Bauhaus* architect named Ludwig Mies van der Rohe

- The scholar Hannah Arendt who, starting in 1940, taught at the New School for Social Research in New York City

Probably the most famous person outcast at the time was Albert Einstein, the theoretical physicist who left Germany for the Institute of Advanced Study at Princeton, New Jersey, and who was the scientist whom Albert Speer had the most in mind when he mocked Hitler for the expulsion the Jews.

The Nazi Atomic Bomb Program

"Dear Mr. President"—so began a letter to President Franklin D. Roosevelt, written and signed by Albert Einstein in August 1939, alerting FDR to the growth of German nuclear research. The letter was nontechnical and it avoided histrionics. "In Germany, nonetheless," Einstein informed Roosevelt, "it is conceivable … that [in Germany] extremely powerful bombs of a new type may be constructed." Einstein went on to say that "a single bomb of this type, carried by boat and exploded in port, might very well destroy the whole port together with some of the surrounding territory."

This may have sounded like science fiction, except for one thing. "I understand," Einstein stated, "Germany has actually stopped the sale of uranium from the Czechoslovakian mines which she had taken over …"

This last statement was enough to lead President Roosevelt to inaugurate the Manhattan Project, America's own (and top secret!) atomic bomb program. For Einstein's letter also had made clear that uranium was a vital ingredient in the production of nuclear weaponry. And if Germany was prohibiting the export of uranium from Czech mines, thus the sale of the ore to Great Britain, which also was working on the bomb, then Germany indeed had a program up and running.

The Super-Bomb Memorandum

Einstein's fears of a German bomb program were well grounded. A document titled "Memorandum on the Properties of a Radioactive Super-bomb," classified top secret, went the rounds of the top scientists in the United States early in 1940. In part, it read:

1. The United States believed that the super-bomb would be practically irresistible.

2. The bomb could probably not be used without killing large numbers of civilians.

3. "… It is quite conceivable that Germany is, in fact, developing this weapon …"

4. It must be realized that no shelters are available that would be effective and could be used on a large scale. The most effective reply would be a counter-threat with a similar weapon."

Led by a theoretician named Werner Heisenberg, Germany indeed was coming into "possession of this weapon."

The Search for Heavy Water

Working in a Berlin laboratory, Heisenberg in early 1941 had reached the point of designing a heavy-water reactor.

But where would they get heavy water? Germany had no facilities for producing it. But Norway did. Near the town of Vemork, the Norwegians had built an establishment called the High Concentration Plant. It specialized in the production of heavy water.

Now recall the American memorandum. It ended with the words, "The most effective reply [to a German atomic bomb] would be a counter-threat with a similar weapon." Who else might have had a "similar weapon"? Believe it or not, Japan; but the Land of the Rising Sun was no threat to Nazi Germany. Then who else had the weapon?

Bet You Didn't Know

Containing more hydrogen than the amount in the familiar formula for water, H_2O, heavy water is used as a moderator in certain kinds of nuclear reactors.

Great Britain. At the Cavendish Laboratory at Cambridge University, the British also were working on an atomic bomb program. They, too, needed heavy water.

Both Germany and Great Britain thus had a good reason to cast longing eyes on Norway, and not for the sake of love. Norway had something else, too, of interest to both countries: the northern Norwegian port of Narvik.

The major raw material lacking in Germany's Ruhr Valley was iron ore. This had to be imported, and the closest mines to Germany were in northern Sweden. Ever since the start of Germany's industrialization, iron ore had been hauled from those Swedish mines by land to Narvik, then by sea along the Norwegian coast to Germany.

Map of Denmark and Norway

The Norwegian coastal route was vital to the maintenance of the German economy. Britain and France also were short of iron ore. Without steel, they could never hope to carry out their war with Hitler.

During the Phony War, therefore, both sides, Germany and France along with Great Britain, prepared to seize Narvik and the heavy-water facilities of Norway. Never mind that Norway was a neutral country. The race to Norway culminated on April 8, 1940.

The Race to Norway Is On

The next day, in a Berlin press conference, Ribbentrop, the Nazi foreign minister, gloated: "Gentlemen," he said to the reporters, "yesterday's Allied invasion of Norwegian territorial waters represents the most flagrant violation of the rights of a neutral country. … However, it did not take Germany by surprise … It was the British intention to create a base in Scandinavia from which Germany's flank could be attacked. The plan included the occupation of all Scandinavia—Denmark, Norway, and Sweden. The German government has the proofs that French and British general staff officers were already on Scandinavian soil, preparing the way for an Allied landing."

Much of Ribbentrop's claim was sheer nonsense. Nonetheless, the Allies and the Germans had engaged in a race for Norway and the Germans had won.

Allied plans for the disruption of the flow of iron ore to Germany had been in the works ever since the German conquest of Poland. Appointed First Lord of the Admiralty in September 1939, Winston S. Churchill had looked for a satisfactory plan of action. But he was not yet in the commanding position of prime minister, and like any other bureaucrat, he found that his ideas had to be vetted by committees—British committees, French ones, military and economic staffs, and so on. All the deliberations took time. Nor were the discussions mere matters of quibbling. In its war with Germany, Great Britain counted on the neutrality of the Scandinavian countries. Yet wouldn't an attack on Norway undermine that land's neutral stance? Churchill had no good answer to that objection.

Then an event in Scandinavia intervened: At the beginning of December 1940, Stalin invaded Finland. The action was an extension of the Nazi–Soviet Pact, which had allowed Russia a free hand along the Baltic. The heroic resistance of the Finns won the hearts of much of the world. For whatever reason, Hitler did nothing to help the Finns. Thus, he gave the British an opportunity to exploit him for the purposes of propaganda. If Great Britain and France went to Finland's defense, they would have to cross the territory of Norway and Sweden; and it would just happen that on the way, the Allies would overrun the Swedish iron ore mines. In fact, Churchill's idea was so great that, at a bilateral conference held on February 5, 1940, the British and French high commands both bought it.

Unfortunately for the Allied planners, early in March 1940, Finland surrendered. So the Finnish pretext for an invasion was removed.

In Paris, the government of Éduard Daladier fell from power; the French people were outraged at the lack of assistance given to Finland and indeed to carry out the wider war. He was replaced by a Paul Reynaud, and Reynaud was under enormous political pressure to take action somewhere, anywhere. Churchill, too, thirsted for action. Britain and France, therefore, organized a joint flotilla to take Narvik and other northern Norwegian ports, no matter the diplomatic consequences.

This was on April 5, 1940, and as the naval staffs in Paris and London knew full well, up along the high Norwegian coast the ice was about to melt. Iron ore shipping would soon resume. So the Allies had to move fast.

At that point Churchill threw a new spice in the pot. As long as we're at it, he asked, why not place mines in the Rhine River? *"Mon Dieu!"* you can practically hear the French saying. Hitler hasn't bombed us at all. If we mine the river, though, he's bound to do so.

All this took up another day. Only on April 7 did a slow-moving convoy of Allied ships rendezvous in the English Channel and start northward.

Denmark and Norway

Berlin in the meantime had its spies. The top brass there were fully aware that the Allies at last were moving. Hitler again unleashed the *Blitzkrieg*, the lightning war. The Nazi strike up through Denmark and Norway was so quick that when Allied troops landed near Narvik and the other ports, they discovered that the Germans were already there. The British and the French scurried away from the Norwegian coast as fast as they could go. The Danish–Norwegian campaign was over practically with a snap of the fingers.

Hitler did face one setback. With his own victory over Finland, Stalin ordered the deportation from all the lands he had seized around the Baltic of the 100,000 or so resident Germans. He was afraid that, as in Austria, the Sudetenland, and Danzig, Hitler would use these German-speakers as a pretext for an invasion of the Soviet Union.

Hitler was outraged over this forced exodus of ethnic Germans. For the moment, however, he did nothing about it. He was now casting his eyes toward the west.

The Schlieffen Plan Revised

From a point in the Maginot Line, just outside Strasbourg in France, a pair of young French sentries hunched their heads down to glance through the slot in their concrete pillbox. It was shortly before dawn on May 10, 1940. The sun was about to peek over the hills of Germany to the east, and the bridge that led across the Rhine to the Nazi fortifications at Kehl still glittered with innumerable little lights. But soon the river would ripple and flash in the sunshine, the air would become dry and clear, and the sky would grow blue and cloudless and warm. One of the sentries leaned against the barrel of his 75mm, knowing that soon he could be off duty far below, sleeping on his bunk in the Maginot Line. In the underground barracks, his comrades were already stretching and yawning as they climbed out of bed, waking to another boring day of the Phony War. Like the sentries far above them, they were weary, restless—and safe.

Just how unsafe they and their fellow French really were would become clear in a matter of hours. After the success of the Scandinavian venture, Hitler believed that the time had come to eliminate the danger from France and Britain on the western frontier. In all likelihood, Hitler had no plans for an invasion of the British Isles: Although he could bomb London and other cities, his navy was not strong enough to cross the Channel. And he may have considered a war between German and Great Britain, almost cousin nations, highly irrational. All the same, if Germany could knock the French out of the war and deprive the British of a base on the continent, the kind of base they had used in the First World War, the *Reich* would be secure on the west. Then he could concentrate on the great foe to the east, the Soviet Union.

Hitler and his top generals spread out their maps and dusted off the old Schlieffen Plan. The basic idea of the plan still seemed valid: The German armies would wheel through Belgium (and this time, Holland—why not?), driving along the Channel coast and striking down toward Paris.

Two points encouraged the resurrection of the Schlieffen Plan. First, with airplanes and tanks, the German forces could move much faster than in 1914. Second, because Germany was not yet going to war with the Soviet Union, there would be no temptation to divert troops to the eastern front, as the German high command had done fatally in the autumn of 1914.

Still, there was a big problem: the Maginot Line. While it possessed no offensive capability, it did allow the French to position huge numbers of troops along the Belgian frontier. They presented the German army with a much more formidable defense than Poland could possibly have mustered.

Hitler's generals were nervous. This time, they were not at all certain of success.

But Hitler had an idea. The principle of the old Schlieffen Plan had been to encircle the French from the north. But what if this time Germany simply turned the Schlieffen Plan upside down, encircling all those French defenders upward by Belgium from the south?

"From the south?" the generals asked, aghast. "But where?"

Through the Ardennes Forest, just above the Maginot Line, Hitler contended.

"Impossible," the generals said. "It's impassible."

Back in the time of the Roman Empire, most of central Europe had been covered with forests so thick that they were practically jungles. In his book on the Gallic Wars, Julius Caesar had gnashed his teeth over how difficult it was to track down the German tribes in those forests. Throughout the centuries since, most of the woodlands had given way to pastures and crop-growing plots. But the Ardennes Forest remained. And it *did* present obstacles.

Hitler pooh-poohed those obstacles. He was convinced that his armored units could traverse the woods successfully (and when they did he fancied himself a world-class military strategist who no longer had to listen to his generals). So the Ardennes Forest it was.

Before dawn on May 10, 1940, just as our French sentries were about to go down for breakfast, the 19th German Armored Corps under the command of General Heinz Guderian was rumbling along with their lights extinguished through the Ardennes Forest. In the lead came the *Panzers*, the tanks, and the armored cars and reinforced motorcycles; next came the troop trucks, the heavy artillery, and the supply echelons;

and finally, stretching 50 miles to the rear, came the columns of German athletes, the elite corps of the Nazi infantry, the blond supermen of the Third Reich.

It was pitch dark in the mountains and the drivers had to exert the utmost powers of vision to avoid ending up in the roadside ditches. The sound of the motors was getting on everyone's nerves. More and more troops who had been quartered in the forest were getting underway; more and more armored vehicles were emerging from the approach roads to join the main columns of tanks. The men were uneasy and nervous, wondering what would happen when they crossed into France.

They need not have worried. *Luftwaffe* (air force) crews were also up and about in their *Stukas* and *Heinkels*, droning off toward Holland and Belgium, diverting the attention northward. The bombers were perpetrating an enormous feint, trying to persuade the French that Hitler was launching the old Schlieffen Plan.

But he wasn't. Before noon, May 10, 1940, the German armored units had driven through the Ardennes Forest, crossed the rivers into France, and begun their race to the English Channel. Not to Paris, not right away. Their objective, designed by Hitler, was to come upon those huge French armies from the rear. Within days they did so. The result was a rout.

Escape from Dunkirk

The story of Dunkirk, the French port right on the Belgian border from which most of the British Expeditionary Force escaped between May 26 and June 4, 1940, has usually been portrayed as one of the utmost heroism. Indeed, there was heroism aplenty. Learning that the Germans surrounded the British by land and were closing in rapidly, hundreds of Britons crossed the Channel in all manner of craft, from tugboats and yachts to skiffs and even rowboats, braving swooping attacks from the *Luftwaffe* to evacuate the troops.

But there was more to the story than that. Large numbers of British officers had deserted their men to climb aboard the earliest boats. Once on English soil, many of those rescued were so demoralized that they threw their weapons out train windows. Some, upon meeting their wives, changed into civilian clothes and simply walked home. In private, Churchill, who on May 10 had succeeded Chamberlain as prime minister, told some of his ministers that Dunkirk had been "the greatest British military defeat for many centuries."

Despite all the attention it has received, the escape from Dunkirk was only one episode in the larger story: Hitler's utter humiliation of the Allies.

The Fall of France

A dozen days after the final escapes from Dunkirk, France surrendered. Hitler's upside-down version of the Schlieffen Plan had worked brilliantly, catching the huge French armies from the rear and causing general panic. With the French in rapid retreat, the Germans marched into Paris almost unopposed.

Thereafter, along with the ministers of the government, what remained of the French army fled, first to Tours in the Loire Valley and then to Bordeaux on the southwestern coast. But it was all over. On June 16, 1940, Premier Paul Reynaud formally surrendered.

The Germans immediately allowed the formation of a new French government. Headed by Marshal Philippe Pétain, the aged hero of Verdun in the First World War, it established its capital in Vichy, a southern resort town. The Vichy government was allowed to administer the southeastern two fifths of France. The rest of the country fell under direct Nazi rule.

In the north of France, Hitler savored a moment of victory. At the end of the First World War, on November 11, 1918, Marshal Ferdinand Foch, then the French commander in chief, had officially taken the German surrender aboard a railroad carriage at Compiègne at a crossing in the fields of Flanders. The French later erected a monument on the spot. Now, on June 22, 1940, Hitler entered into France. He stopped his procession at that monument.

Bet You Didn't Know

William Shirer, an American correspondent, was watching Hitler on June 22, 1940. Hitler's face, he wrote, was "alive with scorn, anger, hate, revenge, triumph. He steps off the monument and contrives to make even this gesture a masterpiece of contempt. ... He glances slowly around the clearing. ... Suddenly, as though his face were not giving quite complete expression to his feelings, he throws his whole body into harmony with his mood. He swiftly snaps his hands on his hips, arches his shoulders, plants his feet wide apart. It is a magnificent gesture of defiance, of burning contempt for this place and all that it has stood for in the 22 years since it witnessed the humbling of the German Empire."

Having ordered Marshal Foch's railroad car extracted from a Paris museum and returned to Compiègne, Hitler stepped aboard and read the terms of surrender to a French delegation. They spelled out the geographical limits of Vichy authority but they made no demands on France's overseas empire. Under German and Italian supervision (at the last moment, Mussolini had entered the war on the side of Germany), the French were to disarm their warships in home ports.

All this the French delegates found more or less acceptable. Then Hitler made one more demand. France was to turn over all the anti-Nazi German refugees who had found safety on its soil. By this, Hitler meant primarily that he wanted the escaped Jews of Germany turned over. One of the French officers, General Charles Huntziger, protested, but Wilhelm Keitel, a German general present in the railroad car, cut him short. "Warmongers and traitors," the German informed the Frenchman bluntly, were to be extradited "at all costs." In that moment began the French participation in the Holocaust.

The Least You Need to Know

♦ Well before the United States began its Manhattan Project, Nazi Germany had embarked on research intended to develop the atomic bomb.

♦ Early in April 1940, the Germans on the one side and the British and French on the other engaged in a race to conquer Norway. Ships along the Norwegian coast were like a huge conveyor belt, transporting iron ore from northern Sweden to the factories of the Ruhr Valley in Germany.

♦ Hitler wanted to avenge Germany's defeat in 1918. So he adopted a variant of the Schlieffen Plan, encircling the French armies through the Ardennes Forest and thus from the south, enabling German armored units to approach the French forces from the rear.

♦ With the French surrender, Nazi Germany was engorged, controlling Norway, Denmark, Holland, Belgium, and Luxembourg. As best he could, Hitler proceeded to impose on those captured countries the same racist policies that had enveloped the Third Reich.

Chapter 20

The Occupied Countries: 1940–1941

In This Chapter

- How Great Britain smuggles Brigadier General Charles de Gaulle out of France
- Life in Poland under the Nazi regime
- Life in Denmark under Nazi rule
- Life in Norway under the Nazi regime
- Life in the Low Countries under Nazi rule
- France's willful participation in the extermination of the Jewish people

On many occasions, after the German troops had marched into Paris, they acted like farm boys seeing the big city for the first time in their lives. They gawked at the Eiffel Tower, took snapshots of the Arch of Triumph, and ogled the girls in the dance halls. They seemed nothing like conquering heroes. Some, to be sure, had affairs with the French. But on the whole the Parisians treated them with disdain. So did most of the people in the other conquered countries, even when the Germans brutalized local populations. Wherever they went, the Germans made themselves thoroughly loathed.

Brigadier General Charles de Gaulle's Escape from France

On the morning of June 16, 1940, the day of the French surrender, a British general named Edward Spears was in Bordeaux. Fluent in French, he was a special aide to Churchill, assigned to bring out of France the sole high-ranking French officer who was willing to continue the fight. The officer in question was the extremely tall Brigadier General Charles de Gaulle.

Spears had flown to Bordeaux on a private airplane. After landing at the airport, he had located de Gaulle in a downtown hotel. Bundling the French general, along with Lieutenant Geoffroy de Courcel, an aide, and a trunk with documents salvaged from the war ministry, into a car, Spears returned to the airport.

On the way, he had to inch past abandoned automobiles and refugees sprawled in the gutters. Policemen loyal to Marshal Pétain stood about by the street intersections. Spears could only hope that none of them would notice the trunk and become curious about his destination.

Spears and de Gaulle were lucky. Not until the airport gate were they stopped. The guard at the gate was peering into the car. He was alert and suspicious, wondering why an Englishman was seated with two French officers in an automobile headed for the runway. Fortunately, de Gaulle's profile—the elephantine nose, the clipped moustache, the pouting mouth, and the receding chin—was not yet famous, and so the guard failed to recognize him.

Spears drove on through the gate, and after a few minutes of searching, he found the twin-engine De Havilland in which he had come. The pilot was waving at them from beside the tail of the plane. He came over to the car to work out plans for departure.

Immediately the pilot spotted a problem. He would have to lash the trunk inside the fuselage, otherwise the weight would shift in flight and cause the plane to crash. But nowhere did he have a rope. So couldn't they simply leave the trunk behind?

General de Gaulle said no. The trunk contained lists of names of persons who could join him in organizing the resistance. Someone, he said, would have to find a rope. Brusquely he gave de Courcel an order, and the lieutenant set off on the double to find one.

This, Spears wrote, rated "high among the unpleasant periods of waiting I have experienced. The possibility of de Gaulle's departure from Bordeaux being detected was increasing. Somebody was sure to think of him in the course of the morning; then steps would be taken to locate him."

Beside Spears in the car, de Gaulle sat chain-smoking gold-tipped cigarettes. He seemed oblivious to the danger.

Spears was not oblivious to the danger, for de Courcel had not yet returned and "if it occurred to anyone that [de Gaulle] had gone, the aerodrome would be the natural place to look for him." And in the bright summer sunshine, someone would sooner or later be able to spot him. Yet there was still no de Courcel.

Spears was frightened. He looked first out through the windshield of the car, and then he climbed up onto a wing of the airplane to search for any sign of de Courcel. "Some would remember having seen me in the car with [de Gaulle]," Spears wrote. "That would be the clue. Then there would be a telephone call." Spears looked over the tops of all the parked airplanes. Nothing.

He was in despair. He gazed this way and that across the airport, then started to clamber down again from the wing. Then something caught his eye.

From under the wing of the next plane came someone running. It was Lieutenant de Courcel. As fast as his "stilt-like legs" were going, Spears thought the man was "moving in slow motion." But he was dashing for the place and in his hand he was clutching a ball of twine.

Very few French were willing or able to escape Nazi-occupied France. But General de Gaulle reached London in safety.

De Gaulle's Attempt to Rally a French Resistance

Two days after de Gaulle's escape, de Gaulle made a broadcast to France from a BBC radio studio. "*Á tous les français*" ("To all Frenchmen"), he began. His brief talk was printed up in the form of posters, and some of the French who joined de Gaulle in London—mostly survivors of Dunkirk—smuggled them into France.

Translated, the rest of the poster read:

> France has lost a battle! But France has not lost the war! The government of
> the moment has capitulated, giving way to panic and delivering the country
> into servitude. However, not all is lost. Out in the free world, immense forces
> have not yet entered the fray. One day, these forces will crush the enemy. It is

necessary that on that day France is present at the victory. Then she will recover her liberty and her grandeur. Such is my goal, my only goal!

That is why I invite all French people, wherever they find themselves, to join with me in action, in sacrifice, and in hope.

Our nation is in danger of dying. Let us struggle to save her!

Vive la France!

From London, on June 18, 1940, General Charles de Gaulle had proclaimed the beginning of resistance to the Nazi occupation. Only a few joined him, but he had taken his stance.

Acts of French Heroism

Back on the continent, furthermore, citizens of various occupied countries engaged in individual bits of heroism. Some of their actions are recorded in photographs. Despite a German ban on tributes to Belgium's *World War I Unknown Soldier*, a retired veteran sneaked flowers past Brussels policemen and placed them on the monument. A young Norwegian couple sitting on the grass of a public park arranged stones to form the monogram of King Haakon VII, who had fled the Nazi invasion. On the back of his silk jacket, a jockey at the Longchamps racetrack wore the Cross of Lorraine, once the emblem of Joan of Arc and now the symbol of Charles de Gaulle and his Free French movement. In Amsterdam, Dutch patriots spread their national flag beside an Amsterdam canal where the Germans had shot 29 of their compatriots; they had been executed in reprisal for a Dutch attempt to assassinate the local SS chief.

Negligible Resistance

Such heroic actions were undeniably brave. But they were isolated and individual acts, part of no organized, general movements of resistance. After the Second World War, occupying Allied forces found that almost nobody would confess to having been a Nazi. In fact, at the war's end, just about everyone in the occupied countries claimed to have been a member of the resistance early on. But it wasn't so. The pattern varied from country to country, but the overall theme was similar to that in France: surrender, resignation, even collaboration with the enemy.

This is not to condemn these populations of people altogether. Who knows how any of us would have reacted when awakened by the sound of jackboots marching on the cobblestones outside or, worse, by loud knocking on our door in the middle of the night.

The fact is that, after the German victory over France and during the Battle of Britain, when it appeared that Hitler might even invade the British Isles, the continental resistance was negligible. With a few exceptions, all the territory from northern Norway to the Swiss border and from eastern Poland to Brittany, the French peninsula that jutted out into the Atlantic, was a geographical extension of Nazi Germany.

> ### Bet You Didn't Know
>
> The massive air campaign in the summer of 1940 was fought to determine air supremacy over the British Isles. If Germany was to have any chance of eliminating its English enemy, it had to destroy the Royal Air Force. The greatest German aerial offensives took place in the middle of August. They succeeded in knocking out most of Britain's airfields. Before the destruction was complete, however, Hitler and Göring, head of the *Luftwaffe*, decided to concentrate on bombing London. While the damage, especially in the East End of the city, was horrific, British pilots were able to concentrate their efforts on oncoming bombers whose course was known. By the middle of September, Germany had lost the Battle of Britain. "Never in the field of human conflict," Churchill said, referring to the pilots of the R.A.F., "was so much owed by so many to so few." It was indeed Great Britain's finest hour.

Poland

A stocky, dark-haired, balding man, Hans Frank was the *Gauleiter* of Poland. A lawyer and an early Hitler supporter, his loyalty had led to his installment in Wawel Castle, the ancient site of Polish kings. He told his wife, Brigitte, that she was going to be the queen of Poland. Once the Germans had subdued Poland, he certainly conducted himself as if he were the monarch. Resplendent in flaring breeches and black boots, he held his official receptions in the throne room. Beneath ancient tapestries, he entertained guests with long tables burdened with Polish hams, cheeses, and bottles of vodka. The guests, needless to say, were not Jewish.

They consisted, rather, of the Nazi elite: Josef Goebbels and Alfred Rosenberg, the Nazi Party's chief theorist. And they included a stream of Aryan movie stars, musicians, and opera singers, a parade of celebrities arriving in Frank's royal railway carriage to take part in his royal parties.

Terms and Translations

Gau means "district," and *Leiter* translates as "leader."

Despite his royalist pretensions, however, Hans Frank knew full well that he served only at Hitler's whim. And he would survive in Wawel Castle just as long as he did his master's bidding: Get rid of the Jews. Under Hans Frank in 1940 and 1941, Poland turned into a grim, gray network of the arrests of Jews, their transportation aboard freight trains from their homes to the concentration camps—Auschwitz in southern Poland was already becoming the most infamous—and their being forced to work as slave laborers.

Those who could work somehow survived, at least for the moment. Those who could not died of exhaustion or were shot.

Frank didn't stop with Jews. Gypsies and Poles also became victims of his not-so-tender mercies. But ironically, he may have been part Jewish. If so, that fact of birth hardly mitigated his rapacious policies.

The corruption of Frank's rule in Poland reached even to his immediate family. His wife, Brigitte, loved to go shopping in the Warsaw ghetto. In their desperation, Jews there were eager to sell their personal belongings, furs, gold, and carpets, at rock-bottom prices. Frau Frank, however, was a sensitive woman. She realized that the Jews hated her very being. So eventually, she took her loot and retreated to her mansion in Bavaria.

If power corrupts, then Nazi power in Poland corrupted absolutely. And for the Jews of Poland, the worst was yet to come.

Denmark

As brutish as they were, the Nazis did know where their bread was buttered—in Denmark. Being a heavily agricultural country, Denmark was a major supplier of meat and butter to the Third Reich. The very food supply of Nazi Germany thus was highly dependent on Denmark: Lots of Germans could eat only if Danish farmers, and actually all the Danish people, were willing to produce and sell.

Even though occupied thus, the Danes were able to drive a hard bargain. They insisted on, and got, the right to self-rule and to keep their constitutional monarch.

They also obliged the Nazis to leave Denmark's Jews alone. About 8,000 Jews lived in Denmark, most of them in Copenhagen. They would have been easy targets for Nazi bigots. Needing the food, however, the Germans at least toned down the persecution.

King Christian X on one of his daily horseback rides through the streets of Copenhagen.

(U.S. Holocaust Memorial Museum)

Norway

The handful of Jews (only 1,800) in Norway were not so lucky. In April 1940, the Nazis desecrated the synagogue in the port town of Trondheim. Soon afterward, Nazi authorities decreed that no Jews could leave Norway. Jewish businesses were confiscated and hundreds of Jews were arrested on trumped-up charges.

Unlike Denmark, Norway, at least official Norway, sanctioned Nazi anti-Semitism. In doing so, Norway introduced a new word into the English language: *quisling*.

Once a military officer serving on the Norwegian general staff, Vidkun Quisling had become the leader of a small group of Norwegians who believed in Nordic racial superiority. Early in the 1930s, he had served as defense minister in a conservative government and had used his post to lash out at the leftist political parties. Later he had formed the Norwegian equivalent of the Nazi Party.

Terms and Translations

A **quisling** is a traitor who serves as the puppet ruler of the enemy occupying his country.

When, on April 9, 1940, the Norwegian government fled from Oslo, the invading Germans set him up as head of a pro-German, anti-British government. In his capacity as prime minister, Quisling insisted that Norwegian schools revise their textbooks, bringing them into line with the Aryan, anti-Semitic slant of those in Nazi Germany. When the history teachers refused to go along with this, Quisling had them arrested. Of the 1,000 or so teachers incarcerated, about 500 were sent to work as dock hands at an Arctic port near the Finnish border. He also revived a defunct passage in the nineteenth-century constitution that had declared Jews and Jesuits to be illegal immigrants. Quisling was laying the groundwork for the deportation of Norway's Jewish community.

Under Quisling's rule, something like 700 Norwegian Jews were arrested and sent to the concentration camps. The rest managed to slip across the frontier into neutral Sweden.

The Jews in the Low Countries, however, were not so lucky. There was nowhere for them to go, except into hiding.

The Low Countries

Holland was a tough place in which to hide. It had no hills or forests to speak of, and the population was dense everywhere. Most important, after the German invasion of France, every country on Holland's borders was Nazi-occupied. The sea afforded no real avenue of escape. Danish fishermen regularly smuggled Jews out of Copenhagen and across a narrow sound into Sweden; however, fishing boats out of Holland were on the high seas, and easily tracked down by German coast guard cutters. The Jews in Holland were trapped.

When the Germans marched through in May 1940, about 1,140,000 Jews lived in Holland. Most were descendants of families that had been fully integrated into Dutch life for centuries: Some of Rembrandt's favorite subjects for his paintings were Jews. On the whole, they were accepted as being fully Dutch.

Bet You Didn't Know

The most famous of refugees was the Frank family of Amsterdam, whose 13-year-old daughter, Anne, began to keep a diary. It would become world-renowned under the title *The Diary of a Young Girl*. Finally captured, she died in March 1945 of typhus in Bergen-Belsen, just days before the concentration camp was liberated.

None of that mattered to the Nazis. In the autumn of 1940, the German occupiers instituted thorough-going anti-Semitic measures: Jews were defined in racial terms and all Jewish business owners had to register with the authorities as Jews. In November, Jewish professors at the universities at Leiden and Delft lost their jobs and, when outraged Dutch students protested, the Nazis closed the classrooms altogether. Then Jews couldn't use buses and taxies; they couldn't buy tickets to the theaters; and they couldn't check books out of the public libraries. Early in 1941, Nazi hoodlums—some of whom were Dutch—began to beat up on Jews at random.

Throughout 1941, the persecution of the Jews in Holland became systematic. All Jews had to register as such and they were forced into ghettos separate from the rest of Dutch society. Then, in July, from Berlin, Heinrich Himmler, head of the SS, ordered the shipment of Jews out of Holland and into the concentration camps, especially in Poland.

Most Gentile Dutch probably were sympathetic to the Jews in their plight. And quite a few tried hard to help. Here and there farmers took in Jewish children, and sometimes city-dwellers allowed Jews to seek refuge in their attics or basements.

The fate of Anne Frank was typical of the Dutch Jews. Aside from individual Dutch families willing to risk their lives, there was simply no one able to help them.

Bet You Didn't Know _____

Belgium was only a little bit better. There, Queen Elizabeth, who had refused to flee, made personal pleas to Nazi authorities, thereby saving thousands of Jews from deportation to the camps. Joseph-Ernest Cardinal van Roey, the highest-ranking Roman Catholic in the country ordered all his institutions to give help to the Jews— at least whenever they could. Priests and nuns, schools and hospitals, joined in a massive effort to conceal Jewish families. So did a well-organized Jewish underground.

At the start of the Nazi occupation, some 65,000 citizens of Belgium were Jewish. 25,000 of them survived. The survival rate was not exactly great, but at least some Belgians in high positions made valiant efforts to save Jewish lives—which was more than one could say about the French.

France

When the Germans entered France, Reichführer Hermann Göring made a little speech to the gauleiters who were going to rule the country:

> What happens to the French is of complete indifference to me," he told them. "Maxim's [the famous restaurant] must have the best food for us but not for the French. ... I intend to plunder in France, and profitably. There will be such inflation in Paris that everything will go for smash. The franc will not be worth more than a well-known type of paper used for a certain purpose.

Göring was true to his word. Wearing the sky-blue uniform of the chief of the *Luftwaffe*, he accompanied Hitler to Compiègne to celebrate the victory over France.

But he didn't stay long. Instead, he slipped away to Paris where he studied the artworks in the Louvre—not for the sake of aesthetics but rather for theft. His aides then spread out all over Occupied France, into museums and private homes, cataloguing and then seizing all paintings, sculptures, carvings, and furniture of any value whatsoever. If the owners were Gentiles, they had to sell at ridiculously low prices; if they were Jewish, the property was declared "ownerless" and simply hauled away.

The Nazi looting of France was also official. France had to pay the costs of the German occupation.

In occupied France, however, Jewish-owned businesses were no longer busy. In September 1940, German authorities promulgated the first of their anti-Semitic measures, defining as Jewish anyone who had at least two Jewish grandparents and ordering a census of the Jewish communities. Once identified as Jewish, shopowners and the like were required to post bilingual signs: "*Jüdisches Geschäft*" and "*Entreprise Juive,*" both meaning Jewish businesses. The lettering was in black on a yellow background.

Most of the French treated their German occupiers with icy disdain. Signs appeared on lampposts and cemetery gates reading: "For Germans only." Referring to the weather in Russia, a few placards made a sardonic joke: "Frost—the best method against pests."

By the spring of 1941, few if any were joking. In May, Parisian police, happy to do the Nazi bidding, rounded up nearly 4,000 foreign-born Jews (most of whom were refugees from Nazi Germany and other occupied countries to the east) and forced them into a sports stadium. They were shipped on cattle trains to an internment camp in northeastern France. And before 1941 was over, 30,000 more such Jews had also been packed away.

Vichy France was no better. This was the unoccupied zone in the southeastern two fifths of France, presided over by First World War hero Marshal Philippe Pétain.

In October 1940, the Vichy regime interned more than 7,000 Jews who had fled from Germany and Austria. These people were hauled by train to camps in the Pyrenees where, during the winter of 1940 to 1941, a good eighth of them died of disease, starvation, or the cold. And that was just the start.

The spring of 1942 witnessed the beginning of the widespread deportation of Jews living in France to the death camps in the east. An order from Himmler of the SS stipulated that within three months France was to send 100,000 Jews to Auschwitz. French authorities out in the departments did their best to comply. Most of the Jewish refugees, however, were not in the countryside but had congregated in Paris.

That fact brought about the horror of the night of July 16, 1942. Several thousand Parisian policemen that night spread out through the darkened streets, tracking down Jews whose names and addresses had been established in the census. Police agents gleefully called the search the *grande rafle*, the clean sweep.

From various sources, anonymous telephone calls, notes in mailboxes, and whispered warnings, many of the refugee Jews knew that the roundup was coming and were able slip out of the city. Others committed suicide.

But on the night of the grande rafle, the police of Paris arrested 12,884 Jews. In time, fewer than 400 of those detained returned alive from the concentration camps. Of those arrested, 4,051 were children. All perished.

The Vichy regime did not last much longer. In November 1942, British, Canadian, and American forces under the leadership of General Dwight D. Eisenhower successfully invaded Morocco and Algeria. Although both had remained French colonies, Vichy had failed to defend them against the Allied attackers. To seal off the southern French coast from another such invasion, the Germans took over power in what had been Unoccupied France. Vichy now was a government in name only.

Hitler had completed his conquest of France. But that victory did not suffice. Hitler had already looked to the whole basin of the Mediterranean for further gains.

The Least You Need to Know

- For the conquering Nazis, Poland became a vast source of loot: Nazis in plunderland. They also turned Poland into a killing field.

- Denmark was different, primarily because the Nazis knew they needed the fruits of Denmark's labor-intensive but very productive farms. The Danes thus were able to mitigate the persecution of their fellow citizens who were Jewish.

- Although various Gentile Dutch and Belgians offered hiding places to the Jews, their efforts could only be sporadic. By 1942, the anti-Semitic terror in Holland and Belgium was full-fledged.

- The French collaboration with the Nazis was, by choice, large-scale. Such collaboration took place in Occupied and Unoccupied France alike. Why, when the French and the Germans had hated each other for decades, did so many French so obligingly accept the occupation and indeed accommodate it? Perhaps anti-Semitism in France was as strong as it was in Germany.

21

The First Warnings: 1941–1942

In This Chapter

♦ Great Britain's retaliation begins

♦ Hitler's campaign to take over the Balkans

♦ Italy's fight in the Balkans

♦ Rommel's initial success in North Africa

♦ Rommel's defeat at El Alamein

Despite the resounding victories in Scandinavia and Western Europe, Berlin greeted the New Year 1941 without much joy. On New Year's Eve, the German capital was nearly deserted. Instead of fireworks, searchlights glided across the black of the sky, scanning the heavens for signs of British bombers. Only a few buses were out in the snow-covered streets; their interior lights were turned off and the top halves of their headlights were hooded with black. No street lights were on and whatever parties took place did so behind shuttered windows. Berliners were experiencing what had become a nightly event: the blackout.

Retaliation Begins

The physical darkness paralleled the spiritual bleakness that had settled over the city. People felt depressed, not the least of them the foreign correspondents. "I vegetated on through the long black night of the second war winter," wrote Howard K. Smith, a young reported with United Press and later an esteemed television commentator. "I was losing my eagerness to see and learn in a tidal wave of despair. My lethargy was not unique. Already old names, long connected with news from Berlin, were disappearing for the simple reason that their owners were sick at heart. ... The pressure that forced them, one by one, to desert Berlin, was finally christened with a name. Those of us who remained called it the 'Berlin Blues.' The name stuck, to describe those awful pits of gloom each of us fell into with periodic regularity, and which grew more severe as the war wore on."

One of those who left was William Shirer, the American reporter we have quoted already. (See Chapter 18 for more information.) He had left just before the New Year. Once he was well away from the Reich, Shirer lashed out against "the Nazi blight and the hatred and the fraud and the political gangsterism and the murder and the massacre and the incredible intolerance and all the suffering and the starving and the cold and the thud of a bomb blowing the people in a house to pieces, the thud of all the bombs blasting man's hope and decency."

But now the bombs were starting to thud away in Germany itself. How was this so? With the defeat of France and the imposition of Nazi control on the occupied countries, Hitler and his legion of propagandists had told the German people that all was well—that they ruled much of Europe and were invulnerable to retaliation.

Yet the retaliation was now underway! Germans hardly dared ask the question: Had Hitler lied to them? The answer was almost unthinkable. Yet here came the bombs as proof.

The Bombing of Germany Commences

The Germans could not deny that they had asked for it. After the failure of Germany's fighter planes to vanquish their English counterparts in the Battle of Britain, Reichmarshal Göring had authorized a new phase of the air war, the massive bombing of Britain. The operation had begun on the morning of August 24, 1940.

The day was a Saturday and for once the skies over southeastern England were clear and bright. "*Luftwaffe* [air force] weather," some Britons worried. They were right. By 9 A.M., more than 100 German bombers, protected by long-range *Messerschmidts*, were up from their new air bases in France and over the English Channel, hitting a British airfield near Dover first. Darkening the sky, they rumbled on toward London. Outside the British capital, they demolished two more landing strips.

They had not yet hit London itself. Göring had strictly forbidden that step. Why, nobody knows. Perhaps he fancied himself marching in triumph from an undamaged Buckingham Palace to the undamaged Houses of Parliament. Or perhaps he was shrewd enough to see that the bombing of London would only raise British morale. Some of Göring's air commanders wanted to have a go at the British capital. Göring was aghast. "Would the people of Berlin capitulate under terror bombing?" he demanded. "I do not believe it. I cannot see the people of London pleading for mercy either." Believe it or not, Hitler backed him up.

On the night of August 24, two German bombers flew off course and, desperate to get back safely to their home bases, dropped their bombs to save fuel. They didn't realize that they were over London: London was living under a black out. The bombing was an accident, as the German high command realized.

But did the British know it? The next night, August 25, Royal Air Force bombers unloaded over a Berlin suburb. At this point all restraint was gone. "When the British declare that they will increase their attacks on our cities," Hitler told an audience, "then we will raze their cities to the ground. We will stop the handiwork of these night air pirates, so help us God! When the British air force drops 3,000 or 4,000 kilograms of bombs, then we will, in one raid, drop 300,000 or 400,000 kilograms. ... In England they are filled with curiosity and keep asking: 'Why doesn't he come?' Be calm. Be calm. He is coming! He is coming! ... The hour will come when one of us will break, and it will not be National Socialist Germany!"

The Nazis Bomb the Coventry Cathedral

Throughout the winter of 1940 to 1941, the damage to London, especially in its East End, was appalling. Yet the greatest damage took place about 100 miles northwest of London at Coventry. During a 10-hour-long attack on the night of November 14, 1940, German bombers dropped hundreds of tons of bombs, killed more than 500 persons, and wounded another 800. The attack leveled a good 100 acres of factories and homes and it gutted the ancient cathedral at Coventry.

Coventry soon stood as a symbol of British resilience and desire for revenge. The revenge did not come about immediately. For German bombers based in Belgium and northern France, skipping across the English Channel and dropping their bombs was an easy matter. For the British to reach Germany, however, was another matter altogether: London and Berlin are about 700 miles apart. Fuel tanks were small, navigational devices were primitive, and the German ground defenses were potent.

Despite the obstacles, the British did make technological improvements. The development of radar, combined with the breaking of the German codes, enabled them to fend off what might have been the worst ravages of Germany's own bombing. Radio-honing devices improved navigation and improved bombsights enabled navigators to single out targets in Germany.

Throughout 1941, the British air attacks on Germany became more and more accurate; British bombers at one point, without destroying the factories, spread terror throughout the Ruhr Valley. But the British raids were still hit or miss. Great Britain simply did not have the financial resources to transform the Royal Air Force into a long-range bombing contingent.

Germany Declares War on the United States

Britain's circumstances changed, however, four days after the Japanese bombing of Pearl Harbor. That's when Hitler declared war on the United States. His doing so may have made some sense. In the summer of 1941, America joined the British in the Battle of the Atlantic, helping track down German submarines and assisting the British in the sinking of the mighty German battleship the *Bismarck*. Washington had also extended substantial financial and military help to Great Britain. (The program was nicknamed Lend-Lease.) So Hitler's declaration of war may well have been simply an acknowledgment of what in the real world already existed: an alliance between Great Britain and the United States.

Whatever Hitler's reasons, the immediate result of America's joining the European war was the infusion of U.S. know-how and wealth into Britain's bombing efforts. Swarming into air bases in East Anglia in the summer of 1942, American military fliers brought with them a new confidence and a new strategy.

The strategy had to do with the American rejection of the British nighttime bombing in favor of daylight attacks. Their own new bombers, the B-17 Flying Fortresses and the B-24 Liberators, were superior to anything the British could put in the air. (We might add that when Hitler declared war on the United States, he didn't have a clue as to the kind of aircraft

---

Modern Day Parallels

Is there anything like Lend-Lease today? Sure. We call it "military aid."

Bet You Didn't Know

The confidence showed up in paintings on fuselages of naked women with suggestive names such as "Ima Vailable" and "Dinah Might." A lot of the British started complaining that the Yanks were "overfed, oversexed, and over here."

that Boeing and other West Coast American factories could make, or to the speed with which they could crank them out.) They could fly higher than any British bomber and, each carrying 10 .50-caliber machine guns, they were far better equipped to fend off Luftwaffe counterattacks. The American bombers also carried the Norden bombsight, so accurate that, it was said, a bombardier could "drop a bomb in a pickle barrel" from 20,000 feet. Such precision bombing, carried out in daytime, appealed to the American frontier pride in marksmanship.

The British didn't warm to the strategy but they soon saw its advantage over anything they could try. By mid-1942, American bombing raids over Germany were wreaking havoc with the industrial production of the Third Reich.

All this added up to a mighty warning to Hitler and his followers in Nazi Germany. They had gone too far. If they had left Great Britain alone, perhaps America would have stayed out of the conflict.

Hitler, ironically, understood full well the consequences of another American intervention in Europe. He had been afraid of that intervention all along. Yet as if obsessed (and perhaps he was), he next embarked on a course of action that could not have been better calculated to ensure his doom. He extended the war again.

Hitler Lays Out the Balkan Campaign

Hitler's attack on the Balkan peninsula stemmed from a lot of things. In 1940, his ally, Mussolini, had invaded Greece and Albania. *Il Duce's* entry into the Hellenic peninsula, however, had led him to a swift defeat and the Albanians were slowly but surely driving the Italians out. With the Italians in retreat, Great Britain was placing troops in Greece. (Throughout the nineteenth century, Greece had been a British protectorate and the Greek and British royal families were united by blood.) With the British nearby, the Yugoslavs in turn were resisting German demands for cooperation, meaning trade concessions and going along with the Reich's anti-Semitic policies.

Yugoslavia, furthermore, had just undergone a palace coup. The pro-German regent, Prince Paul, had been replaced by a pro-British government under the young King Peter II.

You have to wonder: Did Hitler think that the British under Churchill were planning an attack on Germany from southeastern Europe? Churchill called the region Germany's "soft underbelly." And back in the First World War, when he was Lord of the Admiralty, Churchill had presided over the Gallipoli campaign. For the British, the effort had led to disaster. Yet the objective had been getting at Germany from the rear or the bottom. Hitler may have feared the same thing again.

By way of explaining the Balkan attack, there was another factor, too. As early as the beginning of 1941, Hitler was laying plans for the invasion of the Soviet Union. There's no question about this one. A British-supported Greek-Yugoslav bloc—both the Greeks and the Yugoslavs had shown their hostility to German advances—to Hitler was unacceptable. It threatened the flank of his drive toward the east. To Hitler, therefore, the threat had to be removed.

The German invasion of the Balkans began on April 6, 1941. Joining Germany in the assault were Hungary, Romania, and Bulgaria; they all saw an opportunity to take advantage of German power and increase their own holdings in the region. Besides, Hungary, Romania, and Bulgaria all had governments that sympathized with Hitler's anti-Semitism. Racism was hardly contained to Nazi Germany.

German-Occupied Europe

The invasion had a political as well as a military purpose. The largest state in the Balkans, Yugoslavia, was the last remnant of the Versailles Treaty: It had been part of the Allied-conceived *cordon sanitaire* (a sanitary corridor) designed as a buffer against aggression in Eastern Europe. Like Czechoslovakia, it contained a host of ethnic groups, some of which were at odds with the others. In particular, the Serbs, living largely but not exclusively in the old Serbia, tended to be Eastern Orthodox in religion. The Slovenes, living in the north along the border of Hungary, and the Croats, who were concentrated along the Adriatic coast, were Roman Catholic. Wanting to break away from the Yugoslav union and to form an independent country, the Croats were strongly pro-Nazi.

The Germans gave the Croats what they wanted, the separate country of Croatia (which exists again now). And with German support, the *Ustashi*, a Nazilike paramilitary Croat unit, carried out pogroms against local Jews and Serbs. Thus were sown the seeds of hatred that led to the Balkan wars of the 1990s.

Serbian Sentiments

The Germans had little difficulty in overrunning the rest of Yugoslavia. And they did so with a vengeance. After the palace coup in Belgrade, which had taken place in the middle of March, the Serbian people had made clear where their sympathies lay. The new king was distinctly anti-German, and when he took over power, crowds in the street had shouted anti-Nazi slogans and had even spat on the automobile of the German ambassador.

None of this meant that the Serbs were pro-Western. (Although those who staged the coup had had encouragement from an American named William Donovan, who became the first director of the Central Intelligence Agency [CIA].) In a way, what was going on was a replay of what had led to the First World War. Serbia saw Hitler the Austrian as a threat, as the old Austro–Hungarian Empire had seemed a threat; Serbian sympathies as in 1914 lay with Russia. And like the "mad counts of Vienna," Hitler was determined to crush Serbia.

So while the Croats took care of Serbs in their own territory, the Nazis went after Serbs and Jews in Serbia and Bosnia big time. Peter II, the new king of Yugoslavia, and the leading members of his cabinet fled the country, setting up a government-in-exile in London. Lesser members of the defunct government landed in Nazi jails. Then came the Jews. Of the 12,000 Jews who had lived in old Serbia, about two thirds were residents of Belgrade. There, within a week of the German invasion, the Nazis began to register them and force them to wear the identifying Star of David. Then, following the usual pattern, the Nazis stripped them of their homes and businesses and proceeded to "Aryanize" Serbia. Then came the internments and (because Yugoslavia did not have concentration camps) mass shootings. By mid-November 1941, in Serbia, the Nazis had murdered 5,000 male Jews. In December, they rounded up most of the women and children and shot them to death, too.

A few Jews escaped the roundup. But as in France there were Serb collaborators, and they hunted down the Jewish survivors, turning them over to the Nazis. By the beginning of 1942, Yugoslavia no longer had a "Jewish problem."

Isolating Thrace

The German assault in the meantime had continued southward into Greece. The attack began on April 12, 1941; this time Italian and Bulgarian units joined the German attackers. Facing them were combined Greek and British forces.

Isolating Thrace—that's the part of Greece that extends over to Turkey and that lies just below Bulgaria—the Germans and the Bulgarians started down the Aegean coastline. On the western side of the Balkan peninsula, the Italians and the Germans grabbed the Dalmatian coast, soon trapping alot of the Greeks in Albania. In the center of Greece, the Germans took on the British (actually largely Australians and News Zealanders), quickly forcing them back down toward Athens.

German bombers reached Athens early in the morning of April 26. At about 4 A.M., an American scholar working in an archeological institute in the Greek capital heard "a blast of ungodly sound and weird blue light. ... The whole southern sky flamed over Piraeus [the port by Athens], an unearthly brilliance that silhouetted the calm Parthenon to stark ghostly beauty. … From neighboring houses came sounds of maids screaming, and the wild cries of a macaw. Nothing in all the sound effects of catastrophe in Hollywood films could match the crashing thunder, the crackling individual blasts under the greater roar, the howl of the dogs, and human shrieks."

Down in the harbor, all was madness. A British tanker, hit by German bombs, stood there blazing. The flames jumped to a British supply ship loaded with dynamite. A destroyer tried to tow it away, but before they could reach the breakwater, the supply ship exploded, obliterating the destroyer. The explosion shattered windows a dozen miles away, in Athens itself. Refugees started to flee the city.

The British government admitted that it could give Greece no more help. Soon Greece surrendered, King George II fleeing for safety to Alexandria.

The Assault on Crete

Then came Crete, a mountainous 160-mile-long island below Greece and Turkey at the bottom of the Aegean Sea. Crete served as a British naval and air base; it lay within striking distance of Romanian oil fields that Germany needed badly. Besides, for Göring, Crete offered a chance to be reborn. He had lost the Battle of Britain. Now, in the Mediterranean, he could have another go at the British. And this time he was assured of victory.

Thanks to ULTRA, the British knew exactly what they were planning and when. All the same, the British forces on Crete were too weak to defend the island.

> **Bet You Didn't Know**
>
> ULTRA was the special security classification the British gave to information gained from breaking the code of the standard German radio enciphering machine, called the ENIGMA. Just before the outbreak of the war in September 1939, the Poles had given the British and the French reconstructed copies of the German machine. Just how the Poles got hold of an original machine is pretty much of a mystery, even today. Nonetheless, believing their codes safe, the Germans persisted in using ENIGMA until the end of the war. That was a major blunder.

The German assault on Crete came on the morning of May 20, 1941. Shortly after 6 A.M., a group of *Stukas* appeared in the blue sky over the island. They were diving and screaming at the same time, just as they had done over the mountains of Greece.

It got worse. From the ground, the British on Crete next saw contingents of huge planes in mass formations; many of the planes were trailing gliders that looked like "young vultures following the parent bird from the roost." Then suddenly the sky was full of specks, most of them white, but some also red or green or black or yellow, floating to earth and looming ever larger. The Germans were landing glider and parachute troops.

They hit the ground running, and by May 27, Crete was in German hands. Hitler's forces were now in a position to command the eastern end of the Mediterranean.

Like many Austrians and Germans, Hitler had a reverence for classical antiquity. Accordingly, he ordered his forces in Greece and Crete to treat the Greeks with all due consideration.

Not so the Jews. The ghastly old pattern repeated itself. Throughout Greece, Jews were evicted from their homes, humiliated, and arrested. By July 1942, about 10,000 Greek Jews, rounded up for forced-labor battalions, died in malaria-infested swamps. At the same time, Jewish businesses were smashed or taken over.

So the Balkan campaign was really the same old story. Outwardly, Nazi Germany was all-powerful. Inwardly, the stench of anti-Semitism was as strong as ever.

The Italians Surrender in the War in the Desert

In North Africa, the Germans were proving just as potent militarily as they had been in the Balkans. Ironically, however, North Africa would bring Hitler his second warning, if he chose to listen to it.

Back on June 10, 1940, Italy had declared war on France and Great Britain. Mussolini had then given a speech from the marble balcony of his office in the *Palazzo Venezia* in Rome. After announcing the declaration of war, he exhorted the crowd gathered below: "Italian people! Rush to arms and show your tenacity, your courage, your valor!"

He wasn't sending troops to fight against the British in their home island. He wasn't that foolish. What he had in mind was the expansion of his own empire from Libya, already an Italian colony, eastward into Egypt, Somaliland, and Ethiopia, areas largely under British control. Because Great Britain was fighting for its life above the English Channel, Mussolini figured, the time was ripe for him to grab off British interests along the Suez Canal. For the Italians, descendants of the Roman Empire, that shouldn't be a problem.

On June 28, 1940, Mussolini issued orders for the invasion of Egypt. He called it the "great reward for which Italy is waiting." The preparations took most of the summer, but Mussolini kept telling his people, "We are a revived nation! We can fight!" Finally, on September 13, the Italians pushed out of Libya and into Egypt. They moved with five infantry divisions, seven tank battalions, and 80,000 troops—against 36,000 British men in Egypt. Great odds. What they didn't realize was that they had set forth on the road to disaster.

At first the advance went well. In only four days, as they followed the Mediterranean coastline, the Italian legions reached Sidi Barrani, an oasis 60 miles into Egypt. And the British contested the advance.

For the Italians, a few things did go wrong. Their troop-bearing trucks would run up against desert boulders and fall apart. The landscape was barren, the sun was broiling hot, and the food for the enlisted men went bad. But the officers had a good time of it. Their own food was refrigerated, and they had gallons of wine, and they slept on sheets.

December 9, 1940, was the day of disaster. On that date the storm hit. Having built up their forces, the British counterattacked and the Italian advance turned into a retreat. It wasn't just a retreat. It was an utter rout. Chasing the Italians back across the desert, the British, or actually the Australians, on January 22, 1941, reached the Libyan port town of Tobruk. Overrunning the place, some of the Aussies used captured Italian tanks painted with white kangaroos so their comrades would not mistake them for the enemy.

At Tobruk, the Italians gave it up, surrendering and boarding troop ships for home. Disgusted over his ally's failure, Hitler decided to make his own run for the Suez Canal. So down across the Mediterranean he sent a full contingent of German tanks under the command of the officer who had emerged as the hero of the attack on France, Lieutenant General Erwin Rommel.

Rommel Is Triumphant

An officer of keen intelligence and tremendous energy, Rommel handled his desert tank corps with brilliance. His orders from Berlin had been to engage in defensive action only. By the time he reached Africa, however, he sensed that he could easily wage an offensive. So it was. On March 31, 1941, he opened his first desert campaign, sweeping the British almost entirely out of Libya and back into Egypt. On June 21, 1942, he took the Australian-held fortress at Tobruk. Then he penetrated into Egypt much farther than the Italians had gone, to a way station 50 miles west of Alexandria called El Alamein.

In the House of Commons, Churchill paid Rommel a rare tribute: "We have a very daring and skilful opponent against us, and, may I say across the havoc of war, a great general."

Helping Rommel's reputation as a great general was the fact that, for once, the SS didn't follow in the path of German victories. Libya, of course, was a lightly populated country with few Jews. Even so, Rommel's successes were not marred by the usual Nazi atrocities.

Rommel, nonetheless, displayed weaknesses. He was arrogant, as perhaps he had a right to be. But he spent so much time right on the front lines that he could not be in the rear, tending to his line of supplies.

And the supply line for Rommel was getting choked. For Hitler and the general staff in Berlin, the building of air defenses around the German cities, the war in the Balkans, and the invasion of the Soviet Union (coming right up in Chapter 22) took priority over North Africa. In an ideal world, Hitler would have liked to liberate Egypt from the British. But his world was not ideal—increasingly less so. Germany's resources for war were finite and the Russian campaign was eating up more and more of Germany's capacity for waging war.

With American aid, furthermore, the British in Egypt were building up their own supplies, preparing to meet Rommel at El Alamein. The British commander was General Bernard Montgomery, soon known as Montgomery of Alamein.

Rommel Withdraws from El Alamein

Shortly after dusk on October 23, 1942, Montgomery launched his attack on the German forces at El Alamein. Although the Germans were well dug in, the British hit with an overwhelming superiority of men and equipment.

Rommel knew that he could not hold out. On November 2, 1942, he radioed Hitler, asking permission to withdraw. Hitler's response: "… there can be no other thought but to stand fast, yield not a yard of ground, and throw every gun and every man into the battle. … As to your troops, you can show them no other road than that to victory or death."

Although not a Nazi, Rommel had admired Hitler. But this now ended. What Rommel saw as the insanity of Hitler's order was the beginning of the general's disillusionment with the Führer, a disenchantment that would lead to Rommel's death.

Despite Hitler's command, Rommel did withdraw from El Alamein. The British victory there marked the beginning of the end of the

Supporting Actors

Rommel later was stationed in France to fend off the expected American-British invasion. But again he wasn't given the resources to do the job properly. By this point, he had come to doubt Hitler's leadership.

North African war. The downfall of Nazi Germany began with Hitler's invasion of the Soviet Union in the summer of 1941.

The Least You Need to Know

◆ From the start of the Balkan campaign to Rommel's push into the Egyptian desert, Nazi Germany enjoyed a considerable string of victories.

◆ Even in Yugoslavia and Greece, the Nazis instituted their systematic efforts to destroy the local Jewish populations; in Yugoslavia, they had substantial help in this from the Catholic Croatians who went after not just Jews but also Serbs.

◆ This chapter presents two kinds of warning to Nazi Germany: the start of the bombings from bases in Britain, and Rommel's defeat at the hands of the American-supported British in North Africa. Had Hitler heeded the warnings, Nazi Germany might have survived. Of course, he might have gone too far already for survival. In any case, he pushed ahead heedlessly.

Chapter **22**

Barbarossa: 1941–1943

In This Chapter

- ◆ The Nazi attack on the Soviet Union
- ◆ Hitler's early successes
- ◆ Hitler's decision not to invade Moscow
- ◆ The Nazis' failure to take control of Leningrad
- ◆ The role of the *Einsatzgruppen*
- ◆ The Russians' success defending Stalingrad

By the middle of 1941, the European theater of war had settled down to a kind of stalemate. The Germans were bombing Britain and the British were bombing—or at least starting to bomb—Germany. The Atlantic Ocean was the scene of significant naval fighting. German submarines were sinking thousands of tons of foodstuffs and other commodities bound for Great Britain but the Royal Navy, with American assistance, was gradually fending off the submarine menace. Most important, the United States had not yet entered the war officially and massively.

The Consequences of Hitler's Invasion of the Soviet Union

It's easy to look back with hindsight and say that American entry was inevitable. At the time, however, in mid-1941, America's entry into the conflict was far from assured. Isolationists in Congress, the press, and elsewhere—the most famous of whom was Charles Lindbergh, the aviator—seemed to hold sway.

But then, in the summer of 1941, Hitler invaded the Soviet Union. As he did so, a funny thing happened on the way to the Kremlin. For almost a quarter of a century, most Americans had seen the Soviet Union—not Nazi Germany but the USSR—as the world's public enemy number one. Stalin had the reputation of being the breaker of nations. With good reasons, too. Even American Communists saw Stalin's entering into the 1939 pact with Hitler as an act of betrayal, and the Soviet invasions of Poland, the Baltic states, and Finland left just about any remaining U.S. sympathizers horrified.

Then Hitler invaded the Soviet Union and, almost overnight, in the eyes of the American public, Stalin the butcher became kindly old Uncle Joe, a beleaguered leader sticking up for his people. As American sympathy for the plight of the Russian people rose, so sank the influence of the isolationists.

Didn't Hitler realize the effect his attack on Russia would have on American public opinion? If he did, did he care? Was he so obsessed with the idea of *Lebensraum* that he couldn't grasp the consequences of his war with Russia? Or was there something else, too? Had Hitler trapped himself in his own myth as the Führer invincible? Had he so accustomed the German people to victory that he could not resist going after yet another victory?

These are old questions and the answers are probably anybody's guess. But one thing is certain: By the summer of 1941, Hitler's public image of omnipotence and omniscience had never been so visible to the people of Germany. Hitler's image, as expressed in paintings and sculpture, and mounted almost everywhere for the public to see, had never been more pompous.

Image-Making at Its Most Grandiose

Hitler as an art critic? You bet he was. He knew what he liked and he foisted it relentlessly on the German public. He couldn't stand what we call modern art. The paintings of Van Gogh, Gauguin, Picasso, Chagall, and Modigliani (the last two of whom were Jewish) he considered decadent, and down they came from museum walls. Hitler wanted the public to see heroic pictures and statuary. So all sorts of junk, representations of powerful Aryan men and nubile Aryan women, went on display.

Such art was so important to Hitler that he created an arts bureaucracy. Its function was to censor what the public could see. Those artists who met the Aryan criteria became showered with patronage, favorable criticism (Goebbels banned all negative criticism of Nazi art), and exemption from military service. For they were performing service already: The new art was intended to awaken Teutonic pride, turn that pride toward war, and when war came, sustain the spirit of German nationalism.

Yet the art that Hitler loved the most was of himself.

In a studio filled with heroic statuary and busts of Nazi notables, a sculptor named Josef Thorak created a Hitler head, many times the size of life, looking determined, even-featured, even handsome.

All this must have gone to Hitler's head. The allure of the art led him to believe in his own heroic myth. Yet the myth was a trap. He had to sustain the myth: He seemed to recognize that if his heroism lost its forward momentum and that if he allowed Nazi Germany to stagnate, his own popularity and the support of the German masses for the Nazi regime would be undermined, fatally so.

In a sense, Hitler had ceased to be a person but rather the Führer, exalted above mere humankind. But to remain the Führer, the leader, he had to lead. Otherwise he might relive his days in Vienna again, or worse.

In that spirit, in July 1941 Hitler launched his biggest war ever, an invasion of the Soviet Union. The code name for the attack was "Operation Barbarossa."

Terms and Translations

Barbarossa means "Red Beard." It was the name given to a Greek-born Turkish pirate of the mid-sixteenth century. He raided Spanish ports and shipping, captured Algiers, Tunis, and Nice, and for three or four years ruled the Mediterranean. As a code name, Operation Barbarossa was obviously intended to deceive the Soviets about the imminence of the attack. Like America's own military code names, such as Operation Just Cause and Desert Storm, it was also supposed to inspire the troops to victory. The choice of this particular designation, however, contained a startling irony: Barbarossa's rule in the Mediterranean was short-lived indeed.

The Nazi Attack on the Soviet Union

Winter hung on late in Russia in 1941, at least in Moscow and Leningrad. Snow was on the ground even on May Day, and the chilly fogs were still rolling in from the shores of the Baltic well into June. Even the summer carried the promise of winter again, for late June was unseasonably cool. Despite these omens, however, Hitler plunged ahead.

Operation Barbarossa, Hitler's scheme for the defeat of Russia, started off in grand style. From a series of points along the borders of Poland and East Prussia, a massive force of three million soldiers, riding everything they could climb on, from *Panzers* and armored cars to motorcycles, horses, and bicycles, swarmed into the Soviet Union on what proved to be history's largest military assault. The attack went swimmingly, in some cases almost literally. At made points German soldiers waded across streams in Lithuania, Byelorussia, and the Ukraine.

Josef Goebbels at a microphone.

(Eric Stevens)

Engineers threw up pontoon bridges as fast as they could, enabling the infantry to cover as many as 30 miles a day. The *Panzers* moved even faster. By sundown on the first day, June 22, 1941, German armored units had reached more than 50 miles into the vastness of the Soviet Union.

The advance was so swift and so sudden—Stalin and the top officials of the Soviet Union had ignored intelligence warnings of the impending assault—that at one point a German motorcycle unit startled a group of Soviet recruits who were just learning to march. The pace was exhausting. But as in the great triumph the year before in the Low Countries and France, General Heinz Guderian stood high in the turret of his tank and urged his forces ever onward.

By July 10, thousands of Russian troops were dead or prisoners of war. German armored units were approaching Smolensk, more than 300 miles into the Soviet Union.

Even General Franz Halder, the German chief of staff and a man by nature cautious, was ready to celebrate. He had doubted the wisdom of taking on the Soviet Union, with its vast terrain and brutal winters. "It is probably no overstatement," he now however wrote in his diary, "to say that the Russian campaign has been won in the space of two weeks."

The Early Successes

Unfortunately, from Halder's point of view, Russia was an underdeveloped country. The farther the German columns penetrated the countryside, the worse the roads became—when roads even existed. Maps were proving almost useless. Russia furthermore spread eastward like an enormous funnel. The Germans had begun their advance in three coordinated columns. The farther they ranged ahead, however, the farther apart they had to spread. And the farther apart they spread, the more the Russians were able to form guerrilla bands in the fields, marshes, and forests that lay between.

And those guerrillas were fighting unfairly, or so went the German lament. The Russians were breaking the rules, using "Asiatic tricks." They would lie on the ground pretending to be dead, then leap up and shoot at the Germans who were passing over them. Or they would wave white flags of surrender, then fire at those coming to capture them.

The German troops heard such tales all up and down the Russian front. In response, many of them murdered Russians who were genuinely trying to surrender or who were already prisoners. Atrocities raged back and forth. "Our ranks got thinner every day," recalled a German colonel who led a regiment into the Ukraine. "Numberless cemeteries full of our dead appeared along our route."

Impoverished and disorganized, though, the Russian guerrillas could not stop the German juggernaut. The Red Army itself was just about as impotent. The German strategy was to direct the northernmost of its three columns up through the Baltic states toward Leningrad; the one in the middle was to head past Bialystok, Minsk, and Smolensk toward Moscow; and the third was to penetrate the Ukraine, moving toward Kiev.

Germany Takes the Ukraine

In passing through the Ukraine (where at first the Ukrainian population welcomed the Germans as liberators from their Russian oppressors), this third column on June 30 cut off three Russian armies. Some of Hitler's commanders in the field wanted to take Kiev, the Ukrainian capital, but he decided otherwise: Bypassing the city, the German forces pushed on to the Dnieper River that flowed into the Black Sea. The Ukraine was now under Hitler's control.

Wrong! Upon the Nazi arrival, the Ukrainians set up their own government, separate from the Soviet Union. Five days later, the SS knocked it over and jailed its members. In Berlin, Hitler divided the Ukraine into four pieces.

Map showing the German advances into the Soviet Union.

The southern hunk he gave to Romania, one of his Eastern European allies; another piece he turned over to Nazi authorities in Occupied Poland. The other two parts fell under the control of the *Wehrmacht*, the German army.

Sent to administer the latter two parts of the Ukraine, Erich Koch, a Nazi bureaucrat, boasted to his assistants: "I am known as a brutal dog. For this reason I was appointed *Reichskommissar* [regime leader] of the Ukraine. I am expecting from you the utmost severity toward the native population."

Koch's aides took him at his word. To encourage the spread of disease, they tore up sewers and other sanitary facilities. They stopped the shipment of food to hungry areas. And they sent away inhabitants for slave labor in Germany: From Kiev alone, 38,000 Ukrainians were sent off in cattle cars.

"There is no Ukraine," Koch declared. "We are the master race!"

Collaborationist Ukrainians accepted his doctrine, joining the Germans in the murder of Jews. One of the worst massacres of the Second World War took place at Babi Yar, a large gully near Kiev. In two days in September 1941, more than 35,000 Soviet prisoners, Ukrainian partisans, and Jews were executed. Their bodies were dumped in a mass grave.

> **Bet You Didn't Know**
>
> Although their languages are similar and while they share a common history, Russians and Ukrainians are not the same people. There's a Ukrainian museum in Toronto that shows graphically the sufferings of Ukrainians at the hands of the Russians. So when the Germans showed up, the Ukrainians at first thought they had a good deal.

Russia Retreats

Operation Barbarossa so far was an astounding success. In only two months of fighting, the Russians had lost nearly two million men, dead or wounded. Germans controlled a swath of Soviet territory that was almost 500 miles wide. Up along the Baltic, the Germans had pushed to within 100 miles of Leningrad. In the Ukraine, they had overrun half the region, were on the Dnieper, and were ready to advance to the industrialized areas beyond the far bank of the river. And in the central zone, the German forces were only 200 miles from Moscow.

At this point, all the Russians could do was to retreat, trading space for time, or so they hoped. Stalin was prepared to evacuate Moscow.

This was at the end of August 1941. In Russia, winter comes early and stays long. Even at this point the nights were turning quite chilly. The German commanders in the field knew that they had to move fast, before the true onset of winter left them immobilized for months. So General Guderian, in command of the middle column, believed that he had to strike immediately toward Moscow. Once Moscow had fallen, he believed, Russia would surrender and Nazi Germany would have won its greatest victory ever.

Then Hitler intervened.

Conflict over Goals

To the German commanders on the ground, it seemed so easy: Push on just a few days more, take Moscow, and the war on the eastern front would be over. Ordinary soldiers agreed. As they moved east of Smolensk, German troops pounded hand-painted markers along the roadsides. They read "To Moscow."

But Hitler refused to go that way. Perhaps he realized that exactly 129 years before he launched his attack on the Soviet Union, Napoleon had also marched to Moscow. But the Corsican's capture of Moscow had not led to a Russian surrender. Indeed, it had represented a fatal overextension of his supply lines and hence, his ultimate defeat. Perhaps Hitler feared the same fate.

> **Memorable Places**
>
> In the Wolf's Lair, an encampment that served Hitler as a forward headquarters, General Halder kept talking about Moscow. But Hitler would not be dissuaded. "The Führer right now is not interested in Moscow," Halder told aides. "All he cares about is Leningrad."

Whatever his reasons, however, Hitler was adamant about a change of plans. Back in July, he had given orders for the infantry to march to Moscow. Now, though, at the beginning of September, he split the central column in two. Half of the units, commanded by Guderian, headed for the Ukraine. "This means that my *Panzer* Group would be advancing in a southwesterly direction," Guderian complained to his diary, "that is to say toward Germany."

The other half of the central column, led by General Hermann Hoth, was to head for the Baltic. There it was to help the northernmost column in the capture of Leningrad.

The Siege of Leningrad

Built by Peter the Great in the early eighteenth century, Leningrad—the once and future St. Petersburg—was known as the Venice of the North. Bridges arched its many canals, and facing each other over the Neva River were the cathedral-fortress of Sts. Peter and Paul and the graceful spire of the Admiralty Building.

Leningrad was a city of beauty and vulnerability. The Soviet armies had retreated eastward in a gigantic contracting semicircle, leaving Leningrad exposed to attacks from three sides: the Finns (who at least for the sake of exacting revenge on Russia had aligned themselves with Germany) by land from the northwest; the German navy by sea across the Baltic; and the German columns by land from the west and the south. Only Lake Lagoda to the east provided Leningraders any means of escape.

On September 4, 1941, Stalin notified Churchill by cable that the Germans were close to Leningrad. He refrained from telling Churchill, however, that the Germans, controlling the rail lines, had cut off communications between Moscow and Leningrad or that he was on the verge of surrendering the latter city.

What saved the city—if a salvation it was—was the determination of the local Red Army commanders, supported by the populace, to hang on.

The Germans never did capture Leningrad. But they did impose a horrific siege. In the city, constant bombing and shelling compounded the shortage of food. Once food reserves were gone, Leningrad could get sustenance only by boats from Lake Lagoda (and then, after the lake froze, by sled and truck across the ice). But the Germans caught on to that supply route and bombed the supplies to no more than a trickle. Soviet authorities enforced strict food rationing; violators were shot or sent to the front to work in labor units.

The rationing did little good. Starvation and the Russian winter set in at about the same time. Throughout the long, dark, cold months, Leningraders died by the thousands and the streets were littered with corpses.

A question arises, doesn't it? Why, with the bulk of the Red Army hundreds of miles away, with a city ringed with no natural defenses, and with inhabitants dead or starving, could the powerful Wehrmacht not have pushed into the city with ease? If Warsaw, why not Leningrad? Perhaps the Germans were overstretched. Or—perhaps—they *wanted* to inflict horrendous suffering on the Russian people.

That is speculation. But it accords with something else: the sending of the notorious SS *Einsatzgruppen* (inserted groups) into the Soviet Union, whose units followed the regular army and whose explicit task was the extermination of hundreds of thousands of Jews and other so-called enemies of the Nazi state.

The Masters of Death

The *Einsatz* operation almost defied imagination, yet it was for real. The first phase of the plan, opened at the same time as the German invasion of the Soviet Union, called upon the Einsatzgruppen to slaughter the Jews of the Soviet Union. Between 1941 and

1943, the executioners murdered some 1.5 million Jews, lining them up, shooting them, and shoving them into mass graves.

A second phase of the plan, unleashed in December 1941, targeted the Jews in the occupied countries of Western Europe.

An operation of this size needed support. We now know that, in addition to the "ordinary men" who carried out the mass murder, the staff back home in Germany consisted of economists, architects, and lawyers—people we would normally consider the pillars of their communities. Maybe they were, in German eyes. They were also Hitler's willing executioners.

To the Gates of Stalingrad

As expected, the howling winds and deep snowfalls of the Russian winter (1941–1942) saw a cessation of the German advance. The coming of the spring did not give the Wehrmacht much of a chance to progress: The rivers of Russia overflowed their banks with massive floods.

Summertime allowed the Germans to move forward again. This time, intending to finish the Russians off, they drove hard toward the southeast, moving beyond the Black Sea all the way to the Volga River. There, a good thousand miles from the borders of the Third Reich, they reached Stalingrad.

The Germans planned to crush the city in a pincers attack. The offensive was scheduled to start on August 23, 1942. It worked and the Germans entered the city.

This time, however, it was they who were trapped. In 1943, the Soviets instituted their own siege—the beginning of the end of Nazi Germany.

The Least You Need to Know

- Increasingly megalomaniac, Hitler believed that his judgment could never fail—hence the invasion of the Soviet Union.

- At the outset, the invasion went so well that most foreign reporters predicted the quick surrender of the Soviet Union.

- The Germans inflicted stupendous sufferings on the Soviet people, sufferings explicable by no military necessities. With regard to the Jews, the Nazi program had evolved into one of genocide.

- German forces did enter Stalingrad. Here all advance stopped. The ensuing battle of Stalingrad in 1943 proved to be the turning point of the war in the east.

Part 5

The Decline and Fall of Nazi Germany

For Hitler and Nazi Germany, the invasion of the Soviet Union was the beginning of the end. It was, to put it in terms of Grecian and Shakespearean tragedy, the fatal flaw. Representing a vast overextension of resources, the invasion weakened Germany enough in the occupied countries to allow the rise of serious resistance. It also meant that Germany simply didn't have the wherewithal to fend off Eisenhower's landing in France and drive to the Rhine. Insanely, Hitler's henchmen also diverted enough military personnel from the fronts to bring the Holocaust to its hideous climax. In the end, the once invincible Nazi military machine was unable to hold off the destruction of Germany. Germany's surrender was one of total defeat, as you'll see in the following chapters.

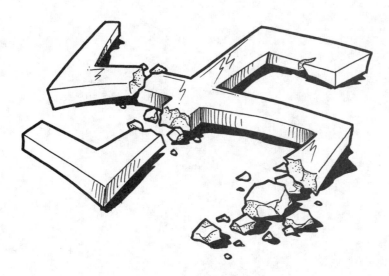

23

The Turn of the Tide: 1943

In This Chapter

- ◆ How the Germans lose Stalingrad

- ◆ With ever-thinning resources, Germany also loses North Africa

- ◆ The Allies take control of Sicily and Italy

- ◆ How the Resistance movement also aids in the fall of Germany

- ◆ The Nazi regime continues its quest to exterminate all Jews, no matter what the cost

It may be hard to do, but for the moment let's put aside the criminality of Hitler and his regime and look at what's happened so far from an international perspective. One of the things that fueled Nazi Germany's drive for the dominance of the European continent was a sense of resentment. Almost to a person, and whether Nazi or not, Germans had felt maligned by the Versailles Treaty. They denied, they vigorously denied, the allegation that Germany had been the sole cause of the First World War. So now, by the end of 1942, they had punished their accusers—the British, the French, and the Russians. Germany appeared to be the master of Europe.

Nazi Occupation in 1942

Almost from the moment of Hitler's rise to power, Great Britain had contested that mastery. As we have seen, the idea that the British under Prime Minister Chamberlain appeased Hitler is largely a myth; as long as they could, the British resisted Hitler's expansion with economic means. Then, when they seemed to have a sufficient arsenal, the British turned to the September 1939 declaration of war. The British, however, were fooling themselves: They couldn't stop Hitler on the European continent. And while they could use the English Channel as a barrier against a Nazi invasion, they could secure a victory only by doing everything in their power to bring the United States into the war. By that very token, however, the British were relinquishing their once unquestionable lead in international affairs.

Hitler's Germany was on the make, and by the end of 1942 he seemed to have replaced Great Britain as the world's leading power. Yet the Nazi invasion of the Soviet Union was an action that assured an equal and opposite reaction.

Slowly, ever so slowly, but surely, the Soviets retreated, regrouped, and revenged. Stalingrad marked the ultimate extension of Nazi power. And when the Germans lost there, the Russians came howling after them like wolves out of the Siberian forest.

In the end, Great Britain and Nazi Germany had something in common. They were both like aging racehorses who suddenly could not keep up the pace. The Anglo–German contest for the mastery of Europe gave way to the division of that continent between the new racehorses, the United States and the Soviet Union.

Stalingrad and the German Retreat

"My Führer," asked General Heinz Guderian, the tank commander, "why do you want us to attack on the East at all this year?"

"You are quite right," Hitler answered. "Whenever I think of this attack, my stomach turns over!"

It was springtime, 1943—"Springtime for Hitler," to use a song title from *The Producers*—and all along the front that stretched the nearly 2,000 miles from Leningrad to the eastern part of the Black Sea, the Germans were experiencing a strange foreboding.

In the Soviet Union, the Germans had fought, and lost, a crucial battle at Stalingrad. The battle had fallen into two phases: the German attack and occupation of the city, which had lasted from August to November 1942; and the Soviet counteroffensive, which had begun in mid-November and ended with the destruction of the German Sixth Army at the end of January 1943.

Most of Stalingrad lay on the west bank of the Volga River; Friedrich Paulus, the German general in charge of the offensive, had believed that once he could cross the river, the Soviets would be finished. His strategy had been to have his infantry and light armored units approach the city from the northwest and a *Panzer* army from the southwest. The city was supposed to fall quickly. Much to Paulus's surprise, however, the Soviets had held the pincers apart: The Germans had not reached even the suburbs until September 1942. Throughout that month and October, a German bombardment had completely destroyed Stalingrad. In November, the Germans had entered an almost wholly deserted city.

In that same month, however, the Soviet Army, under the command of Marshal Georgi Zhukov, had sprung a nasty surprise. From east of the Volga, he had sent two columns across the ice of the river, coming at the Germans from the north and the south. The besiegers had been besieged.

Trapped inside the devastated city, General Paulus had appealed to Hitler for permission to surrender. Hitler had refused permission. Fighting through the snow, the Soviets had forced their own way back into the city, destroying General Paulus's army.

Hitler's Strength Is Waning

By the end of January 1943, the Battle of Stalingrad was over. The Germans had lost more than 200,000 men, and 90,000 more had marched out of the city in captivity.

After Stalingrad, for the Nazis nothing had been the same as before. The German armies on the eastern front had lost their strength and had faced a constantly growing and constantly improving Red Army.

It is little wonder that Hitler, in conversation with General Guderian in the springtime of 1943, confessed to near nausea.

Hitler had more than stomach sickness. He had a great big problem. Hitler's prestige both at home and among his various European allies demanded a show of strength. Yet the strength of his military machine was seeping away.

This fact of life was becoming obvious throughout the Nazi alliance network. Mussolini was looking for a way out of the war. Romania's Marshal Ian Antonescu and

Bet You Didn't Know

Conditions in the Soviet prisoner of war camps had been brutal. In 1955, when the Soviets finally released those still imprisoned, the German survivors numbered no more than 5,000.

Hungary's Admiral Miklos Horthy, the dictators of those small countries, were hoping for contacts with America and Great Britain, accommodations they hoped would shield them from the coming Russian revenge.

Even at home, Hitler's support was starting to crumble. Consumer goods and services were curtailed. Boys as young as 16 and men as old as 65 were being called up for military duty. Women between the ages of 17 and 50 had to work in the munitions plants. Under the leadership of Albert Speer, war production increased: He doubled the output of airplanes and tanks and tripled that of artillery. But he did so at the cost of increasing slave labor and at considerable cost to the civilian economy. Discontent was growing.

Realizing that he could no longer attain victory over the Soviet Union and yet for political and personal reasons needing that victory, Hitler proposed a compromise. He who throughout his career had been extremist was now seeking a middle way. On March 13, 1943, the Führer told his top generals, "It is important for us to take the initiative at certain sectors of the front if possible before the Russians do, so as to be able to dictate their actions in at least one sector."

Gathered around Hitler in the Wolf's Lair encampment in East Prussia, Hitler's generals pored over their maps. Where, they asked each other, could they find a spot where they could be reasonably sure of a victory? After much deliberation, they came up with what they thought was an answer: the Soviet city of Kursk.

Hitler Is Outsmarted in Kursk

Kursk lay about one third of the way up the vast semicircle on the map from Stalingrad to Leningrad. The place had no great value in itself. But it was also situated in the middle of a bulge the Soviets had knocked in German lines. If they could take Kursk, the generals reckoned, they could at least drive the Soviets back and straighten out the front. Maybe that way they could get a stalemate, they thought.

The numbers may not be reliable, but many military historians have considered the Battle of Kursk, fought in the early summer of 1943, to be the largest armored fight in history. It certainly was ferocious. At the end of June, the Germans faced the bulge around Kursk with nearly a million troops, 2,700 tanks and assault guns, 10,000 big guns, and 2,000 airplanes. Confident of victory, Hitler ordered the German offensive, code-named *Zitadelle* (Citadel), to start on July 5.

At first the assault went perfectly. As in the old days, the German armies just gobbled up the land. But the land mass was incomparably greater than in Holland or Belgium. And Marshal Zhukov was about to spring a trap.

German military intelligence, once probably the best in the world, had broken down. What Hitler's generals did not realize was that they were outnumbered. Also with a million men, the Soviets possessed more than 3,300 tanks and armored vehicles, 20,000 pieces of artillery, and nearly 3,000 aircraft.

That wasn't all. Zhukov had ringed Kursk with six concentric defensive belts, meaning 6,000 miles of trenches, and had armed each circle of trenches with 22,400 antitank mines.

How had the Soviets been able to build such potent defenses? For one thing, they had American help. Far more important, at least so the Russians say, soon after the German invasion, they had moved their factories east of the Ural Mountains. Those factories were not as efficient as their German counterparts, but, placed out in Siberia, they were out of Hitler's reach. They were also much closer than before to sources of iron ore and the like. And Russian workers had labored with fervor. None of which the Germans realized.

Here was the scene after the Germans advanced: Surrounded by high stands of wheat, rye, and sunflowers, the forces of both sides hunkered down, blasting away at many places from point-blank range. Then, on July 8, the firing stopped. And when the last wisps of smoke had disappeared into the summer air, the once-feared *Panzers* the Germans had brought forward were no more than charred ruins.

After the Battle of Kursk, the Germans would fight tenaciously. But they were in retreat and the Red Army was rolling invincibly westward. The hope of a Nazi victory over Russia had been lost beyond redemption.

Rommel's Expulsion from North Africa

The fate of the Germans in North Africa was not much different. After the Battle of El Alamein, General Erwin Rommel's *Afrika Korps* began a dismal retreat toward Tunis. Rommel knew full well that he could not hold on any longer. Hitler had refused to allow retreat but at the same time had provided his forces in the desert with no fuel, transport, or reinforcements.

Then, the British out of Egypt (freshly supplied by the United States) and the American forces crossing Morocco and Algeria pinned Rommel in an ever-tightening grip. By the time the Germans were besieged at Stalingrad, their North Africa campaign was over.

Rommel and many of his top aides managed to escape the Allied vise. But by early 1943, nearly 300,000 Germans and Italians in North Africa had surrendered.

What, for the Germans, had gone wrong in North Africa? And why on earth did Hitler send forces there in the first place? Nazi Germany had no vital interest in the region. There weren't many Jews to murder and Gentile Germans certainly weren't going there to live. Hitler's conception of *Lebensraum* lay to the east. Did Berlin see North Africa as a road to Egypt and the British colonies east of Suez? Surely Greece and Crete would have afforded far better jumping-off points.

Then why? Just about the only explanation imaginable is that Hitler wanted to support his ally Mussolini. And that's ironic because Mussolini didn't join the war on Hitler's side until after the Germans were assured of defeating France. However brutal he was, maybe Hitler was a bit naïve.

In any case, the North Africa campaign, like Operation Barbarossa, stretched Germany's resources to the limit and beyond. Hitler had made the fatal mistake of pursuing infinite goals with finite resources. Thus, he left Germany vulnerable to attack from the south, from Sicily up through Italy, a country that by 1942 was virtually a German colony.

The Allied Invasion of Sicily and Italy

When the Americans and British under General Eisenhower landed on the southern coast of Sicily in mid-July 1943, a combined German–Italian force at first put up a vigorous resistance. The resistance soon crumbled. Yet roughly 230,000 defenders, mostly Italian, were still on the island and Eisenhower was determined that they not escape to the mainland. So he sent troops under the British General Montgomery— Montgomery of Alamein—along with the American General George Patton, to Messina, only three miles from the toe of Italy; the assignment was to get to Messina first and stop any escape. The race was on.

Although most of the Italians were left behind, the Germans succeeded in moving most of their own personnel and equipment across the strait to Italy. At the beginning of September, the Allies invaded Sardinia and Corsica, and then Italy itself—the toe, shinbone, instep, and heel. On October 1, 1943, the Americans entered the port of Naples and the British, having crossed the peninsula on the east, overwhelmed the German airfields at Foggia. On November 8, Eisenhower ordered the assault on Rome.

At the same time, the Soviets had pushed beyond Kiev on the Dnieper. The city of Smolensk, near the border of Latvia and Lithuania, was about to fall to the Red Army.

The Germans continued to put up fierce resistance. This was especially so in Italy, where, in contrast to the huge Eastern European plain, the mountainous spine of the country had enabled them to dig in and set up nearly impregnable fortifications. From November 1943 onward until nearly the end of the war, the Allies in Italy would have to pay dearly for every foot of ground they won.

Nevertheless, Germany's alliance with Italy was breaking apart. From almost the moment of the Allied landing in Sicily, leaders of Italy's Fascist Party realized that their country's defeat was imminent and they put Mussolini under arrest. On September 12, 1943, German commandos in a daring raid freed *Il Duce* (The Leader). Hitler ordered Mussolini reinstalled as head of a puppet government at Lake Garda, well to the north of Rome in the Italian Alps.

Mussolini's power, however, was a sham and most Italians knew it. Instead of following him any longer, the Fascist leaders were soon looking for an honorable way to surrender.

They realized that not even the Germans could hold on forever. Indeed, the Nazi defense of Italy was running up against the same problem Rommel had faced in North Africa: a lack of resources. It's often said that under Hitler, Nazi Germany had to fight a two-front war. Wrong. It was a several-front war. There was the Russian front, that devoured just about all the men and materiel Berlin could throw its way; and there was the Italian front. Then there was another front, not exactly in the sense of a battle line, but rather in that of another war that was emerging: the resistance.

The Resistance

Well before dawn on July 4, 1943, a group of half a dozen Frenchmen, all dressed in black, slipped away from a locomotive roundhouse at Troyes, an industrial town about 100 miles southeast of Paris, and disappeared into the night. For half an hour or so, nothing happened. Then an explosion shook the station. German sentries started to investigate, but before they could learn much, another explosion occurred. Then another and another. By the time the sun came up, thirteen bombs had gone off, destroying six locomotives and severely damaging six more.

Three months later, a pair of Frenchmen disguised as shipyard workers talked their way aboard a German minesweeper anchored at Rouen, downstream from Paris on the Seine River. In the middle of the night, an explosion ripped the ship apart and, within minutes, only the top of its funnel was visible above the surface of the water.

On January 7, 1944, two British paratroopers landed near the southern French town of Figeac. Even before they could bury their chutes, the French foreman of a local airplane factory greeted them; the factory turned out propellers for the *Luftwaffe*, the air force. The three men went to a cheese shop, which belonged to another conspirator, and made bombs they covered with the cheese. The owner of the shop, still wearing a chef's hat, carried the cheese balls across town and the foreman, equipped with a key, let the band into the plant. In the middle of the night, the aircraft factory went up in flames. It produced no more propellers for the Luftwaffe.

These and other such operations were coordinated from London. General Charles de Gaulle's Free French organization played a part in the missions: If you recall, in his flight from France, de Gaulle had saved the names and addresses of many whom he thought could eventually play a part in the resistance. But de Gaulle's funds and personnel were limited. Playing a larger part in developing anti-German sabotage missions was the British Special Operations Executive (SOE).

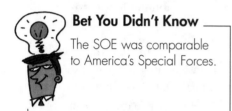

Bet You Didn't Know

The SOE was comparable to America's Special Forces.

Placing trained agents not only in France but also in Belgium, Holland, and Scandinavia, the SOE would radio coded messages, saying where saboteurs could do the most harm. Then airplanes out of Britain would airdrop guns, ammunition, and *plastique*, the puttylike concoction that resistance fighters could wrap around or stick to anything, blowing it practically sky-high.

The Germans were nearly defenseless against such sabotage. Dutch resisters would blow up Nazi trucks. Danish resisters demolished a Copenhagen sports arena that the Germans used as a military barracks. Most important, with the help of British SOE agents dropped in by parachute, Norwegian agents went after that plant that was making heavy water for the Nazi atomic bomb project. Although the plant was heavily guarded and was situated in the deep gorge of a river, the British and Norwegian saboteurs made their way down the icy slope and into the plant. It was the night of Saturday, February 27, 1944. Wrapping their *plastique* around heavy water tanks, they destroyed the operation. In the morning, they also blew up a ferry carrying heavy water to Germany. The saboteurs escaped by skiing to Sweden. The Nazi atomic bomb program never recovered.

Resistance radio operators on the ground also directed Royal Air Force planes in pinpoint bombing of German facilities. These aerial attacks did not cripple German military capabilities in the occupied countries, but they did inflict wounds. And the Germans took the various attacks seriously enough to divert efforts from the Soviet and Italian fronts. The Germans adopted the infamous policy of shooting, say, 10 locals for every German killed. More crucially, the Germans stepped up their efforts to guard their bases in the occupied countries.

It didn't do any good. The more the Germans tried to stave off the attacks by the various national resistances, the more resolve those resisters had in attacking German facilities. The resistance movements created a slow but steady drain on German power. And so did the Holocaust, now mounting to its climax.

The Holocaust, Full Blown

The *Einsatzgruppen* were vicious but they weren't efficient. It was a waste of time to shoot Jews one after another when, instead, the Nazi regime could kill them *en masse* in gas chambers.

The deportation of Jews to the newly constructed gas chambers had begun late in 1942, but gathered steam in early 1943. On February 16, Heinrich Himmler, the SS chieftain, ordered the destruction of the Warsaw ghetto. The liquidation began on April 19. The Jews there fought back but their cause was hopeless: After six weeks, the SS had quelled the uprising altogether. The survivors were sent by trains to Auschwitz.

On and on it went like that. Special trains deported Jews from Minsk, Vilna, and other Soviet cities, from the Baltic states, from France and Rome, Hungary, Greece, and Slovakia. This was the Final Solution, moving at its most rapid pace to date.

Then it might have slowed down. During the Battle of Stalingrad and later, as Germany's military position began to deteriorate, the High Command ordered that all civilian train traffic stop. Trains were to be reserved for the army alone. Himmler, however, went to Hitler and begged for trains. The Führer gave him all the trains he wanted. For Hitler and the Nazi regime, the killing of Jews was more important than saving Germany from the Soviet Union!

Supporting Actors

Were "Hitler's Henchmen" crazy? Judge for yourself. On October 4, 1943, Himmler addressed an SS gathering with the following words:

> I am referring to the evacuation of the Jews, the annihilation of the Jewish people. This is one of those things that are easily said. "The Jewish people is going to be annihilated," says every party member. "Sure, it's in our program, elimination of the Jews, annihilation—we'll take care of it." And then they all come trudging, 80 million worthy Germans, and each one has his one decent Jew. Sure, the others are swine, but this one is an A-1 Jew. Of those who talk this way, not one has seen it happen, not one has been through it. Most of you know what it means to see a hundred corpses lie side by side, or five hundred, or a thousand. To have stuck this out and—excepting cases of human weakness—to have kept our integrity, this is what has made us hard. In our history, this is an unwritten and never-to-be-written page of glory ...

Himmler knew better than to reveal to the world beyond the SS what was happening. At the same time, he saw the destruction of European Jewry as a glorious cause, one that must be pursued even at the risk of defeat and ruin.

Why did the Holocaust mount so intensely at just the time when Nazi Germany was starting its retreat from the eastern front and facing the inevitability of an Allied attack on the western front? The answer does seem to lie in some sort of insanity.

At least that is what quite a number of high-ranking German military figures believed. And only a month after the Normandy invasion that took place in early June, 1944, some of them tried to kill Hitler.

The Least You Need to Know

- The Battle of Stalingrad marked the farthest geographical extension of Nazi power.

- The start of the retreat from Stalingrad coincided with two other critical developments: Rommel's expulsion from North Africa and the ensuing Allied invasion of Sicily and Italy. The German defense of the northern half of Italy was bitter but costly. It put a tremendous strain on Germany's increasingly scarce resources.

- At the same time, the resistance movements in the occupied countries of Scandinavia and Western Europe were becoming ever more potent. In themselves they could not stop the German war machine. But they certainly could give it a lot of flat tires.

- The Holocaust was reaching its terrifying conclusion. It was an act of mass killing but it was also one of mass madness. At a time when the Nazi regime needed all available resources to stem the rising Red tide to the east, the Holocaust represented a massive diversion of those resources into genocide.

- Recognizing the disastrousness of the Holocaust diversion and the ineptitude of Hitler's military leadership, a group of top-ranking German army officers concluded that the only was to save the Reich was to get rid of Hitler. They entered into a conspiracy to murder him.

Chapter 24

The Plot to Kill Hitler: 1943–1944

In This Chapter

- ◆ The landing on the beaches at Normandy
- ◆ How intense Allied bombings begin to cause German dissension
- ◆ The heroic efforts of Oskar Schindler
- ◆ The assassination plot to kill Adolf Hitler
- ◆ Hitler's revenge against his betrayers

In a way, Nazi Germany all along had been based on an illusion. Don't misunderstand this statement. The Holocaust was all too real. And the desire to overturn the Treaty of Versailles was understandable, even accepted in many British and French circles. But the idea that Nazi Germany could then master Scandinavia, the Low Countries and France, the Mediterranean and North Africa, and the Soviet Union, and somehow fend off the power of the United States: All that was just too much. It was a great self-delusion.

As long as Hitler enjoyed success, most Germans denied their country's limits. But when it all began to crumble, as it had to do, then they became more realistic. And the height of realism was getting rid of Hitler.

The Normandy Landing

The Allied landing on the beaches at Normandy on June 6, 1944, was event fraught with hazard. The Germans had prepared well for such an invasion. All along the English Channel coast over to the Atlantic Ocean, *Wehrmacht* (the German Army) engineers had constructed reinforced concrete pillboxes which held machine guns, antitank weapons, and pieces of light artillery. Below the pillboxes, minefields lay below the sand and under the surf. Some of the Allied planners were afraid that the German wall might be impregnable.

Had they been right—had the German defenders thrown back a British and American assault—the consequences could have been grave. America might well have turned from Europe, concentrating its efforts on the defeat of Japan. Great Britain would have stood alone again. Nazi Germany would have been able to send troops stationed along the wall to the eastern front, throwing back the Soviet advance. By the time the American forces returned to Europe—if, indeed, they ever returned—Nazi Germany might well have been the undisputed master of the entire continent.

So the stakes were high, so high that the British had used one excuse after another to postpone the invasion; Churchill's preferred strategy was that of nibbling away at the edges of the Third Reich, continuing the sabotage, counterattacking perhaps in Greece, launching an invasion of France on its southern coastline. Thus, in a war of attrition, like the British naval blockade of the First World War, the Allies could slowly strangle Nazi Germany—without running the risk of failure on the beaches of Normandy.

The man in charge of the operation, General Dwight D. Eisenhower, however, overruled Churchill. "Ike" was all for betting everything on one huge attack. Yet Eisenhower was not above a bit of deception. Following his orders, British and American troops placed dummy tents along with dummy landing craft near the mouth of the Thames. Fake radio broadcasts went out; they indicated that the Allied invasion would take place somewhere around Dunkirk. The idea was to get the Germans to divert troops eastward from the Normandy coast.

Terms and Translations

ENIGMA was the ciphering machine used by the Germans; the British had come into possession of one of these machines. ULTRA was the special security classification given by the British to information gained from breaking the codes sent out by the ENIGMA machine.

The ruse worked. General Rommel, heading the German tank units in northern France, moved units toward the Franco–Belgian border. German intelligence on June 6, 1944, realized that the invaders were coming ashore at Normandy. Rommel rushed back, but it was too late. The Allies were already on the shore in force.

Eisenhower's intelligence units had known of Rommel's move to the east, for ULTRA was transmitting nearly every German message. That knowledge had encouraged Eisenhower and his aides to go ahead with the invasion. Had they possessed one more piece of information, they would have been even more encouraged. The German treasury was nearly bankrupt.

Bombs Away

Or think of the Normandy invasion this way. If Hitler had not invaded the Soviet Union, he certainly would have had a much easier time defending the western front against the Allies. Perhaps he could have staved them off altogether.

The same applies to the ever-mounting Allied campaign of bombing Nazi Germany. The airborne raids might have inflicted substantial damage anyway. But the Reich simply didn't have enough resources left over from the Russian campaign to put an effective air defense system in place.

Bet You Didn't Know

Life in Nazi Germany had been growing progressively tougher. Because of the demands of the eastern front and damage inflicted by British bombing, ordinary Germans in 1941 had been plagued by food shortages. So-called sugar had been made of wood pulp, sausages from beechwood nuts, and beer from whey. Malnutrition had been increasing and so, according to the testimony of many doctors, had the incidence of cancer. Public health was in rapid decline.

In 1942, things grew worse. The British had developed Wellington and Halifax airplanes, bombers that could reach any city in Germany, drop huge tonnage of explosives, and return to bases in Britain. The explosives had been particularly deadly: They had been incendiaries, intended not so much to knock out factories and other buildings as to spread fire; fire (the British had believed correctly) would quickly damage the morale of the German people.

Bet You Didn't Know

All over Germany in 1943 underground shelters such as subways were overwhelmed with people seeking safety from the night bombings. Mob scenes ensued at the entrances and, in the hysteria, people in many cities were crushed to death.

Then came 1943. A case in point: On the night of March 9 and 10, the British celebrated the tenth anniversary of the Nazi seizure of power by unloading on Munich, the Bavarian city that had given birth to the Nazi movement. By the time the Wellingtons and Halifaxes turned back to go home, more than 200 citizens of Munich were dead, more than 400 wounded, and almost 9,000 homeless.

In 1944, American bombers at last joined their British counterparts. Unlike the British, who still flew in at night, the Americans were brazen enough to bomb by daylight. The hell faced by ordinary Germans now continued around the clock. During the first American raid alone, on March 18, 1944, 172 people in Munich died, nearly 300 more were hurt, and more than 4,000 lost their homes. The losses in other German cities were similar.

The Allied air raids exposed Hitler's inability to retaliate as well as the weaknesses of Germany's air defenses. The major attacks were so devastating to industry that the regime had to bring in slave labor. The effect on civilians was also severe. Official propagandists tried to explain the destruction away, blaming the attacks on "Jewish brains" in Washington and "nigger" pilots who hated the white race.

The old appeals to racism, however, were wearing thin on the German population. More and more Germans were becoming hostile to the Nazi regime. Some even began to participate in acts of resistance within the borders of Nazi Germany itself.

Schindler's List

The regime always had had its opponents. Back in 1939, Johann Georg Elser, an unemployed carpenter from nearby Württemberg, had gone into a backroom of a Munich beer hall where Hitler was scheduled to speak, carved a hole in a pillar, and inserted a bomb; the bomb went off just after Hitler and his entourage left.

In 1941 and 1942, conspirators in Munich printed and distributed anti-Nazi tracts signed, "White Rose." In those same years, an American woman, Mildred Fish-Harnack and her husband, Aviv, as members of a resistance group called the Red Orchestra, helped political dissidents escape and provided economic and military intelligence to Washington and Moscow. In 1943, they were discovered, arrested, and executed.

Because of the popularity of *Schindler's List*, an Academy Award–winning movie made by Steven Spielberg in the early 1990s, lots of Americans know of the role played by a few German Gentiles in helping Jews escape. The movie was based on fact. Born in 1908 into a German-speaking family in Moravia, a region that would become part of Czechoslovakia, Oskar Schindler had grown up to become a traveling salesman. Like many Central Europeans, he was fluent in several languages, and he had the charm that allowed him to ingratiate himself into many circles. After the Nazis came into power in Germany, he became a spy for the Reich. In 1939, he set up an enamelware factory in the Polish city of Krakow where, manufacturing dishes for the Reich, he used slave labor. Many of the slaves were Jews.

In 1940, a year after Schindler set up his business, the Nazis built the Auschwitz concentration camp, not far from Krakow. The next year, the Germans established the Ghetto at Krakow, forcing the Jews there to live behind barbed-wire fences and to await whatever fate befell them. Some of them were sent to Schindler's factory, where, perhaps unexpectedly, he treated them humanely.

With the New Year, 1942, the mass killings began at Auschwitz. Aware of the murders, Schindler, again surprisingly for a person of his background, passed whatever information he could get to Jewish underground organizations. The information wasn't much help. In 1943, the Nazis built Plaszów, a slave labor camp, near Krakow, and moved the city's Jews either into it or to the extermination camps. Using his contacts and indeed his charm, Schindler got permission from the authorities to open a "sub-camp" in his factory. There his Jewish laborers were safe from Auschwitz, at least for the moment.

In the autumn of 1944, as the Allied armies were crossing the northern European plain toward Nazi Germany, Schindler pulled off a massive deception. The authorities closed the Plaszów slave camp, preparing to send its inmates to the gas chamber. Wanting to save as many of them as he could, Schindler went back to his hometown in Moravia. There he located an abandoned textile plant and saw that it could be used to manufacture artillery shells. Bribing various officials, he obtained permission to set up a new operation there. With the help of a personnel clerk, he compiled a list of roughly 1,100 Jews slated to be moved from Plaszów to Auschwitz; these Jews, he persuaded his bribed officials, were necessary to run his Moravian shell plant. He got permission to move them there.

Bet You Didn't Know

Schindler continued to bribe officials and even launched an affair with a female SS guard. He may have been a saint, but he was also a sinner.

Schindler, however, had no intention of making shells. He was determined instead to use his plant as a safe haven for even the relative handful of Jews on his list. Some made it safely to his plant, others did not: Schindler's list was full of deletions and typed-in additions. He had to pretend that his factory was for real. All his skills as a sleazy salesman came into play. He purchased shells from other factories and passed them off as his own. He claimed that he had difficulties in obtaining the necessary equipment.

Slave laborers in their bunks at a concentration camp.

(Holocaust Museum)

The Jews in Schindler's plant lived in a state of high anxiety. What if Schindler's lies and bribes should fail? What if the Nazis, in their lust to achieve their greatest aim, the eradication of European Jewry, cared less about getting shells than they did about murdering Jews? Then they would all be dead.

Oskar Schindler himself, and his wife, Emilie, were always in danger. In the eyes of the Nazi authorities, helping Jews was even worse than bribing officials: Many of those who took the bribes still saw Schindler as a criminal.

For the Schindlers and their Jewish workers, it was only a matter of time. If the Americans, the British, and the Russians could close in fast enough, they might survive. Otherwise …

> **Bet You Didn't Know**
>
> Near the end of the war, Schindler and his family, fearing capture by the Russians, made their way across Czechoslovakia to neutral Switzerland. The trip was harrowing but Schindler's silver tongue, along with the diamonds he had hidden in his suitcase and which he used as bribes, eased their way to safety.

The Road to the Wolf's Lair

Quite a few of the high-ranking German officers also realized that it was only a matter of time: The Allies were closing in and Germany's surrender, as they saw it, was inevitable.

But it's fair to say that unlike a few righteous Gentiles like Oskar Schindler, these officers cared little if at all for the imprisoned Jews. Over the years, some of them have been presented as heroes. But it seems just as likely that they were trying to save their own necks. Early in the war, President Franklin D. Roosevelt had made it publicly clear that he intended to treat those who had launched Germany's aggressions as war criminals.

The officers who participated in the plot to kill Hitler on July 20, 1944, claimed that they had switched their loyalty from the Führer to the German state. Maybe so. But they also wished to be able to present themselves to the Americans as "good Germans." They certainly didn't want to fall into the hands of the Russians.

Claus Schenck Count von Stauffenberg

The central figure in the plot to kill Hitler was Claus Schenck Count von Stauffenberg, a handsome officer descended from the Prussian aristocracy. After achieving an outstanding record at the infantry school at Dresden and the cavalry academy at Hanover, he had been commissioned a second lieutenant in 1930. Rising rapidly, he had served as a captain in France. Shifted to North Africa, he had been in a staff car that was strafed by an Allied airplane, and he had received serious injuries. Although barely fit to travel, he was moved to a hospital in Munich. In 1943 he was promoted to lieutenant colonel.

He remained in the Munich hospital throughout the summer of 1943. His injuries were grim—in the attack he had lost his right hand and forearm, his left eye, and the last two fingers of his left hand. During his medical treatment, however, he refused the use of any painkillers. His bravery brought him to the attention of his higher-ups.

Upon his release from the hospital, Stauffenberg's uncle, a Prussian general, arranged his appointment to the army general staff. After all, he was a brilliant officer who could no longer fight.

There was only one catch. Stauffenberg was to serve under General Friedrich von Olbricht. Olbricht was a bespectacled, slender, balding, mild-looking officer who, when Stauffenberg reported for duty in August 1943, asked the least mild of questions. Was Stauffenberg, the general wanted to know, prepared to commit himself to an attack on Hitler's life?

Stauffenberg said "Yes."

How, When, Where, and Other Questions

Under the cover of doing his staff work in the War Ministry on Berlin's Bendlerstrasse (later renamed the Stauffenbergstrasse), Stauffenberg labored at his real job, organizing the assassination of the head of the Third Reich. Consulting with other like-minded officers, he realized that he would have to find answers to three vital questions:

- First, how and when should we kill Hitler? This seemed the easiest of the questions to answer: Hitler was spending most of his time at the Wolf's Lair out on the eastern front. How? With a concealed bomb.

- Second, how, after an assassination, should we set up a new government that can negotiate with the Allies and extract the best terms for surrender? As Stauffenberg and his co-conspirators knew, the post-1918 German government had been hardly a government at all and so the terms of the Versailles Treaty had been onerous indeed.

- And third, how can we ensure that in the wake of the murder, extremist units such as the SS do not seize power? The answer to all these questions evolved into a secret plan called Operation Valkyrie, from the maidens in Wagnerian opera who hovered over the battlefield and conducted the souls of slain heroes to Valhalla.

Operation Valkyrie

Operation Valkyrie involved a gigantic scam. Olbricht went to Hitler. Because of the bombing, the hardships, and the imminence of defeat, he told the Führer, there was arising the strong possibility of a domestic revolution. This part of the scheme was hardly far-fetched. To prevent a menace to the security of the Reich from the inside, therefore, there had to be a Home Army. Germany had to be divided into domestic military districts, each under the command of an officer who could move fast to quell anti-Regime disturbances.

Hitler saw the logic and authorized such a force to be put into effect. What Hitler did not know was that Olbricht was working out a way of issuing secret orders to those commanders to quell *SS* disturbances. That took care of the third question and perhaps the second. But what about the first issue: how to place a bomb near Hitler, or, perhaps, shoot him.

Officers higher than Schauffenberg discussed the elements of an answer. Someone had to be able to get physically close to Hitler out there in the Wolf's Lair.

That someone would have to be able to earn Hitler's trust, and the trust of the SS guards who constantly surrounded the Führer. A genuine war hero! And someone who had been grievously wounded. The SS guards would be unlikely to search thoroughly a valiant warrior who had given so much to his country.

The brass approached Stauffenberg and he volunteered for the assignment. In doing so, he knew that he was risking his life.

But what was he actually to do? It was agreed that Stauffenberg would go to the Wolf's Lair on the pretext of delivering reports from the War Ministry. Given his reputation, such a trip would be easy enough to arrange. The papers would be in his briefcase. So would a bomb. And if an SS officer himself opened the briefcase, it would be all over for each of the conspirators. But if the briefcase went uninspected, then the plot had a chance of succeeding.

The bomb would be equipped with a time-fuse. Here's the way it was to work. Stauffenberg would put the briefcase on the floor beside his chair, unlatch it, and with a tiny pair of pliers snip a wire. That action would release a quantity of acid. The acid would creep along the rest of the wire and trigger the explosion.

But could Stauffenberg, with his right hand gone and only three digits (the thumb and next two fingers) remaining of his left hand, do the job? To avoid arousing suspicions, he performed all his expected duties at the War Ministry.

Only at night and in the secrecy of his Berlin apartment did he dare practice the maneuvers of opening the briefcase and cutting the wire.

At last, however, he was ready. This was the middle of July, 1944. The time had come to kill Hitler.

The Assassination Attempt

On the morning of July 20, 1944, Lt. Col. Claus von Stauffenberg woke up early. As previously arranged, a staff car from the War Ministry picked him up at 6:15; in the car already was Lieutenant Werner von Häften, Schauffenberg's *aide-de-camp* and almost literally his right-hand man. Häften was in on the plot. Together they rode through the Berlin suburbs to an airstrip at Rangsdorf, which lay beside a small lake about 40 minutes by car from the city. At 7 o'clock they were airborne, Stauffenberg with the bomb in his briefcase. Two hours later they were landing at the Wolf's Lair, or *Wolfsschanze*.

Terms and Translations

Wolfsschanze. Wolf is clear. *Schhanze* has two meanings: The first is the same as the English word *chance;* the other is *trench*, which it sort of sounds like; hence also, *entrenchment*. So while we usually translate **Wolfsschanze** as Wolf's Lair, which sounds Teutonic, the term really referred to Hitler's heavily fortified and forward command post.

At the airport by Rastenburg, the nearest town to the command post, another automobile was on hand to take the visitors to the Führer. The drive wound its way through open countryside, then into a dark and gloomy forest, where wolves once might have lived. But pity any wolves that still might have been lurking about: The forest floor was heavily mined. Uniformed SS guards lined the roadway and the car had to pass through checkpoints at two concentric and encircling fences.

Before getting out of the car, Stauffenberg ignited the bomb. Time was of the essence. If Hitler, notorious for his late arrivals, did not show up at the meeting inside the conference room as scheduled, Stauffenberg and not Hitler would be dead.

For once, Hitler was on time, bending over a large table that was littered with maps. Entering the room, Stauffenberg worked his way to a chair that was only six or seven feet from the target. Sitting down, he placed the briefcase on the floor and under the table. With his foot he edged it even closer to the Führer. Then, muttering to an officer in the next chair that he had to make a quick telephone call to Berlin, Stauffenberg walked as calmly as he could out of the room.

Once past the door, he bolted back to the car. Häften was already there. Ducking inside the vehicle, they ordered the driver to return to the airport immediately. The driver did not understand what was going on but he did as he was told.

Just as the automobile cleared the second checkpoint, the men inside heard a distant explosion. Then the alarms went off.

Hitler's Revenge

Adolf Hitler was still alive. The blast had wounded him and killed four of the officers in the room. But the thickness of the table had saved the Führer's life.

Stauffenberg and Häften flew back to Berlin in safety. By nightfall, July 20, 1944, however, an SS investigation had pinpointed him as the would-be assassin; he was executed almost immediately. The other several dozen members of the conspiracy also lost their lives.

Among those arrested was General Erwin Rommel. He was given the choice of standing trial or taking poison. If he chose the latter, he was assured, his family would remain safe. On October 14, 1944, Rommel took the poison. Because of his repute, he was given a state funeral. He had died, the Nazi propaganda machine announced, of earlier wounds.

The Least You Need to Know

♦ The success of the Allied landing in Normandy was for Nazi Germany only the beginning of the end. The Soviet advance from the east and the buildup of Allied bombing from the west were already rendering that end inevitable.

♦ As Nazi Germany crumbled, inversely, the resistance movements gained in momentum. Although the kind of resistance associated with Oskar Schindler, the rescue of Jews, was in no way enough to stave off the Holocaust, it did indicate the growing disillusionment of some Gentile Germans with the Hitler regime.

♦ The most dramatic manifestation of that domestic German resistance lay in the effort of high-ranking officers to get rid of Hitler. These officers, such as Stauffenberg, had not suddenly become pacifists. They had come to believe, rather, that the Hitler regime was dooming Germany to vast and mass destruction.

♦ The July 20, 1944, anti-Hitler conspirators certainly hoped that a deal with the Americans could save Germany from the coming vengeance of the Soviet Union. But they hoped in vain.

Chapter 25

The Closing of the Trap: 1944–1945

In This Chapter

- ◆ Mussolini's capture and execution
- ◆ The Russians' revenge on Berlin
- ◆ The Allied attack from the western front
- ◆ The implementation of the Final Solution continues
- ◆ The Allied annihilation of Dresden

Readiness to risk one's life in protest occurred not only among the martyrs of the German aristocracy but also among the humbler members of German society. Here and there simple couples of the working class decided to voice their protest against Hitler: Some of them secretly wrote and disseminated postcards criticizing the Führer for his waste of German youth in an unnecessary war. Such humble acts may have seemed less dramatic than the assassination attempt at the Wolf's Lair, yet these deeds came from the people the most accustomed to being ruled. And when the protesters were caught, their fate was inevitable.

But by late 1944 and on into 1945, the fate of their persecutors was also becoming inevitable. For Hitler, Mussolini's death was an omen.

Mussolini's Execution

After Mussolini's fall from power in mid-1943, he had been placed under arrest. But the Germans had sprung him and taken him to Hitler's encampment in East Prussia. After thanking the Führer, he had put on one of his old uniforms and gone back to rule something called the Fascist Republic of North Italy.

His headquarters was on Lake Garda, near the Brenner Pass that led through the Alps, a location that might have afforded him a quick escape if things went bad. In the early spring of 1945, when it was obvious that Germany was in retreat everywhere, Mussolini tried to flee Italy. He thought he would make his way to Switzerland.

> **Bet You Didn't Know**
>
> *Il Duce* (Mussolini) had once said to a biographer: "Everybody dies the death that corresponds to his character." Mussolini had fooled his people but they had fooled him into believing that they were truly his supporters. Now he was dead—and Hitler had deluded his own people into believing that Nazi Germany could last a thousand years.

But he was found by partisans on a road that went along the shore of Lake Como. He was hiding in a German truck, dressed in the heavy coat of a German enlisted man and a German helmet. Claretta Petacci, his mistress, was with him.

The next morning they were both shot in front of the ornate gate of a ponderous villa. The woman tried to shield his body and was mown down with him. The bodies were taken to Milan and hung from the roof of a gasoline station.

The Russians' Next Target: Berlin

Throughout the autumn of 1943 and the winter of 1943 to 1944, the Soviet army had ground steadily ahead, gradually forcing the Germans back to a line about 300 miles west of Moscow. In May 1944, however, the rains became heavy, the rivers rose, and the advance of the Soviet forces came to a halt.

At this point, Hitler thought he might be able to recoup his losses. As he studied the military maps of the eastern front in the spring and summer of 1944, he saw that the German line was actually a bulge with the Red Army almost at Estonia in the north, the bulk of the German force was still ballooning out back toward Byelorussia, and another extension of the Soviets into Poland in the south. What, Hitler and his intelligence officers asked, was going to happen next? Allied bombings and partisan warfare were already pushing the Germans up and out of Crete, Greece, and Yugoslavia. So much of southeastern Europe was up for grabs. The Russians had long wanted to get their hands on Bulgaria, Romania, and Hungary, and the Germans now could no longer stop them from doing so. Furthermore, once the Soviets had Hungary (the strategists in the Wolf's Lair calculated), they could go straight on into Austria and then Bavaria, in southern Germany itself.

Believing that Stalin would be unable to resist the temptation of such a southern strategy, Hitler in May 1944 stripped much of his strength from the Baltic states and the bulge into Byelorussia, and sent those forces south. Hitler was proud of that move: At last he had outsmarted Stalin. The truth, however, was that he had played directly into the Soviet dictator's hands.

Stalin could wait. Most of southeastern Europe was his for the taking, whenever he wanted it. He had set his sights, rather, on the much bigger prize: Berlin. So while the waters of May 1944 rose, crested, and receded, Stalin and his commanders used the halt in the fighting to plan an assault upon the bulge in the German line.

Operation Bagration

There was nothing subtle about the Soviet scheme. It was named Operation Bagration, after Peter Bagration, the warrior-prince who had won fame by demolishing another invader from the west, Napoleon Bonaparte. And the starting date for the new Soviet offensive was June 22, 1944, exactly three years after the opening of Hitler's invasion of the Soviet Union.

The Soviets prepared well for the attack. A fleet of some 12,000 trucks (many supplied by the United States under the Lend-Lease program) transported a force of two and a half million to the front. Supporting them were more than 5,000 tanks, some 7,000 fighter planes, and at least 31,000 field guns and mortars. During the month and a half of preparations, the Soviets moved 100 trainloads of ammunition, food, and fuel to the front.

Yet our genius of military strategy and tactics, Adolf Hitler, refused to listen to intelligence reports of the buildup. The massing of Soviet forces on the eastern bank of the Dnieper River, he told his aides, was only a ruse. Stalin definitely was going to go south! Hitler could divine it!

Soviet Assault

Opening on June 22, 1944, the Soviet assault was unstoppable. Aircraft equipped with precision bombsights took out German artillery all around the bulge in the front. At

4 A.M. two days later, the Soviet Union's own artillery began to fire in a barrage that left the Germans stunned.

Memorable Places

Observing the bombardment from a village on the Dnieper, Vasily Grossman, a Soviet reporter, wrote:

> The pounding blows of the headquarters artillery, the thunder of the divisional cannon, the heavy strokes of the howitzers, the sharp, rapid reports of the regimental guns merged in an uproar that shook the very foundations of the earth. Through the rumble of the artillery came a piercing whistle, like an enormous locomotive letting off steam.

> Hundreds of fiery sickles rose into the air and fell into the German trenches. The trench mortars of the Guards had opened fire. A cat ran down the deserted village street, dragging its tail in the dust. It must have been mewing desperately, but its cry could not be heard. The leaves were trembling on the Byelorussian maples, oaks, and poplars. In the deserted houses windowpanes were shattered, brick stoves fell crumbling to the floor, and doors and shutters swung wildly.

Then the Soviet tanks and troops moved forward, supported by aircraft. Grossman continued:

> The sky was in tumult with the rhythmic roaring of the dive bombers, the hard metallic voices of the attack planes, the piercing whine of the fighters. Fields and meadows were splashed with the darting outlines of hundreds of planes.

Six days after it had begun, the Soviet attack was a complete success. Dazed by the catastrophe, thousands of German soldiers surrendered. Those who did not surrender rushed westward in a panicked retreat. Nothing stood in the way of a Soviet march into Poland.

The Western Front

After landing successfully on the beaches of Normandy, the Allies—the British, Canadians, Americans, and a small contingent of Free French under the leadership of General de Gaulle—expected to make rapid progress across northern France. Once Normandy and Brittany to the west were under control, Allied planners had thought, they could dash on to Paris, then launch a massive drive across northern France and Belgium into Germany. Estimates were that all this would take about three months.

By the middle of June 1944, however, the invaders were way behind schedule. The Germans still held Caen, the major city in Normandy, and Cherbourg, on the

Channel coast; and the Allies were nowhere near Paris. The Germans were fighting back fiercely, but that wasn't the only thing that slowed the Allied advance. Much of Normandy was hedgerow country (the French called it *bocage*), dense thickets of hawthorn, brambles, vines, and trees centuries old that often stood as much as 15 feet high. Individual fields looked as if they were surrounded by the walls of forts. These natural forts in turn were surrounded by narrow lanes and drainage ditches.

These thickets brought the Allied advance to a crawl. Tanks were bogged down in the lanes and ditches and when they tried to crash through the brush they often upended or exposed their undersides to German bazooka fire. Infantrymen had to proceed with the utmost caution: The hedgerows were so thick that Allied soldiers sometimes would step around a bend only to find themselves eyeball-to-eyeball with a German counterpart. The hedgerows provided almost perfect cover for machine gun nests. The lanes were laden with mines.

Nevertheless, the Allies substantially outnumbered the Germans and—Germany's scarcity of resources was showing up again—the defending tanks and airplanes were running out of fuel. As usual, Hitler dismissed this problem as a fantasy. By the end of June and the beginning of July, he was ranting and raving, demanding that his forces in France create a new Dunkirk.

No Dunkirk was in the offing. Everywhere along the slowly eastward-moving Normandy front, Allied artillery repulsed counterattacks. By July 10, 1944, most of Normandy was in Allied hands.

Operation Cobra

Also on July 10, Omar Bradley, the American general, mapped a plan for a breakout. Called Operation Cobra, it went into effect a week later and on August 19 it led to a decisive German defeat by the banks of the Seine River. There the Allies caught the Germans in a hurricane of tank and artillery fire. Flames from German ammunition dumps leapt skyward. Ammunition exploded. So many fleeing Germans crowded onto a bridge that many fell into the river in a tangled mass.

As a Canadian soldier later remembered:

> Germans charred coal-black, looking like blackened tree trunks, lay beside smoking vehicles. One didn't realize that the obscene mess was human until it was poked at. I remember wishing that the Germans didn't have to use so many horses. Seeing all those dead animals on their backs, their legs pointing at God's sky like accusing fingers, their bellies bloated, some ripped open ... That really bothered me.

The defeat was the worst the Germans had suffered since Stalingrad and Tunisia. That night, in a pouring rain, American soldiers walked single-file over a narrow dam on the Seine, each man touching the one ahead to keep from falling into the water. In the morning, engineers laid the first of many bridges across the flow. The Allies now had a clear shot at Paris.

The Liberation of Paris

Starting at 8 A.M., August 25, the first of the Free French armored units entered the outskirts of Paris. Followed by an American infantry division, de Gaulle's tanks had come to liberate Paris. Their arrival touched off one of the most tumultuous celebrations in recorded history.

Despite gunfire from Germans and their collaborators, still cooped up in parts of the French capital, Parisians poured out onto the streets to welcome their liberators. They showered their soldiers with champagne and flowers and smothered them with hugs and kisses. Along the route to the center of Paris, open windows displayed the Nazi-forbidden French tricolor flags. People cried out *"Vive de Gaulle!"*

Riding into the city at 4 P.M., de Gaulle first established his headquarters at the Ministry of War, the same building from which four years earlier he had departed with his trunk-load of documents pertaining to the building of a resistance. Then he proceeded to the Arc of Triumph where he headed a victory parade down the *Champs Élysées*.

Bet You Didn't Know

Parisians also extracted vengeance from French women who had been mistresses of the Nazis. Such women had their heads shaved and their bared breasts painted with swastikas. Forced to parade through the streets, they carried signs that said, "I whored with the *boches*" (rather like our use of the word *Hun*).

While the parade was taking place, the German occupiers suddenly became prisoners. Parisians at last had a chance to extract their revenge. They cut up or shot portraits of Nazi leaders and ripped down swastikas, setting them afire. When General Dietrich von Choltitz, the former military commander of Paris, was hauled off to jail, people spat on him and clawed at his uniform; they did not realize that earlier, by disobeying orders from Hitler to burn Paris to the ground, Choltitz had actually saved the city.

In the meantime, the great parade was nearing its climax, heading out of the *Champs Élysées* and into the *Place de la Concorde* on the way to the Cathedral of Notre Dame. Just at that point, the marchers heard the sound of a gun going off. Thousands of people fell to the pavement or took cover behind vehicles parked along the street.

General de Gaulle, however, sought no refuge. Walking straight and tall, he approached a waiting car that took him to the *Hôtel de Ville*—city hall—where he stopped briefly. As he reemerged from the building, rifles and machine guns went off from nearby windows and rooftops. Apparently the Germans were making their last stand in Paris. Soldiers in the parade began firing back.

Indifferent to the danger, de Gaulle rode on to the cathedral. There was more shooting there, too. Calmly and without hurry, de Gaulle entered the massive front doors.

In the gloom inside, still more shooting broke out from the balconies high above the nave. De Gaulle paid no attention. Unflustered, he strode 200 feet down the aisle to his place of honor in a pew facing the altar. "He walked straight ahead in what appeared to me to be a hail of fire," a BBC correspondent reported, "without hesitation, his shoulders flung back. It was the most extraordinary example of courage that I've ever seen."

De Gaulle stayed at his place in front of the nave throughout the singing of the "Magnificat." When he left the cathedral, an American journalist wrote, he "had France in the palm of his hand." His performance symbolized France's revenge for its defeat at the hands of Nazi Germany in 1940.

Battle of the Bulge

Hitler, however, was not finished, not quite yet. Even as the German armies were streaming back across France and Belgium in the late summer of 1944, the Führer was mulling over the idea of a counteroffensive against the Allies. If he could deal them a major setback and aggravate jealousies between the British and American high commands, then maybe he could win a separate peace and finally hurl everything against the ever-advancing Soviet army.

His thoughts returned to where, turning the Schlieffen Plan upside down, he had scored his major strategic triumph in 1940: the Ardennes Forest. Hitler believed—correctly—that Eisenhower and the other Allied commanders were making the same mistake the French had made in 1940: regarding the Ardennes Forest as impenetrable and so throwing the weight of their forces to the north. Hitler figured that if he could feint with armored units toward Antwerp, almost at the Belgian North Sea coast, he could lure Eisenhower away from the Ardennes region altogether. Hitler called the plan *Wacht am Rhein* (Watch on the Rhine). Its target date was December 6, 1944.

Hitler ordered absolute secrecy. Sensing perhaps that the Allies might have broken German codes (which, through ULTRA, they had indeed done), he forbade any radio or telephone discussions of the operation. All preparations took place at night. Not until the first day of December were the corps and division commanders given their orders, and not until the night of December 5 and 6 did the troops learn what they were supposed to do.

The German secrecy was remarkably effective. At dawn on attack day, some 200,000 German troops made their way through the snow of the Ardennes Forest and, coming up from the rear, took the American army in Belgium by surprise.

The fighting turned out to be the largest pitched battle in which American soldiers had ever engaged.

Because the Germans pushed heavily into the middle of the Allied lines, the fight has been called the Battle of the Bulge. Its correct title is the Battle of the Ardennes.

As the scope and depth of the German attack became apparent, General Eisenhower realized that they had split his forces in two, making communications between his troops down near Luxembourg and up by the Belgian coast impossible. Americans in the town of Bastogne, in southern Belgium, were besieged.

The siege went into effect on December 20. Two days later, the commanding officer of the surrounding *Panzer* corps sent a message into the town, demanding surrender. The American response was: "Nuts!"

The Germans celebrated Christmas by mounting a huge bombardment of Bastogne. But for the trapped Americans help was on the way. Under the command of General George S. Patton, an American armored division on the day after Christmas broke through the ring that surrounded Bastogne.

Heavy fighting ensued. Soon, though, the Germans ran into what by this point was becoming their usual and customary problem: a lack of gasoline. Shortly after Christmas, the German field commanders realized that for them time was running out. They were right. The first major American counterattack came on January 3, 1945. By January 22, the Germans were in full withdrawal; on that date, General Eisenhower eliminated altogether the bulge created by the German offensive. On January 28, it was all over: The Germans were now in full retreat.

The Battle of the Bulge, as the papers called it, had slowed the Allied advance but it had not stopped it. Both sides had suffered huge casualties: the Germans 100,000 and the Americans about 81,000. They both had lost heavily in weapons and equipment—800 tanks each, and the Germans a thousand airplanes.

The crucial fact of the war, however, was that the Americans could replace their losses in a couple weeks and the Germans could not do so at all. The Allied armies resumed their march toward Nazi Germany, and from this point onward Germany was incapable of serious resistance.

The Climax of the Holocaust

Despite the retreat, the Final Solution reached its finality. All over the parts of Europe that the Nazis still occupied, SS agents, joined often by local Nazi supporters, Latvians, Poles, Hungarians, and others, joined in the destruction of the ghettos into which the Jews had been forced. Labor camps, too, were closed down, as most of the remaining Jews were shipped to the gas chambers.

Some Jews had managed to escape the dragnet so far: perhaps 10,000 Jews had tried to live in the forests, surrounded by nature's own hostile milieu. Others, equipped with false papers, had tried to survive in the cities as Aryans. In the forests, unfriendly peasants found it convenient to lead the Gestapo to Jewish caves and other hiding places. In the cities, local police, spies, blackmailers, and the like exposed Jews who had tried to pass as Gentiles.

As the winter of 1945 gave way to spring, however, almost all of those who had sought to hide had been exposed. Every day the number of surviving Jews dwindled.

Throughout Central and Eastern Europe, the Jewish communities were gone. There were no synagogues, no Jewish schools, no Jewish life. In Poland, blood-soaked books in Yiddish and Hebrew strewn along the banks of the Vistula were all that remained of the thousand-year-old civilization of the Jews.

Yet, in a sense, the Nazi destruction of the Jews in Central and Eastern Europe did not go unavenged. Between the middle of February and of April 1945, Allied bombing reduced the German city of Dresden to rubble.

The Destruction of Dresden

About 100 miles south of Berlin, Dresden was one of Germany's most ancient and beautiful cities. Established in the thirteenth century, it boasted much of Europe's finest baroque and rococo architecture. Its galleries and museums housed invaluable paintings by Holbein, Vermeer, Rembrandt, Rubens, Botticelli, and Canaletto. Dresden contained an engravings collection that by 1945 numbered at least half-a-million pieces. Dresden was famous worldwide for its porcelains. For centuries the city had been a center for music and musicians on a European scale—Bach, Handel, Telemann, Wagner, and Strauss. The sculptures and bas-reliefs on the public buildings were from the classical age of Greece. The skyline of bridges and spires were unsurpassed anywhere in Europe.

Dresden also was a city of no military value. Allied bombers destroyed it all.

American and British raids on Dresden were acts of deliberate terror bombing, ruthless expedients to hasten the German surrender. It seems fair to say that, if the Manhattan Project had been completed in the spring of 1945, Dresden would have experienced the fate of Hiroshima and Nagasaki.

The Least You Need to Know

- ◆ Mussolini's death foretold the fate of his ally to the north, Hitler.

- ◆ The Soviet westward advance in 1944 and 1945 was an unstoppable force. Hitler's delaying tactics proved irrelevant. For despite the long-standing economic and technological backwardness of the Soviet Union, Hitler had committed the fundamental error of overexpansion.

- ◆ No matter how determined the German defenders were to resist the Allied landing and advance, they were simply overwhelmed by the superiority of American personnel, firepower, and economic prowess. Had the Allies not attacked from the west, Nazi Germany might have survived. Hitler, however, from the beginning had committed Germany to a war it could not win.

- ◆ With the final elimination of the Jews and the utter destruction of Dresden, Nazi Germany was fast approaching its Wagnerian *dénouement*.

Götterdämmerung: 1945

In This Chapter

- ◆ Russia's march into Poland
- ◆ The meeting of the "Big Three" in Yalta
- ◆ Hitler's reaction to FDR's death
- ◆ The annihilation of Berlin
- ◆ Hitler's death
- ◆ Germany's surrender

At the end of *Die Götterdämmerung* (*The Twilight of the Gods*), Richard Wagner's climactic opera first performed in Bayreuth in 1876, comes the "Immolation Scene." Following the death of Siegfried, the hero, Brünnhilde, his lover, rides horseback into flames. The fire billows fiercely and seems about to devour the entire stage and the chorus of terrified onlookers crowd to the foreground. When the flames die down the Rhine surges up in a mighty flood, bearing the Rhinemaidens on its crest. On seeing them, Hagen, the villain of the opera (played of course by a bass), leaps into the river like a madman to gain the ring they are holding. The ring—this opera ends the "Ring Cycle"—stands for all that is good and righteous and is the object the good guys have been looking for. Hagen cries out, "*Zurück vom*

Ring!" ("Away from the ring!"). The Rhinemaidens, however, drag him beneath the waves, then reappear, one of them holding up the ring in a gesture of joyous triumph.

The Rhine subsides. In the distance a glow breaks through a dark band of clouds, revealing Valhalla (the Wagnerian heaven) and Wotan, the chief god, facing his flaming doom. The music storms to a great climax, and then dies away as the theme of redemption through love soars high in the violins. The curtain falls.

Is this symbolic or what? Led by Hitler, the people of Nazi Germany, or most of them, had persuaded themselves that they were pursuing all that was good and righteous, only (in their eyes) to have it snatched away. In the end, Hitler, whom so many Germans had invested with godlike qualities, faced a flaming doom. Then, and only then, was Germany able to experience a kind of redemption, entering as it had never done throughout its history, into the community of nations as a normal country.

Reds over the Vistula

Not long before the destruction of Dresden, namely on January 17, 1945, the Soviet army crossed the Vistula, the river that ran up through the middle of Poland. The Reds had come into Poland from the southeast, a path that brought them close to the concentration camp at Auschwitz. Ten days later, Russian infantrymen pushed their way through the front gate, under the banner that proclaimed Work Makes Freedom.

Inside they came upon about 5,000 survivors, so feeble from hunger that they could barely cheer. The Soviets almost immediately dynamited the gas chambers. Later, officials from the Red Cross went into the camp. Nazi authorities at Auschwitz had tried to cover up evidence of their crimes. They had burned all sorts of personal effects of their victims. The Red Cross nevertheless discovered almost 400,000 men's suits, more than 800,000 women's coats, seven tons (that's a correct figure!) of human hair, and mountains of eyeglasses, toothbrushes, and shoes. The Holocaust Museum in Washington, D.C., has an exhibit of the shoes. And there were mass graves of hundreds of thousands of human corpses.

In Berlin, on the day the Soviets crossed the Vistula, several top German military officials, Generals Keitel, Jodl, and Guderian, and Hermann Göring, approached Hitler's office in the Chancellery, right in the center of the city. The building had been bombed already and they had to pick their way through back corridors where windows were covered with cardboard. At the door to the office, SS guards took their side arms and searched their briefcases: Hitler had retreated from the Wolf's Lair but his guards were super-vigilant for any repetition of the assassination attempt.

At 4:20 P.M., Hitler shuffled in late. His shoulders were stooped and his left arm hung limp, whether from the July 20 episode or from a stroke was unclear. He had been wounded, however, and with an incapacitated right hand he could barely shake hands with his visitors. He sank heavily into a chair.

The mood of the conference was grim. Nazi Germany obviously could not survive for long. What to do? Hitler had an idea. Put Heinrich Himmler, head of the SS, in charge of a special unit that would march forward into the face of the Soviet advance. Guderian thought the idea was crazy and said so. That was the end of his influence in what was left of Hitler's court.

On the last day of January 1945, Soviet tanks crossed the Oder River, the traditional boundary between Poland and Germany. No natural barrier lay between them and Berlin.

Three days later, nearly 1,000 American bombers appeared over Berlin. In the ensuing bombing, Hitler moved his headquarters down into a bunker, well below the Chancellery. Overhead, the Führer's headquarters were in ruins. In the reinforced cave underground, water and electricity were uncertain; the air was always stuffy. In the midst of all the ruin, Hitler spent much of his time studying cardboard models of a new Munich and a new Linz. At last it was within his power to be an architect!

Yalta

Meeting at Yalta, a resort town with old Russian palaces that overlooked the Black Sea, on February 12, 1945, the Big Three announced their demand for Germany's unconditional surrender. Roosevelt, Churchill, and Stalin jointly made clear that they intended to dismember Germany and force it to pay crushing reparations. Remember: at the end of the First World War, President Woodrow Wilson had insisted on keeping Germany almost intact. Not so this time around. Although Roosevelt had resisted the demand of Henry Morgenthau, his treasury secretary, to turn post-war Germany into a pasture, the president was fervent in his wish to see Germany eliminated altogether as a great power.

For some years after the Second World War, historians and others debated the wisdom of the "unconditional surrender" declaration. It only gave the Nazis, the argument went, the determination to fight to the end. In some cases it may well have done so. But if you're going to fight to the bitter end, you'd better have something to fight with! And by the time of the Yalta statement, the Nazi war machine was almost nonexistent.

Churchill, Roosevelt, and Stalin at Yalta.

(FDR Presidential Library)

After the bombing of Dresden, Josef Goebbels proposed that captured Allied bomber crews be killed in retaliation. Down in the bunker, Hitler was tempted to go along with the idea. But Ribbentrop and others persuaded him otherwise. Such executions would clearly be war crimes and most of the top Nazis realized they themselves would soon be prisoners.

Peace "Negotiations"

Throughout the second half of February 1945, newspapers in neutral Sweden reported that a certain high-ranking Nazi was suing for peace. The personage in question was Heinrich Himmler, the paper-filing sadist who headed the SS.

The news stories exaggerated. Nevertheless, Count Folke Bernadotte, a Swedish nobleman, had been in Berlin and had conversed with Himmler at a sanatorium some 75 miles north of Berlin. This was Himmler's unofficial headquarters. Bernadotte was surprised: Far from looking diabolical, Himmler was affable, even quiet and polite.

"What did the man want?" the Swedish diplomat asked. The SS chief raised the issue of a German surrender *with* a condition: His own safety in Sweden. But would Himmler grant any concessions, such as releasing even some Jews from the concentration camps? The answer was no, and so any deal was off.

Ribbentrop also made an approach to the Swedes. Through an agent named Hesse, he put out feelers to a Stockholm banker, Raoul Wallenberg. The banker's message back to Ribbentrop was blunt. The Big Three were determined to destroy Germany, period.

The Oder and the Rhine

A thousand years before, the borders of the German-speaking people had been the Oder, which flowed to the Baltic just a bit east of Berlin, and the Rhine. By the beginning of March 1945, the Reich that had been supposed to last another thousand years was squeezed back between those same two rivers. And the compression was going to continue. From both east and west Hitler's enemies were poised for the advances they were sure would bring an end to Nazi Germany. Having crossed Poland into Germany, Marshal Zhukov's Red Army was encountering almost no resistance. On the west, where the British and the Americans had reached the Rhine, engineers threw a pontoon bridge across the river.

Leading the American armored units, General Patton walked to the middle of the bridge and said, "I've been waiting a long time to do this!" Then he urinated in the water.

Back in the bunker, Hitler was physically falling apart. He walked with a shuffle; his face was deathly white except for large red blotches; his hands trembled. He was almost alone. Eva Braun and a few others from the old days were with him and the Goebbels family was in regular attendance. But Himmler was out in the field, pretending to lead an army. Göring had ensconced himself in the villa at Berchtesgaden. (Berlin was not for him; from the mountaintop near Munich, he figured he could surrender to the Americans.) Completely disgusted, General Guderian took his leave of the Führer. As a parting comment, the general said that he would look for a quiet place in the country that wouldn't be overrun for another weekend.

On Easter Sunday the Ruhr, that economic heart of the German economy, stopped beating, indeed overrun by the Allied advance. A few days later, the Red Army entered Vienna; hordes of people, even the police, fled the onetime imperial capital.

Hitler's Last Hope

Across the Atlantic Ocean, in a cottage in the southwestern Georgia village of Warm Springs, on April 12, 1945, President Franklin D. Roosevelt stayed in bed nearly all morning. An adult victim of polio, FDR back in the 1920s had built the cottage and bought a nearby hotel, an establishment that had access to a pool with supposedly restorative local waters. He had visited the place regularly ever since, and had loved to frolic with the other "polios," as they were called, in the warm waters.

By 1945, however, he was a sick man, suffering from hypertension and congestive heart failure. The long trip by airplane to Yalta and back had left him exhausted. This time, though, Warm Springs afforded him little rest. He slept late on the morning of April 12 because he felt terrible.

Only with the help of his valet was he able to get up, bathe, and dress. He dressed rather formally, in a blue suit and a red necktie; he was due to sit for a portrait. With him were the artist, a Russian named Madame Shoumatov, and Lucy Mercer Ruth-erford, who had been his wife's social secretary and who, although married and living in South Carolina, had remained the woman he loved. In inviting her to Warm Springs, he probably realized that it was the last time he would see her.

As he sat for the portrait by a card table, he shuffled through a few official papers. Suddenly he said, "I have a terrific headache," and collapsed unconscious. Two hours later the president of the United States was dead.

Hitler and the others in the bunker were overjoyed at the news. With the archenemy gone, they believed, surely the Reich would experience a reversal of fortune. Hitler made a broadcast to the troops, exhorting them to have faith that now they could be saved.

The next day, April 13, all German troops in the valley of the Ruhr surrendered. Zhukov also crashed across the Oder and started along the road to Berlin. The bunker was only 45 miles away.

In the bunker on April 20, Hitler and his remaining minions drank the last of the champagne. They were celebrating the Führer's fifty-sixth birthday.

Bombs over Berlin

The British and the Americans celebrated the birthday with a 1,000-bomber attack on the German capital. The same day, one Red Army unit advanced to within 20 miles of Berlin.

In the bunker, Hitler's top officers, Grossadmiral Karl Dönitz and Field Marshal Wilhelm Keitel, were frantic. Keitel had organized the search of the would-be assas-sins at the Wolf's Lair and later had engineered Hitler's return to Berlin. He had proven his loyalty.

Now, however, he urged Hitler to send out peace feelers.

Hitler refused to do anything of the sort.

Then, Keitel and Dönitz advised, leave Berlin! The road to Berchtesgaden is still clear! Leave while there is still time!

Hitler ignored the advice.

Himmler got away as best he could. After paying respects to the Führer on his birthday, the SS chief drove several hours to meet Norbert Masur, a representative of the World Jewish Congress. After all the monstrous things he had done, Himmler apparently believed that by making some last-minute concessions he could save his own hide.

Of course he was betraying Hitler. But Heinrich Himmler was the ultimate rat leaving the ultimate sinking ship.

On April 21, 1945, the Red Army had come into artillery range of Berlin. Even down in the bunker, people started to hear the thud of Soviet shells.

Martin Bormann, a top Hitler aide, knew it was all over. Finding a telephone that was still working, he called his wife, who was at Berchtesgaden, telling her that he had located a hiding place for her and their children in the Tyrol. He himself would stay with Hitler in the bunker until the end.

On April 22, Eva Braun promised that she, too, would remain until the end. With that promise, Hitler did something that no one around him had ever seen. He kissed her on the lips.

On April 23, Göring at Berchtesgaden learned from telephone calls that Hitler had collapsed. What was the Reichsfuhrer to do? The answer was obvious. He prepared to walk out.

Death in Berlin

Holed up with his wife and butler at Berchtesgaden, Göring had thought himself safe. Allied bombers on their way to Salzburg and other Austrian sites had passed overhead but had left the villa untouched. But Göring had only been deluding himself. On the morning of April 25, at exactly 10 A.M., a wave of British Lancasters swept in from over the mountain, dropping explosives all around the perimeter of the villa. Göring apparently thought they were just trying to trap him. Later in the morning, however, another wave appeared, then another and another, unloading blockbusters directly on the estate.

How Göring survived is unknown. But Hitler was furious at Göring's not being in Berlin and the *Luftwaffe* chieftain did not dare wait around until the Russians moved in. He had only one choice. With his wife, he fled Berchtesgaden, starting to walk westward toward the American lines. Somewhere in his clothing he was carrying a hidden cyanide pill.

That same morning the Soviet pincers were about to close on Berlin. By dawn two days later the city was completely encircled.

Hitler Decides His Own Future

Down in the bunker, Hitler started to worry—in conferences at least—about his own future. He knew the end was near but he had no intention of letting Stalin exhibit him like a bear in a cage. Yet there was no way he could or would leave Berlin. He was still the Führer, he said; how could he ask others to die for Germany if he himself tried to flee?

By the morning of April 26, the Soviets had overrun the Berlin airports and were making their way toward the center of the city. The resistance was disjointed and officers were trying to sneak out of the capital so they could surrender to the Americans. In her quarters in the bunker, Frau Goebbels wrote to her son by a previous marriage and now an Allied prisoner of war, that the "glorious ideals" of Nazism were shattered.

The next morning, April 27, an officer bought word to the bunker that all ammunition and supply dumps were in Russian hands. In two days' time, with all supplies gone, the troops still in the city would be unable to resist any longer. He urged Hitler to risk a breakout.

Hitler had other plans. Abdicating all his titles, he signed two documents. The first made Admiral Dönitz president of the Reich and commander in chief of the armed forces; the second appointed Goebbels as chancellor.

Then, down in the bunker, seated at the conference table and surrounded by the loyal aides, Hitler dictated his will and launched into his last speech. "Since I did not feel that I could accept the responsibility of marriage during the years of struggle, I have decided now, before the end of my earthly career, to take as my wife the girl who, after many years of loyal friendship, came of her own free will to this city, already almost besieged, in order to share my fate. Death will compensate us as for what we were both deprived of by my labors in the service of my people." The next could have been straight out of a Wagnerian opera:

> My wife and I choose to die in order to escape the shame of overthrow or capitulation. It is our wish that our bodies be burned immediately, here where I have performed the greater part of my daily work during the 12 years I served my people.

Hitler's Pre-Death Marriage

The marriage ceremony took place on the evening of April 28, down in the bunker. Eight guests were present, including the Goebbelses, husband and wife. Someone had found a bureaucrat who had the authority to officiate: His name was Wagner. Eva wore a dress of black silk and Hitler was in uniform, the swastika band on his left arm. The newlyweds signed the marriage certificate; Martin Bormann and the Goebbelses appended their signatures as witnesses. The time was just before midnight, April 28.

The Final Days

By the middle of the next morning, April 29, Soviet troops had entered the *Tiergarten*, the zoo. Other units, coming in from the east, south, and north, were heading for the bunker. Just outside the bunker, Martin Bormann was picking his way through the rubble to the headquarters of Admiral Dönitz; Bormann needed to give the admiral Hitler's document appointing him head of state. Down in the bunker, Eva Braun-Hitler slept until noon.

Early evening brought the news of Mussolini's death. "I will not fall into the hands of the enemy dead or alive!" Hitler said in response. "After I die, my body shall be burned and so remain undiscovered forever!"

Shortly after midnight, Hitler entered the bunker's canteen. There he said good-bye to a group of about 20 secretaries and officers.

After he left, going down the staircase to his bedroom, the people in the canteen erupted with wildness. Dancing and drinking champagne, they whooped and hollered so loudly that an aide to Martin Bormann looked in at the door, telling them to quiet down. Bormann was in his office nearby, composing a telegram to Admiral Dönitz. Hitler, the message said, written already in the past tense, would have wanted the new head of state to execute all traitors.

Late in the morning of April 30, a Soviet advance guard was in the street next to the bunker.

Knowing that Hitler wished to be immolated, an aide sent out for canisters of gasoline. The only ones available, he learned, were buried under the zoo, too far away to reach. He told an orderly to siphon gasoline out of nearby wrecked cars.

In his bedroom suite, Hitler bade farewell to Hans Baur, for many years his personal pilot. He gave the man his beloved portrait of Frederick the Great. "He, too," Hitler said, "was the victim of his generals."

Afternoon came. Soviet soldiers had spotted the gate to the bunker.

Inside, on the top floor, one of Hitler's secretaries was telling the Goebbels children a fairy story to keep them from going down.

The time was 3:30 P.M., April 30, 1945.

Then, from below, they heard a shot. Young Helmut Goebbels thought it was a bomb. It was not.

Eva Braun-Hitler had taken cyanide. Adolph Hitler had shot himself in the temple with a revolver. For both of them it was all over.

As quickly as possible, guards got them upstairs and burned the bodies.

The next morning, May 1, as Soviet infantrymen were entering the courtyard, Frau Goebbels gave her children cyanide pills. On their way out of the bunker, she and her husband were shot to death, possibly by Soviet arms.

Martin Bormann disappeared. Later some thought he had escaped to Argentina. It was more likely that he died in a hail of Soviet gunfire, for Berlin was now under Soviet control.

Two weeks later, Heinrich Himmler fell into British hands. Before a doctor could examine him thoroughly, he swallowed a cyanide pill.

Surrender

With Hitler's death, the remaining German leaders harbored the hope that the Allies would now see Germany as a bulwark against further Soviet expansion into Europe. From the naval base at Kiel, Admiral Dönitz on May 4 sent an aide to Allied head-quarters at Reims, the ancient cathedral town in northeastern France. Dönitz was hoping for a separate deal.

Eisenhower would have nothing to do with it. Refusing to see any German officers, Ike sent word back through General Walter Bedell Smith that there would be no bargaining at all: Germany was to surrender unconditionally and to the Allies and the Soviets at the same time.

The Germans surrendered three days later. Led by Chief of Staff Alfred Jodl, a small German delegation climbed the front steps of the Reims schoolhouse that served as Eisenhower's command center. They were ushered into a former classroom where the walls were covered with maps. The room was small and Allied officers bumped into one another as they made their way to their assigned chairs around a heavy oak table. Jodl stood before them, tall, erect, his uniform crisp, a monocle in his eye, the very model of a Prussian army general. He bowed, then stood erect again.

While Eisenhower waited in his private office next door, Jodl signed the papers of surrender. Only then did Ike consent to see the German. It was shortly after 2 A.M., May 8, 1945. As General Smith led Jodl into the inner chamber, Eisenhower sat down behind his desk. Jodl bowed again, and stood at attention. Did he understand the terms? Eisenhower asked. *Ja*. Was he ready to execute them? *Ja*. Did Jodl realize that he would be held personally accountable if fighting erupted again? *Ja*. Jodl was escorted out of the building.

With that, Eisenhower went into the old classroom. All the British and American officers broke out into cheers. Flashbulbs exploded and newsreel cameras whirred. Flashing his famous grin, Ike held up the pens with which the surrender had been signed in the form of a V for victory.

Dead tired, Eisenhower went back into his office. He dictated a telegram to the War Department in Washington. It read: "The mission of this Allied force was fulfilled." The story of Nazi Germany was over.

As the war was ending, thoughts of punishing those responsible for the atrocities began to emerge. Back in April 1945, just a few days after Roosevelt's death, Robert Jackson, an associate justice of the United States, in his Supreme Court chambers received a visitor, Samuel Rosenman. Rosenman had been a speechwriter and confidant to the late president. The president wanted to know, Rosenman said, meaning Truman but speaking as if FDR were still alive, if Jackson would prosecute remaining Nazi leaders as war criminals. After some consideration Jackson agreed to do so. Soon he was off to Germany to serve as the chief American representative in the Nuremberg war crimes trials.

The Least You Need to Know

- With the Battle of the Bulge over and the Soviet forces crossing the Vistula River in Poland, Roosevelt, Stalin, and Churchill, the "Big Three," felt confident enough to issue the demand for Germany's unconditional surrender.

- As the borders of Germany contracted steadily, Hitler and other top-ranking Germans harbored the hope that the Allies would accept Germany as a partner in stopping the Soviet advance.

- For quite a few years to come, many persons in the United States criticized the Allies for not accepting a deal, continuing on against the onrushing Soviets.

- Aside from the questions whether the Allies-plus-Germans could have won, the major consideration was simply this: For the British and the Americans, Germany was the enemy, and the overwhelming priority was to ensure its defeat.

♦ The defeat was inevitable. Hitler and Goebbels died in Berlin. Himmler committed suicide in the northern part of Germany. Terrified of a Russian revenge, the rest of the top Nazis fled to the American and British lines.

Chapter 27

Judgment: 1945–1946

In This Chapter

- ◆ A full account of the Nuremberg trials
- ◆ The verdicts and the sentences handed down
- ◆ A reflection of why Germany's recent history happened they way it did
- ◆ How the rise of Nazi Germany was possible
- ◆ Why Germany failed

An issue has always hung over the Nuremberg war crimes trials (as well as over the similar ones in Tokyo): Can judicial proceedings imposed by the victors be fair? Is there such a thing as "victors' justice"? Without question, the Nazis committed horrible atrocities and indeed started the Second World War in Europe. But did they violate previously created and widely accepted international laws? Or were the surviving top Nazis tried on an *ex post facto* basis, on the basis of laws put forth after the deeds had been committed?

Justice Robert Jackson and the Start of the Nuremberg Trials

A dignified man in his 50s, somewhat balding, who usually wore a blue pin-striped three-piece suit with a gold chain stretched across his slight paunch,

Justice Robert Jackson conveyed the solid air one expected in a member of the United States Supreme Court. Everything about his background suggested that same solidity. After a stint in law school in Albany, he had become a prosecuting attorney in rural upper New York State. In many ways he was the classic conservative lawyer. But, a Democrat, he also had a populist streak that led him sometimes to defend the little guy against the forces of the big corporations. In 1932, he also publicly denounced corruption in the New York Democratic Party. His scathing attacks on the political hacks brought him to the attention of Franklin D. Roosevelt, who, once in the White House, gave Jackson a job in the Justice Department. Jackson rose rapidly through the ranks and, in 1942, FDR appointed him to the Supreme Court.

Jackson became renowned for his sense of justice in Supreme Court cases. In a 1943 case involving a Jehovah's Witness family in West Virginia who had not let their children salute the flag at the start of school days, Jackson struck off one of the golden passages in the literature of the Supreme Court:

> If there is any fixed star in our constitutional constellation, it is that no official, high or petty, can prescribe what shall be orthodox in politics, nationalism, religion, or other matters of opinion or force citizens to confess by word or act their faith therein. If there are any circumstances which permit such an exception, they do not now occur to us.

Jackson's fairmindedness was exactly what recommended him to President Truman in the weeks after the death of FDR. The governments of the victorious powers, Great Britain, the Soviet Union, and the United States, had agreed quickly on the need to place all the surviving Nazis they could find on trial for war crimes. They also agreed to hold the hearings in Nuremberg (Nürnberg), the medieval city about 100 miles north of Munich where many of the Nazis' most dramatic rallies had taken place.

But lots of people, especially in Britain and America, raised a troubling question. Would such a trial represent justice or just revenge? There was no already existing international court in which such a trial could take place. Even more important, there was no significant body of international law that defined crimes of war—as opposed to standard military action. The American Constitution had banned the passage of *ex post facto* laws, statutes designed to punish people for committing acts before those acts were deemed criminal. Were the Nazis then to be tried on an *ex post facto* basis?

The question troubled President Truman greatly. He hoped that the appointment of Justice Jackson as chief prosecutor would make the proceedings in Nuremberg look fair.

After months of preparation, Justice Jackson, in early November 1945, flew to Germany and took a train to Nuremberg. After eleven Allied bombing raids, the city was almost wholly in ruins. He took a room in the only hotel still standing. The trials opened on November 20, 1945.

The Nuremberg Trials

The Palace of Justice had been rapidly restored. It was a four-storied building with three courtyards and lots of gables on its pointed roofs. Behind it stood a long semicircular cement wall that housed the Nazi prisoners.

Of the 22 prisoners to be tried (Martin Bormann, one of Hitler's top administrators, was tried *in absentia*—without being present; he later was found to have committed suicide), the most important ones were:

◆ **Albert Speer,** the slightly balding, lean-faced architect who had presided over German arms production for most of the war; he stood accused of using slave labor.

◆ **Colonel General Alfred Jodl,** who had served as the chief of operations of the German armed forces and who, then, as commander in chief, had surrendered to General Eisenhower. The Soviets insisted on his being put on trial.

◆ **Grand Admiral Karl Dönitz,** the head of the German navy and Hitler's chosen successor, had the deceptive air of a meek college professor. Even in the dock, his tone of voice was one of snarling authority.

◆ **Hans Frank,** the balding, swarthy Nazi governor general of Poland who was known as the butcher of Jews.

◆ **Joachim von Ribbentrop,** the one-time champagne salesman who had worked his way into Hitler's good graces and become the Nazi foreign minister.

◆ **Rudolf Hess,** a dark-haired, heavy-browed man who had been with Hitler since the earliest days in Munich, and had risen to the rank of third-highest Nazi. A pilot in the First World War, in May 1941, Hess had made a solo flight from Germany to Scotland. Why he made the flight remains a mystery: The British, who incarcerated him for the duration of the war, have never released the results of their many interviews with Hess. But we have several possible reasons for his flight. He was trying to escape. He was crazy. Or he was on a mission from Hitler, trying to persuade the British to join the Reich in Hitler's upcoming invasion of the Soviet Union. Convinced that the last explanation was the correct one, the Soviet Union demanded that Hess be put on trial.

◆ **Hermann Göring,** the former flying ace and luxury-loving number-two Nazi after Hitler, Göring had been a marked man. Hugely overweight from his excesses of food and drink, Göring upon getting away from Berchtesgaden had crossed Allied lines under the illusion that he would be treated with great respect. He ended up in prison.

These and the other Nazi prisoners had been kept one to a cell. Their food was slop. Their only clothing consisted of prison gray sacks of prison uniforms; none was allowed shoelaces, neckties, belts, razors, even nail-clippers, anything that might have let them commit suicide. Each cell door had a peephole, so that guards from the United States, Great Britain, and the Soviet Union could keep watch on their prisoners 24 hours a day.

On November 29, 1945, the defendants were awakened by the banging of washbasins out in the corridor and the raucous chatter of their guards. Since none of the Germans had clothing appropriate to a courtroom, the civilians among them were provided with ill-fitting cheaply made suits; outside their cells they were allowed to use shoelaces and to put on neckties. The military were given back their uniforms, with all insignia patches torn off.

Then, moving single-file, they were marched through the prison corridors into the courtroom. They were ushered into an oblong wooden box filled with two rows of straight-backed chairs. There they sat, surrounded (on both sides of the box and behind it) with American military police, standing at ease but armed. There they heard the formal charges read against them.

The Proceedings

On the first day of the trial, the defendants pleaded "not guilty."

Justice Jackson then introduced massive documentary evidence that in effect was a history of Nazi Germany presented in terms of four main charges:

- First: That the Nazis had conspired criminally to seize power in Germany.

- Second: That Nazi Germany had planned, prepared, initiated, and waged wars of aggression, in violation of foreign treaties.

- Third: That the Nazis had committed war crimes in the countries and territories occupied by the German armed forces—murder and ill-treatment of civilian populations, deportations for slave labor, killing of prisoners of war and hostages, wanton destruction of cities, towns, and villages, and the conscription of civilian labor.

- Fourth: Crimes against humanity—murder, extermination, enslavement, deportation, and persecution on political, racial, and religious grounds.

Jackson followed these charges against the individual defendants with indictments against the organizations of Nazi Germany: the party, the cabinet, the SA, the SS, the Gestapo, and the high command of the German armed forces.

The justice based these charges not so much on eyewitness testimony as on hundreds of thousands of pieces of paper gathered from captured Nazi archives: The record of the trials filled 23 volumes and the documentary evidence another 19 volumes. Time and again, Jackson shot down the claims of the defense by producing incriminating orders signed by the defendants themselves.

The Nazis in the dock were divided between those who were penitent (Hans Frank had recently converted to Catholicism and Speer was particularly cooperative, especially in bearing witness against his colleagues), those who, being the military brass, claimed that they had only been following orders, and those who, such as Göring, were defiant.

Because of his former rank in the Nazi Party, Göring was the most challenging of the defendants. Although he denied prior knowledge of the death camps, he insisted on upholding the principles, such as *Lebensraum*, that dream of living space spelled out in *Mein Kampf*. Lucid, entertaining, sometimes funny, and always domineering, Göring displayed a remarkable memory for the details of Nazi history. "I am determined to go down in German history as a great man," he told an Allied psychiatrist; in the dock he certainly was playing the greatest role of his life. Göring's interruptions were so frequent and his assertions so impertinent that at one point Jackson lost his temper. The trial had to be recessed for several days.

Supporting Actors

The Hess Mystery. Hess provided plenty of dramatic moments. When the British turned him over for trial, he claimed that he suffered from amnesia. In the dock on November 30, 1945, however, he suddenly stood up and declared that his memory had returned. He accepted full responsibility for what he had done as a Nazi. But when he sat down again, he seemed to relapse into his earlier obliviousness.

The Nuremberg trials dragged on for month after month. Because the court had ruled out a *tu quoque* defense—Latin for "everybody else, the British, the Russians, etc., did it, too"—the defense attorneys had the task of challenging the authenticity, sheet by sheet, of the documents Jackson had collected. Even cross-examining the 21 defendants took a long time. The judges—Soviet, British, and American—took a full month to reach their verdicts.

The Verdicts and the Sentences

At last, on September 30, 1946, the judges delivered their verdicts and the sentences.

Three of the defendants, including Franz von Papen, who had been forced to resign as chancellor during the machinations of Hitler's rise to power, were found innocent.

Seven were found guilty and were sentenced to prison terms of various lengths. Hess got life; Speer got 20 years; and Dönitz, who had not been involved in the death camps, got 10 years.

The rest were found guilty as charged and were sentenced to death by hanging. Göring alone avoided the hangman's noose. Playing out his macabre role to the end, he had managed somehow in the prison to hide his cyanide capsule. Somewhere, sometime, he got access to that pill. Like Hitler before him, Hermann Göring took his own life.

The Reasons Why

At last, it's time to sum up. A lot of questions still pop up about the history of Nazi Germany:

 ◆ Were the Nuremberg trials legally valid?

 ◆ What brought about Nazi Germany's defeat?

 ◆ What motivated Hitler? How and why did the Nazis rise to power in the first place? Further, what were the distant influences on the Nazi movement? Most important of all, what was it specifically about Germany in the 1920s, 30s, and early 40s that led to Nazism, the Second World War, and the Holocaust?

The following sections address these questions.

The Trials' Validity

As a number of commentators have pointed out, the prosecutor and his assistants, and the judges, were from the same countries: Great Britain, the Soviet Union, and the United States. The independence of the judges therefore was open to question.

But as for the matter of precedent, Justice Jackson need not have worried. The Charter of the League of Nations, which Germany had joined, called for international sanctions against aggressors. As a further assurance against war, in 1925 at Locarno in Switzerland, the European powers signed a number of treaties—including one in which Germany guaranteed the borders of Belgium and France unconditionally. By that same token, by its own volition and not under compulsion by the Treaty of Versailles, Germany had accepted its own borders, both east and west, and had renounced unilateral military action even in the east. Three years later, in 1928 at Paris, the French foreign minister Aristide Briand and the American secretary of state Frank B. Kellogg negotiated a treaty that condemned recourse to war as a solution to international problems; 65 nations signed, including Germany. And the Geneva Convention of 1929 mandated the humane treatment of prisoners of war. By any reasonable standard, the Jews and others who died in the extermination camps were prisoners of war: What else were they?

Back in the late 1940s, Senator Robert A. Taft, a Republican of Ohio, charged that the Nuremberg trials had amounted to a kangaroo court, handing down *ex post facto* judgments. But there was plenty of legal precedent for the verdicts. The Nuremberg Trials were far more than a matter of victors' justice.

Germany's Defeat

Yet if Germany had won the war, obviously there would have been no Nuremberg trials. So the next question on our own docket is: Why did Germany lose the war? It's easy to pin the blame on Hitler's tactical mistakes:

♦ The Soviet campaign was full of his bungling. Much to the anguish of his generals, he diverted forces from Moscow to Stalingrad, a city which had less value to the Soviets than did their capital; by taking Stalingrad, he stretched Germany's supply lines to the breaking point.

♦ He allowed his troops to mistreat local populations, especially the Ukrainians, who would have been natural allies in the struggle against the Russians.

♦ In the face of inexorable pressure from the Soviets after Stalingrad, he persisted in carrying out the extermination of the Jews. This diverted men and resources from the eastern front.

Yet even without these errors, Germany most likely could never have won. No matter what the Germans did, the Soviet Union had two resources against which even a sanely led German army would have bogged down: space and people. Even German-built machinery does wear out, and in the nearly thousand miles from Warsaw to Moscow, German tanks, armored cars, and other mechanized vehicles broke down at unprecedented rates. The farther the remaining units penetrated into the Soviet Union, furthermore, the more vulnerable did they become to guerrilla attacks from the sides and the rear. And the Soviet population was much larger than the German: Soviet troops at Stalingrad came at the Germans in human waves, were shot down, and simply came again. Hitler's invasion of the Soviet Union was a classic example of military overextension. He thought he could avoid Napoleon's mistake and he just could not do so.

But the campaign in the west was also a case of overextension. As we have seen, the British escape from Dunkirk was heroic. It was also a defeat: From that point onward, as in Greece and Crete, Great Britain's role in the war was relatively negligible. Individual cases of valor did not disguise the fact that in the British–American alliance, the United States was distinctly the first between equals. Germany had little or nothing to fear from Britain alone. And if Hitler and Göring had refrained from launching air attacks on Britain, including the nighttime air raids of British cities, a stalemate could have well ensued and Germany might have held on to northern France for decades.

In June 1939, however, President Roosevelt had promised King George VI that if London were bombed, the United States would intervene. Hitler could not have known about that conversation. Yet he did remember quite well the consequences of the American entry into the First World War. In fact, he remembered it so well that long before Pearl Harbor he ordered his submarine commanders at all costs not to sink vessels with Americans aboard. The last thing Hitler wanted to do was to risk another *Lusitania*.

Yet the German bombing of London had much the same effect as the sinking of the *Lusitania*. Winston Churchill's words of defiance reached American radio sets, and the grim voice of the radio correspondent Edward R. Murrow stirred the wrath of the American public against Nazi Germany. That's why, in the summer of 1941, Congress, and behind it the people of the United States, let President Roosevelt wage an undeclared naval war with Germany in the Atlantic Ocean.

Nonetheless, Hitler authorized the bombing of cities in the southeastern and central parts of England, especially London and Coventry. This was an overextension of German power almost guaranteed to bring America in.

So why the bombing of Britain? The best answer would seem to lie in the very nature of Nazi Germany. Nazi Germany resembled a child's toy car that, once wound up, keeps going until it crashes into a wall.

The Rise of Nazi Germany

On the surface, at least, Nazi Germany seems hard to explain. It was both familiar and unfamiliar.

Consider how many of the bits and pieces have existed in other countries and other times. Lots of other countries, the Soviet Union and Communist China being the most famous examples, have had to endure the cult of personality—Josef Stalin and Mao Zedong, for example. Other places have succumbed to virulent racism: Think of South Africa or the history of the American South. Anti-Semitism has existed elsewhere, as with the notorious Russian pogroms; modern Yugoslavia (a country that no longer exists as such) was notorious for its so-called ethnic cleansing. Holocausts have existed elsewhere: In December 1937, the Japanese perpetrated what the Chinese to this day remember as the "Rape of Nanjing." Other countries have had their extreme right and left-wing elements, replete with flags, banners, symbols, and mystical ideologies of sorts—the Ku Klux Klan, for example. Other countries have committed aggression: Japan, Iraq, the Soviet Union, perhaps even the United States in Vietnam.

But all these bits and pieces of horror came together in *Nazi Germany*. Why?

We need to review generally the circumstances that followed the First World War. Germany lost the war; but other countries, too, such as Japan in 1945, have lost wars without going Nazi. All right, then, the terms of the Versailles Treaty were restrictive: Germany was partially dismembered. But the operative word here is "partially." Most of Germany was kept intact. President Woodrow Wilson saw to that. But other countries have been ripped up, moved around, distorted geographically without turning into Nazi-like war machines: Think of Poland.

Other countries also have experienced the hyperinflation that afflicted Germany in the early 1920s: China in the late 1940s suffered a similar fate, and the hyperinflation there contributed mightily to the rise of the Communists to power. But they didn't turn to aggression: China's intervention in the Korean War in 1950 was largely defensive.

The Great Depression hit Germany hard, no question about it. But it also afflicted the rest of industrialized Europe and North America. In the Depression years the United States witnessed right-wing protest movements, such as that spearheaded by Huey Long of Louisiana. The heavily Roman Catholic population of Montreal flirted with Mussolini's fascism. Yet both countries remained democratic.

Then, too, there was the matter of Hitler's dramatics. He picked up a lot of hints of dramaturgy from the Viennese theater (at least when he could afford tickets) and he practiced facial expressions and hand gestures before a mirror in Munich. Nazi rallies in Nuremberg and elsewhere were marvels of stagecraft. But politicians around the world have striven to put on good shows: In 1907, Teddy Roosevelt sent the Great White Fleet around the world and it returned to coastal Virginia exactly one week before the end of his presidency: In politics as in the theater, timing is everything. Yet TR hardly overthrew the government of the United States as Hitler overthrew the government of Germany.

So what was it about the time and the place and the culture specifically that gave rise to the phenomenon known as Nazi Germany? The answer, it seems to this author, lies in an idea that goes back to the recorded beginnings of western civilization: The ancient Greek *hubris*, the pride that precedes the fall.

The Fatal Flaw

Hubris is more than just pride. It is overbearing pride, arrogance, and insolence. It can refer to a person who lives by his or her own rules, when there's a larger set of rules that will prevail. It's believing in yourself only. It's an overweening confidence that one is in charge of one's own destiny when indeed the gods are mocking. It's the conviction that one can remake the world in one's own image. *Hubris* is the fatal flaw.

> ### Modern Day Parallels
>
> The history of drama and literature is full of the working out of the fatal flaw. The Greek tragedies revolved around the theme. So are Shakespeare's: MacBeth's belief that he could murder the king and get away with it led to his own death; King Lear's refusal to listen to the words of wisdom of his daughter Cordelia produced his ruin. Tolstoy's Anna Karenina's flouting of the rules of society against adultery turned into her suicide. Flaubert's Emma Bovary suffered a similar fate. So did the Don Juan, or Don Giovanni, of legend. Always excess led to doom.

Then there was Germany's own Richard Wagner. Convinced that his own opera would demolish all other forms of art, he composed and wrote huge works of tremendous intensity: the highest pathos of passion; the darkest pessimism; uncontrollable sensual fervor; and a tormented desire for fulfillment and redemption, all carried to a point where the boundaries of the world and the beyond were no longer recognizable.

Richard Wagner was also a specifically German musician and dramatist. Staging his works in the mid- to late nineteenth century, he saw Germany as having fallen from a golden age, which it absolutely must regain. He saw himself as the instrument of that redemption. It was by no accident that Wagner drew his themes from German folklore. He exalted the German people, the *Volk*. And it followed from that exaltation that he wished the extermination of the Jewish people.

Here are some of Wagner's own words: "The Jew speaks the language of the nation in whose midst he dwells from generation to generation, but he speaks it always as an alien. … Judaism is the evil conscience of our modern civilization." For Wagner, the Jewish people had been the agents of Germany's decline; it followed that Germany could find its redemption only by eliminating the Jewish people.

None of this is to say that Wagner caused Hitler. It is to say that in a remarkable way Wagner foretold the tragic story of Nazi Germany.

Nationalism in Response to Inferiority

Very briefly, let's review that story. And let's add a little bit about that so-called golden age. On Christmas Day, in the year 800, Pope Leo III placed the crown of the Roman Empire on the head of Karl, King of the Franks; we know him as Charlemagne, but the Germans claimed him as their own, Karl der Grosse. His coronation marked the advent of the Holy Roman Empire, for it symbolized the union of the Roman and the Teuton. His was a golden age in the sense that his conquests ranged from the border of Spain down past Rome, into Moravia and Croatia, and over to Danzig.

In the course of the Middle Ages, the Holy Roman Empire degenerated into being neither holy nor Roman nor an empire. Compared to the other European great powers, Prussia (which was the remnant of the Holy Roman Empire) in the eighteenth and early nineteenth centuries was a poor country cousin.

The nationalism that affected and afflicted German speakers in the middle of the nineteenth century was a response to that inferior status. Then Bismarck came along and fixed it, creating the German Empire. Here we had the first of the Germanic tragedies: Bismarck deluded himself into believing that he could construct a behemoth and not scare the rest of the European continent half out of its wits. The second tragedy lay in Germany's entry into the First World War. While Kaiser Wilhelm II may not have been the sole aggressor, he clung irrationally to his alliance with Austria-Hungary, allowing the Viennese tail to wag the Berliner dog. In believing he could keep Austria's conflict with Serbia localized in the Balkans, he was subjecting himself to a gross self-deception.

Germany lost the First World War. To that obvious fact, however, we must add a point that's not so obvious: It was *Germany* that lost. The very terms of the Versailles Treaty were humiliating enough. But the fact that they had been imposed upon a proud, even arrogant, nation was even worse, especially because the Germans did not accept guilt for the coming of the war. Exactly as David Lloyd George feared, the peace settlement was practically a guarantee of war.

Hitler's Promise of Redemption

It's important to recognize that Hitler didn't make much political headway in the 1920s. What really propelled him into power was the Great Depression. Other countries, granted, also suffered from the economic collapse. But in Germany, the mixture of pride, grievance, and privation was explosive in the extreme.

Hitler promised redemption: That was his Wagnerian theme. As in Wagnerian opera, moreover, redemption was to be total. There was a great faith that Hitler could and should slay *all* the dragons: The Czechs and Poles who had allegedly deprived Germanic peoples within their borders of their rights; the Allies who had imposed the Versailles Treaty, and that meant especially the French; the Communists, who had stood in the way of Hitler's rise; and, naturally, the Jews, who supposedly had stood in the way of the resurgence of Germany itself.

The Lack of Resources in Spite of the Pride

The tragedy of Nazi Germany, the pride that preceded the fall, the fatal flaw, was that the country simply didn't have the resources to pull it all off. That's why, toward the end of the Second World War, Albert Speer used slave labor in his arms factories. That's why Rommel's efforts collapsed in North Africa. That's why Germany lost at Stalingrad. That's why Hitler couldn't fend off Eisenhower's invasion on the beaches of Normandy. The reach of Nazi Germany exceeded its grasp.

The Jewish Holocaust Proves Aryan Superiority a Myth

And, in the end, the Holocaust. Why the Jews, who had contributed so much to the economic and cultural life of Germany, should have been slaughtered is almost inexplicable. Except maybe for just this: In their very successes, they showed beyond a doubt that the idea of Aryan superiority was a myth. Their mere presence showed that Nazi Germany was a sham.

The Least You Need to Know

- The Nuremberg Trials of course represented judgments imposed by the victors on the vanquished. But at least they were trials: The American government wanted to show the world that it did not indulge in Nazi-style summary executions. The trials also stood to show future generations what fate would await those who ever tried to repeat the course of Nazi Germany.

- Contrary to what some people alleged in the 20 years or so that followed the end of the Second World War, the Nuremberg verdicts were not *ex post facto* ones. They were based on legal precedent.

- Through its *hubris*, its overweening arrogance, Germany, once a great country, under the Nazis collapsed in ruin. As it did so, it took six million of the Jewish people down with it, committing the crime of the centuries.

Appendix A

Chronology

The following list gives important dates pertaining to the rise and fall of Nazi Germany. It's worthwhile to remember that Nazi Germany didn't just come out of nowhere: this chronology gives a sense of the background.

1870–1871	Franco–German War; unification of Germany and founding of German Empire under Bismarck.
1890	Dismissal of Bismarck by Kaiser Wilhelm II.
1914	Assassination of Franz Ferdinand, Archduke of the Austro–Hungarian Empire (June 28).
1914	Outbreak of World War I (July 28–August 4).
1918	Armistice; German revolution.
1919	Treaty of Versailles.
1923	French occupation of the Ruhr; peak of the German inflation and final stabilization of the German currency.
1929	Beginning of Great Depression; worldwide unemployment; felt extremely hard in Germany.
1932	Nazi electoral victories.

1933	Hitler becomes chancellor of Germany.
1935	Remilitarization of Germany.
1936	Occupation of the Rhineland.
1938	Annexation of Austria.
1938	Munich agreement; annexation of German-speaking parts of Czechoslovakia (September).
1939	Occupation of the rest of Czechoslovakia (March); Nazi–Soviet Pact (August); invasion of Poland (September).
1940	Conquest of Denmark, Norway, Luxembourg, Belgium, Holland, and France.
1941	Invasion of the Soviet Union.
1943	Defeat at Stalingrad (January 31).
1944	Landing of Allied troops on the French coast.
1945	Collapse of Germany and Hitler's death (April 30).

Appendix B

Additional Reading

I hope I've whetted your appetite for more. The following titles are informative and worth your time.

Brecher, Elinor J. *Schindler's Legacy: True Stories of the List Survivors.* New York: Plume, 1994.
Stories of persons featured in the movie *Schindler's List.*

Bullock, Alan. *Hitler: A Study in Tyranny.* New York: Harper & Row, 1964.
The first major biography of Hitler in English.

Craig, William. *Enemy at the Gates: The Battle for Stalingrad.* New York: Penguin, 1973.
Probably the best single work on the Battle of Stalingrad.

Dawidowicz, Lucy S. *The War Against the Jews, 1933–1945.* New York: Holt, Rinehart and Winston, 1975.
A powerful year-by-year, country-by-country account of the Holocaust.

Deathridge, John and Carl Dahlhaus. *Wagner.* New York: Norton, 1984.
A biography of the composer, so adored by the Nazis.

Erickson, John. *The Road to Berlin: Stalin's War with Germany*. London: Weidenfeld & Nicolson, 1983.
The story of the Red Army's epic struggle to drive the Germans out of Russia.

———. *The Road to Stalingrad; Stalin's War with Germany*. London: Weidenfeld & Nicolson, 1973.
Covers Hitler's invasion of the Soviet Union.

Frank, Anne. *The Diary of a Young Girl; The Definitive Edition*. Otto H. Frank and Mirjam Pressler, eds. Susan Massotty, trans. New York: Doubleday, 1995.
The classic story of the Holocaust told from the point of view of Anne Frank, a young Jewish girl whose family went into hiding during the Holocaust.

Goldhagen, Daniel Jonah. *Hitler's Willing Executioners: Ordinary Germans and the Holocaust*. New York: Knopf, 1996.
A brilliant and controversial view of the support of the German citizenry for the Holocaust.

Hamann, Brigitte. *Hitler's Vienna: A Dictator's Apprenticeship*. New York: Oxford University Press, 1999.
A vivid view of Hitler's days in Vienna.

Hamerow, Theodore S. *On the Road to the Wolf's Lair: German Resistance to Hitler*. Cambridge: Harvard University Press, 1997.
The definitive story of the plot to kill Hitler.

Hitler, Adolf. *Mein Kampf*. Boston: Houghton Mifflin, 1971.
This comes in lots of editions, but they're all his own words.

Large, David Clay. *Where Ghosts Walked: Munich's Road to the Third Reich*. New York: Norton, 1997.
An excellent biography of the city that gave birth to Nazism.

McKee, Alexander. *Dresden 1945: The Devil's Tinderbox*. New York: Dutton, 1984.
The best picture of the bombing of Dresden.

Newman, Simon. *March 1939: The British Guarantee to Poland: A Study in the Continuity of British Foreign Policy*. Oxford: Clarendon, 1976.
A dissent from the usual view of British appeasement of Hitler.

Persico, Joseph E. *Nuremberg: Infamy on Trial.* New York: Viking, 1994.
The most vivid portrayal of the Nuremberg trials.

Rhodes, Richard. *Masters of Death: The SS Einsatzgruppen and the Invention of the Holocaust.* New York: Knopf, 2002.
The immediate origins of the Holocaust.

Rosenbaum, Ron. *Explaining Hitler: The Search for the Origins of His Evil.* New York: Random House, 1998.
A recent and fascinating survey of contending theories about Hitler's character.

Shirer, William L. *The Rise and Fall of the Third Reich: A History of Nazi Germany.* New York: Fawcett Crest, 1959.
An early view—massive and worthwhile—of Nazi Germany by a reporter who was there.

Toland, John. *Adolf Hitler.* 2 vols. Garden City: Doubleday, 1976.
Toland was a journalist who became a best-selling historian of the Second World War.

Waite, Robert G. L. *Kaiser and Führer: A Comparative Study of Personality and Politics.* Toronto: University of Toronto Press, 1998.
Despite their backgrounds, as this work shows, Hitler and Wilhelm II were very much alike.

Appendix C

Citations

The sources of the most important quotations are listed in this appendix.

Chapter 3

"If he laughs … enjoyment of any joke …": quoted in Michael Balfour's *The Kaiser and His Times*. London: Cresset, 1969, p. 63.

"Our navy … if God helps us": quoted in Balfour, p. 206.

"What more can I do … holds a dagger …": Louis Snyder's *Basic History of Modern Germany*. Princeton: Van Nostrand, 1957, p. 74.

Chapter 4

"It was a beautiful evening … starting a war.": Georg Alexander von Müller, *The Kaiser and His Court*. New York: Harcourt, Brace & World, 1961, p. 7.

The Page–Grey dialogue: John Milton Cooper's *Walter Hines Page*. Chapel Hill: University of North Carolina Press, 1977, p. 314.

Chapter 5

"On the first day of February … Texas and Arizona …": quoted in Barbara Tuchman's *The Zimmermann Telegram*. New York: Ballantine, 1959, pp. 201–202.

Chapter 7

"I was a young … clear conscience …": quoted in Adolf Hitler's, *Mein Kampf.* Boston: Houghton Mifflin, 1971, p. 23.

"Now the first shrapnel … outside [the trenches]": quoted in Hitler, p. 159.

"I was eating … was killed": quoted in Hitler, p. 170.

Chapter 10

"The Horst Wessel Song": quoted in Snyder, p. 72.

Chapter 16

"The bright faithfulness … know any better": quoted in David Irving's *The War Path: Hitler's Germany, 1933–1939*. New York: Viking, 1978, p. 171.

"I wonder if … did like about him": quoted in Irving, p. a73.

Chapter 18

"Life here is still quite normal …": quoted in William L. Shirer, *Berlin Diary.* New York: Popular Library, 1940, pp. 153–156.

"No one in our class … were mentioned": quoted in Richard Bessel, *Life in the Third Reich.* Oxford: Oxford University Press, 1987, p. 27.

"… that if the Allies planned …": quoted in Simon & Schuster's *Encyclopedia of World War II*, p. 447.

Chapter 19

Einstein's Letter: quoted in Martin J. Sherwin, *A World Destroyed.* New York: Vintage, 1977, pp. 27–28.

Hitler's facial expression: Shirer, *Berlin Diary*, p. 307.

Chapter 20

Scene at Bordeaux airport: quoted in Edward Spears, *Assignment to Catastrophe*. London: Heinemann, 1954, p. 18.

Chapter 21

"I vegetated … war wore on": quoted in William Shirer, *The Rise and Fall of the Third Reich*. Greenwich, CT: Fawcett, 1959, p. 889.

"The Nazi blight …": Shirer, *The Rise and Fall of the Third Reich*, p. 890.

Chapter 25

The Canadian soldier's recollection: Earl F. Ziemke, *The Soviet Juggernaut*. Alexandria: Time-Life, 1980, p. 126.

Chapter 26

Wagner's attitude toward the Jews: Albert Goldman and Evert Sprinchorn, eds., and H. Ashton Ellis, trans. *Wagner on Music and Drama*. London: Victor Gollancz, 1977, pp. 51–59.

Index

H

O-P

Y-Z

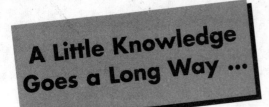
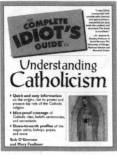

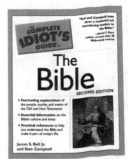

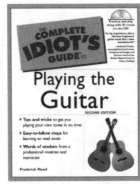

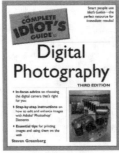

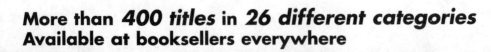